The Jo Anne Stolaroff Cotsen Prize Imprint
honors outstanding studies in archaeology in
commemoration of a woman whose appreciation
for scholarship was recognized by all those whose
lives she touched.

Cotsen Advanced Seminars 1

COTSEN INSTITUTE OF
ARCHAEOLOGY AT UCLA

Theory and Practice in Mediterranean Archaeology: Old World and New World Perspectives

An Advanced Seminar in Honor of Lloyd Cotsen

EDITED BY
JOHN K. PAPADOPOULOS
RICHARD M. LEVENTHAL

COTSEN INSTITUTE OF ARCHAEOLOGY
UNIVERSITY OF CALIFORNIA, LOS ANGELES
2003

Library of Congress Cataloging-in-Publication Data
Theory and Practice in Mediterranean Archaeology: Old World and New World
Perspectives / edited by John K. Papadopoulos and Richard M. Leventhal
p. cm. — (CIOA Seminar series ; v. 1)
Includes bibliographic references
ISBN: 1-931745-10-2 paperback
ISBN: 1-931745-11-0 hardcover

Theory and Practice in Mediterranean Archaeology

To Lloyd Cotsen for his vision and generosity

Contents

Preface

This book is dedicated to Lloyd Cotsen, a benefactor and friend to archaeologists around the world. When Lloyd agreed to make a major contribution to the then UCLA Institute of Archaeology, he catapulted the Institute into the top ranks of archaeological research centers throughout the world. It will take time and much energy for the newly named Cotsen Institute of Archaeology at UCLA to achieve the goals it has set for itself. But it is clear that Lloyd has provided UCLA with a wonderful gift that will allow the Institute to build on the strengths it has already developed.

Lloyd Cotsen's gift will fund much of the basic infrastructure of the Cotsen Institute. In addition, his largess will support a variety of new programs, including the development of annual or semi-annual Advanced Seminars. The latter were conceived of as a gathering of ten to fifteen leading scholars who would meet at UCLA to examine a critical issue or issues in the study of the past. This volume publishes the first Cotsen Advanced Seminar, held in Los Angeles from March 23 through 25, 2000. The seminar, originally cast as a workshop, was largely limited to the participants and moderators and began as a discussion among many members of the Cotsen Institute about what topic we might choose. We wanted to highlight, first of all, the enormous breadth and diversity of the UCLA archaeological community. The Cotsen Institute brings together archaeologists from many different departments—and disciplines—in the Humanities and Social Sciences (Anthropology, Art History, Classics, Germanic Languages, History, and Near Eastern Languages and Cultures), who work in various countries of the Americas, Africa, Asia, and Europe. We also wished to bring to the fore not only Lloyd's gift but his own diversity of interests.

In the end, we decided to focus upon one geographic area—a region of almost constant study and (re)assessment over the course of centuries—the Mediterranean, and more particularly, the Aegean. This region ignited Lloyd's own interests in archaeology and in the past. We decided, however, to move away from a purely regional conference as we identified areas of study or broader themes and thus included responses from New World archaeologists. The goal was to focus discussion not only on issues related to the Mediterranean but also to the broader assessment of archaeological methods and theory throughout the world. The combination of both a regional—Old World—focus with responses and ideas from the New World created, we believe, a most exciting intellectual dialogue over the two days of the gathering.

Lloyd Cotsen came to all of the sessions and gatherings, commented on the discussions, and produced voluminous notes from each session. We hope that this is a fitting volume to thank Lloyd for his generosity, together with his interest in the archaeological present and the distant past. It is also a fitting volume to initiate what we hope will be a long series of important publications based upon future Advanced Seminars of the Cotsen Institute.

John K. Papadopoulos and Richard M. Leventhal

Acknowledgments

We are grateful to a good many friends and colleagues who made the original meeting, and the publication that developed from it, possible. We are grateful, first of all, to the participants and moderators of the seminar: John Cherry, Lynn Gamble, Richard Lesure, Claire Lyons, Jerry Moore, Sarah Morris, Tom Palaima, Clairy Palyvou, Colin Renfrew, Steve Rosen, Curtis Runnels, James Sackett, Charles Stanish, Nicholas Stanley-Price, Ruth Tringham, and Lothar von Falkenhausen. One of the invited participants, John Henderson, was unable to attend at the last moment, and we are very grateful to Joyce Marcus and Charles Redman for agreeing to submit written contributions without enjoying the benefits of having taken part in the workshop. We are also grateful to Jack Davis, who worked with Lloyd Cotsen at Ayia Irini on the Greek island of Kea, for his tribute to Lloyd and Greece. Special thanks are due to Wendy Ashmore for reading the volume in its entirety and for her many comments on the individual contributions, which greatly strengthened the volume as a whole; we are also grateful to the anonymous readers for their useful comments. The assistance of a number of UCLA graduate students, and former graduate students, throughout the seminar was critical to its smooth running. In this respect we are particularly grateful to Dr. Brendan Burke, who worked tirelessly in organizing the logistics of the meeting and for serving, with Cynthia Skvorec Colburn, as rapporteur for the various sessions. Special thanks are also due to Julia Sanchez, the Assistant Director of the Cotsen Institute, for her administrative help throughout the workshop; to Helle Girey for all she has done and continues to do for the Archaeology Program at UCLA; and to Petya Hristova for her assistance during the editing of this volume.

We owe an especial debt of gratitude to two scholars who form the backbone of the Cotsen Institute of Archaeology: Sarah Morris assisted in the early stages of planning the workshop and helped us to articulate the themes we finally chose. Charles (Chip) Stanish not only rose to the challenge of responding to two Old World presentations, but as the current Director of the Cotsen Institute, he has been instrumental in supporting this publication. Finally, we are grateful to Margit Cotsen for helping us keep this tribute to Lloyd a secret and, most of all, we would like to thank Lloyd Cotsen for making all this possible.

John K. Papadopoulos and Richard M. Leventhal

Biographical Notes about the Contributors

John F. Cherry is Professor of Classical Archaeology and Greek at the University of Michigan, where he is also Director of the graduate-level Interdepartmental Program in Classical Art and Archaeology, and a Senior Fellow of the Michigan Society of Fellows. His principal interests are regional analysis and archaeological survey in the Mediterranean lands, Aegean prehistory, state formation, lithic analysis, island archaeology, and archaeological theory. He has taken part in archaeological fieldwork (almost all of it survey based) in the United Kingdom, Texas, Italy, and especially Greece, with involvement in projects on Melos, Keos, in the Nemea Valley, and in Messenia. Recent publications include *Landscape Archaeology as Long-Term History* (with J.L. Davis and E. Mantzourani, Los Angeles, 1991); *Provenance Studies and Bronze Age Cyprus* (with A.B. Knapp, Madison, 1994); and *Pausanias: Travel and Imagination in Roman Greece* (with S.E. Alcock and J. Elsner, eds., New York, 2001).

Jack L. Davis is an Aegean prehistorian and Classical archaeologist, who has a particular interest in regional studies. He has directed or co-directed surface surveys on the island of Keos in the Cyclades (1983–84), at Nemea (1983–89) and Pylos in the Peloponnese (1991–97), and at Apollonia (1998–present) and Durres (2001) in Albania. He is participating in a multidisciplinary team that is attempting to reconstruct patterns of settlement and land use in Messenia ca. 1700 AD by integrating the study of material culture with information gleaned from Venetian and Ottoman archival documents. Since 1993 he has been Carl W. Blegen Professor of Greek Archaeology at the University of Cincinnati.

Lynn Gamble received her degree from the University of California, Santa Barbara in 1991. She is an Associate Professor of Anthropology and Director of the Collections Management Program at San Diego State University. Active in California archaeology for twenty-two years, her research interests focus on the development of sociopolitical complexity of southern California Indian societies, exchange systems, mortuary analysis, spatial archaeology, and ethical issues in anthropology. She has an article published in *American Antiquity* on archaeological evidence for the origin of the plank canoe in the New World. Other recent and pending articles include a 2001 *American Antiquity* article entitled "An Integrative Approach to Mortuary Analysis: Social and Symbolic Dimensions of Chumash Burial Practices," an article entitled "Fact or Forgery: Dilemmas in Museum Collections" to appear in *Museum Anthropology*, and an article entitled "Social Differentiation and Exchange during the Historic Period among the Kumeyaay" to be published in *Historical Archaeology*.

Richard Lesure, Associate Professor of Anthropology at the University of California, Los Angeles, is a specialist in ancient Mesoamerica. He has conducted excavations at Formative period sites in southern and central Mexico and is particularly interested in the archaeology of social life in early villages, including the challenge of investigating prehistoric religions. Recent publications include "Animal Imagery, Cultural Unities, and Ideologies of Inequality in Early Formative Mesoamerica" in *Olmec Art and Archaeology in Mesoamerica: Developments in Formative Period Social Complexity* (Studies in the History of Art, National Gallery of Art, Washington, DC, 2000) and "On the Genesis of Value in Early Hierarchical Societies" in *Material Symbols: Culture and Economy in Prehistory* (Center for Archaeological Investigations, Southern Illinois University, 1999).

Richard Leventhal is President and CEO of the School of American Research, an anthropological think tank located in Santa Fe, New Mexico. From 1992 to 2001, he was Director of the Cotsen Institute of Archaeology at UCLA and Associate Professor in the Department of Anthropology at UCLA. He received his B.A. in 1974 and his Ph.D. in Anthropology from Harvard in 1979. He has done extensive field research in Belize and other parts of Central America for over twenty-five years. Most recently he directed a major program of excavation at the ancient Maya city of Xunantunich located in Belize. He is a Trustee of the Archaeological Institute of America and an advisor to the Government of Belize concerning the development of a National Museum. In addition, he works with several Maya indigenous groups in Belize.

Claire Lyons is Collections Curator at the Getty Research Institute in Los Angeles. A specialist in Sicilian and South Italian archaeology, she is the author of *Morgantina: The Archaic Cemeteries (1996)*, as well as co-editor of *Naked Truths: Women, Sexuality and Gender in Classical Art and Archaeology* (with A. Koloski-Ostrow, 1997) and *The Archaeology of Colonialism* (with J.K. Papadopoulos, 2002). During her 1994–98 tenure as Vice President for Professional Responsibilities of the Archaeological Institute of America, she oversaw the area of ethics and contributed to initiatives in cultural heritage policy, lobbying, and illicit antiquities. Essays on these topics have appeared in *Antichità senza provenienza II* (2000) and *Claiming the Stones/Naming the Bones: Cultural Property and the Negotiation of National and Ethnic Identity* (2002). Claire Lyons sits on the advisory boards of the *International Journal of Cultural Property* and the *American Journal of Archaeology*.

Joyce Marcus has excavated in Mexico, Guatemala, Peru, and the western United States. She is the Elman R. Service Professor of Cultural Evolution at the University of Michigan. Her interests include the origins of rank, the origins of writing, and the political dynamics involved in the rise and fall of ancient states. Her books include *Mesoamerican Writing Systems* (Princeton University Press); *Archaic States* (with G.M. Feinman; SAR Press, Sante Fe); *Emblem and State in the Classic Maya Lowlands* (Dumbarton Oaks, Washington, DC); *Zapotec Civilization* (with K.V. Flannery; Thames and Hudson, New York); *Women's Ritual in Formative Oaxaca: Figurine-making, Divination and the Ancestors* (Memoir 33, Museum of Anthropology, University of Michigan); and *Late Intermediate Occupation at Cerro Azul, Peru* (Technical Report 20, Museum of Anthropology, University of Michigan).

Jerry D. Moore is Professor of Anthropology at California State University, Dominguez Hills. Dr. Moore has directed archaeological research in Peru, Mexico, and the western United States. His research interests include the archaeological analysis of ancient architecture, the development of sociopolitical complexity in the Andes, and hunter-gatherer adaptations in Baja California. His recent publications on ancient architecture include *Architecture and Power in the Prehispanic Andes: The Archaeology of Public Buildings* (Cambridge University Press, 1996); "La Place dans les Andes Anciennes: Le Contrôle des Espaces Ouverts dans les Villes Précolumbiennes" in *La Ville et le Pouvoir en Amérique: Les formes de l'autorité*, edited by J. Monnet (L'Harmattan, Paris, 1999 edition); and "The Archaeology of Plazas and the Proxemics of Ritual: Three Andean Traditions" in *American Anthropologist* (1996, 98:789–802). An article entitled "Life Behind Walls: Patterns in the Urban Landscape on the Prehistoric North Coast of Peru" will appear in *The Social*

Construction of Ancient Cities, edited by Monica Smith and published by Smithsonian Institution Press, Washington, DC.

Sarah Morris is a classicist and archaeologist in both the Department of Classics and the Cotsen Institute of Archaeology at UCLA. A graduate of the University of North Carolina at Chapel Hill, she received her doctorate in Classics at Harvard University, and taught for eight years at Yale University before joining the UCLA faculty in 1989, where she served as Department Chair from 1997–2000. Her training and research involve the interaction of Greece with its Eastern neighbors in art, literature, religion, and culture. Her chief book on the subject, *Daidalos and the Origins of Greek Art* (Princeton, 1992), won the James Wiseman Book Award from the Archaeological Institute of America for 1993. She has also edited (with Jane Carter) a volume of essays, *The Ages of Homer* (Texas, 1995), regarding the archaeological, literary, and artistic background and responses to Greek epic poetry. A practicing field archaeologist, she has excavated in Israel, Turkey, and Greece, and is currently engaged in research in the Ionian islands of Greece (Leukas) and in the Cyclades. She chairs the Interdepartmental Ph.D. program in Archaeology at the Cotsen Institute of Archaeology at UCLA, and in 2001 was named Steinmetz Professor of Classical Archaeology and Material Culture at UCLA. Her teaching and research interests include early Greek literature (Homer, Hesiod, and Herodotus), Greek religion, prehistoric and early Greek archaeology, Near Eastern influence on Greek art and culture, and Modern Greek literature and culture.

Thomas G. Palaima is Dickson Centennial Professor of Classics and Director of the Program in Aegean Scripts and Prehistory at the University of Texas at Austin. He is interested in Aegean civilization (especially kingship, religion, economy, and administration); writing systems, literacy, and decipherment techniques; war and violence in ancient and modern societies; and general cultural and higher educational issues. His recent work includes "Courage and Prowess Afoot in Homer and the Vietnam of Tim O'Brien" in *Classical and Modern Literature* (20[3]:1–22), "Religion in the Room of the Chariot Tablets" in Potnia (Aegaeum 22:453–461), and "Special vs. Normal Mycenaean: Hand 24 and Writing in the Service of the King?" in *Minos* (forthcoming). He regularly writes reviews for the *London Times Higher Education Supplement*.

Clairy Palyvou, born in Piraeus, Greece, studied architecture at the Aristotle University of Thessaloniki (1965–71) and is now a professor at the same university. She worked for the Greek Ministry of Culture for fifteen years and has been a member of the excavation team of the prehistoric town at Akrotiri, Thera, since 1977. She received her Ph.D. from the National Technical University of Athens in 1989. She has been awarded the Michael Ventris Memorial Award and has lectured extensively in the United States (Fulbright and Samuel H. Kress scholarships) and elsewhere. Her field projects on site management and restoration involve Knossos, Mycenae, Thorikos, and Thera. A major project, recently completed, was the "Unification of the Archaeological Sites of Athens." Among her most important publications is *The Art of Building at Akrotiri, Thera* (Athens, 1999, in Greek). See also "Concepts of Space in Aegean Bronze Age Art and Architecture" in *The Wall Paintings of Thera* (Athens, 2000, 413–436).

John Papadopoulos is a classical archaeologist in the Department of Classics and the Cotsen Institute of Archaeology at UCLA. A graduate of the University of Sydney, he has worked at various sites in Australia, Greece, and southern Italy. Since 1986 he has served as field director of the excavations at Torone in the north Aegean. His books include *Torone I* (with Alexander Cambitoglou and Olwen Tudor Jones, published by the Athens Archaeological Society, 2001); *Ceramicus Redivivus: The Early Iron Age Potters' Field in the Area of the Classical Athenian Agora* (published by the American School of Classical Studies at Athens, 2003); and *The Archaeology of Colonialism* (co-edited with Claire Lyons and published by the Getty Research Institute, 2002). Forthcoming monographs include two volumes on the Early Iron Age in the *Athenian Agora* series and a volume on the Archaic votive metal objects from the site of Francavilla Marittima in southern Italy.

Charles Redman received his B.A. from Harvard University and his M.A. and Ph.D. in Anthropology from the University of Chicago. He taught at New York University and at SUNY-Binghamton before coming to Arizona State University. Since then, he served for nine years as Chair of the Department of Anthropology, and in 1997 assumed the directorship of the Center for Environmental Studies. Redman's interests include human impact on the environment, historical ecology, rise of civilization, urban ecology, environmental education, and public outreach. The author or co-author of nine books, including *Explanation in Archaeology, The Rise of Civilization, People of the Tonto Rim*, and most recently *Human Impact on Ancient Environments*, he has directed archaeological field projects in the Near East, North Africa, and Arizona. Redman has served as Principal Investigator or Co-principal Investigator on thirty-five research grants from federal, state, and private agencies totaling over $24 million. Five years ago he began co-directing the Central Arizona-Phoenix Long Term Ecological Research project, the first established by the National Science Foundation in an urban arid locale. He is also co-directing the recent expansion of this urban ecological research to include an innovative interdisciplinary Ph.D. program sponsored by the National Science Foundation. Redman is also a founding member of the Southwest Center for Education and the Natural Environment, an officer of the state chapter of The Nature Conservancy, and subcommittee chair of the Governor's Groundwater Management Commission. He has served as a member of several state and national councils, including Chair of the State's Archaeology Advisory Commission and the Arizona Advisory Council on Environmental Education, and a member of the Science Advisory Committees of Biosphere 2 and The Wenner-Gren Foundation.

Colin Renfrew is Disney Professor of Archaeology in the University of Cambridge and Director of the McDonald Institute for Archaeological Research. He has conducted excavations at Saliagos near Antiparos (with Professor J. Evans), at Phylakopi in Melos, at Sitagroi in East Macedonia, and (in collaboration with Professors Lila Marangou and Christos Doumas) at Markiani in Amorgos and Dhaskaleio Kavos on Keros. He was made a Fellow of the British Academy in 1980 and a Foreign Associate of the National Academy of Sciences of the USA in 1997. His publications include *The Emergence of Civilisation: the Cyclades and the Aegean in the Third Millennium BC* (1972), *Archaeology and Language: the Puzzle of Indo European Origins* (1987), and *Loot, Legitimacy and Ownership: the Ethical Crisis in Archaeology* (2000).

Steven Rosen is head of the Archaeological Division at Ben-Gurion University in Beersheva, Israel. His current research interests focus on desert adaptations, especially the archaeology of pastoral nomadism and the analysis of lithic assemblages from protohistoric and historic periods in the Near East. Major publications include *Archaeological Survey of Israel Map of Makhtesh Ramon – 204* (Jerusalem, 1994); *The 'Oded Sites: Investigations at Two Early Islamic Pastoral Encampments in the South Central Negev* (with G. Avni, Beersheva, 1994); *Lithics After the Stone Age: A Handbook of Stone Tools from the Levant* (Walnut Creek, 1997); and numerous professional papers. Current research projects include excavations at the desert cult site of Ramat Saharonim in the central Negev, at the lithic workshop at Titris Hoyuk in Turkey, and at Early Bronze Age pastoral nomadic encampments in the Negev.

Curtis Runnels is Professor of Archaeology in the Department of Archaeology at Boston University. Educated at the University of Kansas and Indiana

University, he taught at Indiana University, Stanford University, and since 1987 at Boston University. Runnels is a specialist in Aegean prehistory. He participated in the Franchthi Cave excavations in Greece and since 1973 has directed or participated in survey projects and museum studies in Greece, Turkey, and Albania. Among his recent monographs are *Greece Before History: An Archaeological Companion and Guide* (with Priscilla Murray, 2001); *Beyond the Acropolis: A Rural Greek Past* (with Tjeerd H. van Andel, 1987); *A Greek Countryside: The Southern Argolid from Prehistory to the Present Day* (with Michael H. Jameson and Tjeerd H. van Andel, 1994); and *Artifact and Assemblage: The Finds from a Regional Survey of the Southern Argolid, Greece* (edited with Daniel J. Pullen and Susan Langdon, 1995), all from Stanford University Press.

James Sackett, Professor emeritus of Anthropology at UCLA, is director of the European Laboratory of the Cotsen Institute of Archaeology at UCLA. He periodically conducted late Stone Age archaeology over more than three decades in the Perigord region of southwestern France, excavating both rock shelters and open-air stations. The latter include the site of Solvieux, one of the archaeologically richest and areally most extensive complexes of Upper Paleolithic occupation known in Western Europe. Sackett's interests include the history of archaeology and the play of style in material culture, topics that have in fact dominated most of his research and writing during the past few years.

Charles Stanish is Professor of Anthropology and Director of the Cotsen Institute of Archaeology at UCLA. He has worked in Guatemala, Bolivia, and Peru for the last twenty years. Since 1988 he has directed the Programa Collasuyu in the Lake Titicaca Basin in the southern highlands of Peru. His earlier books include *Ancient Andean Political Economy* (1992), and *Ritual and Pilgrimage in the Ancient Andes* (with B. Bauer, 2001), both by the University of Texas Press; and *Ancient Titicaca* (2003), published by the University of California Press. He continues to work in western South America studying the evolution of political and economic complexity in the archaeological record.

Nicholas Stanley-Price, who received his B.A. and D.Phil. from Oxford University, trained as an archaeologist and carried out archaeological research and administration in the East Mediterranean and Middle East for 12 years. His doctoral research was on the early prehistory of Cyprus, after which he held archaeological posts in Jerusalem and the Sultanate of Oman. He then was on the staff of ICCROM, the intergovernmental conservation organization in Rome (1982–86) and the Getty Conservation Institute in Los Angeles (1987–95), specializing in archaeological conservation and professional education. At the Institute of Archaeology at University College London he taught site conservation and management (1998–2000), introducing a new M.A. program on the topic. Since August 2000 he has been Director-General of ICCROM in Rome. The books he has edited include *Conservation on Archaeological Excavations* (1984); *Preventive Measures During Excavation and Site Protection* (1986), both published by ICCROM; and *Historical and Philosophical Issues in Conservation of Cultural Heritage* (Getty Conservation Institute, 1996). He has also published many articles on archaeology and conservation. He founded and edits the quarterly journal *Conservation and Management of Archaeological Sites*.

Ruth Tringham is Professor of Anthropology at the University of California, Berkeley. Her research during the last thirty years has focused on the transformation of early agricultural (Neolithic) societies of Eastern Europe, where she directed archaeological excavations in the former Yugoslavia and Bulgaria. Some of this work was published, for example, in the monograph *Selevac* (UCLA Institute of Archaeology, 1990). Her early book *Hunters, Fishers, and Farmers of Eastern Europe* became a classic on these subjects. Since 1997 she has expanded this research interest to include Turkey, directing a team in the excavation of the 9000-year-old site of Çatalhöyük. Her current research focuses on the life histories of buildings and the construction of place. Much of her recent practice of archaeology incorporates the utilization of digital, especially multimedia, technology in the presentation of the process of archaeological interpretation. This work was published, for example, in *The Chimera Web*, about the Neolithic site of Opovo, Yugoslavia, and in *Dead Women Do Tell Tales*, her current project about Çatalhöyük.

Lothar von Falkenhausen is Professor of Chinese archaeology and art history at UCLA. His main area of research is the Chinese Bronze Age, as evidenced by numerous publications (for example, *Suspended Music: Chime-bells in the Culture of Bronze Age China* [1993] and "The Waning of the Bronze Age: Material Culture and Social Developments" in *The Cambridge History of Ancient China* [1999]). He is the American Co-principal Investigator in a multiyear joint archaeological project investigating ancient salt production in the Upper Yangzi river basin. He is also the founder and co-editor of the *Journal of East Asian Archaeology* (1999–present).

INTRODUCTION

CHAPTER 1

Engaging Mediterranean Archaeology: Old World and New World Perspectives

JOHN K. PAPADOPOULOS

Our original goals for this publication of the first Cotsen Advanced Seminar were modest: to select a few key themes of cross-cultural significance in the discipline of archaeology and to bring together a number of Old World and New World archaeologists to discuss them. The focus on the Old World was inspired by Lloyd Cotsen's interest in and contributions to the field of Aegean prehistory, not least as architect of the excavations at Ayia Irini on Kea and Lerna, and for his work at the Palace of Nestor at Pylos (Davis chapter 2). The New World response acknowledges the interdisciplinary strengths of the Cotsen Institute of Archaeology at UCLA, which brings together archaeologists and specialists from various departments in the humanities and social sciences.

Finding a suitable title for the workshop and for this volume has not proved straightforward. Originally, the title was cast as "Archaeology in the Mediterranean: The Present State and Future Scope of a Discipline." For scholars of early Greece—Classical or Hellenist archaeologists as they have come to be known (see I. Morris 1994)—the subtitle was an open tribute to Anthony Snodgrass's *An Archaeology of Greece: The Present State and Future Scope of a Discipline* (1987). Indeed, the first four chapters of that book provided something of a backdrop for some of the themes covered in the workshop and in this publication: the health of a discipline, archaeology and history (writ large), the rural landscape of ancient Greece, and the rural landscape of Greece today. Our focus was sharply on the Aegean, but the issues covered were not confined to just the Aegean. Although the workshop was, in part, an overview of where we have been and where we might be going with the discipline of archaeology as a whole, particularly in parts of the Mediterranean, it is not an archaeology of the Mediterranean—*sensu strictu*—nor was it conceived as such. Ours was not an endeavor shaped by the seminal contribution of Fernand Braudel (1966), nor was it an attempt to deal with the expansive history and cultural ecology of *The Corrupting Sea* (Horden and Purcell 2000). After exploring a number of alternative titles, we finally settled on *Theory and Practice in Mediterranean Archaeology: Old World and New World Perspectives*, which seemed to describe best both the workshop and this volume. From the very outset we wished to avoid an introspective overview of Aegean or Mediterranean archaeology, and one way of achieving this was to open the discussion to scrutiny by scholars working in the New World. Consequently, this book concerns a number of general archaeological themes from the perspective of Old World archaeologists, with responses by New World colleagues or by colleagues working in very different parts of the Old World.

The themes covered were at the same time broad, attempting to address issues of cross-cultural significance, as well as specifically focused. They were chosen to stimulate discussion on a variety of issues common to archaeology as a discipline: the future of large-scale archaeological fieldwork, particularly at "the site"; archaeology and text; interpretation and preservation of archaeological sites; regional survey, landscape, and settlement archaeology; and new approaches to the archaeology of the Stone Age. Many of the original sessions in which these papers were aired were titled to promote reaction and response. Each of the Old World participants was asked to provide a basic overview of the subject by summarizing a history or historiography of the work done; reviewing major successes and shortcomings; identifying critical issues that determined and defined the field, both in the past and present; and pointing to future directions. These presentations served as a springboard for discussion and response by archaeologists working in the Americas. In the publication of these papers, we have kept to the basic structure of the workshop, although we have rearranged slightly the order of the papers and have asked the moderators and some of the more vocal participants to contribute to the volume. We have also added two papers by scholars (Redman and Marcus) who were not part of the original workshop.[1]

Archaeology and Text

The themes covered in this book begin with what was framed by the late Emily Vermeule (1996) as "the dirt and the word." Archaeology and text have enjoyed a special relationship in the study of Greece and of the eastern and central Mediterranean more generally, as they have in Central America and in other parts of the world. The parallel lives of Michael Ventris and Linda Schele and their respective roles in the decipherment of Mycenaean

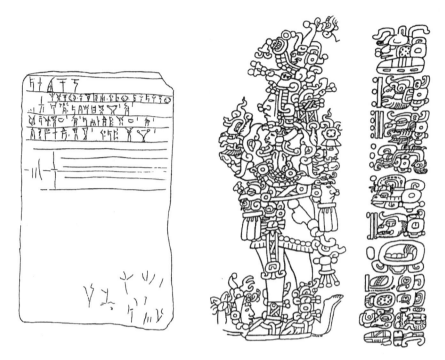

(ABOVE LEFT): FIGURE 1.1. Linear B tablet in Mycenaean Greek, Pylos Tn 316. Late Helladic III B, ca. 1200 BC. *Line drawing by Emmet L. Bennett, Jr. Courtesy of the Program in Aegean Scripts and Prehistory, the University of Texas at Austin.*

(ABOVE RIGHT): FIGURE 1.2. Line drawing of the front and back of the jade celt known as the Leiden Plaque. Maya, Early Classic Period, ca. AD 320. *Drawing by Linda Schele. Courtesy of the Program in Aegean Scripts and Prehistory, the University of Texas at Austin.*

and Maya writing (figures 1.1, 1.2) are strikingly similar in the manner in which they affected the study of the Greek Bronze Age and the Classic period of the Maya and opened new vistas of interpretation (for example, Palaima, Pope, and Reilly 2000). In the Old World, the decipherment of Linear B was a relatively late event in terms of other decipherments. It is worth remembering that in the late eighteenth century virtually nothing was known about the ancient civilizations of Egypt and the Near East, except what was recorded in the Bible and by the ancient Greeks and Romans (Trigger 1989:39; Larsen 1996). The systematic investigation of Egypt was begun by French scholars who accompanied Napoleon in his invasion of Egypt in 1798–99 (figure 1.3)—archaeology, colonialism, and orientalism go back a long way (Lyons and Papadopoulos 2002)—and culminated in Jean-François Champollion's (1790–1832) decipherment of Egyptian script. This was followed by Georg Grotefend's (1775–1853) early attempts to translate cuneiform and by Henry Rawlinson's (1810–95) success, in the mid-nineteenth century, in deciphering an older Babylonian language through the study of the Old Persian version of the trilingual text carved by Darius I on the cliff at Behistun (Daniel 1967:197–210; Trigger 1989:39–40; see also Brunner-Traut 1984).

These linguistic developments were accompanied by the spectacular finds of Paul-Emile Botta at Nineveh and Khorsabad, and Austen Layard's discoveries at Nimrud and Kuyunjik, to mention only a few, adding a whole new arena to the impressive array of Egyptian art and material culture that Giovanni Belzoni and others had laid before Europe (Trigger 1989:39–40; Fagan 1975; Clayton 1982). These developments in Egyptology and Assyriology added over 3000 years of history to two crucial regions of special interest to biblical studies and ushered in a boom in archaeological fieldwork. The steady flow of new textual material, as well as vast amounts of sculpture and other ancient Near Eastern finds, aroused enormous interest in Europe, because the texts in particular not only paralleled early stories in the Bible but took them back to an even more remote past (see also Trigger 1989:40).

The fantastic "telescopic" view looking south up the Nile from Alexandria to Philae (figure 1.3) adds a further element to the archaeology of the "East," namely the framing and claiming of, in this particular case, Egyptian antiquity. As D.M. Reid (2002:3, Fig. 1) writes: "The landscape shows no Cairo, Islamic monuments, or modern inhabitants" (see Said 1978). From early on, Western scholars viewed Egypt and the Near East through their own filtered lenses.

In "Archaeology and Text: Decipherment, Translation, and Interpretation" (chapter 3), Thomas Palaima diachronically reviews the subdiscipline, as he puts it, of Mycenology. Well before Michael Ventris showed Linear B to be an early, syllabic form of Greek, archaeology and texts were inextricably connected. The ramifications of the decipherment in 1952 were immense in Greek prehistory and archaeology; in Homeric studies; in Near Eastern, Mesopotamian, and cross-cultural documentary evidence; and in Indo-European studies (see also Barber 1974; Bennett 1989; Robinson 1995: 108–119). Palaima reviews the successes of decipherment and how they contributed to archaeology, anthropology, and history, including the history of religion.

Despite the enormous advances in our knowledge of Aegean prehistory brought about by the decipherment of Linear B, the close relationship of archaeology and text in the Greek world, particularly in the Classical period,

FIGURE 1.3. Vivant Denon, frontispiece to the *Description de l'Egypt*, 1809. Fantastic "telescopic" view looking south up the Nile from Alexandria to Philae in the distance. Features on the west (right) bank include, from near to far, the Sphinx and a pyramid, Dendera, the Ramesseum, Colossi of Memnon and Medinet Habu, Armant, and Edfu. On the east bank, in the foreground, is the obelisk of Heliopolis; beyond lie Antaeopolis, Karnak, Luxor, and Kom Ombo.

has been a stormy marriage—not exactly the same but not unlike that between Old Testament history and archaeology in modern Israel (compare Rosen chapter 11). It is a relationship in which one of the two parties is subordinate (Snodgrass 1987:37). The tyranny of the text has loomed large in the study of ancient Greece (Papadopoulos 1999), and as Snodgrass (1987: 37) has argued, Greek archaeology "has been married to, or waiting on, the wrong kind of history." For many scholars in various parts of the world, archaeology continues to remain "the handmaid of history" (for which see Snodgrass 1987).

In "Writing History: The Maya and the Mediterranean" (chapter 4), Richard Leventhal not only notes the similarities between the process of decipherment of Mycenaean and Maya script but also the fact that the decipherment of the ancient Maya writing system has led to a controversy—a divide or polarity—between archaeologists, on the one hand, and epigraphers and art historians on the other. The decipherment of Maya hieroglyphs a quarter century ago led to a new development in Maya studies: the self-proclaimed writing of *history*. Leventhal points to the multiplicity of meanings of the script and the fact that words and pictures are an integral part of ideology and expressions of power within both modern and ancient societies. He points to three basic types of analysis of the text: translation and the assignment of meanings to any given text; hieroglyphs as "historical activity"—or, as Kent Lightfoot (1995) put it in a very different context, the continued practice of using historical records as direct historic analogues—and, finally, the fact that culture can be constructed by texts. Leventhal argues that Maya iconography and writing should be analyzed in terms of the construction of power relations, the construction of kingship, and the construction of the state. In this, he echoes what is often stated: that history is written by the winners (see also Paynter 1990:59; Papadopoulos 1999).

New and Old World perspectives on archaeology and texts are elaborated by Sarah Morris in "New Worlds, Ancient Texts: Perspectives on Epigraphy and Archaeology" (chapter 5). She begins with the quinquecentennial of the arrival of Columbus in 1492, an event that generated many revisions of the confrontation between a world still reliant on Mediterranean traditions and an unsuspected continent of new cultures and languages. She compares and contrasts the role(s) of the Maya and Mycenaean scribe and the essential part they played in creating and maintaining systems of power. In so doing, Morris uncovers the prehistory of the adage: the pen is mightier than the sword. Morris also points to a systemic difference between New World archaeology, which has maintained a primary allegiance with anthropology—and in some sectors a deliberate distancing from texts in seeking answers independently from the material record—whereas in the Mediterranean world, Aegean prehistory has maintained its academic home in the humanities. This is a theme echoed in Charles Stanish's paper on settlement archaeology (chapter 10). Morris effectively explores what keeps archaeology in North America linked—or chained—to other disciplines in both the

New and Old Worlds and where these bonds might lead in the future. Both Leventhal and Morris turn to the vast range of meanings or messages communicated in the symbols of the Maya script—what Colin Renfrew (chapter 21) would refer to as its "dazzling variety and multiplicity." Here it would be useful to look, albeit briefly, at the language that the ancients themselves used to describe the process of writing. In ancient Greek there is no distinction between the word *to write* and *to paint* (Papadopoulos 1994). The word *graphein* may denote any number of meanings, including to scratch; to sketch, draw, or paint; to write; to inscribe; to brand; or, generally, to write down. In the formative period of the creation of the Greek alphabet, language and iconography were not the monoliths they have come to be. In a related vein, Maya hieroglyphs—which were syllabic in value although some signs functioned ideographically or morphemically—could be written, painted, inscribed, or even sculpted.

Large-Scale Archaeological Fieldwork in a New Millennium

Throughout the Mediterranean, the archaeological site has loomed large as a focus of memory and identity. Ruins contain the remnants of former worlds, a living reminder of the past in the present. Some sites, like the Acropolis of Athens (figure 1.4)—albeit a nineteenth-century restoration defined by the neo-Classical sensitivities of the archaeologists of the time (McNeal 1991;

FIGURE 1.4. The Athenian Acropolis from the Hill of the Muses (Philopappos). Albumen print by Anonymous ca. 1865. *Gary Edwards Collection, Getty Research Institute, acc. no. 92.R.84 (04.01.04).*

FIGURE 1.5. The Temple of Poseidon at Sounion, built in the middle of the fifth century BC, with boat in the foreground. Albumen print by Petros Moraites ca. 1865–1870. *Gary Edwards Collection, Getty Research Institute, acc. no. 92.R.84 (06.02.01).*

FIGURE 1.6. General view of Mycenae. *Drawing by Sir William Gell, after Gell 1810: Pl. 13.*

see also Hurwit 1999:301)—or the Temple of Poseidon at Cape Sounion (figure 1.5), have never been lost from human view. The same is true for prehistoric sites throughout the Mediterranean and well beyond. Figure 1.6 shows the ruins of Mycenae within its greater landscape as sketched by Sir William Gell (1810) at the turn of the nineteenth century. With the

FIGURE 1.7. The Gate of the Lions at Mycenae constructed in the middle of the thirteenth century BC. Albumen print by Anonymous ca. 1859. *Gary Edwards Collection, Getty Research Institute, acc. no. 92.R.84 (03.18)*.

invention of photography in 1839, early photographers of Greek antiquities had an array of monuments to choose from in their creation of "true illusions," as Andrew Szegedy-Maszak (1987) so cogently described. The detail of the Lions' Gate at Mycenae (figure 1.7) with debris in the portal was taken in 1859 and predates Heinrich Schliemann's 1876 excavations at the site. Similarly, the detail of the "Cyclopean" walls of the Bronze Age acropolis of Tiryns by Constantine Athanassiou was taken in 1875 (figure 1.8), more or less at the same time as Schliemann's historic excavations at the site. The Gate of the Lions was constructed sometime around 1250 BC, and is roughly contemporary with the fortification walls of Tiryns. In a similar vein, archaeological sites in the New World became a legacy neither fully remembered nor fully forgotten. The image of the so-called Second Palace at Mitla in Oaxaca (figure 1.9) was taken by the French photographer Désiré

FIGURE 1.8. Detail of the Cyclopean masonry of the Bronze Age acropolis of Tiryns built in the thirteenth century BC. Albumen print by Constantine Athanassiou ca. 1875. *Gary Edwards Collection, Getty Research Institute, acc. no. 92.R.84 (04.25.05).*

Charnay in March 1859, the same year as the photograph of the Lion's Gate at Mycenae (figure 1.7) (see Roth, Lyons, and Merewether 1997:26–27). Dating to the years between AD 800 and 1200, the ruins of Mitla became the site of a large Christian church—itself partly built using the stones of the Mixtec ruins—and continued to exert its influence in a different way. The photograph of the site of Palenque in Mexico (figure 1.10), taken by Alfred P. Maudslay in the 1880s, vividly shows how archaeologists reclaimed a lost civilization from the wilds of the jungle.

In Aegean as in Mediterranean prehistory, however, whole sites—and cultures—were resurrected, even *invented* in the course of the nineteenth and early twentieth centuries. Heinrich Schliemann's sensational discoveries at Troy, Mycenae, and Tiryns laid bare the Late Bronze Age civilization of the Aegean. As Bruce Trigger has shown, Schliemann's discoveries, more than anything else, awakened not only classical scholars to the realization that ancient mythology and epic poetry might be connected with historical events and actual places. From this time forward, the public has often looked

FIGURE 1.9. The "Second Palace" at Mitla in Oaxaca, Mexico, dating to ca. AD 800–1200. Albumen print by Désiré Charnay ca. 1859. *Getty Research Institute, acc. no. 95.R.126*.*

FIGURE 1.10. Detail of the clearing of the site of Palenque, Mexico. Albumen print by Alfred P. Maudslay ca. 1880s. *Getty Research Institute, acc. no. 94.R.31.*

to archaeology to support or uproot diverse historical, political, and social movements throughout the world (Trigger 1989:3). Unlike Schliemann, however, Arthur Evans's excavations at Knossos (figure 1.11) took him back before Classical Greece and even before Schliemann's Homeric Greece. Without the aid of substantial texts, he ventured into a realm of interpretation based purely on objects and architecture, the very stuff of the archaeological record, and his own vivid imagination (Papadopoulos 1997).

Knossos and Mycenae were only two Mediterranean sites, albeit among the most prominent, investigated in the nineteenth and early twentieth centuries. In "(Re)-digging the Site at the End of the Twentieth Century: Large-scale Archaeological Fieldwork in a New Millennium" (chapter 6), Ruth Tringham turns to her own personal experience in directing large-scale excavations at Selevac and Opovo in Yugoslavia, Podgoritsa in Bulgaria, and Çatalhöyük in Turkey. The focus—past and present—on investigating large visible sites and the ramifications, including paradigm shifts, of large-scale exposure by excavation form only part of Tringham's study. She looks at the nature of large-scale archaeological fieldwork in a new millennium: large

FIGURE 1.11. The "Grand Staircase" of the "Palace of Minos" at Knossos during restoration in 1910. Arthur Evans, dressed in white, is seen in the upper center right. Duncan Mackenzie, wearing a pith helmet, served as Evans's assistant and the supervising field archaeologist. Next to him is architect Christian Doll, wearing a wide-brimmed hat. *Courtesy of the Evans Archive, Ashmolean Museum, Oxford.*

scale in terms of time and personnel, and at the very root of the term "large scale," the essential question: What is the objective of the excavation? In looking at new trends at the beginning of the twenty-first century in eastern Mediterranean archaeology, Tringham notes that the traditional dichotomy of site-oriented research versus regional research had become clouded at the end of the twentieth century. She stresses the great advances in geophysics, satellite imagery, ground-penetrating radar, sonic physics, and other developments of the later twentieth century and how they have radically changed the character of fieldwork. To these she adds the digitization of archaeological data, moving beyond the quantification and statistical manipulation of information to the use of EDMs, GPS receivers, GIS, and CAD software, together with digital video and image cameras, and the emerging role of digital publication and dissemination of fieldwork. Tringham also turns her attention to the destructive nature of archaeology, the more destructive effects of looting, and how archaeologists themselves have become more sensitive to their responsibilities in conserving local cultural heritage. Many of these themes are also addressed by other papers in this volume. The demystification and democratization of digitization and multimedia—the low-tech digitization revolution—has facilitated the practice of a more reflexive methodology and has led to exciting ideas about the way in which archaeology can view prehistory and the many voices of the actors who participated in this prehistory.

Many of the challenges Tringham poses are confronted in "Archaeology for a New Millennium" (chapter 7) by Charles Redman, who goes on to pose a number of challenges of his own. He begins with several themes that archaeologists of a generation ago looked to in order to work on a larger scale. These include an expanded geographical scale, a sufficient sample of phenomena of interest to determine the scope of variability, and a fuller recovery of the range of material in the archaeological record. He notes that Tringham's approach goes considerably beyond these goals to a new level of detail and sensitivity, but Redman returns to the conundrum posed by Tringham herself: whereas research demands are increasing, the modest financial resources and growing conservation ethic are working against the freedom of archaeology to devote adequate energy to individual archaeological sites. Redman reviews several trajectories that archaeologists have pursued to overcome this conflict, and in so doing turns his gaze to the growth of culture resource management in the Mediterranean, Europe, the Near East, and United States. He also focuses on the dichotomy between salvage projects and those larger-scale expeditions conducted by universities or related institutions. Indeed, the divide between archaeologists working on salvage projects—often under the shadow of angry landowners, developers, and bulldozers—and those working on larger-scale and longer-termed excavations is profound in many Mediterranean countries. Following Tringham, Redman sees a great deal of potential in the changing nature of interdisciplinary research, but he does not underestimate the difficulty of bridging disciplinary boundaries. The basic issue, according to Redman, is whether we should train researchers to be sufficiently skilled at a number of necessary disciplines or whether we should be training them to retain their disciplinary focus but be more collaborative. In a world of intense competition for limited resources, Redman believes that archaeology is not holding its own and that it is certainly not growing. He tempers this pessimism, however, with the fundamental strengths of archaeology and looks to these for the future. Not only are archaeologists good at deriving meaning from spatial patterns—something that ecologists are only beginning to recognize—but as the primary purveyors of time depth, the *longue durée* remains the preserve of archaeology. More than this, archaeology controls a unique database concerning, among other issues, human-environmental relationships, religious fundamentalism, multiculturalism, and urban growth. Redman urges archaeology to situate itself more strategically in major research initiatives, and urges archaeologists to take a leadership role in the integration of the social and life sciences.

In "Monumentality in Archaic States" (chapter 8) Joyce Marcus turns to the lessons learned from larger-scale excavations of the past and in the process casts her net wide to encompass a variety of Old World and New World cultures. Complementing Tringham's focus on houses and individual life histories, Marcus turns to public buildings and monumental structures, including some of the most enduring archaeological monuments in Egypt and Central and South America. In so doing, Marcus questions a number of endemic assumptions:

- That monumentality equals power

- That early states had less power than later states

- That the bigger the monument, the more powerful the ruler or the government that commissioned it

- That the most elegant tombs are those of legitimate rulers in the direct line of succession

Although many of these assumptions are seemingly simplistic, Marcus argues that many archaeologists continue, whether consciously or subconsciously, to treat them as universally valid. By looking behind these assumptions and their motivations, Marcus points to a variety of issues, including the use of labor and broader economic policies, the politics of power, and the power and meaning of texts (see also Marcus 1995). The most essential issue is that archaeologists cannot directly observe power. Marcus reviews a number of blatant cases, such as the Great Pyramids of Egypt and similarly imposing monuments at Teotihuacan, the Moche State, and the Maya pyramids at Palenque and Tikal, and concludes with a cautionary tale drawn from the Zapotec civilization of Oaxaca, Mexico. The Egyptian, Peruvian, Maya, and Zapotec cases that Marcus examines warn that monumentality in ancient states is not a direct reflection of political power.

The Recent Past and the Remote Past: Regional Survey and the Archaeological Landscape

The old dichotomy of site-oriented research versus regional research is an issue taken up by John Cherry in his penetrating paper on "Archaeology Beyond the Site: Regional Survey and Its Future" (chapter 9). Some twenty years ago, Cherry's (1983) robust defense of survey as an approach to regional research questions—in his own words, one adopting "a strongly evangelical tone about survey"—was highly influential. Between then and now, there has been an immense volume of fieldwork, analysis, and publication. The past developments, current issues, and a look to the future that Cherry reviews underscore the significant contributions that regional survey has had on the landscape of the Mediterranean. At the same time, it shows how far our knowledge of the landscape of ancient and modern Greece has developed since Snodgrass's 1987 review. As Cherry stresses, the picture has not always been a rosy one, but the various debates have invariably led to a healthier discipline. In looking to the future, Cherry enumerates several selective critical issues for survey. The astonishing developments in computing capabilities and the possibility of conducting meta-searches of numerous Web-based survey databases, together with the remote sensing revolution with its far-reaching implications for research at the regional level, are only a few conceivable future avenues.

At the same time, Cherry is mindful of the political and cultural implications of the tourist industry, national and European Union agricultural policies, and economic development and their irrevocable effects on the landscape. He also effectively brings to the fore the fact that current legislation regarding heritage preservation is based on the assumption that there are a finite number of locations or "sites," whereas Mediterranean-wide surveys have demonstrated that the surface archaeological record is considerably more interesting and complex. Here it is worth drawing attention to the archaeology of Australia, where surveys along parts of the Murray and Darling Rivers of eastern Australia have brought to light palimpsests of repeated short-term use where whole stretches of a riverbank—effectively a continuous landscape—are virtually a continual site of human activity by mobile people rather than discrete "sites" of sedentary activity (compare Lesure chapter 14). More than this, Cherry, following the seminal contributions of Michalis Fotiadis (1993, 1995, 1997), exposes the often orientalist, nationalist, romanticized, touristic, and urban-based motivations that underlie the colonialist character of many archaeological survey projects. In so doing, Cherry moves toward reconciling survey projects that have followed a broadly processual approach with the more postmodern "archaeologies of landscape" that have emerged in recent years (for example, the introduction of Ashmore and Knapp 1999; Ucko and Layton 1999), which stress experimental and phenomenological approaches, as well as human perception and the symbolic ordering of space.

Charles Stanish, in "A Brief Americanist Perspective on Settlement Archaeology" (chapter 10), returns to the familiar Old World dichotomy of site-oriented research versus regional research and argues that, in the Americas, settlement studies and excavation are usually integrated in single project research designs.[2] He turns, first of all, to the methodology and theoretical underpinnings of settlement archaeology in the New World and the strong intellectual and professional bonds between archaeology and anthropology in the Americas. This approach echoes Bruce Trigger's (1978:75–95; see also Moreland 2001) contention that archaeology in Europe tends to be traditionally linked with history, whereas in North America it is linked with anthropology. Beyond this, Stanish argues that the development of settlement archaeology in the Americas was intimately tied to the emergence of cultural ecological theory associated with the developments of the still-called "New Archaeology" a generation ago. Stanish reviews the contributions of pioneers, such as Gordon Willey, Julian Steward, and others working in the New World, but also the seminal contribution of Robert McC. Adams (1966, 1981), whose research in Mesopotamia—cited by Stanish as a "methodological canon of anthropological archaeology"—was ironically more influential in the Americas than it was in the Mediterranean. In this, Stanish echoes Cherry's concern for the importance of dialogue between archaeologists of various persuasions in the New and Old Worlds. The considerably weaker link between archaeology and anthropology in the Mediterranean, particularly in Greece, is an issue effectively explored by Michael Herzfeld, who notes the "curious silence" that "enfolds the connection between Modern Greek culture and the practice of anthropology" (Herzfeld 1987:1). As Herzfeld (1987) has intimated, since ancient Greece was the idealized spiritual and intellectual ancestor of Europe, anthropology—the study of humankind that emerged from the heyday of European dominance—has found disproportionately little theoretical use for the Greece of today.

Following on the Aegean experience outlined by Cherry, particularly the link between the Homeric texts and Aegean prehistory, Steve Rosen looks to the development of landscape archaeology in the Levant in "Settlement and Survey Archaeology: A View from a 'Periphery'" (chapter 11). Rosen characterizes the late nineteenth and early twentieth century development of survey archaeology in the Levant as part of a quest to identify places associated with the Bible. Indeed, the deep symbolic power of the Bible, as the source text for both fundamentalist Christianity and nationalist Zionism, continues to this day. In contrast, settlement archaeology in the Americas, without the burden of a Homer or the Bible, fast-forwarded from early explorers to a universalist theoretical paradigm: cultural ecology. This difference between the trajectory of settlement and survey archaeology in the Classical world and the Near East, on the one hand, and the Americas, on the other, is reflected, as Rosen cogently notes, in the near absence of overlapping bibliography in Cherry's and Stanish's papers. Another difference Rosen notes is that, in both the Classical and Near East worlds, survey archaeologists were largely investigating their own past, not that of someone else. Rosen goes on to provide a synthetic overview of the development of survey archaeology in the Levant, beginning with the pioneering work of Nelson Glueck in the 1930s and including the very specific situation of Israel. Beginning in the 1950s, archaeology in Israel was dominated by a local cadre of archaeologists whose research agenda was dictated by the needs and concerns of a larger society, a society building a national identity (Silberman 1989; Silberman and Small 1997; Zerubavel 1995), though Israel is not alone in using archaeology in the forging of a nation. Despite important advances, Rosen sees the development of survey archaeology lagging behind both the Americas and the Aegean, much of which is the result of the enduring legacy of the biblical texts. Turning an eye back to the Americas, Rosen points to the irony that, in the world of the Maya, the decipherment of Maya script led to something of a schism between text and non-text-based archaeologies (Coe 1992; Leventhal chapter 4; Morris chapter 5, even though many Maya scholars have found the availability of texts constructively stimulating for archaeological research [for example, Fash and Sharer 1991]), thereby mirroring a situation in the Levant and the Aegean that was there from the beginning. Beyond the texts, the more recent influence of prehistoric archaeology in the Levant, particularly the archaeology of the Paleolithic and Neolithic periods, has led to greater integration of prehistoric and historic archaeologies. Echoing Redman (chapter 7), Rosen looks to future collaborations, partnerships, and joint projects, not only among specialists but also among local and foreign archaeologists, as the next phase in the ongoing development of survey archaeology in the Levant.

One of the points that Cherry (chapter 9) stressed is the complex nature of the surface archaeological record. One aspect of this is the study of open-air sites and regional settlements in the Old Stone Age. In "The History and Future Prospects of Paleolithic Archaeology in Greece" (chapter 12), Curtis Runnels effectively shows how the outmoded research model in Greece that focused on cave sites was largely abandoned in the 1980s for a new paradigm of regional survey and land use studies based on the catchment analysis of Eric Higgs and Claudio Vita-Finzi. Echoing Cherry, Runnels stresses that the antiquities laws of Greece, formulated in the nineteenth century and based on the assumptions of that time, have severely limited future prospects in the study of Paleolithic land use beyond the cave. Runnels provides a cogent history of Paleolithic archaeology in Greece and its present state, as well as an attempt to assess future prospects. The recognition and systematic investigation of the Paleolithic and Mesolithic periods in the Aegean lagged far behind that of the Neolithic and was comparatively recent with respect to Paleolithic studies in Western Europe. Despite this, Runnels effectively summarizes the progress of regional surveys and interdisciplinary research in the Greek Paleolithic, particularly from the 1960s to the end of the twentieth century. In assessing future prospects, Runnels identifies a number of political, social, economic, and cultural factors, including education, legislation, and government administration, that may lead to a more uncertain and less productive future for Paleolithic studies in Greece. As in the past, the prominence of large sites, coupled with a focus on their excavation and preservation, has contributed to a more general neglect of the greater landscape.

In "Exploring the Paleolithic in the Open Air: A View from the Perigord" (chapter 13), James Sackett comments on the specific situation of Paleolithic archaeology in Greece from the perspective of Western Europe, more particularly southwest France, where the study of the Paleolithic has enjoyed a longer history. Although cave sites have long been favored by Paleolithic specialists because their archaeology, as Sackett so nicely puts it, comes neatly packaged by nature itself, the so-called "cave people" of the Old Stone Age spent most of their time in the open air. In comparing the Paleolithic in France and Greece, Sackett focuses on the empirical makeup of the Paleolithic open-air record, something that has to be addressed before issues such as demography and economic and social organization can be fruitfully discussed. Sackett argues that it takes much more than the conventional sort of field walking survey to explore an open-air Paleolithic landscape in a part of the world, such as Greece, that is covered by post-Pleistocene topsoil. He also emphasizes that a major commitment to excavation is critical, noting that the "quick-and-dirty" methods advanced by archaeologists working with Neolithic or Bronze Age horizons are entirely inadequate. Sackett concludes that "serendipity, opportunity, an intimate and day-to-day familiarity of the landscape and the people who work it, freedom of entry to private property, and . . . a cultivated eye for the odd flint"—collectively the métier of the local amateur prehistorian—are the essential ingredients in exploring the Paleolithic in the open air.

The tyranny of the site—echoing the earlier tyranny of the text—is effectively explored by Richard Lesure in his paper on "Archaeologists and 'The Site'" (chapter 14). Although there is no Paleolithic in the New World, Lesure compares the state of Paleolithic studies in Greece with the situation in preceramic archaeology in Mexico. Indeed, Runnels's comments on the failure of standard field walking techniques for recovering Pleistocene or early Holocene sites resonate with the case of Mexico. Lesure turns his focus to the apparent schism between the archaeology of mobile and sedentary peoples, and the fact that not only antiquities laws, but archaeologists themselves, reify and fetishize the site. Whereas archaeologies of mobile peoples have been forced to confront the complex relationships between sites, as viewed by archaeologists, and the social phenomena they seek to study, archaeologies of settled peoples have tended to under-theorize "the relationship between the site as identified by archaeologists and the town as experienced by ancient inhabitants." In looking at appropriate approaches for the study of mobile peoples, Lesure effectively shows how the archaeology of mobile peoples, following the seminal contribution of Lewis Binford (1980), has freed itself from the fetters of the site in theoretical and methodological terms. Lesure ends by looking at what an archaeology of sedentism can draw from current trends in the study of mobile peoples.

Archaeology and Architecture

The power of architecture and the built environment, as living physical entities with which humans are constantly interacting, has been underestimated by many archaeologists. The layout of a hunter-gather camp, a Neolithic house, or an urban nucleus reinforces all manner of social relationships, hierarchies, and authority. Architecture is one of the most penetrating methods that permeates day-to-day social encounters, thereby infiltrating human minds and bodies (Bourdieu 1977). Such methods, practices, and techniques cultivate behavior and beliefs and mold the tastes, desires, and needs of any individual or society (see also Foucault 1977; Smart 1986:160). Architecture is not simply a residue of social behavior or interaction, but an active and primary agent in shaping identities and communities. More than this, the cultural symbolism of architecture is both real and blatant, because it serves as a powerful focus of memory: the illustrations of the Sphinx and Great Pyramid of Egypt (figure 1.12), the ruins of Angkor Wat in Cambodia (figure 1.13), and the remains of Stonehenge (figure 1.14) are only a few examples of the symbolic power such monuments exert.

Discussions exploring the site form the ideal backdrop to Clairy Palyvou's "Architecture and Archaeology: The Minoan Palaces in the Twenty-first Century" (chapter 15), which focuses on the so-called Palace of Minos at Knossos (figure 1.11) and explores in a penetrating manner the history of the common involvement of archaeology and architecture. Palyvou begins with architects' contributions to the interpretation process in archaeology, especially the contribution of various architects who worked for and with Sir Arthur Evans: Theodor Fyfe, Christian Doll, F. G. Newton, and Piet de Jong. She then turns to the drawings produced by the Knossos architects and shows that what seem to be missing are depictions of the ruins as found. We have, instead, published drawings, including watercolors, that are interpretational and one step ahead of the study of the archaeological remains. Such drawings are reminiscent of those that architects would prepare to implement their own work, and anticipated from the beginning the future restoration work at Knossos. Palyvou then asks the question of how can architecture be read

FIGURE 1.12. The Sphinx and the Great Pyramid. Photograph ca. 1857. From Francis Frith, *Lower Egypt, Thebes and the Pyramids*, London, 1862. *Getty Research Institute, acc. no. 84-B8850.*

FIGURE 1.13. French colonial mission to cast sculptures and photograph archaeological ruins, Angkor Wat, Cambodia. Albumen print by Urbain Basset ca. 1890–1899. *Getty Research Institute, acc. no. 96.R.127.*

FIGURE 1.14. Stonehenge. *From William Camden,* Britannia, *London, 1600 edition.*

through a drawing alone? To this end she effectively examines the three basic constituents of architecture: structure, form, and function (Vitruvius's *firmitas, utilitas, venustas*). Unlike many other sites, however, where antiquity was depicted through drawings (figure 1.14; a subject cogently explored in Piggott 1978), Knossos was subjected to full-scale restoration, or reconstitution, the term that Evans preferred (Papadopoulos 1997).

By 1930, three decades after Evans began his excavations at the low mound he was eventually to call the Palace of Minos, the monument was transformed from poorly preserved ruins into a sensational multistoried, brightly painted, concrete vision of the past. Palyvou turns to the technical aspects of this restoration and the ultimate Knossos that Evans and his architects left behind. In looking beyond Knossos to architecture and archaeology in the twenty-first century, Palyvou stresses that measuring and drawing—whether done with an electronic theodolite and a computer or a measuring tape and a pencil—still involve an interpretive process. She assesses the role of computer technology in architecture and adds that one new development is that architects working on archeological sites are expressing themselves in writing, in addition to drawing, more than at any other time in the past. Palyvou returns to the triad of structure-form-function to understand Minoan architecture and to assess its new and changing interpretations. Her final question is: how do our changing interpretations of Minoan architecture affect site presentation? The issue of site presentation and preservation is further treated in both Nicholas Stanley-Price's and Lynn Gamble's contributions to this volume (chapters 18 and 19, respectively).

Following on from his 1996 monograph on *Architecture and Power in the Ancient Andes: The Archaeology of Public Buildings*, Jerry Moore contends, in his paper entitled "Archaeology in Search of Architecture" (chapter 16), that the objectives and methods of archaeology and architecture are fundamentally divergent. Rather than advocating that archaeologists indiscriminately borrow the ideas and terminology used by architects, Moore recommends that archaeologists should invest in the creation of an anthropologically informed, holistic approach to the built landscape. The central objective of such an approach should be how past societies shaped and were shaped by their culturally constructed environments. His perspective provides a useful complement to Palyvou's contribution and a contrast between how things are done in the Old World and New World. Building on the comments of master architects, such as (Charles-Edouard) Le Corbusier, Louis Sullivan, and Frank Lloyd Wright, as well as architectural critics like Charles Jencks, Ada Louise Huxtable, Paul Goldberger, and Nicolai Ouroussof, Moore exposes fundamental differences between architecture and archaeology as disciplines. In moving toward an anthropological archaeology of architecture, Moore advocates a holistic approach because architecture and the built environment are inherently multidimensional. As he stresses, no building ever solely reflected "function," "style," "engineering," "energetics," "ideology," or "gender" to the exclusion of all other decision domains. At the same time, archaeologists have been slow in developing cogent analytical techniques for the study of architecture, and most "analytical methods" usually employ nonsystematic inferences derived from visual inspection of two-dimensional plans. Indeed, what may be termed "ground-plan" archaeology has been a mainstay in the study of architecture in many Mediterranean archaeological sites. In turning to new methods for the study of architecture, Moore discusses several recent examples of methods informed by a phenomenological approach to the built environment, directed toward the experience of the constructed landscape.

From the outset, Lothar von Falkenhausen's paper, "Architecture and Archaeology: A View from China" (chapter 17), stands in opposition to Moore's perspective that archaeologists have no intellectual common ground with architects. Von Falkenhausen emphasizes that, through excavated remains, architects of the present can commune in a very real sense with architects of the past, because "the physical remains of any ancient building embody its builders' conscious intentions in ways that are at least partially verifiable." Von Falkenhausen enumerates the links between architecture and archaeology and, echoing Palyvou, the fundamental significance of including an architect in any archaeological field project involving architecture. As immovable entities, buildings constitute part of the site matrix that is destroyed by the process of excavation, thereby necessitating the study of architecture in tandem with excavation. Moreover, given their size and the considerable investment of labor in their construction, buildings are usually more complex, culturally important, and potentially informative about a society than is a broad range of artifacts alone. This is because buildings not only exert a dominant impact on the landscape, they condition the spatial experience of local inhabitants in fundamental ways.

Von Falkenhausen goes on to provide a most useful overview of architecture and archaeology in China, beginning with the early studies by European and Japanese scholars, and the critical role played by Liang Sicheng and Lin Huiyin. The history of architectural and archaeological monuments in China has followed a trajectory very different from that of Europe or, indeed, much of the New World. With wood-framed constructions standing on top of stamped earth platforms constituting the predominant building type, the state of preservation of buildings is particularly poor. Coupled with this, wars and economic modernization have decimated China's architectural patrimony. The reliance on wooden architecture and of rebuilding in wood has not only contributed to the poor state of preservation of the archaeological remains—the earliest surviving Chinese wooden structure dates to the eighth century AD—but has led to a questioning of the applicability of the Venice Charter to the unique cultural circumstances of China. The charter was first developed at the Second International Congress of Architects and Technicians of Historic Monuments in Venice in 1964 and was officially adopted by the International Council of Monuments and Sites (ICOMOS) in 1965 (see Demas 1997). Despite these difficulties, the study of Chinese architecture has progressed a great deal in the last half century, thanks largely to the insights gained through archaeological discoveries. Following this overview, von Falkenhausen provides an account of the work of Yang Hongxun, the only full-time specialist currently working in China; in the process he uncovers a number of important contrasts, particularly with the Aegean and Mediterranean spheres. In the final section of his paper, von Falkenhausen turns his attention to the present and future issues of education, entertainment, tourism, architectural reconstruction, and heritage preservation, issues that are explored further in other parts of the world, as discussed in the next three chapters.

Site Preservation, Conservation, and Archaeological Ethics

A number of papers in this volume stress the importance of the conservation of archaeological sites and the pace of destruction of the landscape. Colin Renfrew notes in his paper (chapter 21) that it "is now very clear that the present of 2001 is not that of 1995: the present is changing more rapidly than it used to." The surviving remains of the past are finite and vulnerable, and the intrinsic importance and exhaustible nature of archaeological resources have been recognized in various international charters (Demas 1997). The conservation, management, and presentation of archaeological sites are subjects of great complexity and continued importance. Archaeological sites are of value to numerous individuals and groups (archaeologists, local populations, visitors, national authorities, and many others). In "Site Preservation and Archaeology in the Mediterranean Region" (chapter 18), Nicholas Stanley-Price begins by reviewing the historical development of policies for archaeology in the Mediterranean, and from there considers current issues in site preservation, which in turn point to possible future trends. Historically, issues such as site preservation, presentation to the public, and site management have tended to be addressed once fieldwork was completed. Stanley-Price emphasizes that, in contrast, contemporary thinking would stress that they need to be considered in advance of any fieldwork, and especially in advance of any destructive technique such as excavation.

Some key issues concerning site conservation and presentation in the Mediterranean revolve around what to do with exposed excavated remains. Apart from reburial (backfilling), which often comes up against numerous legal, ethical, and practical difficulties, most conservation solutions have fallen into one of two traditions: preserving the remains as excavated, and restoration or reconstruction. Stanley-Price assesses both alternatives. He notes that there is much more emphasis today on reducing the rate of deterioration of excavated remains by using a variety of preventive measures. He stresses that caution is needed with regard to the use of synthetic materials on archaeological sites, and notes that, although high-tech approaches still exist, there has been something of a return to more traditional methods of protection. Stanley-Price goes on to discuss the importance of documentation and publication. His main argument is that, in the emerging field of archaeological heritage management, the issues of conservation, presentation, and site management are no longer to be tackled after archaeological fieldwork. Instead, archaeology is considered but one use of a heritage site. Its potential impact must be foreseen as part of a systematic approach to the management of heritage sites that integrates research, conservation, and public access goals. In dealing with future trends, he notes that several current approaches to archaeological site management in the Mediterranean region go beyond the single site to treat whole landscapes; they also move away from the traditional model of sole management by a department of antiquities. Alternative models involve various interest groups, academic specialists, professional planners, tourism promoters, and local communities. In discussing these modes, he features a variety of rural and urban examples from the Côa Valley in Portugal to Butrint in Albania, and the Parco della Rocca di San Silvestro in Tuscany to the cities of Athens, Rome, Carthage, and Beirut.

Standing in stark contrast to the situation in most countries of the Mediterranean region is the practice of cultural resource preservation in the United States. In her paper "Obstacles to Site Preservation in the United States" (chapter 19), Lynn Gamble identifies three major obstacles in the history of the United States that have affected the conservation and preservation of archaeological heritage, particularly Native American heritage. First, America's colonial foundations not only affected the entire discipline of archaeology as practiced and taught in the United States, they are pervasive in the heritage management legislation of the nation. Gamble traces the tragic history of neglect of American Indian cultural heritage and the effects of national legislation on the protection of cultural resources, beginning with the Antiquities Act of 1906 and culminating in the Native American Graves Protection and Repatriation Act (NAGPRA) of 1990 and beyond. Recently invoked in the case of Kennewick Man (Thomas

2000), NAGPRA, like other similar laws in the United States, does not affect the excavation of archaeological remains on private lands unless federal oversight is required. The question of private landownership thus forms the second major obstacle. Cultural resources in the United States are protected differentially based on the type of landownership, and the legal ownership of land overrides the significance of heritage sites. Private property owners in the United States are granted legal rights over archaeological resources that far exceed such rights in the Mediterranean and in most regions of the world (about 60% of the 2.3 billion acres of land in the United States is privately owned). The third obstacle has to do with the limited number of sites with architectural remains. Gamble poses the question effectively: how do you save a site when no one knows it exists? The relative dearth of sites with blatantly visible archaeological remains has meant that preservationists must overcome great barriers to convince the public that sites with more subtle significance are worth preserving. Despite the fact that the United States has fallen behind many countries in the world in the preservation of cultural resources, Gamble discerns, nevertheless, something of a shift in attitudes, particularly within the archaeological community, and it is to these changes that she turns in the final section of her paper on the future of conservation in the United States.

In "Archaeology, Conservation, and the Ethics of Sustainability" (chapter 20), Claire Lyons focuses on the deepening respect for the physical and social consequences of field excavation. The realization that the past is an endangered and contested commodity represents one of the most fundamental sea changes in archaeology. As Lyons stresses, the mission of archaeology today goes well beyond (re)discovery and interpretation: it aims to reconcile three goals that stand at odds: scientific research, public access, and long-term preservation. Such a mission is no longer conducted introspectively but on a public stage before an audience whose demands can be inconsistent or even incompatible. In a similar vein, the mission of conservation professionals has gone far beyond the treatment of deteriorating objects, to playing a leading role in shaping policies that take contemporary values into account. Lyons not only emphasizes many of the issues described and discussed by Stanley-Price and Gamble, as well as those of other contributors to this volume, including Tringham, she highlights the critical issue of ethics in archaeology and conservation. Lyons goes on to review various codes of ethics and the momentum of ethical consciousness, particularly in the light of looting and the illicit traffic in antiquities. She turns to the role of collectors, dealers, and museums, as well as to the changing role of archaeologists, conservators, and archaeometry laboratories, and the impact and ramifications of national and international legislation. She notes that, when it comes to its own "best practices," archaeology still has some way to go. But looting is not the only threat. Agriculture, development, tourism, hydroelectric dams, environment degradation, ethnic conflict, religious iconoclasm, and plain neglect have all contributed to the destruction of monuments and sites throughout the world.

Against this backdrop, Lyons cautions that, as long as we think of excavators and conservators as partners in the introspective project of "archaeology as usual," the two professions will fail to make any real impact. What is required are changes in archaeology's field of operation, which in turn necessitates changes in ethics and practice. Echoing Redman, Lyons looks to cultural resource management and particularly the participation of community interests at all levels, that is, identifying the various stakeholder interests. Acknowledging the many voices and the fact that archaeological heritage is nonrenewable, Lyons borrows a page from environmentalists by embracing the notion of "sustainability," which involves satisfying the needs of the present without rendering those of the future impossible. Lyons ends by enumerating several guiding principles: caution (in that excavation should only be undertaken as a last resort and not solely as a means of satisfying curiosity or training students), utilizing resources carefully, better leveraging of existing data, proper documentation, equity among the various stakeholder groups, planning for diversity, and education. These recommendations underscore both remedial steps and the greater responsibility to redirect our ethical ideals. Lyons concludes that archaeology's ethical challenge is to publicly demonstrate its essential contribution to the issues that society will face in the next millennium.

Traditions, Polarities, and Divides: The Present State and Future Scope of Archaeology in the Mediterranean

As has often happened in the past few decades, the final word belongs to Colin Renfrew. In "Retrospect and Prospect: Mediterranean Archaeology in a New Millennium" (chapter 21), Renfrew attempts to look beyond the polarities of the past in order to focus on the future potential of Mediterranean archaeology in a new millennium. The themes he singles out include the tyranny and opportunity of technique, where he echoes many of the statements made by other contributors to this volume. Beyond the digital and remote sensing revolutions, Renfrew looks toward the potential of mitochondrial DNA and Y-chromosome studies to reconstruct male and female lineage histories. He also looks to survey as a data source, noting that an emerging issue will be the standardization of methods and techniques, as well as categories of classification. One area of real progress that Renfrew identifies is the advent of better descriptions—the result of the much fuller data now available—and matching realities. One of the success stories he singles out is the contribution of Mycenaean epigraphy to the study of the material culture of the Greek Bronze Age (see Palaima chapter 3). The effective integration of text, representation, and material culture has been realized in archaeological studies in various parts of the world, not least in historical archaeology (for example, Falk 1991). Indeed, as Kent Lightfoot (1995) has cogently argued, the discipline of archaeology is poised to play a pivotal role in the reconfiguration of historical studies. Renfrew's optimism is tempered, however, in his lamenting the decline of comparative studies. He points, in particular, to the fact that there is nothing in Aegean or Mediterranean archaeology to set alongside Robert McC. Adams's (1966) classic juxtaposition of the Mespotamian and Mesoamerican paths toward statehood, though he does mention several notable exceptions, and many would point to his own contributions (for example, Renfrew 1972) as refreshing exceptions. Renfrew ends by returning to a particular polarity: the divide in Aegean studies between prehistory and history, a subject he wrote about more than two decades ago (Renfrew 1980).

The polarities in the conventions and traditions of archaeological research that Renfrew spoke of, and the multiplicity of polarities within polarities, are a fitting way to both end and begin this volume. Within the framework of the Mediterranean, one polarity was the "divide" between the great tradition of classical archaeology and the then current trends in British and Americanist archaeology. This in itself harked back to an earlier polarity, one between "culture history" and "culture process." But an even earlier polarity was lurking behind the scenes, one expressed in Robin Collingwood's *The Idea of History*, in which the historical and scientific approaches to the past were contrasted (Collingwood 1946). And Renfrew points to more polarities, many of which are reinvented or rehashed versions of earlier ones, including the now somewhat "diminished" polarity, as he puts it, between "processual" and "post-processual" or "interpretive" archaeology. Although such terms help us categorize certain perspectives or approaches, they are nowhere near as black and white as some scholars maintain. The vehemence of the polemic has abated or diminished somewhat, precisely because such terms mean very little. In reality, most—if not all—archaeologists are, at the same time, many things (see also Chippindale 1995). The great majority of archaeologists are culture historians who care intensely for ancient particulars—the devil is in the details—whether they are Minoan palaces, Asian burial practices, Maya architecture, Athenian vases, Australian Aboriginal rock art, Mesopotamian states, Pacific island glyptic, or the late prehistoric lithics of the California coast. Whether they know it or not—or whether they like it or not—most archaeologists have to be processualists at one level or another, for the only way to grasp the specifics of culture history is by general frames of inference that bridge across the worlds we know to those we do not know through the common processes at work in both. At the same time, many archaeologists are post-processualists in spirit if not in declared practice, and this is because generalizing accounts do not do justice to the enticing texture of the human specifics we discern in the material record, a point so well brought out by Ruth Tringham.

In many ways, the polarities are part and parcel of understanding the past, and they are, in themselves, something of a measure or gauge of the health of a discipline. I would also contend that such polarities spiral back to a past much more remote than that of Robin Collingwood or Benedetto Croce and his classic statement: *ogni vera storia è storia contemporanea* (all history is contemporary history) (Croce 1927:4). It goes right back to the earliest attempts of writing about and interpreting the past. The earliest "archaeology" ever written is in Book I of Thucydides' unfinished and unnamed history of the Peloponnesian War, penned in the fifth century BC.

Thucydides' history was cast, in the author's own words, as a *ktēma es aiei*—a possession (or legacy gift) for all time (I. 22). In the preface to his 1907 book on *Thucydides Mythistoricus*, Francis Cornford (1907:vii) begins with a word of explanation, if not an apology: "for to any one who is accustomed to think of Thucydides as typically prosaic, and nothing if not purely historical, the epithet *Mythistoricus* may seem to carry a note of challenge, or even paradox." Despite severe criticism then and now from the historical establishment (Chambers 1991), and dismissed as wrong-headed and pernicious by many historians (see Calder 1991:v), Cornford's great achievement was to see Thucydides in context and to bring out the essentially artistic aspect of his history (Cornford 1907). His book, which predates the seminal contributions of Collingwood (1946), Ricoeur (1971), and Gadamer (1975; 1981) (see also DiCenso 1990) by decades, goes well beyond a discussion of Thucydides's "trustworthiness." It embraces a meaning of history "cast in a mould of conception, whether artistic or philosophic, which, long before the work was even contemplated, was already inwrought into the very structure of the author's mind" (Cornford 1907:viii). Cornford went on to issue a warning to all historians and archaeologists by saying about Thucydides that

> He chose a task which promised to lie wholly within the sphere of positively ascertainable facts; and, to make assurance double sure, he set himself limits which further restricted his sphere, till it seemed that no bias, no preconception, no art except the art of methodical inquiry, could possibly intrude. But he had not reckoned with the truth that you cannot collect facts, like so many pebbles, without your own personality and the common mind of your age and country having something to say to the choice and arrangement of the collection. He had forgotten that he was

an Athenian, born before Aeschylus was dead; and it did not occur to him that he must have a standpoint and outlook from which the world, having a long way to travel in a thousand or two thousand years, would drift far indeed. Thus it came about that even his vigilant precaution allowed a certain traditional mode of thought, characteristic of the Athenian mind, to shape the mass of facts which was to have been shapeless, so that the work of science came to be a work of art. (Cornford 1907:viii–ix)

Archaeology in the Mediterranean has developed a great deal in the close to 2.5 millennia since Thucydides; it is still changing (for a history of archaeology from antiquity to the era of Charles Darwin, see Schnapp 1993). Although much of the old order has remained with us—a cultural and academic baggage that is difficult to shake—new configurations are constantly appearing. Simple explanations of culture change and development have given way to a deeper understanding of cultural dynamics and the multiplicity of the human past. New interpretations, both by scholars working in the Mediterranean and those beyond, have not only revealed a more compelling picture of the past but have offered a sharper awareness of the preconceptions that we ourselves bring to its reconstruction and interpretation. In so many ways, the health of a discipline is often better gauged by colleagues looking in from the outside, and the exercise of subjecting the practice of archaeology in the Old World to scrutiny by practitioners in the New World proved to be, for better or worse, a worthy gauge. The papers in this volume provide a sense of how far archaeology has come in parts of the Mediterranean, where the discipline finds itself today, and a look toward some of its future prospects.

Notes

1. As was noted in the Acknowledgments, John Henderson, who was originally to have responded to Ruth Tringham's paper, was unable at the last moment to attend the workshop. I am therefore grateful to Professors Marcus and Redman for accepting an invitation to contribute to this volume without enjoying the benefits of having taken part in the workshop.
2. It is important to stress that in some Mediterranean countries, notably Greece, the government treats permits for excavations and surveys separately. Each foreign archaeological school in Greece, for example, is permitted annually three excavation permits, three survey permits, and three collaborative survey or excavation permits with an official Greek partner (normally a local Ephoreia or Superintendency of Antiquities). This administrative and legislative fact is not conducive to research projects that combine settlement and survey research with excavation (see also Kardulias 1994). In other countries, the opposite is true. In Turkey, for example, since 1993, the excavators of a site are required to conduct a survey in the area around that site.

CHAPTER 2

Lloyd Cotsen in Greece: Some Reminiscences from the Field

JACK L. DAVIS

Lloyd Cotsen is a man with many friends in archaeology, and it would be presumptuous of me to write a memoir without drawing on the assistance of others. Certainly none of our colleagues who worked with Lloyd on Kea or at Lerna in the Argolid is likely to disagree that he was usually the most popular member of the staff. For that reason, my strategy in this brief review has been to mix my reminiscences with facts of Lloyd's career and the memories that other colleagues of mine have so generously shared.[1] What emerges is, I hope, a portrayal of an individual that Lloyd may, despite his remarkable modesty, recognize as himself.

In the summer of 1974, Professor John (Jack) L. Caskey (a.k.a., JLC) invited me to become a member of his excavation team. Shortly after I arrived at Kea, old hands began talking about the imminent arrival of Lloyd Cotsen—an occasion that I soon learned was tantamount to the advent of Santa Claus. Like St. Nick, he could be expected to arrive with presents for all, beef jerky for the children, and samples of Neutrogena toiletries aplenty for his colleagues.[2] On the archaeological side of the ledger, I had already heard tales of the other magic Lloyd could work: how as architect at Lerna he had painstakingly connected on paper individual cobbles mapped over several seasons, and found that they described a circle bordering a mound heaped over the ruins of the "House of the Tiles" (figure 2.1; Caskey 1956:165; Wiencke 2000: s.v. *tumulus*).

As a rookie I was assigned to help Lloyd that first summer to produce an underwater contour map of the sea bottom off the peninsula of Ayia Irini. Lloyd had an enormous love for swimming and diving. Suggesting me as a human float, he tied a rope around my waist with a rock at the other end. I was to swim designated distances out from shore, tread water, drop the rock to the bottom, and report the depth. I survived, and by such an improbable,

33

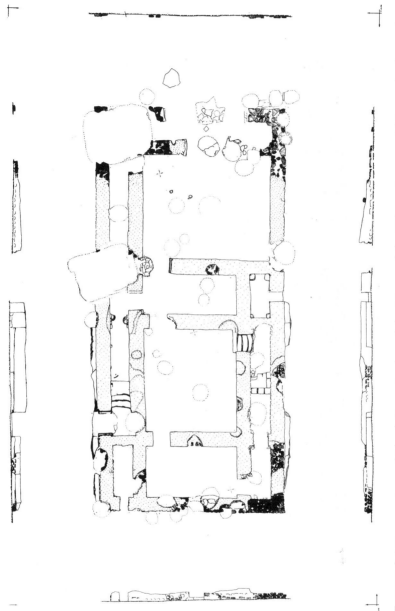

FIGURE 2.1. Two versions of Lloyd Cotsen's plan of the House of the Tiles at Lerna: a (this page), plan and section as preserved; b (facing), actual state plan.

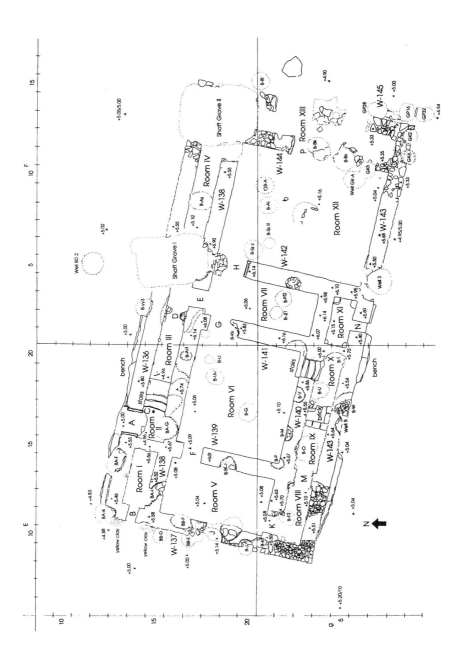

yet ingenious, method, an excellent map was produced. A friendship ensued
that yields many vivid memories out of the field, as well as in Greece: talking
archaeological theory and method in the Oyster Bar in Grand Central station; discussing the results of archaeological survey on Kea on the harbor
mole in Laurion while waiting for a ferryboat; diving into a pile of seafood
that he dumped on my bed at an Archaeological Institute of America annual
meeting. I came to know Lloyd as a gentle and genial companion. His impish
sense of humor delighted us with good jokes in the doldrums of the summer
when our spirits flagged. His appetite was legend; it was not uncommon for
him to eat several evening meals in Vourkari, the town where we lived. The
cook Tassos was amazed, and Eleftheria, his wife, kept me abreast of Lloyd's
culinary accomplishments. Lloyd ate early with the older Americans, then
joined us youngsters, and closed his gastronomic odysseys in the wee hours
with his circle of Greek friends.[3] In 1986 he flew to Kea in secret expressly so
that he could treat the entire publication team to an aerial tour of the island.
When the helicopter appeared on the horizon, only Stella Bouzaki, long-
time conservator at Ayia Irini and Corinth, guessed what was up and
exclaimed: "Oh, he couldn't have!"

Lloyd's archaeological career now spans nearly five decades. After com-
pleting a B.A. in History and graduate work in the School of Architecture at
Princeton, he came to the American School of Classical Studies at Athens
(ASCSA) as a student in 1955–56, where he formed a lifelong partnership
with archaeologists at the University of Cincinnati, notably Jack Caskey,
then director of ASCSA. Carl Blegen also benefited from his talent. At
Pylos, Lloyd, "who was serving as architect at the excavations at Lerna, spent
a few days at Englianos, during which he measured, drew, and added to the
general plan the various elements brought to light in that season" (Blegen
and Rawson 1966:ix). Already Lloyd's modesty and characteristic sense of
humor were evident: Lloyd claimed in his end-of-the-year report to Caskey
that "Greek lessons were taken each week but little penetrated." Both his
gregarious nature and his comprehension of the benefits of cultural plurality
can also be appreciated from the gentle criticisms that he offered the administration of ASCSA. Lloyd was concerned about "the insular aspect of the
school and the students. Outside of the trips there is very little effort
expended on getting out and seeing Greece on one's own. I think there is little effort on the school's part in that it treats the students somewhat on the
continuation-of-college basis, in a word, sheltered."

At Lerna, Lloyd served as architect in all but the first season, and it is
clear from the memories of his friends that he had changed very little in the
intervening years before I met him in Vourkari. Betty Banks recently wrote:

Things I remember were his voracious appetite (three brizoles [chops] at the Nauplion restaurant under the tree on Saturdays; the quantities of peanut butter he could consume at tea, which totally shot Betty Caskey's carefully planned supply list; his gentleness with the rather wild village boy Hari he took on as his assistant in the field and his and Joanne's generosity with Hari's family in which the father was disabled, a generosity which continued long after the excavation was over; the dark cloud which enveloped him when work didn't go well on the excavation which even led to his missing meals!—we knew to stay clear and let him work it out.

Martha Wiencke remembered:

He was a welcome sight, impervious to the sun in his shorts while the rest of us were muffled in our trousers and long-sleeved shirts; and he was good humored in all circumstances, coming round whenever we summoned him, to draw our boasted scraps of walls (and how I have relied on those careful pencil drawings ever since!), taking daily measurements of levels as we progressed, always on hand to help. He could always be depended on for good company, on the site, at meals (to which we all did more than justice), on Saturday jaunts to Nauplia when we wandered round the shops, watched the sunset over the bay, sat round the table at the old Ficus restaurant. I remember one occasion when we were taken to Nauplia by boat across the bay, instead of by road along the shore, Lloyd and Joanne sitting close together, and all of us enjoying the view of the gulf and the peacefulness of the whole experience. Those were cheerful days and Lloyd was a prime factor in that good cheer.[4]

At Ayia Irini, Lloyd had already served Jack Caskey as an architect for more than a decade when I arrived (figures 2.2, 2.3). From the first full season in 1961 until 1964, when the management of Neutrogena became too complicated for him to spend the entire season there, he prepared the architectural plans of the site shirtless; clad only in shoes, shorts, and a burnoose, he was assisted by a young Greek named Lefteris, whom he dubbed "Lefty" (figure 2.4).[5] His beard was a fixture at Kea, as it had been at Lerna, until one day in 1963, he shaved half of it and, with the help of a colleague, recorded a video to send before and after views to Joanne back home. After 1964, Lloyd returned nearly every summer to assist his replacements, Roger Holzen and Wil Cummer, in special projects where his assistance might be required and desired: in 1968 "a careful analysis of the architecture of House A, with a revised plan and elevations of all the basement walls"; in 1973 a study of "structural problems in the Temple"; in 1974 the underwater map; and in several years the drawing of primary sections through Early and Middle Bronze Age levels of the site. Once, he sat up all night to finish his analysis

FIGURE 2.2. Lloyd Cotsen at work at the draftman's station. *Courtesy of the Department of Classics, University of Cincinnati.*

of the Temple stratigraphy and entitled it: "Separating the Wheat from the Chaff." Lloyd's commitment to Kea continued to the end of that project and beyond. In the very last season in 1988, when the storeroom was being cleaned for a final time, he could still find humor in the melancholy. When two boys charged with painting failed to clean their brushes, Lloyd exclaimed: "One boy is half a man. Two boys are no man."

Jack Caskey depended on Lloyd, honored his opinions, and trusted his judgment. Those of us who lived and worked with Jack know that he could bestow no greater praise. Elizabeth Schofield has written succinctly that Lloyd

> . . . acted as advisor, good-will ambassador, and moral supporter, both to my predecessor as director, Prof. John L. Caskey, and to myself. We both depended on his fund of good sense, businesslike advice, willingness to liaise with difficult people, and great good humor. He was always immensely kind and caring to all members of the excavation staff, who in turn all greatly love and value him.

In a 1994 letter addressed to the Department of Classics at the University of Cincinnati, Emily Vermeule described Lloyd's contribution to archaeology in the following words:

> He has always been a passionate archaeologist, discerning with three-dimensional vision into the earth, careful but brilliant in interpretation. His plans for both the Cincinnati excavations of the Greek Bronze Age, Lerna and Kea, have become internationally famous. . . .

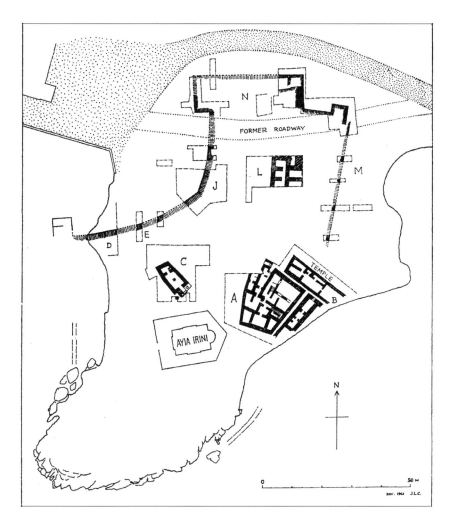

FIGURE 2.3. Lloyd Cotsen's 1963 plan of Ayia Irini, Kea.

FIGURE 2.4. Lloyd in shorts at work on site at Ayia Irini, Kea.

And this same loyalty to fieldwork was recognized in 1994 when an honorary degree from the University of Cincinnati was awarded in recognition of his archaeological achievements. I quote from it:

> No one has been more creative in strengthening archaeological research. . . . His distinction is . . . his effective leadership which has created opportunities and institutions that will continue to serve the scholarly community well beyond his lifetime.[6]

Notes

1. I am grateful to Betty Banks, Aliki Bikaki, Mary Eliot, Carol Herschenson, John Overbeck, Elizabeth Schofield, Natalia Vogeikoff, and Martha Wiencke.
2. Neutrogena is the company with which Lloyd was long associated.
3. Mary Eliot writes: ". . . although we were always well fed on Caskey digs, the menu always improved with the arrival of Lloyd. In the early days of Lerna, Joanne [Cotsen, Lloyd's wife] decided that Lloyd was losing weight and maybe energy. She threatened to fly in steaks from the States. Thereafter, on our Saturday night out in Nauplion, JLC would weigh us at the scales in the pharmacy and record the weights in his neat little figures. One Saturday when Lloyd was a couple of ounces lighter than the previous week, he treated us to a particularly good dinner. Finished? Enough? No, says Lloyd, and so we went on to a second restaurant and another dinner with JLC and his wallet in attendance. Still not enough and so there was a third restaurant. I could not eat the third meal but Lloyd did. It was an amazing tease. I think you can imagine JLC's unfailing politesse. Not a crack in his façade."
4. Another colleague at Lerna was adamant that Joanne Cotsen was sometimes more precious than anyone else. She took great care for the purity of the water supply, but this was the least of her contributions. "It was her presence that was a blessing and a pleasure."
5. Even on Kea urgent business could break Lloyd's serenity, such as the day that NASA rang to inquire about the melting point of Neutrogena soap, part of a payload of a spacecraft with its window stuck in a nonprotective position.
6. Lloyd once explained to a friend "how easy it is to make money, how difficult it is to spend it in a meaningful fashion. The money makes itself. The spending is a heavy responsibility."

PART I

ARCHAEOLOGY AND TEXT

CHAPTER 3

Archaeology and Text: Decipherment, Translation, and Interpretation

Thomas Palaima

This is necessarily a selective discussion of the history of the subdiscipline of Mycenology (the study of records from Crete and the southern and central Greek mainland [figure 3.1] during the period ca. 1450–1200 BC that are written in the so-called Linear B script and represent the Greek language) and its relationship to anthropological and archaeological work in what is known as Aegean prehistory (the study of the cultures of the Aegean basin pre-1200 BC). My primary objective throughout is to explain with a few well-chosen examples the prevailing methodological *Zeitgeist* of each main period in the development of Mycenology and what sorts of information Mycenological scholars were interested in and capable of providing to and using from scholars in related fields. This leads to a critical assessment of the current state of Mycenology as a subdiscipline (of linguistics, epigraphy, and prehistory) now linked with archaeological and anthropological research.

Stage One: The First Fifty Years

Archaeology and Texts Inextricably Connected from the Beginning

The study of Minoan and Mycenaean writing is slightly older than the discovery and definition of Minoan archaeology. The recognition of a distinctive "Minoan," as opposed to a "Mycenaean," prehistoric archaeology resulted from the excavations of Sir Arthur Evans at Knossos (figures 3.2, 3.3) beginning on March 23, 1900 (A. Evans 1900a). The discovery of three distinctive classes of writing (as defined by Evans himself in A. Evans 1909) at Knossos and at other major Cretan sites during the first two decades of the twentieth century, and not at any of the Mycenaean mainland centers, reinforced the

45

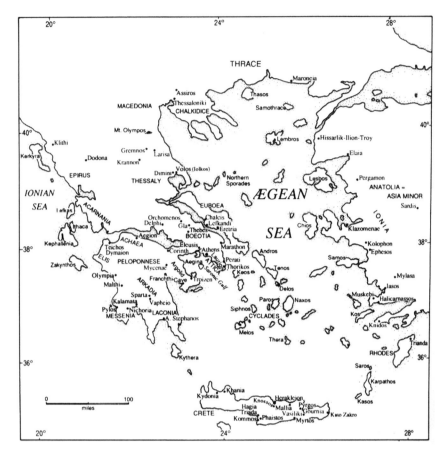

FIGURE 3.1. Map of the Aegean area. *After McDonald and Thomas 1990:514.*

impression gained from the rest of the material record that Cretan palatial civilization well into the second half of the second millennium BC was not only separate from the Mycenaean but more advanced and dominant.

The first Linear B tablet finds from a controlled excavation were uncovered by Evans and Duncan Mackenzie at Knossos beginning on March 30, 1900, the eighth day of excavation (figures 3.4, 3.5). Evans described the first piece uncovered as "part of an elongated clay tablet with a chisel-like end, engraved with what appeared to be signs and numbers" (A. Evans 1900a:18, 55–58; MacGillivray 2000:177–178, 181–185). He had earlier seen a "graffito fragment" of a clay tablet from brief local excavations by Minos Kalokairinos at the site of Knossos in 1878 (A. Evans 1900a:18 n. 1), and he had already formulated ideas about the cultural context and evolution of what he

FIGURE 3.2. Sir Arthur Evans at Knossos. *Courtesy of the Evans Archive, Ashmolean Museum, Oxford.*

then called "Mycenaean" writing from his studies (most fully in A. Evans 1894 and 1897) of stone seals and other objects. The stone seals were inscribed with discrete pictorial forms that Evans recognized as characters in what he called the Cretan Hieroglyphic writing system. He acquired many of these on the antiquities market. He also observed a few examples of writing of a different kind, in linear characters inscribed on objects like a bronze axe and a libation table (Myres 1941:334–335).

We should keep in mind that Evans was first and foremost a student of Cretan writing. His interests in early writing systems led him to become an excavator (Myres 1941). Mycenologists, strictly defined as scholars who work with the primary documents (as epigraphers or pinacologists)[1] or texts (as linguists) of Aegean scripts, in fact view the monumental publication of

FIGURE 3.3. Left to right: Sir Arthur Evans with David Theodore Fyfe (architect) and Duncan Mackenzie. *Courtesy of the Evans Archive, Ashmolean Museum, Oxford.*

(*FACING PAGE*): FIGURE 3.4. Plan of the "Palace of Minos" after the first season of excavation. *After Evans 1899–1900: Plate XIII.*

the results of the excavations at Knossos (A. Evans 1900b, 1901–02, 1902–03, 1904, 1921–35)[2] as a major distraction. It kept Evans from finishing the field-defining work he had begun on Cretan writing systems during the late 1890s (and in A. Evans 1909; see also Palaima 2000b). He worked on the publication of the Linear B material from Knossos until his death in 1941 and left a substantial manuscript to the charge of Sir John L. Myres (A. Evans 1952; Palaima, Pope, and Reilly 2000:10).

Linear B: The Slow Pace of Publication

Serious work toward decipherment was hampered by the slow pace of publication. Only in 1935, with the appearance of the fourth and final volume of *The Palace of Minos* (A. Evans 1921–35), was any sizable number of photographs and drawings made available to scholars interested in Linear B writing, and even then this was a small and unsystematic selection. In 1936,

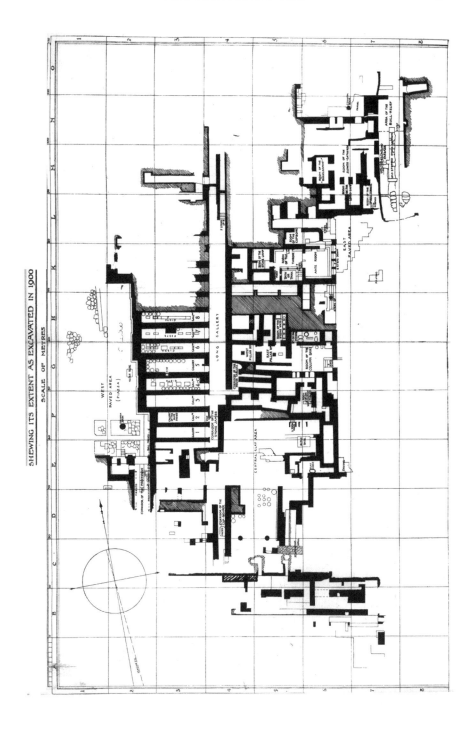

FIGURE 3.5. The first published photograph of Linear B tablets from Knossos.
After Evans 1899–1900: Plate I.

besides Evans, there were three scholars seriously interested in Linear B (see
Palaima, Pope, and Reilly 2000:11–14):

- Alice Elizabeth Kober (Palaima n.d.a), a thirty-year-old professor of
  Classics at Brooklyn College (figures 3.6, 3.7). Kober had as yet published nothing in the field, was trained in Classical philology—not
  archaeology or linguistics—and had no knowledge of any ancient languages beyond Latin and Greek. Moreover, she taught traditional
  courses in Latin and Greek authors and what we would now call topics
  courses in classical civilization. Yet upon her graduation from Hunter
  College in 1928, Kober had declared that she would decipher the
  "Minoan" scripts. In the decade from 1935 to 1945 she would master, by
  participating in various summer linguistic institutes and making frequent trips to Yale University during her own busy school terms at
  Brooklyn College, the principal ancient languages and scripts of Anatolia and the Near East, all with a view to knowing them well enough to
  see if their linguistic patterns matched those she was discovering
  through meticulous and comprehensive analysis of the data for the
  Minoan linear scripts.

FIGURE 3.6. Alice Elizabeth Kober, approximately age 35, as a professor at Brooklyn College. *Courtesy of the Program in Aegean Scripts and Prehistory Archives, University of Texas at Austin.*

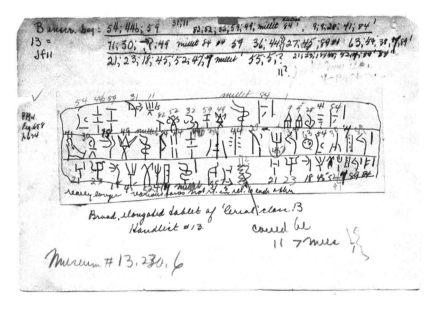

FIGURE 3.7. Alice Kober's drawing and notes of Knossos Linear B tablet Fp 13, now known to be a record of offerings of oil to religious sanctuaries, "all the gods," "priestesses of the winds," and a likely Minoan deity *pi-pi-tu-na*. Length 7.7 cm × height 5.0 cm. *After Palaima, Pope, and Reilly 2000: Fig. 7.*

FIGURE 3.8. Linear A tablet HT 117 from Hagia Triada in south central Crete. Length 6.7 × height 10.9 × thickness 0.8 cm. A deep scoring crosses the tablet just above the third to last line of the text. Small dots separate the three words in the opening header. Then come ten entries, each with a single phonetically written word followed by the vertical stroke for "1." This first "section" ends with the entry of the two-sign Minoan word for "total" and the horizontal stroke for "10." *Courtesy of the Program in Aegean Scripts and Prehistory Archives, University of Texas at Austin.*

- Johannes Sundwall (Palaima n.d.a), Professor der alten Geschichte an der Academie zu Åbo (Finland). Sundwall was at this point the one systematic scholar of relatively long standing in analyzing the structure of the texts and patterns of sign occurrence mainly on the Linear A tablets from Hagia Triada (figure 3.8). He worked carefully at analyzing accounting procedures and units of measurement in the Minoan scripts (for example, Sundwall 1920, 1932a, 1932b, 1936) and knew enough later to recognize that Kober was the most knowledgeable figure at work in the field (Ventris 1988:86).

- Michael Ventris (Palaima, Pope, and Reilly 2000:6–15), a fourteen-year-old schoolboy at Stowe School. Ventris (figure 3.9) had been interested in ancient scripts at least since the age of eight. The Institute of Classical Studies at the University of London has among its Ventrisiana a book he purchased on Egyptian hieroglyphs at this age. In 1936 Ventris happened to meet Sir Arthur Evans during an excursion for boys from Stowe School to Burlington House to see an exhibition of materials from fifty years of excavations sponsored by the British School of Archaeology in Athens.

Remarkably, the efforts of Kober, Ventris, Sir John Myres, and Emmett L. Bennett, Jr. (the latter also shown in figure 3.9), although hampered by the disruptions caused by the Second World War, made it possible for Ventris to

FIGURE 3.9. Photograph of Michael Ventris, John Chadwick, and Emmett L. Bennett, Jr. (first three facing, left to right) in April 1956. *After Palaima, Pope, and Reilly 2000:3, Fig. 1.*

decipher Linear B. Ventris produced his decipherment in just over fifteen years of sporadic part-time work. From 1949 to 1952, his circumstances made it possible for him to devote stretches of several months at a time to rather intensive work on the linear scripts (Robinson 2002).

The lamentable situation concerning text publication prevailed even after the discovery of Linear B tablets at the site of Pylos in 1939. In 1947 when Alice Kober began collaborating with Sir John Myres on the publication of Evans's unfinished study (A. Evans 1952, working on the unfinished manuscript left by Sir Arthur Evans at his death in 1941), the sum total of published data available to scholars was:

- About 45 published photographs, 103 drawings, and 120 transcriptions (by Johannes Sundwall) of Knossos tablets

- Seven photographs of Pylos tablets (see Blegen and Kourouniotis 1939; Blegen 1939; Chadwick 1999:31 overlooks the three tablets presented in the latter)

- A few painted stirrup jar inscriptions from Thebes and Eleusis

- Some dubitanda that could not be properly evaluated given the unexamined state of most genuine texts and the writing system as a whole

The Major Addition: Linear B at Pylos

In March 1939 Carl W. Blegen of the University of Cincinnati began excavation in Messenia in southwestern Greece at what he hoped would prove to be a mainland "palatial complex" (Blegen and Kourouniotis 1939) (figures 3.10, 3.11). Just as at Knossos, on one of the first days of work, the team of excavators found tablets. They had laid out their very first exploratory trench to avoid damaging olive trees on the site at Ano Englianos. By good fortune it was placed directly over what would eventually be identified as the tablet storage room (Room 8) of the central Archives Complex of what Blegen called the Palace of Nestor (Blegen and Kourouniotis 1939:562–570, Figs. 6–10; Palaima n.d.b). By equal good fortune, Blegen set William A. McDonald to record precisely the position within the trench of every fragment of the clay tablets. Some 636 tablets in all were excavated and photographed during that first season.

As noted already, photographs of a mere seven tablets were published in the preliminary excavation report and the *Illustrated London News*. These created a sensation because they convinced some—and reinforced Blegen's own strongly argued position—that the mainland Greek Mycenaean civilization was much more independently vigorous than Evans's theories of pan-Minoan cultural hegemony suggested (McDonald and Thomas 1990:233–

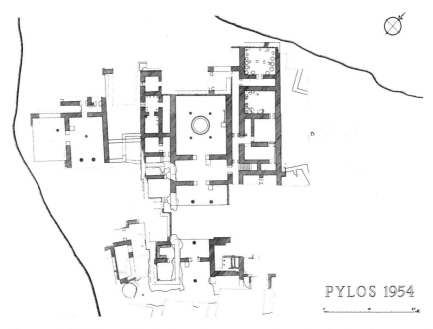

FIGURE 3.10. Plan of the "Palace of Nestor" at Pylos after the fourth season of excavation (1954), revealing the central *megaron* complex and Southwest Building. *After Blegen 1955: Plate 24*.

FIGURE 3.11. Pylos tablet Ta 641. Length 25.2 × height 3.6 × thickness 1.5 cm. This leaf-shaped tablet shows the advances in systematized formatting, the increase in lexical information, and the developed calligraphic appearance of the script from the Minoan Linear A period (cf. figure 3.8). The first entry describes two tripods of Cretan workmanship "of *Aigeus* type." The first entry in the second line is of three vases known as $k^w e$-*to* (historical Greek "pithos"?). Then follow entries for four-, three-, and no-eared (that is, handled) *di-pa* (historical Greek *depas*). The tablet belongs to a set compiled as an inventory of special vessels, fire equipment, sacrificial implements, and furniture connected with a ritual banquet. *Courtesy of the Program in Aegean Scripts and Prehistory Archives, University of Texas at Austin. With permission of the University of Cincinnati.*

241, 247–291). Again, however, publication of the material was delayed, in this case by the outbreak of the Second World War and the widespread disruption of normal life that continued well after the cessation of hostilities. For example, the Knossos tablets in the Herakleion Museum in Crete were never accessible to Alice Kober or any other scholars during the 1940s. For their work on Evans's unfinished monograph (A. Evans 1952), Kober and Myres studied photographs taken by Evans years before, the small selection of tablets in the Ashmolean Museum, Oxford, and photographs and drawings of dubious quality in scattered publications (Palaima n.d.a).

In 1939, Blegen entrusted to Emmett L. Bennett, Jr., then a first-year graduate student at the University of Cincinnati, the work of publishing the Linear B tablets uncovered at Pylos. During the Second World War, Bennett was called to work on the early stages of decoding Japanese documents. Bennett, in his post-war Ph.D. dissertation (Bennett 1947), working from photographs made of the tablets before the war, completed the first scientific paleographical analysis of a body of Linear B documents. He investigated the core signary of the script and the workings of the scribal system.

The Final Years of Stage One

During the period 1947–50, Ventris at first made an attempt at assisting Sir John Myres and Alice Elizabeth Kober intermittently on their revision and expansion of the manuscript Sir Arthur Evans had left behind (see A. Evans 1952). Ventris eventually withdrew, it seems mainly for personal reasons. But by this point he had begun his own "group working" approach to Linear A and Linear B, and he was circulating letters to scholars worldwide whom he himself had tracked down through their interests in the scripts (Palaima 1993). In so working he was adapting a theory of problem solving that had just come into vogue in his chosen professional field of architecture (Palaima 1993; Palaima, Pope, and Reilly 2000:6–15). Ventris had published an unfocused and methodologically flawed article in the *American Journal of Archaeology* for 1940—the British *Journal of Hellenic Studies* had turned it down— which proposed that the language behind the Minoan scripts was Etruscan-related Pelasgian (Ventris 1940). The paucity of data available made possible his continued belief in this "solution" until literally months before the decipherment (Bennett 1989). In December 1949, Ventris sent out to over twenty scholars letters containing twenty-one questions about Linear B (and Linear A) and proposed that he would compile the answers and circulate them to members of this working group. In the hand-penciled postscript of his letter to Emmett L. Bennett, Jr., Ventris comments on "what little we have to show for the first 50 years' work" (Palaima, Pope, and Reilly 2000:30, item 10). Bennett's replies to this questionnaire were minimal. Kober absolutely refused to answer it, calling it "a step in the wrong direction and a complete waste of time" (Ventris 1988:37–38, 67; Palaima, Pope, and Reilly 2000:6–15).

Between 1945 and 1950, the main work that accelerated progress in our understanding of Linear B was done by Alice Elizabeth Kober and Emmett L. Bennett, Jr. As already mentioned, Bennett, in his dissertation on the Pylos tablets (Bennett 1947), completed the first scientific paleographical analysis of Linear B, fulfilling a prerequisite in working with data from an undeciphered script by establishing what the core character repertory of the script was. His study of the Minoan fractional system (Bennett 1950) showed how pure analysis of the tablets could lead to unquestionable results. Ventris later cited this article as one that encouraged him to continue his own work.

Kober, however, was in the forefront of advances. In four methodologically spare and clean articles (Kober 1945, 1946, 1948, 1949; Palaima n.d.a), she presented the evidence for inflection in the Linear B tablets (sign alternations at word endings occurring as the so-called "Kober's triplets") and also laid out what could be known and what remained unknown with regard to Minoan scripts. Kober (1948) effectively defined the proper program of research toward the decipherment of the Minoan scripts and the principles that should be followed in conducting this research.

Stage Two: The Last Fifty Years

The First Two Years of Stage Two: Decipherment, 1950–52

On May 16, 1950, Alice Elizabeth Kober died of the critical illness that had progressively impaired her health and limited her activities during the last two years of her life. Michael Ventris and Emmett L. Bennett, Jr. became the prime movers in the attack on Linear B on opposite sides of the Atlantic. On the epigraphical side, Bennett helped Myres with correct readings of the Knossos tablets, traveling to the Herakleion Museum in 1950 to study them firsthand (Melena and Palaima 2001). His publication of the Pylos tablets in the next year greatly expanded the repertory of inscriptions available to researchers and set a high standard for accuracy of presentation (Bennett 1951). The texts were edited in normalized transcription, which meant that most problems with interpretation of individual scribal variants had been examined and resolved. Thus for the first time those working on decipherment had direct access to secure texts of the lengthier and syntactically more revealing Pylos documents.

In March–April 1952, Michael Ventris gained full use of the Myres-Kober-Bennett-edited Knossos tablets (A. Evans 1952) and an early version of Bennett's index of Minoan words (Bennett 1953), which accurately laid out the occurrences of signs and sign-groups in the Knossos and Pylos tablets. Within three months, using these increased data and improved means of analyzing them, Ventris abandoned the "Etruscan solution" (Ventris 1940) and deciphered Linear B as Greek.

Old Archaeology, Homeric Studies, Near Eastern Studies, and the Mycenaean Greek Texts, 1952–73

The Ventris decipherment had to be presented to an understandably skeptical scholarly world. Michael Ventris and his postdecipherment collaborator John Chadwick (who also appears in figure 3.9) did this in a superb joint article (Ventris and Chadwick 1953) and then in the first edition of the "bible of Linear B" (Ventris and Chadwick 1956; Ventris and Chadwick, second edition, 1973). Ventris and Chadwick (1956) used 300 selected sample texts to illustrate the problems, results, and resources of the new field of Mycenology. Their 1953 publication presented the writing system and its Cretan forerunners (Cretan Hieroglyphic and Linear A), its regional paleographical variants, the status of the Greek language between 1400–1200 BC, and its dialectal affinities. It then discussed the individual texts by subject categories relating to almost all aspects of Mycenaean civilization and material culture: social organization, religion, political structure, agriculture and land tenure, industry and trade, geographical names, categories of personnel, livestock and agricultural produce, landownership and land use, proportional tribute and ritual offerings, textiles, vessels and furniture, metals, and military equipment.

A paradoxically healthy development was the appearance of L. Palmer's (1963) study, which offered, let us say, many alternative perspectives on interpretations to those proposed in Ventris and Chadwick (1956) while maintaining similar categories of presentation. In reality, if Ventris and Chadwick said "black," Palmer was apt to say "white"—and in some cases say it in a way that tested the ground rules of polite scholarly discourse. Such polarities of interpretation meant that, on most crucial issues, those interested in the Mycenaean textual evidence could consult at least two well-reasoned points of view by well-trained scholars and then navigate a course between, toward, or beyond one or the other.

It should be noted that Chadwick was a lexicographer who had pursued a private interest in deciphering the linear scripts based on his war experience in the Naval Intelligence Division (Chadwick 1999:29–34). Ventris was an architect with public school Greek—and absolutely no experience at decoding during the war—and a basic polymathic understanding of the contents of ancient records from societies roughly contemporary with the

Minoan and Mycenaean. Palmer was an Indo-European linguist. None of them had serious archaeological or anthropological interests.

The linguistic sophistication required for the first phase of interpretation of the Linear B texts reinforced the separation between material archaeology and textual scholarship. The continental school was devoted almost entirely to linguistics, a trend starting and seen clearly in the papers of the first international Mycenological colloquium (Lejeune 1956).

The interpretation of the Linear B texts in this first postdecipherment stage was influenced by four fields of scholarship:

1. *Homeric studies.* Although those who approach Bronze Age studies with training primarily as classical philologists, historians, or archaeologists often think of the Homericist side of scholarly inquiry as the baby that got thrown out with the old archaeological bathwater, it is a truth of the history of scholarship that the first phases of interpretation in Mycenaean archaeology and in Linear B studies, from Schliemann and Ventris onward, were determined, and in Schliemann's case even inspired, by Homeric scholarship (McDonald and Thomas 1990:3–110; Nilsson 1932). Most of the textually oriented interpreters of the newly readable Linear B texts had no appreciable background in the study of material culture. This trend continues among most contemporary continental European Mycenologists with the notable exception of the collaborative work that produced a number of important studies (for example, Hiller and Panagl 1976; Treuil et al. 1989) and individual exceptions like José Melena and Jan Driessen. What such scholars assimilated in the way of archaeological information only reinforced their predisposition to view the Mycenaean period by comparison or contrast with the features of the Homeric age.

   The discovery that key Mycenaean texts referred to the production of chariots, spear points, armor, swords, and even to strategic military assignments was consistent with notions derived from the original interpretation of the excavated materials from the shaft graves at Mycenae: that Mycenaean culture was dominated by a warrior elite and that warrior-kings (each called a *wanaks*) in each region stood at the top of steep social, political, and economic organizational pyramids (L. Palmer 1963:83–95; Palaima 1995a; Wright 1995b).

   In the religious sphere, many of the main deities of the historical—and Homeric—pantheon could be identified, and commensal ceremonial texts, like the Pylos Un series in which Poseidon is a main focus, suggested an easy parallelism with Homer, for example, the Pylos Un tablets and Book 3 of Homer's *Odyssey* (Ventris and Chadwick 1973: 125–129, 275–312, 410–412, 456–485). Thus the Mycenaean texts were used effectively to give a sound track to the silent movie of Aegean pala-tial cult and ritual that had been forming through the study of iconogra-phy, architecture, and artifacts from the time of Evans (1901) until Nilsson (1941–50).

In the social sphere, in stunning contrast to the non-Homeric pros-opography of the historical period (Ventris and Chadwick 1973:103–105 with no update from 1956; Page 1959:196–202), scholars could identify many individuals in the Linear B tablets who bore Homeric names, Achilles and Hector among them. Sociopolitical terminology like *laos* (collective male fighting force or Volk), *basileus*—in the Myce-naean form *g^w asileus* (king), and *wanaks* (exalted king) could also be made to harmonize with a Homericist view. This evidence suggested that some form of heroic oral poetic tradition existed during the late Bronze Age (Page 1959:187–188).

Likewise, details of material culture lent themselves to interpreting this period and the Mycenaean textual evidence through a Homericist filter, for example, the use of the rare word *phasganon* to describe swords in Linear B, and in Homer the use of the term *pharweha* to describe cloth, and the inventory of precious furniture, vessels, and fire imple-ments in the Pylos Ta series. Gray's (1959) paper was an immediate "proto-literate" successor to the monumental *Homer and the monuments* (Lorimer 1950).

The clearest examples of this tendency to "Homericize" are publica-tions such as Webster (1958) and Wace and Stubbings (1962). Both exploit the Linear B data and have among their objectives comparing the image of society in the Homeric poems to the image formed from the Mycenaean texts (see also Page 1959:118–296). Webster's (1958) intro-ductory remarks encapsulate how the Homeric poems were mined as sources postdecipherment, and especially predecipherment, during the time when they were the only written texts that archaeologists had to assist in the interpretation of Aegean Bronze Age cultures. In this regard there had been little advance in methodology in nearly 2500 years—from the period when Thucydides in Book 1.3–1.12 (see Strassler 1996:4–11) looked upon the ruins of Mycenae and analyzed the artifacts in "Carian" graves on the island of Delos and compared them with Homeric and other oral traditions relating to the late Bronze Age.

Michael Ventris's decipherment of Linear B in 1952 proved that Greek was spoken in the Mycenaean world (Ventris 1952). This fact had long been suspected by archaeologists and, to quote two outstanding examples, Nilsson (1932) had maintained that much of Greek mythol-ogy was Mycenaean in origin, and Lorimer (1950) claimed that Homer's knowledge of perishable Mycenaean objects came from a poetic tradition that went back to the time of the shaft graves of Mycenae. On the linguistic side, Bowra (1934) had shown the probability that words common to the Homeric poems and Arcado-Cypriote came from Mycenaean Greek (Webster 1958:1).

Because Beattie (1962) was a lifelong disbeliever in the Ventris decipherment, his contribution to "Aegean languages of the heroic age" (Wace and Stubbings 1962:311–324) omitted all mention of the results of nearly a decade of work on the correctly deciphered texts and their significance for understanding the language picture of Greece in the late Bronze Age. On the purely archaeological side, such specialized volumes as Hope Simpson and Lazenby (1970) directly tested the correlation between sites listed in Book 2 of the *Iliad* and sites identifiable through excavation and survey within the regions mentioned in the catalogue in the *Iliad*.

2. *Near Eastern, Mesopotamian, and cross-cultural documentary evidence.* Notebooks of Michael Ventris still preserved in the Institute of Classical Studies at the University of London show that during the 1940s, well before he deciphered the Linear B script, he immersed himself deeply in the published interpretations of cuneiform and Egyptian records. He kept detailed lists of the kinds of economic, political, and social information, and transactional terminology such records contained. Although Ventris was doing this work to have a means of controlling his own speculations about the patterns of information possibly exhibited in the undeciphered Linear A and Linear B tablets, it gave him the ability, postdecipherment, immediately to use such documentation for cross-cultural comparisons in interpreting the Linear B tablets. Ventris and Chadwick (1956) contains numerous references to tablet records from Nuzi, Alalakh, Lagash, Ur, and Ugarit (as well as to Egyptian and Hittite record-based information). Ventris and Chadwick (1973), published seventeen years after Ventris's tragic death in 1956, contains little in the way of additional Near Eastern comparanda, thus offering further proof, if we needed it, that this element of the original edition was decidedly Ventris's contribution.

While Ventris's contribution did not represent sophisticated cross-cultural anthropology or archaeology, it did establish as an important research technique in Mycenology the comparative study of records from other cultures and historical periods. In this respect an early trendsetting article was Killen (1964). It used medieval sheep and wool records as comparanda for the meticulous management of breeding and production flocks in the Knossos Linear B tablets. Most recently, Killen has even used a manual of sheep husbandry in the Great Plains of the USA published in 1931 to corroborate an interpretation of the use of a Mycenaean technical term (o-pa) within livestock and other economic contexts in the Linear B tablets (see Killen 1999a:332 n. 34). Killen (1999a) advances our understanding of this term beyond the parameters that Melena (1983) was able to establish by closely studying parallel terminology in Mesopotamian texts.

3. *Greek prehistoric archaeology.* In a mutually reinforcing way, discoveries in the field, which had heretofore been interpreted through a Homericist filter, were now also Mycenologized, and meanwhile Mycenologists were using discoveries from the field to interpret Linear B texts. The most conspicuous example of this may be the site of Pylos. The material remains from the architectural complex known as the Palace of Nestor were viewed and interpreted as a Homeric palace (Blegen 1962; Blegen and Rawson 1966:419–424; Blegen and Rawson 1967:31–32). Nonetheless, the excavators and their associates showed admirable restraint. For example, the few scattered finds of La, Ae, and Xa tablet fragments from Room 6 of the central megaron (figure 3.10) make reference to women and cloth working. Their unusual find spots might be viewed by analogy with the "Homeric" use of upper floors of the palace of a *basileus* like Odysseus as a location for women to work cloth. The collected tablet fragments could have been interpreted from this perspective and the upper floors above the megaron assigned this function. Blegen and Rawson (1966:81) refrain from doing so.

Their restraint has now been proved correct. In 1999, José Melena, in continuing his masterfully precise work in directing the definitive *corpus* edition of the Pylos tablets, has hypothesized *per vocem*, while visiting the Program in Aegean Scripts and Prehistory at the University of Texas at Austin, that these fragments have, in fact, nothing to do with work on the upper floor but were random old and discarded scraps of Linear B tablets worked into the materials used to construct walls on the upper floor. This conclusion finds support in research on the small finds from the Palace of Nestor (Hofstra 2000), where it has been pointed out that the loom weights or spindle whorls that one would find, if the upper area were devoted to cloth manufacture, are conspicuously absent from the destruction debris. Otherwise, the material artifactual evidence was mined fully to explain the detailed terminology used in describing manufactured objects in the tablets, whether armor, chariots, furniture, or vessels. The seminal work here is Gray (1959), which examined Mycenaean ideograms (signs for objects) and their archaeological correlates.

Whole tablet sets could also be interpreted by assuming that their material environments were understood, often in Homeric terms. Thus, for example, the tablets of the Pylos Ta series that list vessels, tripods, fire equipment, tables, thrones, "footstools," sacrificial knives, and what have now finally been correctly identified as "stunning axes" were interpreted by Ventris (1955) as an inventory for a kind of Homeric reception room, while Leonard Palmer interpreted them by analogy to the rich burial gifts found in the shaft graves and imagined for the Mycenaean *tholoi* (Palmer 1960).

A major advance late in this stage was the development of multidisciplinary scientific intensive surveys of specific regions within the Aegean basin. McDonald and Rapp (1972) aimed at reconstructing the Bronze Age regional environment of Messenia, the district of the Greek mainland controlled by the Mycenaean palatial center at Pylos, and they were careful to include contributions by scholars specializing in documentary evidence of the Mycenaean (Chadwick 1972), Greco-Roman, and post-Classical periods. Chadwick (1972) took what was known about administrative geography (see also Chadwick 1963) and exploitation of natural resources from the Linear B tablets and related it to what archaeology, survey, and scientific studies could reconstruct about the actual natural landscape and settlement patterns of late Bronze Age Messenia.

Another positive development was the attention paid to the Mycenaean textual evidence in what for a generation was the most widely used general handbook of the Greek Bronze Age in the English language (Vermeule 1972:232–266). Vermeule took care to use the Linear B data to reconstruct the "society and history of the Mycenaean world."

4. *Indo-European studies.* Despite the comparativist inclinations and abilities of Michael Ventris and other second-generation scholars like Killen and Melena, the Linear B tablets were viewed primarily through the same Indo-Europeanist filter through which Bronze Age Greek archaeological discoveries had been viewed since the discovery of the shaft graves at Mycenae. Thus, basic institutions and basic patterns of social and political organization were reconstructed according to what was considered to be an invariable Indo-European model as laid out in the works of Dumézil (1958) and Benveniste (1969). As with the use of any interpretive templates, subtleties and cautionary nuances of the original formulators of such theories were overlooked. The identifiable Indo-European features of Mycenaean culture were emphasized, while the components that were adapted from the merging of the Greek speakers with preceding population groups (in general terms, Minoans and the

so-called Aegean substrate, by which was meant the inhabitants of the Cycladic islands and "Helladic" mainland) were left underexplored. Such tendencies were naturally reinforced by the influence of Homeric studies.

For a good example of this process and its effects, see the concise reappraisals of the Indo-European nature of the Mycenaean *wanaks* (Linear B texts and Indo-European theory, Homeric studies, and evidence of iconography, archaeology, and anthropology) in Palaima (1995a) and the multidisciplinary general reexamination of Aegean rulership in Rehak (1995; see also Renfrew 1998 and Shelmerdine 1999).

This second period of the second stage was also marked by the publication of specialized monographs necessary to work with the information in the Linear B texts. From this time come our only complete onomastic study (Landau 1958), our first lexicon (Morpurgo 1963, written in Latin!), our only full-scale "historical" prosopography (Lindgren 1973), our only full grammar (Vilborg 1960: called at the time "tentative" and now at last just about to be replaced by a definitive grammar), our only full study of how the Mycenaean evidence affects our understanding of the history of Greek phonology (Lejeune 1972), and our only systematic overviews of Mycenaean religious references (Gérard-Rousseau 1968) and economic terminology (Ruijgh 1967; Duhoux 1976, which was finished in 1972).

During this period, too, Mycenologists took advantage of the relative paucity of tablets from their sites and the relatively careful documentation of the archaeological contexts of the inscribed records to begin to develop archival, paleographical, pinacological, and sphragistic approaches to Mycenaean administration to a level of sophistication unparalleled in the study of most ancient Near Eastern and Mesopotamian cultures (Bennett 1959; Palmer and Boardman 1963; Gill 1966; Olivier 1967; see the overview in Palaima n.d.b).

New Archaeology, Hyperspecialization, and the Mycenaean Greek Texts, 1974–2000

The final stage in the hundred-year history of study of Aegean scripts is marked by many positive developments and two serious negative developments. Among the positive developments is an integrative approach to studying the tablets in relation to their archaeological contexts (Shelmerdine and Palaima 1984a, 1984b; Bennet 1985, 1988; Driessen 2000; Olivier 1997; Palaima 1995b, 1999, 2000c, n.d.b; R. Palmer 1994; Pini 1997; Piteros, Olivier, and Melena 1990; Varias 1993) as now understood through more sophisticated anthropological and archaeological methods of interpretation.

Moreover, cross-disciplinarity has become *de rigeur*. This does not mean that many Mycenologists have been trained at the feet of leading anthropological archaeologists, or vice versa that many anthropologists have developed the epigraphical and linguistic skills to work with the Linear B tablets at the level of sophistication now required by nearly fifty years of accumulated linguistic study and textual interpretation. In fact, I can think of only one true "switch-hitter": John Bennet, now at Oxford University. But there has been some satisfying interdisciplinary awareness, discussion, and collaboration across the great divide identified by Renfrew (1980).

Many of the latest students of Mycenaean texts have been trained within programs that at least include or tolerate emphasis on archaeology or even ancient history and philology rather than linguistics per se, and have therefore been disposed to collaborate more closely with practitioners of New Archaeology or at least to try to answer questions posed by more sophisticated theoretical approaches to archaeological evidence. The work of Jan Driessen is exemplary in this regard (most notably Driessen 1997, 2000; Driessen and MacDonald 1997). The seminal work of Cynthia Shelmerdine relating Mycenaean toponyms to archaeological topography (Shelmerdine 1973, 1981; see also Chadwick 1972) and her recent textually informed overview of the Mycenaean palatial period (Shelmerdine 1997), plus the work of R. Palmer (1989, 1992, 1994, 1999), demonstrate the gains to be made by studying the tablets in conjunction with the material record and comparanda from well-documented cultures of the ancient Near East, although neither scholar has been required to use sophisticated anthropological theory to achieve those gains. Palaima (2000c) brings together the evidence of intensive interdisciplinary and diachronic scientific field survey work, dialect studies and lexicography, toponymy, and economic history to propose a more probable interpretation of a significant place name in the Pylos corpus. In so doing, there are ancillary gains because the discussion casts light on regional resource management and exploitation in the Mycenaean palatial period, the mixing and layering of speakers of different languages (Indo-European and non-Indo-European), and even the paucity of references to the legal sphere in the Linear B texts.

Moving in the opposite direction, Paul Halstead has exploited the Linear B evidence in his discussions of Mycenaean systems of agricultural and pastoral resource management, taxation, and production (for example, Halstead 1992, 1995, 1999a, 1999b) and thereby given purely textual scholars new tools and perspectives for approaching their data. R. Palmer (1992) and Halstead (1995) well exemplify the need to question critical assumptions made in interpreting Linear B documents in the first generation of scholarship. For instance, the values of the two fundamental ideograms for grains may yet have to be reversed. The scholarly jury is still out, but a wide array of evidence has now been brought to bear on original interpretations that were based on assumptions rather than full reasoned argument.

In turn, leading figures such as Colin Renfrew (1987, 1998) have gone back to other fundamental questions and major assumptions about interpreting Mycenaean culture largely from an Indo-Europeanist, Homericist, and historical Hellenist—one almost wants to say a "Thucydidean"—perspective. Renfrew (1980) is credited with triggering the entire debate about how and why to bring New World anthropologically oriented methods of research to bear on Old World archaeological questions. Fortunately for us, he was interested *inter alia* in Aegean prehistory. Thus such questions as the arrival of Greek speakers in the Balkan peninsula, the nature of trade and cultural contacts between east and west, and most recently the composition of the language features of the pre-Greek Aegean have come in for restudy. This is an extremely healthy trend. Non-Mycenological archaeologists and anthropologists have forced Mycenologists to rethink evidence and to reformulate questions.

At the same time, at least from my perspective, interpreters of Linear B tablets have acted—and I hope will continue to act—as sober police officers curbing the tendencies of anthropological and archaeological theorists to speed ahead of the limits of available textual data or even to overlook the implications of closely nuanced interpretations of the details in the texts (see Killen 1999b; Palaima n.d.d responding to Wright 1994). In some ways, to paraphrase Oscar Wilde, this amounts to the importance of being, if not earnest, at least stodgy. But, as I have already noted, there are now a number of more senior Mycenologists (for example, Killen, Melena, Driessen, Hiller, Shelmerdine, Bennet, and R. Palmer) whose primary approach to the interpretation of the documents has always been grounded in at least attempting to understand the material culture of Mycenaean and related societies, and to pay attention to questions raised by archaeological theory, methods, and interpretations. That anthropologists and archaeologists can do their own "policing" is proved by Cherry and Davis (1999).

The collaboration between Mycenologists and archaeologists has brought about a questioning of old assumptions concerning topics as important and fundamental as the nature of Mycenaean kingship (Palaima 1995a; Rehak 1995), the function of Mycenaean palaces (Galaty and Parkinson 1999), the dating of destruction(s) at the Palace of Minos at Knossos (Driessen 1997, 2000), the formation and operation of Mycenaean palatial territories (Bennet 1990, 1998a, Bintliff 1977), the nature of Mycenaean trade (Duhoux 1988; Palaima 1991; Olivier 1996–97), the operation of specialized Mycenaean industries (R. Palmer 1994; Shelmerdine 1985), the nature and location of religious rituals (Hägg 1997), the whole apparatus and organization of economic administration (including the important nonliterate sphragistic component), and the methods used to identify cultural components within the Greek mainland and Cretan archaeological record (the old Minoan vs. Mycenaean dichotomy in areas such as religion and political organization and even in the history of the site of Knossos and its relationship to other sites in the Minoan neo-palatial and Mycenaean palatial period).

There are ramifications in a number of other area and related fields; these include:

- Indo-European questions relating to language and ethnic identity, religion, and political and social institutions (Renfrew 1998; Burkert 1997; Palaima 1995a)

- Archaeology and texts, regional geography, and reassessment of the function of the Mycenaean palatial complex (Bintliff 1977; Shelmerdine and Palaima 1984a, 1984b; Bennet 1988, 1990, 1998a, 1998b; Galaty and Parkinson 1999; Palaima 2000a)

- Sphragistics (the comparative study of clay sealing devices as used within administrative and economic systems in ancient Aegean, Near Eastern, Mesopotamian, and Egyptian civilizations, especially cross-cultural and systems-oriented analyses with broad implications for economic matters and social and political organization) (see Weingarten 1986, 1988; Palaima 1987, 1990, 2000; R. Palmer 1994; Ferioli et al. 1994; Ferioli, Fiandra, and Fissore 1996; Hallager 1996; Pini 1997; and Perna 1998)

- Mycenaean "dialects" and their implications for the structure of Mycenaean society (archaeologically invisible with implications for the relationship between the palatial centers and outlying communities and districts) and also for major archaeological questions like the "Dorian invasion" (Risch 1966, 1979; Chadwick 1976a; Duhoux 1994–95; Varias 1994–95; Thompson 1996–97; Palaima 2002)

- Palatially organized commensal banqueting ceremonies and their significance for reinforcing social unity and stratification (comparative study of sphragistics, technical terminology, relevant Linear B tablet series, palatial architecture and iconography, the artifactual record, regional geography, and anthropological and cross-cultural parallels) (see Melena 1983; Piteros, Olivier, and Melena 1990; Killen 1992, 1994, 1998, 1999a; Davis and Bennet 1999; Palaima n.d.c; Sacconi 1999; and Speciale 1999)

- Reappraisal of a key ritual document with the assistance of anthropological discussion about prestige ritual artifacts and through an understanding of the history of scholarship surrounding earlier interpretive approaches (Palaima 1999; Sacconi 1987; Wright 1995a).

- Scribal administration and archival studies (understanding the environments and procedures and purposes of the inscribed documentation and relating them to reconstructions of social, political, and economic prehistory) (see Palaima 1988, 1995b, n.d.b; Pluta 1996–97; Bennet 1985; Driessen 2000; and Driessen and MacDonald 1997)

- The exploitation of Mycenaean textual information for an understanding of the spread of cult locales that have been so far virtually unidentifiable, even through intensive regional interdisciplinary archaeological survey, and for addressing problems relating to religious continuity from the prehistoric to the historical period (Hiller 1981; Palaima n.d.d)

A major positive development has been the integration of textual scholars into conferences primarily focused on iconography or archaeology. The current workshop is a good example, as are the many Aegaeum conferences cited as the sources for the publication of many articles in the bibliography, and the kinds of cross-disciplinary workshops that have been held in the field of ancient texts (see Palaima n.d.b) or sealing systems (Palaima 1990; Ferioli et al. 1994; Ferioli, Fiandra, and Fissore 1996; and Perna 1998).

Other advances have been achieved by Spanish scholars in the field of lexicography where we now have a fairly up-to-date comprehensive lexicon and detailed studies of words relating to specific aspects of the Mycenaean world (Aura Jorro 1985, 1993; Luján 1996–97; Bernabé et al. 1990–91, 1992–93).

One important negative development, or rather nondevelopment, during this period is that no comprehensive study of the Linear B documents on the scale of Ventris and Chadwick 1956 and 1973 has made up-to-date information about the general evidence in the tablets readily available to nonspecialist scholars. The last collaborative state-of-the-art survey was by Davies and Duhoux (1985), which for our purposes is noteworthy for its comprehensive survey of textual evidence for the Mycenaean economy (Killen 1985), its convincing demonstration that particular Homeric verses predate the earliest Linear B texts (Ruijgh 1985), and its cursory treatment of small-scale topics in Mycenaean religion.

The failure to produce a serious new source volume for the Linear B evidence is due partly to the fact that the techniques of interpretation have become so sophisticated and the questions asked of the tablets so complicated that work on a single tablet, a single tablet series, or a single technical term, if done correctly (for example, Del Freo 1996–97), can now take years to complete satisfactorily. There is also a tendency among Mycenological scholars not to review comprehensively the history of scholarship on related topics, so that underlying assumptions are perpetuated and problems and questions ignored because they are considered resolved. Moreover, we have had periodic discoveries of new tablets. Delays, however justifiable or unavoidable, in the publication of these new tablets create a disincentive for Mycenological scholars to bring specialized studies to completion, if they know that data relevant to their topics are contained in the new inscriptions.

Palaima (n.d.c) restudies the Ta series in the context of commensal cere-monies, administrative *realia*, and an exhaustive review of pertinent scholar-ship. Palaima (1999) interprets Tn 316 in its archival, ceremonial, and social contexts, and traces the history of scholarship back to observations made in an unpublished letter by Michael Ventris predecipherment. Each is a good example of technical, yet combinatory, scholarship that is ensconced or soon to be ensconced in the specialist literature. Each represents about four years of intensive, albeit sometimes intermittent, work and even longer back-ground periods while looking at specific side topics impinging upon the proper interpretation of such texts. Some of these side topics were identified by pursuing the neglected area of the history of scholarship, whereby it has been possible to identify assumptions and even forgotten side avenues that have steered scholarly interpretation along particular paths. Recall the prob-able misidentification, or at least ill-reasoned identification, of fundamental Linear B ideograms for grain, cited above, as another good example of how potentially "false" ideas can be perpetuated uncritically.

Specialized publications (for example, Palaima 1998) can have serious ramifications for the general interpretation of key texts of interest to archae-ologists, anthropologists, and specialists in the history of culture. But they risk being virtually inaccessible to such scholars, if the results do not make their way into readily accessible and up-to-date handbooks. We should note that the problem is exacerbated by "mainstream" journals in archaeology, history, or philology not providing any room for technical articles in subdis-ciplines like Mycenology, papyrology, or epigraphy.

Nonspecialists wanting to exploit the evidence of the Linear B texts are now working with a "bible" (Ventris and Chadwick 1973) that has an inter-pretive outlook on the documents set in the early 1950s. At that time, under-standing of the Linear B material was primitive. Ventris and Chadwick did not have available the results now achieved by refinements and advances in paleographical, pinacological, linguistic, dialectal, and archival studies, and by the vast array of new approaches and newly posed questions derived from the fields of archaeology and anthropology.

The second edition of the Mycenaean "bible" is nearly a full scholarly generation old. It is a partial updating that, of course, does not take into account any of the significant new tablet discoveries at Thebes, Tiryns, Midea, Khania, Pylos, and Knossos during the last three decades. Chadwick (1976b) is now outdated and presents the interpretive views of a scholar who did not have deep interests in archaeological or anthropological data, theories, and questions. Hiller and Panagl (1976), of the same date, is a solid, condensed overview. The most advanced, concise thematic overview that incorporates discussion of new texts and the latest interpretive theories is by Ruipérez and Melena (1996), an update of their popular handbook (Ruipérez and Melena 1990). But it focuses on fewer than 100 Linear B texts of the approximately 5000 we now possess. Ventris and Chadwick (1973) covers only about 400.

The hyper-technicality of the field and the proliferation of specialist publications devoted to problems in sub-areas of research within the field of Mycenology often make the tracking of scholarship problematical for archaeologists and general prehistorians. There are now three volumes of a specialist Polish periodical devoted to Mycenology (Sharypkin et al. 2000–01). The annotated analytical bibliography for the field, entitled *Studies in Mycenaean Inscriptions and Dialect* (SMID), suspended publication in 1978. It has now been revived by the Program in Aegean Scripts and Prehistory (PASP) at the University of Texas at Austin. Volumes for 1978–83 and 1994–99 have appeared. The volume for 1984–85 is almost set for publication. An on-line version of an integrated database for the new volumes will become available when our limited technical resources are sufficient to keep it up and on-line. But there are constant worries about sustainability, given the resources and person-hours of specialized technical research that go into producing a single volume of a resource like SMID.

Sustainability is also a chief concern for graduate programs that conduct research and train new scholars. The field has lost solid footing in some countries as senior scholars have retired and not been replaced at their universities, or as research centers have gradually shifted focus. This is true even of the general field of Aegean prehistory. In Palaima (n.d.e) I cited Sweden as an example of a country in which what appeared to be a well-established tradition of research in Aegean prehistory has collapsed. It spanned nearly the entire century and included major field excavators and excavations, major specialist scholars (in Mycenaean pottery, Minoan and Mycenaean religion, Linear B prosopography, onomastics, and grammar), scholarly symposia and colloquia in Sweden and at the Swedish Archaeological Institute in Athens, a major monograph series (*Studies in Mediterranean Archaeology*) and for a brief period a main philological journal (see *Eranos* 1952–55), and posts for professors at three of the four major Swedish universities. There will soon be no Aegeanists occupying the chairs once held by such great figures as Nilsson, Persson, Furumark, Åström, and Hägg at the Universities of Lund, Göteborg, and Uppsala; and minor posts have also disappeared.

It might also appear shocking to outsiders—or even to insiders who have remained obtuse to the "corporatization" of universities worldwide—that Cambridge University made a first choice to have no scholar in a permanent position who has a primary research focus on Mycenology and could sustain the pioneering tradition of John Chadwick and John Killen. This situation has rectified itself, as it were accidentally, with an unexpected resignation and the appointment of Rupert Thompson. Likewise in the United States, Harvard University, Bryn Mawr College, and the University of Wisconsin have not sustained the traditions that could have developed from eminent scholars (and related programmatic resources) such as Emily Vermeule, Mabel Lang, and Emmett L. Bennett, Jr. Each of these scholars represented a range of approaches to Aegean prehistory coordinated with other subjects. Vermeule was a prodigious and wide-ranging intellect adept at addressing archaeological, art historical, and general cultural problems in prehistory while paying fair attention to textual evidence. Lang did the primary work of editing Linear B tablets from Pylos in the 1950s and early 1960s and taught Linear B at Bryn Mawr throughout a long career during which she produced major studies of the Pylos frescoes, historical-period graffiti and *dipinti* from the Athenian Agora, and the classical historian Herodotus. Emmett Bennett, of course, was the leading Mycenaean epigrapher and a brilliant scholar of the history of writing per se. The noncontinuation of their Aegean prehistorical components is part of a worrisome general pattern of declining support for the humanities in general and particularly for specialized subfields within the humanities.

There have been some pockets of growth as scholars of the caliber of J. Bennet, Driessen, R. Palmer, Shelmerdine, and Varias have obtained good permanent posts. The Eleventh International Mycenological Colloquium met in Austin, Texas, on May 7–13, 2000, sponsored by PASP. In attendance were approximately seventy junior and senior participants who gave and discussed fifty-eight papers that covered a broad range of topics.[3] There were more young scholars presenting papers in Austin and a much larger number of auditors than at the previous three colloquia.

There is then reason for guarded optimism about future integrative results from research in the fields of Mycenology, archaeology, and anthropology, and for an expectation of the normal course of lurching progress in areas where archaeologists, anthropologists, and textual scholars can talk across divides that are no longer so great. In some cases, the conversations are being held at last within single human minds and psyches, or among scholars who have become used to collaborating with one another as team-mates on opposite sides of traditional disciplinary boundaries. To cite one good example of a healthy trend, Van Alfen (1996–97) proposes a sound interpretation for the painted Linear B inscriptions on a limited number of Mycenaean stirrup jars. The author was able to use his extensive knowledge of Aegean and extra-Aegean trade and nautical archaeology in both the pre-historic and historical periods and considerable understanding of numismat-ics, sphragistics, literacy, and "closed systems" of economic marking. He has completed a dissertation on "trade and economic interaction between the Levant and Aegean during the Persian Period." His research is likely to remain cross-cultural and interdisciplinary. It will certainly extend across the divide between history and prehistory in a way that will inform specialists in either period.

There is also good reason to hope that synthetic volumes will continue to appear, especially given the changing mandates of university presses that are reluctant to publish specialist studies purely in narrow areas of archaeol-ogy or textual studies. As mentioned, there have also been considerable new discoveries of texts in the last decade and vastly improved editions of extant texts. These lie outside the scope of this paper.

I shall close by sounding a further optimistic note relating to two areas treated at length above: Homeric studies and history of religion. Bennet (1997) provides a fine progress report on the current status of our under-standing of how the Homeric poems relate to the archaeological record and to the development of Greek society from the Bronze Age into the Iron Age. His survey ably exploits recent work with the Linear B texts, the linguistic reconstruction and dating of Homeric verse, and our understanding of differ-ent cultural periods based on archaeological and anthropological data and methods. Cook and Palaima (n.d.) will be reinvestigating the "historicity" of the Homeric vision of Nestor's Pylos using modern literary and narrative analysis and our contemporary understanding of the transition to the Greek Iron Age and of the Mycenaean textual, archaeological, and iconographical evidence for cult practice. Likewise, there are non-Mycenological scholars of the history of religion who are attuned to the Mycenaean evidence and are able to use it judiciously (Burkert 1985; Schachter 1981, 1986, 1994; Hägg 1997a; Gulizio, Palaima, and Pluta 2001).

In sum, I think we have reached the stage where Mycenological special-ists rarely will work as if hermetically sealed within their specialties. The greater challenge seems to me to ensure that there are enough specialists and enough support for specialists to do the highly technical work in Mycenology that provides us with secure data for addressing larger questions and issues of interest to archaeologists, anthropologists, prehistorians, and Mycenologists. For example, someone has to continue to be interested in such questions as whether new Linear B tablets from Khania are paleographically identical to or just similar to Knossian tablets (Palaima 1992–93; Olivier 1996; Driessen 2000:110–112). This kind of question, though argued on a very technical level, has serious implications for more general reconstructions of Aegean prehistory. Without at least three experts worldwide willing to take on such detailed questions and to disagree with one another openly and politely, the field will make only illusory progress, and we run the risk of constructing the kinds of houses of cards that long have plagued the study of Minoan Linear A. Again, I stress that it was healthy for the field in the 1950s through the 1970s to have Chadwick and Palmer producing radically different interpretations of virtually the same data.

Mycenological interpretations of the textual "evidence" emanating unchecked from even the most rigorous single scholarly minds well might introduce a factor of error that will contaminate the work of archaeologists who resort to the Linear B tablets for help in their reconstructions of the late Greek Bronze Age. I hope we can make sure in the generation ahead that archaeologists and anthropologists who resort to the Linear B evidence will always have relatively convenient ways to obtain second and third opinions, and to get them from Mycenological scholars who speak the language and understand the methods and issues of archaeology and anthropology.

Notes

1. Pinacology (deriving from the Greek *pinax* or tablet) is the technical term used in Mycenaean scholarship for the study of clay documents.
2. This four-volume work includes a general synthesis of those facets of Minoan civilization that most interested Evans: cultural reconstruction; seal and fresco iconography; inscribed materials, religion, and ritual; and the use of architectural space within the palatial center.
3. Interested parties should consult the PASP web site for the titles of papers and subjects covered: *http://www.utexas.edu/research/pasp*.

CHAPTER 4

Writing History:
The Maya and the Mediterranean

RICHARD M. LEVENTHAL

It is interesting to see the similarities in the process of decipherment between the stages defined by Tom Palaima and the stages that can be defined for the decipherment of the ancient Maya script. The imposition of personalities, preconceived ideas, and lengthy side transects that characterize Palaima's description of Linear B decipherment are similarly found in the work on the Maya script.

The story of the decipherment of the Maya hieroglyphic script has been told many times, most recently in a book by Michael Coe entitled *Breaking the Maya Code* (Coe 1992). With the story of decipherment already related, it is therefore not necessary for me to repeat the tale here.

The decipherment of the ancient Maya writing system is a major step forward in our study of this ancient society. But rather than bringing people together with a new, finely tuned focus, this decipherment has resulted in a strong controversy between the archaeologists on the one hand and the epigraphers and art historians on the other:

> You might reasonably think that the decipherment of the Maya script would have been greeted with open arms by the archaeologists. Not a bit of it! The reaction of the digging fraternity (and sorority) to the most exciting development in New World archaeology this century has been . . . rejection. It is not that they claim, like Champollion's opponents, that the decipherment has not taken place, they simply believe it is not worthy of notice (at least overtly). (M. Coe 1992:271)

The wielders of trowels finally got their revenge, at Dumbarton Oaks in a conference held in early October 1989 [Sabloff and Henderson 1993]. It was called "On the Eve of the Collapse: Ancient Maya Societies in the

Eighth century, A.D." I (luckily) wasn't there, but there can be little doubt that the whole conference was a negative reaction to the decipherment and to *The Blood of Kings*. (M. Coe 1992:272)

With these words behind us, let me try to stake out a middle ground between what epigraphers and archaeologists have been arguing about for the past two decades.

A common adage in today's world of television, videos, and glossy periodicals is that a "picture is worth a thousand words." It is clear, however, that even in today's world, words and pictures are an integral part of the presentation of ideas and are integral in the expressions of power within our societies. I want to suggest that this was particularly true for the ancient Maya civilization of Middle America.

The Maya writing system and its complex series of calendars are fully integrated with pictures throughout the Maya lowlands. In fact, I would argue that the writing system was a, or possibly the, primary mode utilized by the elite within Maya society to exercise and present their conception of power (see also Johnston 2001).

Let me begin my analysis with a methodological statement and several basic definitions. First, the Maya hieroglyphic system, as with all writing systems, must be perceived as a complex symbol system that was utilized to express concepts and ideas. The study of any such symbol system must proceed with several types of analysis. For this paper, I would like to define three such lines. The first is the basic decipherment of the text or individual hieroglyphs. Terms such as "reading" the text or "translating" the text are often used to describe this type of study. The multiplicity of meanings that have been ascribed to these terms makes them useless, however, in the description of this type of study. For example, the phrase "to read the text" may refer to either the act of reading or to providing an interpretive structure to the text. Perhaps the best definition or phrase that describes this type of analysis is "to assign meaning" to a text. A good example of this assignment of meaning might be the English translation of a foreign language text or book. As we will see, however, even this assignment of meaning is not completely clear cut and basic in its format and result. The phrases and words utilized in the translation will very much reflect the translator's own background and cultural milieu. This is why there are multiple translations of foreign language books—there are hundreds of translations into English, for example, of *Don Quixote*.

This brings me to the second type of analysis that can be conducted with a text such as those from the Maya area now being deciphered. This effort focuses upon the attempt to define whether an event, recorded in the texts, actually took place in the past. As the Maya hieroglyphs have been deciphered over the past twenty-five years, we have seen a variety of types of events presented as historical activities. It was argued at Dumbarton Oaks in 1989 (Sabloff and Henderson 1993), the same conference mentioned by Mike Coe (see above), that it is important to attempt to document the existence of these events. The documentation of any specific "historical" event in the past is, however, a most difficult task archaeologically or even epigraphically.

Let me divide these events into two broad categories. First, there are events that are specific individual activities that do not have an impact upon a large number of people or even a broad material culture. Such events would clearly include the basic genealogical structure of a ruling family or an elite family, the identification of individuals as associated with a particular social or political position, or even ritual activities such as individualized bloodletting. I believe it would be difficult, if not impossible, archaeologically or even epigraphically to attempt to demonstrate that any of these events actually occurred in the past.

A secondary category of events might be possible to delineate. These events are broader in their scope and have a greater impact upon a large population and therefore may be identifiable within the archaeological record. Such events may include wars between sites or large population displacements or movements. As will be discussed below, even these types of events will be very difficult, if not impossible, to identify and should be attempted carefully.

A third type of analysis does not focus upon "events" but rather upon the constructed nature of the world and of society as embodied within the texts. As Edward Said (1983:5) has stated, "Discourse is not mere formalization of knowledge; its aim is the control and manipulation of knowledge, the body politic, and ultimately the State." Texts and images are produced by the state in its efforts to develop and maintain power. These texts and images can be used to examine the construction of the state or of kingship, and therefore can be examined as evidence for a set of power relations within the social and political structure, as argued by Michel Foucault (1973). The people in the past, and in the present, who control representations and the interpretations of representations control the social and political power within society. A reading of a text that makes a direct correlation between word and action is an acceptable model, but is not necessarily, by definition, the most viable.

I argue that scholars of the ancient Maya civilization must begin to analyze the iconography and writing, not purely in terms of "actual" events, but rather in terms of the construction of these power relations and the construction of kingship and the state. An analysis of the texts and images will reveal a series of strategies utilized by the Maya kings and elite to construct and maintain their power.

The attempt to directly correlate what the Maya wrote on their monuments with an identification of some sort of "historical past" does not take into account the fact that power in ancient Maya society may lie less in physical action and more in the ability to state that events occurred. The expression of power through writing can be more important and more powerful than physical events or activities. Although this view of the present and the past may seem anathema to us in the twenty-first century, this age of technology, it remains clear that words remain the prevailing force in the creation of the elite expression of power. This is the form of the argument presented by Jean-François Lyotard in his book entitled *The Postmodern Condition: A Report on Knowledge* (1984).

Let me present two very brief examples from the present-day world. One of the best examples over the past several years is the events—or now specifically—the writing about the events in Tienamien Square in Beijing more than a decade ago. The events played on world television, newscasts, and throughout the newspapers—combining images and words. Who can forget the sharp image of the makeshift Statue of Liberty constructed in the Square or the lone individual standing in front of an advancing tank. Similar pictures associated with different words, spoken or written, resulted in a series of very different competing interpretations of these events in Tienamien Square. The two ends of the spectrum identify this individual as a hero standing up to the totalitarian army or, in contrast, as a villain fighting against the will of the people and the state. It is not a question of which representation is the "accurate" one or which is "more correct." It is a question of who created each representation and how these representations were used to express, argue for, and legitimize power.

The concept of competing representations and/or competing interpretations is an important one, for it is within this context that change within the political, social, or religious organization can occur. It is the presentation, acceptance of, and then future control over these representations that allows for change and the creation of a system of power symbols.

A second example within the United States, and I am sure that there are many examples throughout the past and present worlds of the Mediterranean, focuses upon the Iwo Jima Memorial in Washington, DC. Along the base of the monument are listed all the great battles in which the US Marines have engaged. These include battles in Europe and the Pacific during the First and Second World Wars. At the same time, the "invasion" of Grenada is listed. The simple listing of this minor incursion, along with other apparently large battles, creates and maintains an expression of power and authority associated with the US Marines within today's world of the United States.

Power is in the word and the image, as long as this representation is not challenged. A text and image representing action can, if unchallenged, have as significant a consequence as the action itself. Patricia O'Brien (1989:35), in her discussion of Foucault's concept of power, states: "Most challenging of all is the realization that power creates truth and hence its own legitimation."

An analysis of the narrative of the Maya, as well as Linear B Mycenaean texts, must therefore become the focus of future research rather than simply the translation of the texts themselves.

In closing, I would like to return to Tom Palaima's paper and some of his conclusions. He identifies one very positive development within Linear B studies, along with two strong negative developments. From Palaima's perspective, the growing integration of epigraphers and iconographic scholars with archaeologists in terms of thinking, conferences, and interpretations is a good, positive force in the field. It is clear from the material presented above that this integration is still needed within the Maya area. In addition, the nature of the integration is crucial—it cannot be purely an exchange of information but must also be an integration of the theory of writing and history.

Only one of Palaima's two negative developments relates to the Maya area. His second point is that there is a decreased interest and therefore a decreased number of jobs available for people working on Linear B or on Mycenology. Within anthropology and art history departments throughout the United States there continue to be jobs for Maya scholars. This area of study remains strong.

Palaima's first negative relates specifically to the lack of good information flow from the epigraphers to other interested scholars—or the lack of an up-to-date "bible" or dictionary. This difficulty also exists within the Maya area for the same reasons Palaima discussed: the constant shifting of ideas and the incredible detail required to assess and develop translations and interpretations.

In the end, the parallels between the decipherment of Linear B and Maya writing are striking. Also striking are the similarities in terms of how these decipherments and new interpretations have not brought an immediate accord among all scholars in the Mediterranean or within the Maya area. I believe that the theoretical concepts of writing, translation, and history must remain central to our work in both the Maya area and the Mediterranean in the future.

CHAPTER 5

New Worlds, Ancient Texts: Perspectives on Epigraphy and Archaeology

SARAH P. MORRIS

The history from the Incas onward must be learned by heart, even if we do not teach of the riches of Greece. For our Greece is preferable to that Greece which is not ours.

Jose Martí, Nuestra America

The phrase above was invoked by a self-described "Italian born, French national archaeologist with Mexican professional commitments" in lamenting the failure of Caribbean archaeology to advance beyond colonial models (Sued-Badillo 1992:599, 605). The quinquecentennial in 1992 of the arrival of Columbus in a land unknown to Europeans generated many such revisions of the confrontation between a world still reliant on Mediterranean traditions and an unsuspected continent of new cultures and languages. The very discovery of the "New World" across the Atlantic was a shock and a challenge to the inherited wisdom based on ancient texts, as analyzed by scholars from the European tradition on the other side of the Atlantic (Grafton 1992). As John Locke put it succinctly, "In the beginning, all the World was America," one expression of the impact of prehistoric civilizations in the Americas on the kind of learning that relied on biblical and classical texts for an understanding of the world. So, one chief novelty of the regions we still call "new" inhered in their displacement of the written word as a source of authority, in the face of cultures unknown from ancient writings. In radical movements that still seek to liberate indigenous and oppressed populations from overlords imported from Spain, France, Portugal, and England, the words of Jose Martí epitomize the desire to transcend those inherited texts as one step toward cultural as well as political autonomy. And in some sectors, New World archaeology has retained that deliberate distancing in seeking answers independently from the material record of textual authority. Thus a recent Dumbarton Oaks roundtable convened around the theme of "Art and Writing" evolved, in its published version, into "Writing without Words" (Boone and Mignolo 1994). These vivid postures struck on this issue in the New World no doubt enhance the efforts of archaeologists to bridge or widen the gap between the study of texts and the practice of archaeology.

At this workshop we heard from two scholars engaged on both sides of the Atlantic in the encounter between texts and prehistory (a self-described Aegean pinacologist and an archaeologist who has sought to engage scholars of glyphs in a dialogue in Maya studies). Both reviewed the impact of the decipherment and looked closely at its future. What common lessons are there to be learned for the study of ancient texts in coordination with archaeology?

In both regions, the decipherment of previously unread texts has had a revolutionary effect on local research, groundbreaking for progress in certain directions, if not always salutary for the discipline as a whole. In the Aegean in the half century since Ventris and others succeeded in reading Linear B as an early form of Greek, a new form of specialization soon developed, as Palaima traces so thoroughly. And that new discipline also developed a distance from archaeology within the first generation. In Palaima's final stage (1974–2000), it has been the second generation (Bennet, Palaima, Shelmerdine, and Wright, to name the most prominent practitioners in English) that has set out to integrate the study of texts with their archaeological context. A new era was heralded with the AIA symposium published as *Pylos Comes Alive* (Shelmerdine and Palaima 1984a), an examination of the location and distribution as well as contents of Linear B texts by archaeologists and epigraphers working and publishing in collaboration. The synoptic reanalysis of the archives room at Pylos by an archaeologist and an epigrapher (Palaima and Wright 1985) demonstrated the fruits of such collaboration.

But only certain kinds of "texts" qualify as suitable for integration with Bronze Age archaeology. For example, my comparison of later Greek poetry with Aegean narrative art (S. Morris 1989) has been criticized for lifting the iron curtain drawn between classical Greece and its Bronze Age past (Muhly 1992:15–16; Starr 1992:2; I. Morris 2000:102–103). Yet in the New World, understanding the Popul Vuh, a Quiché Maya epic tradition recorded in the sixteenth century (Tedlock 1985), is a delicate exercise of comparison with Classic Maya imagery ever since Michael Coe first detected forerunners of Popul Vuh myths in Classic Maya art (M. Coe 1973).

An advantage to archaeologists in the world of Mycenaean texts is the predominantly economic thrust of most documents in Linear B: they record property holdings in land, animals, manufactured goods, and raw materials, often regionally recorded in a way that has inspired conjoined studies of regional systems. The recent Cotsen Institute volume, *Rethinking Mycenaean Palaces* (Galaty and Parkinson 1999), derives from a Society for American Archaeology panel convened by specialists in lithics, ceramics, and zooarchaeology, and by archaeologists focused on religious ritual, political power, and regional analysis. The survey of Messenia that drew many of these experts together, published as *Sandy Pylos* (J. Davis 1998), exemplifies how such collaboration can produce long-term regional histories based on landscape archaeology as well as written sources.

One reason that texts and archaeology will stay close in the Mediterranean world is that the academic home of Aegean prehistory has remained, for better or for worse, in humanities departments, if not in classics departments, strongly shaped by research and training in ancient languages and texts. Thus the guarded optimism Palaima expresses at the end of his paper for a future of integrated studies is justified by the guaranteed fraternity that will continue to keep Aegean prehistorians and specialists in Linear B linked (if not chained) to the same agenda. New World archaeology, however, maintains primary allegiance with anthropology, particularly since the advent of "New Archaeology" in the 1960s, under the umbrella of the social sciences. Thus scholars who specialize in Maya glyphs are rare in anthropology departments and are far more welcome among those who pursue the integrated study of texts and images, usually in art history departments. Notable exceptions in Mesoamerican archaeology include a chief contributor to this volume, Joyce Marcus (see chapter 8, which is cross-cultural, as well as interdisciplinary, in comparing texts and monuments); in the Aegean, John Bennet remains a "switch-hitter" in a class of his own (see Palaima chapter 3, and recent exceptions such as Driessen 2000).

In the New World, as Richard Leventhal stressed in his presentation at the Cotsen Seminar, the decipherment of Maya glyphs offered early hopes of "history" (absent in Aegean texts) by yielding the names of rulers, places, and alleged "events" such as battles and conquests. This led, on the one hand, to ambitious new titles such as *The Lost Chronicles of the Maya Kings* (Drew 1999) and *Chronicle of the Maya Kings and Queens* (Martin and Grube 2000), along with a newly specialized cadre of epigraphers. It also led, on the other hand, to the rejection of glyphs and images as "unscientific" by archaeologists who mistrusted the propaganda behind the inscription and display of glyphic texts linked to images (Schele 1996:412). This manipulation of messages by Maya rulers and scribes makes these texts similar to the self-aggrandizing monuments promulgated by rulers in Egypt and Mesopotamia (Marcus chapter 8) rather than the more pedestrian economic and temporary records of a single year that survive from the Greek Bronze Age. And the status and treatment of Maya scribes only reinforce the enormous role they played in maintaining these systems of power (see Johnston 2001).

Understanding Maya glyphs as part of a symbolic system aimed at maintaining power calls for postmodern strategies, as Leventhal demonstrates in chapter 4. At the same time, the contents and purposes of these texts are bound to elude archaeologists who are more focused on economic and processual developments where change and its forces can be examined. In point of fact, the revelations of Maya epigraphy emerged in a period experiencing a paradigm shift of another kind, as anthropologists (primarily in Europe) explored beyond the boundaries of process and rediscovered the individual and history (Hodder 1986). The aftermath of decipherment coincided with, and may have reinforced, a deep divide in anthropological archaeology. Postprocessual archaeologists were attracted to the study of inscriptions that manipulate the reader and the environment and embody agency in the names of individuals and their professed deeds. But processual archaeologists can afford to ignore the complications of these texts in preference for a "text" of their own, an evolving set of social hypotheses first generated by the New Archaeology. To illustrate this divergence, it is worth recalling that the journal that once publicized seminal steps toward full decipherment of Maya glyphs (Proskouriakoff 1960) was *American Antiquity*, now quite distant from such research.

Aspects of this conflict have fostered wider anxiety over the value of written sources, and even rejection of them. Social archaeologists stake out a "text-free zone" for research (Moreland 2001:19, 31) and disparage research driven by historical sources as "text-hindered" archaeology (Smith 1997:6), or one laboring under the "tyranny of the text" (Champion 1990; Papadopoulos 1999). This conflict plays itself out dramatically in historical archaeology on both sides of the Atlantic, in medieval archaeology in Europe, and in the New World in Maya studies. But this conflict is shadowed in the Old World by an early history of archaeology as a simplistic and positivistic verification of such texts as Homer and the Bible, such that invoking ancient texts at all now risks being compared with Schliemann, as I have experienced (I. Morris 2000:102–103).

In the Aegean, new texts (Linear B) offered the opposite to prehistoric archaeologists: many names but few individuals exercising power outside hierarchies implied through property holdings, but a treasury of commodities and manufactured goods, deployed across regional territories, that illuminate systems of subsistence as well as surplus. Thus written evidence did not pose the same threat to anthropological approaches that it did to scholars of the Maya. In fact, unlike the opposition noted elsewhere between field survey and historical archaeology (Moreland 2001:19–20), reconciling the regional picture offered by Mycenaean tablets with the landscape through intensive survey became a common goal for a new generation, shaping the mother of all Aegean surveys, the University of Minnesota Messenia Expedition (see Cherry chapter 9).

Thus, the rubric of a "text" conceals a vast range of messages, as Leventhal articulates for the case of Maya glyphs, and presumes a range of human symbols in communication that transcends the traditional expectation of what a text could deliver to an archaeologist (Marcus 1992). In both hemispheres, more than mutual reinforcement of existing assumptions is called for, beginning with an interdisciplinary understanding of the discourse behind any text.

Beyond such comparative speculations, what does the future hold for practitioners of Mediterranean archaeology, the focus of this conference, in consort with the study of texts? Several developments, as well as the structure of a discipline that keeps epigraphers together with archaeologists (see above), are at play here. For one thing, departments of classics have advertised more frequently in recent years for specialists in "material culture," a discreet way of identifying a kind of research with which philologists feel comfortable. This rubric does not always welcome "real" archaeologists who are active in the field or engaged in primary processing of large assemblies of excavated data, in my experience. So this process may have further stranded plenty of archaeologists who pursue an anthropological approach in their training and research. They are not readily employed in the social sciences (where any connection to research in Greece brands one a "classical" archaeologist), yet these same archaeologists are now displaced in classics departments by philologists who can fill the "material culture" bill.

At the same time, the new focus on material culture sends out a message dear to any archaeologist's heart with every such advertisement: philologists in training had better obtain some minimal exposure to archaeology in the classroom or the field for the sake of a future appointment or career. The latter keeps archaeology secure in the classics curriculum and may lead to new generations of classicists congenial to material culture and more informed about it. While this offsets slightly Palaima's negative picture of fewer positions for Aegean prehistorians and epigraphers, it also reinforces the notion that, at least in the Mediterranean, there is safety in numbers and that scholars of texts and artifacts have more to gain through collaboration. In American archaeology, it remains to be seen whether specialists in different kinds of evidence can be reconciled across boundaries generated by theoretical approaches and disciplinary divides to form partnerships in and for the future.

PART II

LARGE-SCALE ARCHAEOLOGICAL
FIELDWORK IN A NEW MILLENNIUM

(Re)-Digging the Site at the End of the Twentieth Century: Large-Scale Archaeological Fieldwork in a New Millennium

RUTH TRINGHAM

This paper was first given as a PowerPoint presentation with animation and even sound effects. In its transferral to text, much has been lost. What I have tried to retain is the format of this paper as a self-reflective and impressionistic one that, I hope, avoids the pitfalls of self-indulgence. This paper is based on my personal experience in directing large-scale excavations at Selevac and Opovo in Yugoslavia, Podgoritsa in Bulgaria, and Çatalhöyük in Turkey. It is also based on my experiences and observations in the field and in the literature in southeast Europe and the east Mediterranean area in general.

The paper explores a number of questions that are problematic for me concerning the nature of large-scale, site-focused excavation. I see these questions as challenges that those of us who work in such contexts will have to face increasingly. And those who read the reports that publish the results of such work would find more productive reading if they are also aware of these challenges. You will see that in this paper I have not been able to resolve these questions and challenges. I personally think that there are no single responses to the challenges of how to do fieldwork in the current socio-economico-political context of the United States and the east Mediterranean. Perhaps other papers from the symposium have been able to address them and come up with answers.

The Nature of Large-Scale Archaeological Fieldwork in a New Millennium

The use of the term "large scale" in archaeological fieldwork covers a number of characteristics of archaeological research in the east Mediterranean area, all of which are important to consider in terms of their future relevance and appropriateness in the twenty-first century.

Investigating Large, Visible Sites

A focus on large, visible sites, especially tells or settlement mounds and/or urban centers, has been a characteristic of fieldwork in this region. The renewed research at Çatalhöyük since 1993 brings to the forefront the question of the feasibility and ultimate purpose of research focused on large visible sites. The site was first excavated by James Mellaart in the 1960s. In three seasons, with a large local workforce (35, by no means the largest being used in the Near East at that time), he succeeded in excavating close to 200 rooms distributed in 13 building horizons constructed of well-preserved clay brick (Mellaart 1967:54–66; Todd 1976:15–23). From these data he created a narrative of the significance of the site for the origins of city life, agriculture, and goddess worship, as well as art and symbolism (Mellaart 1967). The site is still referred to in these terms in many popular and academic works on these subjects (Gadon 1989:25–38; Shane and Küçük 1998).

The excavation of tell settlements in Europe and the Near East has been privileged as contributing to the investigation of early continuous occupation of a place—that is, sedentism—and therefore as a correlate to the investigation of the evolution of social complexity (D. Bailey 1999). By contrast, non-tells, smaller settlements, and areas peripheral to large tells have received lower priority in research agendas and, I suspect, less funding for field research.

There are two points to be made here about such a privilege. First, we cannot assume that the "complexity" of tell settlements and their apparent continuity of occupation is greater in terms of the construction of continuous places (Tringham 2000:117–120). This means that the absence of tell settlements in most of European prehistory and many areas of the east Mediterranean must indicate not so much a lack of social complexity among their inhabitants but a very different intention in the production of continuity and a very different use of architecture in the construction of remembered places. Thus, investigations away from large tell sites have provided data concerning the occupation of smaller settlements that did not form mounds (D. Bailey 1999; D. Bailey et al. 1998).

Second, there is the important point of how to excavate a large site with respect to time, funding, and personnel, given the conditions and constraints in the twenty-first century.

Large-Scale Exposure by Excavation

Traditionally, the "building horizon" concept has provided the basis of excavation strategies of settlements in southeast Europe, Anatolia, and the east Mediterranean (as well as other areas of the Near East). One obvious benefit of this strategy is that it enables a relatively rapid exposure of a broad expanse of the site using unskilled labor, as in Mellaart's own excavations. Another advantage is that, on a large site, it allows extrapolation from a small spatial sample in one area to the entire settlement (Hodder 1996; Mellaart 1967:54–66; Todd 1976:24–32). What may have begun as a convenient excavation strategy, however, has tended to become an underlying assumption: that all houses in a village are occupied at the same time, that they are abandoned or destroyed at the same time, and that they are then replaced at the same time as a single depositional event, forming a "new building horizon." Continuity—if it is thought of as a subject for investigation—is done by matching house plans from the different horizons, but this strategy makes it difficult to follow the individual histories of the houses (D. Bailey 1990, 1996). In other words, individual building events (architectural features) are lumped into one generic time frame called "building or occupation horizon."

The dominance of this strategy of excavation has been driven by questions such as the evolution of social complexity and population growth that can be addressed by an investigation of the architectural ground plan of a settlement and an understanding of the sequence of building horizons (Mellaart 1967; Todd 1976). Thus large stratified settlements have provided an opportunity to trace the evolution of social complexity through many generations, even millennia (D. Bailey 2000:156–161; Georgiev 1961; Mellaart 1967; Todorova 1978).

The link between the building horizon strategy and these questions is made through an understanding of architecture as a finished object whose constructional style or complexity of ground plan can be recorded, compared, measured, and grasped, focusing on house construction, form, elaboration, furnishings, and subdivisions. Traditionally, such a perspective has dominated the study of archaeological architecture as it has the study of the history of architecture. Tim Ingold has referred to this perception of architecture as "the building perspective" (Ingold 1995). The building perspective is characterized by the idea that:

- Dwelling is an epiphenomenon of building

- Buildings are regarded as passive containers of dwellers

- Organization of space cognitively precedes its material expression

From this follows the archaeological perception that buildings are best perceived and treated as finished objects whose design in shape and construction provides a window into the cultural attribution and technological and social complexity of their builders. The limitations of the building horizon strategy were only revealed by a conceptual change concerning the relationship between humans and material culture and concerning the meaning of the term "continuity of place."

Paradigm Shifts

The New Archaeology from the 1960s was interested in cultural transformation as a process, but this paradigm shift did not extend at first to material
culture, which was still regarded as something that should be quantified in its
finished form. I believe that it was an interest in the site formation processes
and other transformative processes that empirically linked archaeological
data with the behavior that changed this perception of material culture.
From the mid-1970s the manipulation of materials, including the built environment, was also treated as a process—"a production process." Thus artifacts and buildings were said to have "use-lives" during which their form and
utilization could be modified (McGuire and Schiffer 1983; Tringham 1990:
10–11). According to this viewpoint, the ultimate aim of the study of the
built environment is to link the occupants of the building to the process of
the evolution of social complexity. Toward this end the reconstructed use-
life of a building—the container and reflector of social behavior—is used as a
monitor of more generalized evolutionary trends and regional patterns of
social behavior (Tringham 1994:175–179).

In designing the projects at Selevac and at Opovo, I was very much part
of this intellectual movement. The interest in use-lives of buildings led us to
introduce some innovative excavation techniques at Opovo. It also led us far
away from traditional aims and assumptions. For example, for us, the causes
and context of the house fires and the nature of house replacement became
priority objects of investigation rather than a taken-for-granted background.
We needed to investigate each house fire in the context of its use-life. In
doing this we were able to conclude that, in each case, the fire was set to
deliberately interrupt and end the life of the house (Stevanovic and Tringham 1998).

Although there appeared to be a paradigm shift from treating material
culture as finished artifact to a process of production, and although detailed
recording and retrieval of individual buildings was developed as an innovative strategy of excavation, the results of these small-scale detailed examinations were extrapolated toward the reconstruction of social and economic
trends at the scale of the corporate village, preferably a regional social unit.
Thus the aim of site-oriented excavation in the end remained not that much
different from the traditional large-scale excavation: to investigate settlement patterns via village-wide building and occupation horizons.

A more startling change in the strategy of large-scale excavation projects
was the result of a paradigm shift in terms of the relationship of history, social
practice, and material culture that was incorporated into the research of the
archaeologists whose ideas of the construction of knowledge bring them
under the collective umbrella term of "post-processual archaeology" (Hodder

1985). Emerging in the early 1980s, post-processual archaeology is essentially interpretive in nature, contrasting with the hypothetico-deductive epistemology of New (processual) Archaeology. The epistemological challenge that this represents has been explored in many places (Preucel 1995). The relevance of the paradigm shift for the argument presented here is that it has broadened the treatment of architecture and associated features to suggest that the histories of individual places have significance within a multiscalar context of history.

My use of the term "place" here, rather than "space," is deliberate and denotes another dimension in which the post-processualist paradigm manifests itself. In contrast to the processualist view of (archaeological) architecture, the built environment is embedded with meaning that may be ambiguous even to those who move through it but which nevertheless plays an active role in creating, maintaining, and changing social practice. Thus it is much more than a passive container and bystander of social action. A place is a space that is given meaning by and creates meaning for people who pass through and within it.

Tim Ingold expresses this contrast in describing his "Dwelling Perspective," which he contrasts to his building perspective described above (Ingold 1995):

- The concept that the forms people build arise with the current of their involved activity (practice)

- Houses are living organisms

- "To Build is in itself to Dwell" (Heidegger 1971)

- Architecture is a social process

In Allan Pred's "Theory of Place," the production of "place" is a historically contingent process by which universally present components, such as an unbroken flow of local events and "projects" (the reproduction of social and cultural forms), the formation of biographies of social actors, and the life histories of made objects such as the built environment are interwoven differently with each local historical circumstance (Pred 1984; 1990:25–33). Places are constantly changing, as is their meaning to the actors involved in their production and as are peoples' relations with one another. Local places are interwoven with larger places, and daily paths and practices are interwoven with life paths and generational and long-term paths.

It is the interweaving of the universal components in the formation and transformation of actual places in real historical situations that became the object of knowledge in our research at Opovo and has become so at Çatalhöyük. Each house is considered an individual, a dynamic entity whose every month of life is significant for the men and women who act in and around it. Continuity of place, whether tell or open site, is the study of the interweaving of individual house life histories (as well as that of each of its individual human actors): this means the duration of the house, the continuity of its next generation (that is, its replacement), its ancestors and descendants, the memories of it held by its actors, and the ghosts that are held within its walls and under its foundations.

The prehistoric houses and their surrounding landscape become the tangible expression of the continuity of place through which the inhabitants passed and to which they gave meaning in their own biographies. Thus the burning of the houses and the placing of a new house in relation to the old becomes meaningful within the context of social action in the village and beyond (Tringham 1994:188–198). The deposition of their rubble in garbage pits and even in a well at Opovo is perhaps part of the "burial rites" of the dead house to ensure continuity of place. The mass of burned clay becomes a "monument" of that place, blocking the fertile soil forever. How different is the ensuring of the continuity of place at Çatalhöyük by placing the dead under the platforms and floors of the house, and by building new houses on the foundations of the old (Tringham 2000:126).

The theoretical models of Pred and Ingold provide the basis for the investigation of the organic formation of a tell or open stratified site through its intertwining histories comprising the becoming of a place. This is a grand interpretive task from which there are no shortcuts. The building horizon strategy of excavation, which has provided speed and economy of excavation by itself, is at odds with the writing of such an organic history.

Archaeologically, the history of a building comprises thousands of depositional events that took place in its building, modification, destruction, and abandonment, and in its relationship to other houses, older and later, each of which has its own life history. These depositional events can be defined by microstratigraphy and micromorphological analysis, but such analysis slows down the excavation process (Courty, Goldberg, and MacPhail 1990; A. Rosen 1986). The strategy of excavation, in which each place—room, building, midden, or garden—is investigated as a meaningful place in the context of a web of interlocking places, producing an anthill or a beehive of a tell rather than the "layer gateau" metaphor of the building horizon strategy, has enormous implications for other aspects of large-scale field research that I consider below.

Thus, the use-lives of individual buildings are relevant not only as samples from which can be extrapolated the larger-scale picture, but also for their own historical trajectory and context. One important result of such thinking is that it becomes as important to understand the histories of

FIGURE 6.1. Aerial photograph of the Neolithic mound of Çatalhöyük from the southwest showing the two distinct excavation areas: "North" with the tents and "South/Mellaart" closest to the camera. *Photograph courtesy of the Çatalhöyük Research Project.*

domestic places as it does the more conventionally prioritized world of supra-domestic public buildings. All places—whether public or domestic—meaningfully articulate with one another in a dialectical sense. Another result is that arechaeologists are encouraged to excavate buildings in even greater detail in order to gather data concerning the events of their individual histories. And detail means intensification of labor in terms of time and money spent in the field and afterward.

At Çatalhöyük a major challenge has been to link the histories of individual buildings, yards, dumps, and gardens in particular areas and to link those of one area (such as the North area) with another area (such as the South or Mellaart) into the rich mosaic of intertwining histories that caused the mound to form (figure 6.1). The strategies to do this range from such labor-intensive methods as the identification of linking paths and microstratigraphic links through micromorphology, and the refitting of faunal and ceramic remains, to those that rely on some form of essentializing, such as ceramic typology and macrostratigraphy of the identification of building horizons. Total excavation—for example, Ovcharovo, Bulgaria (D. Bailey 1996, 2000; Todorova et al. 1983) (figure 6.2)—and large-scale exposure—for example, Asikli Höyük, Turkey (Esin and Harmankaya 1999) (figure 6.3), or Dipsisca Mogila, Bulgaria (Georgiev et al. 1979) (figure 6.4)—per se are not necessarily the answer for the very reasons I discussed above.

Is intensive long-term investigation the answer?

a

b

FIGURE 6.2. Ovcharovo, Bulgaria, July 1972: a, excavation of the total Eneolithic tell settlement with the exception of a central baulk; b, central baulk showing stratified deposits interpreted as building horizons. *Photograph by Ruth Tringham.*

FIGURE 6.3. Asikli Höyük, Turkey, August 1997. Large-scale exposure by excavation of the Neolithic tell settlement. *After Essin 1999: Fig. 4.*

FIGURE 6.4. Dipsisca Mogila/Ezero, Bulgaria, August 1967. Large-scale exposure by excavation of the Early Bronze Age tell settlement. *Photograph by Ruth Tringham.*

Large Scale in Terms of Time

Many of the fieldwork projects in southeast Europe, the east Mediterranean, and Near Eastern areas have been characterized by long duration, continuing season after season. In some cases this has been a long-term nibbling at a site, with a small-scale exposure—for example, Vinča, Yugoslavia (Chapman 1981; Srejovic 1988). The anticipated length of a project is, surprisingly, one that is often avoided. Recently at Çatalhöyük we were asked how long the project is anticipated to last and how long it would take to dig Çatalhöyük. These are two very different questions. Ian Hodder has suggested that the excavation at Çatalhöyük is designed as a twenty-five-year project. But in twenty-five years, at the rate of five years per building, very different results will be achieved by the current teams and strategy than would have been achieved in the same time period by, for example, Mellaart excavating using his strategy. At the rate that the current Çatalhöyük teams are excavating, it would take several hundred years to excavate the entire site. And is that a desirable aim (see below)? The excavation of house life histories takes much longer than the excavation of building horizons. The ever increasing exciting possibilities of information from scientific analyses of varying kinds (DNA, soil chemistry, flotation, phytoliths, and microsediments, to name just a few) encourage the ever increasing number of samples. But the care with which these must be taken and recorded increases the time frame of an excavation. The question is: Should that put pressure on the excavator? Is it not more fruitful to have a slow, productive excavation than a quick, less productive one?

But who is to say what is productive? The answer to that question is: those who fund the research (see below). For example, the National Science Foundation of Washington, DC, obviously expects highly productive results in two years, since that is currently the maximum duration of their senior research grants. Private and corporate funders have different demands and expect different results.

Another strand of this complex question is in terms of personnel. Long-term excavation is best served by continuity of teams (see below).

Large Scale in Terms of Personnel

The term "large scale," when applied to field projects in archaeology, conjures up visions of huge teams of laborers distributed at the bottom of excavation trenches, handing baskets of earth out of the trench from one hand to another in a human chain to the ever-growing dump pile. Movies such as *Indiana Jones* and the *Raiders of the Lost Ark* have fostered these visions. But they have been an accurate representation at certain times in the history of field archaeology in Europe and the Near East. In excavations until the 1970s and perhaps later, large amounts of earth were moved by local village

FIGURE 6.5. Ovcharovo, Bulgaria, July 1972. Excavation of the Eneolithic tell with "brigada" youth labor. *Photograph by Ruth Tringham.*

labor, which started out unskilled, although in time many of these laborers became highly skilled excavators. They were supervised by a few archaeologists through a complex hierarchical system of supervisors and foremen. In Eastern Europe laborers were used, but some of the largest excavations (for example, Ovcharovo in Bulgaria) were carried out by unskilled youth labor using the brigades of schoolchildren sent from the cities during the summer to various "useful" projects (figure 6.5). The result of this organization of labor was that large amounts of matrix could be removed, and quick—and often visually spectacular—results could be achieved in a relatively short time. As already noted, Mellaart, for example, with a team of 35 workers and a few archaeologists, was able to excavate 200 rooms in three seasons (Todd 1976:17). Much was achieved and much was lost by this strategy of work. The transformation of this traditional organization of labor has occurred along at least two trajectories.

First, in the late 1950s and early 1960s government funds were applied to large research excavations that incorporated advanced experts in diverse specializations within and affiliated with archaeology (such as archaeobotany, pedology, archaeozoology, and mineral sourcing) working together in an interdisciplinary team. In addition, a growing body of graduate student apprentices was trained by these specialists in the field. For example, Robert

Braidwood's large interdisciplinary teams at Jarmo and then Cayönü were part of the growing trend toward the incorporation of biological and physical sciences into archaeological research at this time (Braidwood 1974). Many students who later became leaders in the movement toward a New (processual) Archaeology in the later 1960s and 1970s trained in the field with him (for example, Charles Redman and Patty Jo Watson) (Watson, Leblanc, and Redman 1971). This transformation in the nature of the projects led to a larger ratio of research specialists and students working in the field with local laborers (who were often more experienced at excavating than they).

The second trajectory that changed labor relations in the field was the growth of professional field archaeologists—not necessarily associated with research institutions—who are engaged in what has become known in the United States as cultural resource management (CRM) and is still known in the United Kingdom and elsewhere in Europe as rescue or conservation archaeology associated with heritage management. These archaeologists could work in the field year round; they were paid a salary or wages for their field service (unlike most academically based archaeologists) and were used to start and finish a field investigation project according to a contract in a given span of time. To achieve these aims, their projects have developed and adopted standardized procedures of excavation, recording, and analysis that emphasize efficiency in terms of a project's purpose. In the United States, United Kingdom, and some European countries, local unskilled labor might be hired, but for the most part these projects are characterized by a very high archaeologist-to-laborer ratio. CRM projects have also increasingly played an important role in field projects in the Near East and east Mediterranean.

The projects I directed at Selevac and Opovo were both research projects out of an academic institution. We used more students (undergraduate and graduate) than was usual at that time in Yugoslavia and fewer local laborers. Very unusually, the workers were engaged for the most part in screening and earth moving rather than in actual excavation. And even more unusually, graduate students doubled as field supervisors and specialist laboratory analysts (for analyses of, for example, macroflora, fauna, lithics, and ceramics) rather than as specialist experts (Tringham 1990:11–12; Tringham et al. 1992). My Yugoslav collaborators were frequently frustrated by the fact that this made the investigation go more slowly, but I argued that the results in the long run would be much more productive. The apprentices training in Opovo stayed together as a team at Opovo and Podgoritsa (D. Bailey et al. 1998), and some have become valued members of the Çatalhöyük team. Others have gone on to direct their own projects. I have argued that the research this kind of team produced was far more integrated in terms of research themes than if I had used specialist experts.

In the project at Çatalhöyük we can see characteristics of all of these trajectories. The Çatalhöyük team, in fact, comprises multiple research teams working under the umbrella of the permit granted to Dr. Ian Hodder and the British Institute of Archaeology in Ankara (Hodder 1997b; Hodder 2000:3–14).[1] Each team is independent in terms of funding but takes advantage of the facilities developed and established at Çatalhöyük by the Çatalhöyük Research Project under the direction of Dr. Ian Hodder. The research objectives and recording procedures are standardized across all the different teams, and data are freely shared and made available through the umbrella project's Web site (Wolle and Tringham 2000:207–210).[2] There are, however, some interesting differences in excavation procedures and the organization of the work force which I have noted in another publication (Farid 2000; Tringham and Stevanovic 2000). For example, the team from Cambridge University comprises a high proportion of professional archaeologists who are contracted to work at Çatalhöyük, whereas the team from Berkeley (BACH) is an academically based team comprising, for the most part, students who are not paid a salary, because this experience is considered part of their training. The BACH team tends to work more slowly than the Cambridge team (figure 6.6).

Large-Scale Questions

At the root of the term "large scale" lies the essential question: What is the objective of the excavation? Does it demand or justify the expenditure of time, labor, and money on the projects discussed here? In requesting funds for large-scale projects, the director of a project becomes accustomed to setting the detailed tasks of an excavation in the context of large-scale questions: the early development of food production, the origins of an urban way of life, the establishment and demise of Old Europe. This requirement becomes so familiar that it is hardly questioned. Clearly, the larger the scale of the project, the larger the scale must be of the questions. But is this really so? I have argued that, although we should not deny the importance of making general statements, these larger questions should not be privileged to the extent that they deny the relevance of the myriad of complex events and diversity of practices that make up the rich interconnected life histories of a woman, man, or child; or a household; or a building or a village (Tringham 1994; Tringham and Conkey 1998). We have tended in the last 100 years of archaeology to meld these histories into a generic set of evolutionary or regional trends. In advocating a multiscalar curiosity about the past, I am not alone in suggesting that small-scale projects do not mean small-scale questions. And large-scale projects, for example at Çatalhöyük, can gate life at an intimate scale.

FIGURE 6.6. Çatalhöyük, Turkey, 1997–99. A variety of different excavation styles by two excavation teams. *After Tringham and Stevanovic 2000: Fig. 9.3.*

New Trends at the Beginning of the Twenty-First Century in East Mediterranean Archaeology

In this final section of the paper, I summarize some of the points already presented in the context of the trends in east Mediterranean archaeology at the end of the twentieth century:

1. The traditional dichotomy of site-oriented research versus regional research became clouded at the end of the twentieth century. Moreover, there is a growing trend of integrating survey with large- as well as small-scale excavation. The multiscalar nature of archaeological field research in the twenty-first century is the result of techniques that allow a multiplicity of geospatial mapping styles and scales to be examined as a whole. Here I am referring especially to the various forms of geographic information systems (GIS) mapping (Allen, Green, and Zubrow 1990). It is also the result, however, of the growing popularity of a suite of theoretical standpoints, including postmodern, post-structural, and post-processual standpoints, that have found such a multiscalar and multisited approach to the cultural construction of landscape, place, and history a significant object of investigation (Hodder 1999:129–147; Tringham 1994:183–187).

2. During the latter half of the twentieth century there was a constant development of ever more accurate and detailed windows through which to observe the ground surface and its contents below the surface, thanks to advances in geophysics, satellite imagery, ground-penetrating radar, sonic physics, and so on (Avery and Lyons 1981; Clark 1990). At the beginning of the twenty-first century it is not unusual for the public taxpayer to wonder: Is digging the site with its intensive expenditure of money and labor really essential? Could the same answers not be gained through observation alone? Is excavation the most economic way of doing archaeological research?

   The same question is asked by interest groups whose aim is to conserve the past heritage. In their case, the argument is for nondestructive methods of investigation, contrasting with the renowned destructive nature of excavation. The answer is that all of these "scales" of observation are needed, from the very distant satellite observation to the local interpretation of these observations through "ground-truthing," and to the interpretation of "ground-truths" through observation and touch below the ground.

   Through excavation an archaeologist engages in a most intensive way with the remains of the past and produces a record of the past that is unique in the complexity of its observation and interpretation, and then she/he destroys the very data that have been collected. At the end of the millennium, through what has been termed "reflexive methodology" (Hassan 1997; Hodder 1997a; 1999:80–104; 2000:4–9), this experience has become a self-conscious blending of the construction of a multivocal and ambiguous past created by the multiple voices of modern archaeologists who are required to know themselves and their positioning in life in the same way that budding psychiatrists are required to understand their own psyches first (Bartu 2000; Hamilton 2000; Hodder 1999:80).

3. Excavation is intrusive and it is destructive, but so are looters (figure 6.7) (D. Bailey 1993). In the earlier history of the discipline of archaeology, the archaeologists themselves were viewed as "looters" as they carried the "spoils" of their excavations back to their own imperial centers. It is not surprising at the end of the millennium, with the upswing of interest in national and cultural heritage in those countries that had formerly been the targets of imperialism, including a number of countries around the east Mediterranean, that a careful inventory and control of what archaeologists (particularly foreign ones) excavate has become the norm. In addition, the archaeologists themselves have become more sensitive to their responsibilities in conserving local cultural heritage (Bender 1993; Chippindale et al. 1990; Diaz-Andreu and Champion 1996; Hodder 1999:161-177; Renfrew 2000). There are a number of often contradictory results of these trends.

First is the question: Who owns the past? This question foregrounds the multiple groups interested in controlling cultural heritage. At the one end of the broad spectrum of these groups is World Heritage[3] spearheaded by UNESCO, with perhaps some international financial consortia lurking

FIGURE 6.7. Podgoritsa, Bulgaria, July 1995. The Eneolithic tell settlement from the southeast, showing a looters' trench cut into its east side. *Photograph by Ruth Tringham.*

in the background. Is the prize title of "World Heritage Site" a burden of lost control or a bounty of financial grants for a local population (Hodder 1999:202–204)?

And who is the "local population"? At Çatalhöyük it might be the government in Ankara, the financial backers in Istanbul, the local museum and provincial center of Konya, the proud mayor and his neighbors in Çumra, or the villagers at Küçükköy who live nearby and work there (Bartu 2000; Shankland 2000). This same complexity and multi-sited arena is repeated at many other sites described in this volume and has been well articulated by Ayfer Bartu (Bartu 2000). For the case of Çatalhöyük, Bartu has also drawn attention to other interest groups, some of whom cross national boundaries, such as tourists and goddess enthusiasts. None of these interest groups are themselves monolithic, and at the beginning of the twenty-first century the trend is to recognize and respect their diversity, to listen to their voices and their ideas about the archaeological practice and research at Çatalhöyük (Hodder 1999:148–167).

"Listening" may be done at the site or on the Internet (Shane and Küçük 2000; Wolle and Tringham 2000:211–212). It is expensive of time and often of labor, but it is part of modern fieldwork. The presentation of the results to the public has always been a problem and presents a real contradiction to the aims of archaeology. In addressing this problem, I would repeat a root set of questions: Why do we excavate? What is the ultimate purpose of excavation? When do we stop excavating?

Do we excavate to expose a building in order to see what it looked like? Or do we excavate a building to see how it fell down and was abandoned, to see how it was built, and to see the nature of its foundations and precursors? The latter destructive strategy of excavation is at odds with presentation of the site to the public. The former strategy preserves the building to be viewed later but could be construed as leaving the job undone. As usual, there is no single answer, but the problem does pose a potential basis for conflict among local authorities who would preserve the heritage site and archaeologists who wish to investigate the lower depths.

Conservation of excavated sites is very expensive. For example, the shelter over Building 5 at Çatalhöyük cost many thousands of dollars (figure 6.8). One solution might be found in the digital revolution that characterizes the twenty-first century—for example, through detailed scans of site and buildings leading to "virtual tours" of the site before destruction, and libraries of digital images, these available on the Internet or at a local "interpretive center" (Addison 2000).

If we ask "Who owns the past?" I am sure we would all agree that it definitely does not belong to international private collectors of antiquities any

FIGURE 6.8. Çatalhöyük, Turkey, August 2000. The new tent built to preserve Building 5 for visitors. *Photograph by Michael Ashley-Lopez.*

more than it belonged earlier to the large museums of imperial centers. The problem of the antiquities trade is worldwide, and no less present in the east Mediterranean area (D. Bailey 1993; Holloway 1995; Staley 1993).

4. One of the results of the contradictions discussed above is the ongoing careful scrutinization of archaeologists, both local and foreign, before they are granted permission to excavate. The authorities entrusted with protecting cultural heritage are certainly justified in the care with which they carry out their responsibilities. The downside for foreign research teams is the unpredictability of the permit process in terms of whether or not permission will be granted, and if so, when. The unpredictability reverberates in many domains, including funding, logistical planning, and personal planning, as well as academic careers (D. Bailey 1998).

5. The unpredictability of granting permits is compounded by the unpredictability of funding for large-scale field projects. Government funding is highly competitive and with no promise of long-term commitment. Yet long-term commitment (at least more than two years) is what is needed to ensure that the postexcavation process is funded to the end, including the analyses of all of those increased numbers and varieties of samples discussed earlier in this paper. Alternatives comprise private foundations, corporate sponsorship, and individual gift. Is this an ethical problem?

6. Digitization of archaeological data has been part of archaeological research as a regular aspect of the quantification and statistical manipulation of data since the second half of the twentieth century. The digital revolution of the late 1990s and continuing into the twenty-first century is of a different nature. By this time digitization has become embedded in every

aspect of archaeological research, including the archaeological experience (Hodder 1999:120–127).

Recording mapped points in the field during excavation and during surface and subsurface mapping has been speeded up. With the use of "total stations" (electronic distance measurers) and global positioning system (GPS) receivers, the number and detail of points that can be recorded in a short time and overall is enormous. The points can be quickly manipulated by software, such as geographic information systems (GIS) and computer-aided design (CAD) programs, producing two-dimensional maps and three-dimensional reconstructions of landscapes and buildings in which a rich mosaic of descriptive and numerical data are embedded (Addison and Gaiani 2000; Forte and Siliotti 1997; Llobera 1996).

Instead of points, as mentioned above, landscapes and buildings can be scanned as a virtually continuous digitized surface in which data are embedded (Addison 2000). The more detailed and precise the scans of real objects or the modeling of reconstructed ones, the more expensive the imaging becomes in terms of both technology and expertise. I have argued elsewhere that the ultimate purpose of the scans and/or models needs to be considered before embarking on a costly program to use this technology. In many cases, virtual realism is less effective than Surrealism (Wolle and Tringham 2000:213–215).

Digital video and image cameras have been extraordinarily effective in facilitating a detailed audio-visual record of the excavation process. The detailed photographic recording of the process using conventional image photography would be prohibitively expensive. Moreover, the use of digital still and video cameras enables the postexcavation process of editing, indexing, and cataloging the thousands of images to be carried out quickly and effectively. The storage of images on photo-CDs and other digital storage media is also arguably easier to preserve and certainly takes up less space and raw materials.[4] At Çatalhöyük we use an audio-visual recording of the field diary to provide a running interpretive record of the process, allowing us to put into practice the "reflexive methodology" advocated by Ian Hodder (Brill 2000; Hodder 1999:178–187; Stevanovic 2000). Slide film is used only for archival purposes of a selected sample of events and images during the excavation. A final advantage of a digital audio-visual record is the ease with which this record can be integrated into the textual and numerical record of the field research. Thus, the audio-visual record itself begins to play a privileged, rather than a supplemental or illustrative, role. Not much has yet been written about this aspect of the digital revolution, but I believe it will become important in the twenty-first century.

Digital publication and dissemination of field research has also begun to play an increasingly important role for a number of reasons. The *samizdat* nature of digital publishing is attractive to small-scale archaeological enterprises with low budgets but a rich source of research results. The lower costs of digital publication compare favorably to printing costs in general, but especially in contrast to the costs of printing color photographs (Krasniewicz 1999). Moreover, the data (including an audio-visual database) can be published in a way that links it directly to the text, so that the text through hypertext links can be navigated in a multitude of ways (Tringham n.d.; Wolle and Tringham 2000:212–215). Digital publication on the Internet, I am sure, is a medium of distribution that will become increasingly popular in combination with printed paper publication and/or digital publication on CD-ROM.

In contrast to the pre-1990s, much of the technology through which these wonders of digitization and multimedia are achieved has now been demystified and democratized so that it is possible for archaeologists themselves, on a relatively low budget, to produce professional results. The low-tech digitization revolution has also facilitated the practice of the reflexive methodology described earlier, through, for example, standardized formats for the audio-visual recording of the archaeological experience.

Conclusion

Perhaps we should look forward to the large-scale nature of fieldwork in the twenty-first century as leading toward some wonderfully creative ideas about the construction of prehistory as a web of interlocking histories, about the actors who participated in these histories, and about how we can gain insight into our own lives by considering theirs. The grand contradiction, however, is that the more interested we become in the complexity of the social life of the past, the more complex becomes our task in terms of the practical logistics and the less satisfied we become with the shortcuts into which our optimistic "history writ large" in the twentieth century has drawn us. What is the solution? I have no idea—but just to plunge in.

Notes

1. See also the following Web pages: *http://www.catalhoyuk.com*, *http://www.smm. org/catal*, and *http://www.mactia.berkeley.edu/catal/default1.html*.
2. *http://www.catalhoyuk.com*.
3. The best resource for the officially perceived role of World Heritage is found at: *http://whc.unesco.org/nwhc/pages/home/pages/homepage.htm*.
4. The UCLA Digital Imprint group, however, and the Archaeological Data Service have drawn attention to important caveats concerning the optimism for digital archiving of archaeological data: *http://www.sscnet.ucla.edu/ioa/labs/digital/imprint/imprint.html*.

CHAPTER 7

Archaeology for a New Millennium

CHARLES L. REDMAN

A generation ago a series of archaeologists argued strongly that we had to work at a larger scale if we were to achieve our newly proclaimed objective of culture process as well as culture history (Binford 1964; Struever 1968; Redman 1973). Three themes about how to work at an enlarged scale resonated through these and other articles: first, geographical scale had to be expanded to the region in order to encompass the extent of many of the issues we wanted to address; second, we had to sample a sufficient number of examples of the phenomena of interest (that is, sites, houses, activity areas) to allow an evaluation of the range of variability; and third, we needed to recover a fuller range of material in the archaeological record (that is, screening, flotation, and other recovery techniques). Archaeologists the world over have devoted enormous energy operationalizing these ideas and have brought the discipline to a new level of coverage and reliability.

Ruth Tringham, in her excellent chapter, has challenged the discipline to expand further the scope of data collected in order to answer new questions posed by an evolving substantive paradigm and to confront some of the crosscurrents impeding this expansion. Tringham's suggestions are part of a broader intellectual initiative, commonly referred to as "post-processualism," which promotes the more detailed reconstruction of individual events (Hodder 1985). This initiative directs researchers to reconsider how they partition the excavation of their site so that it can reflect the complex patterns of history and social change. Instead of perceiving the stratified site as a series of chronologically separate levels, each with its own "horizon" of contemporary houses, Tringham suggests that each house be considered as having an individual history so that these histories can be linked together more as a web or an ant hill than as an idealized layer cake. In this way the architecture itself is viewed as a social process that becomes an integral part of the multi-scalar context of the people who occupied the site. Hence, we need to study the changing character of each architectural unit: its "micro" history and what other houses coexisted with it. This is quite different from the traditional approach of digging in levels or horizons with the tacit assumption that each level represented a coherent and in many ways uniform community. Clearly, the physical character of deeply stratified mounds led archaeologists to conceive of them as layer cakes and to excavate and interpret them accordingly. In my own large-scale excavations in the Mediterranean region, I, too, sought to use the house and its immediate surroundings as the behavioral unit, but I assembled them for reporting into a series of contemporary phases (Braidwood et al. 1974; Redman 1986). My rationale was to seek not just a normative view of the typical household but to understand the variability during each phase of a community's history, as well as variability among those phases (Redman 1978:153–164).

Tringham would have us go considerably further and suggests that houses, and their inhabitants, do not live in discrete contemporary phases but change and intermingle in unique and complex patterns. The implication of this interpretive stance is that individual life histories of each house should be reconstructed and then cojoined in flexible frameworks that reflect the organic way in which a community grows and changes. She also rightly recognizes that excavating with the sensitivity to identify the detailed life histories of individual houses takes more labor and time than unearthing building horizons. Given all the onerous demands already enumerated above for modern excavations, this effort now adds new recording procedures and slower excavation strategies. To recover this enhanced detailed information, do we have to give up something else, or do we, as Tringham recommends, become more patient and recognize that large-scale fieldwork really means longer-term fieldwork?

A willingness to devote more time and energy to our excavations seems reasonable, but Tringham herself presents the fundamental conundrum facing modern archaeologists: our research demands are increasing while our modest financial resources, competing needs for potential funds, and conservation ethic all may be working against allowing us the freedom to devote this kind of energy to individual archaeological sites.

Archaeologists have pursued several trajectories to overcome this conflict. One approach is to involve an increasing proportion of skilled excavators, recorders, and analysts among one's fieldworkers. The transition from three or four "supervisors" with dozens of unskilled "diggers" to a larger proportion of supervisors has continued to where, in many situations, virtually all the fieldworkers are either students, trained local workers, or professional archaeologists. The increased participation of local universities and museums in the Mediterranean countries has accelerated this process, as has the growth of culture resource management (CRM) in the US, Europe, and now the Near East. With this greater professionalization of archaeological fieldwork, it is possible to excavate with the precision and record with the richness of information that Tringham seeks. Yet attaining a satisfactory level of completeness requires enormous financial resources if there is a short time limit, as in CRM deadlines, or a willingness to excavate at a site for a very long period of time. Even with the patience to devote one's team to a single site for a decade or more of field seasons, there remains the question of adequate funding to keep such work going and the ability to obtain excavation permits over those many seasons. Long-term excavations at a few key sites clearly was the pattern in the Near East a century ago, but the question is whether in the twenty-first century funding agencies, permitting governments, and the archaeologists themselves have the patience to adhere to this approach.

Even if all of the above parties do have the patience, there is a further complication, and that involves our desire and duty to salvage information from archaeological sites that are to be unavoidably destroyed by "development." Over the past thirty years in the United States, it is clear that the proportion of archaeology done on threatened sites has increased dramatically. This same transition has been going on in Europe and is becoming significant in the Near East and elsewhere. Whereas salvage projects often have an easier time obtaining permits and funding, there is a fundamental obligation to recover "all the data" about a site before it is destroyed. Agreeing on the extent and nature of information to be recovered is no simple matter, and the interpretive issues that Tringham outlines have increased the complexity of this decision. It may be possible to decide to extend the excavation at Çatalhöyük for twenty-five years or more, but at most sites being excavated today the timeline will have to be much shorter.

Clearly, we can adopt two very different strategies for field excavations in the twenty-first century, but I doubt if archaeologists of either processual or post-processual persuasions would be satisfied. Whatever one's theoretical perspective, it is important that we, as researchers, feel that appropriate data collection has occurred before a site is lost forever. Does there need to be a single, best approach? Does this approach involve extensive coverage or intensive data recovery? I would not try to answer that question in a uniform way; in fact, I would not try to answer it for sites I am not involved with. As Tringham rightly brings up, who should be involved in answering this type of question for a site is an important issue in its own right. Increasingly, archaeologists have become willing to share their "intellectual" control of archaeological sites with various local constituencies. This sharing was made necessary by laws and permitting agencies, but it also has become a way for us to work more closely with local communities and with individuals who feel strong affiliation with the ancient societies. Clearly, the evolution of this set of relationships will have a significant imprint on the nature of archaeological fieldwork in the twenty-first century.

Tringham also addresses the changing nature of interdisciplinary research on archaeological field projects. This is a subject of intense interest to me because five years ago I shed my hat as strictly an archaeologist and became director of our university's Center for Environmental Studies, a unit devoted to promoting interdisciplinary research. Among other things, I now codirect two large NSF projects, the Central Arizona-Phoenix Long Term Ecological Research project (CAP LTER) and the Integrative Education, Research, and Training program in Urban Ecology (IGERT). In both of these cases, the major challenge is to promote collaboration and integrate the research activities of earth, life, and social scientists (including archaeologists). The promise of this type of integration is great and has been long recognized, but I do not underestimate the difficulty of bridging disciplinary boundaries (Redman 1999; van der Leeuw and Redman 2002).

Tringham refers to the interdisciplinary teams that Robert Braidwood employed at Jarmo and Çayönü as examples of the former approach of bringing specialists trained in other disciplines into the field versus the more recent tendency to rely on archaeological graduate students and Ph.D.s trained in those specialties. I had the good fortune to spend three field seasons with Braidwood at Çayönü as a graduate student and young Ph.D. It was a field camp with mainly archaeologists (both American and Turkish), but also with a senior zoologist, botanist, geologist, and architect. Although putting together these specialists in a field setting was very exciting, the next generation of archaeologists (including myself) has come to rely on archaeology graduate students who have taken it upon themselves to learn the necessary elements of those sister disciplines to serve our archaeological needs. From Tringham's article it seems that she has had a similar experience and is promoting the close integration and shared ideas of "intradisciplinary" specialists trained in both archaeology and an allied field.

There is no question that a certain efficiency has been gained by using archaeologists to study the faunal and floral remains. They share our objectives, they are better at identifying the categories of data most useful for archaeological interpretation, and since in many cases they are graduate students, they cost less to take to the field. Although I have endorsed this approach through the formation of my own field projects (Redman 1986, 1993), in my new role of pursuing interdisciplinary research questions I now question my own decisions. The basic issue is whether we should train researchers to be sufficiently skilled in a number of necessary disciplines or whether we should be training researchers to retain their disciplinary focus but be more collaborative. I do not believe there is a simple answer to this question, but I do think we need to consider carefully what is gained and lost in each approach.

To work with full-time zoologists in the field was somewhat inefficient and certainly frustrating because we had to convince them to focus continually on what was important to our interpretations and us. I cannot help thinking, however, that full-time zoologists also had an impact on what we were doing and how we were thinking, which combined with their own studies, kept our field a bit more relevant to theirs. There is no question that over these past thirty or forty years archaeology has become better at what we do and more interesting to us. But the bigger question is whether we have become more interesting and are viewed as more important by our colleagues in other disciplines, including those who allocate university and research resources. Viewed dispassionately, I doubt most of us would like the answer. I would argue that we have borrowed widely from other disciplines but that, for the most part, we have taken their ideas or approaches and taught ourselves or our students to employ them. The result is that archaeology is internally a diverse and rich discipline but that we have grown insulated from other fields; hence, our work is often viewed as interesting but only peripherally relevant to theirs. In a world where there is intense competition for limited resources, I believe we are not holding our own, and we are certainly not growing.

Despite this pessimistic view I believe there can be cause for optimism. The past is a fundamentally rich source of information that must play an increasing role in our understanding of the way the world works and what to do about the future. I think we must situate ourselves as key players on interdisciplinary teams that address some of the big questions confronting society. We control a unique database concerning human-environmental relationships, religious fundamentalism, multiculturalism, urban growth, and many other pressing issues. We can contribute to these issues; in fact, I believe the response to many major controversies will be seriously incomplete without our cooperation. There is good evidence that some of our colleagues have been successful in this new integrated arena. Archaeologists have been quite successful in the NSF's cross-disciplinary Human Dimension of Global Change and Biocomplexity in the Environment grant competitions. It is important to note that virtually all the successful teams included both archaeologists and non-archaeology colleagues as senior personnel.

My own experience is focused on trying to integrate social and ecological sciences. I believe both the information we normally control and the perspective our training promotes can be valuable aspects of this new inte-gration. Increasingly, ecologists are recognizing that the current condition and future operation of an ecosystem is significantly impacted by legacies of its past condition. Hence, archaeological information on past social sys-tems, extractive technologies, and paleoenvironmental reconstructions are becoming viewed as essential aspects of ecosystem analysis. The anthropol-ogist's focus on recording actual human behavior, cultural traditions, and perceptions of the world around them are all becoming of greater interest to our colleagues.

It is our perspective, however, that will be most valuable in situating us in the future integrated approaches to human ecosystems. First, archaeolo-gists have from the beginning been trained to work collaboratively, because we knew we could not answer the big questions by ourselves. We have always relied on a variety of sciences and hence are well suited to organize multidis-ciplinary teams. Second, because of the nature of our evidence we are com-fortable in deriving meaning from spatial patterns, something that is only beginning to be recognized by most ecologists. And finally, I would argue that archaeologists are among the very best trained to cope with the growing realization that social-ecological processes work at varying scales of time and space. As archaeologists we are the main purveyors of significant time depth, and have learned to adjust our inquiry to processes of varying speed. We also have recognized that some questions can be addressed only at the regional level, while as Tringham reminds us, other questions can be best investigated at local, household, or even smaller scales. This flexibility of data collection and interpretation I believe positions us to take a leadership role in the grow-ing integration of social and life sciences and the ensuing large-scale field projects of the twenty-first century.

CHAPTER 8

Monumentality in Archaic States: Lessons Learned from Large-Scale Excavations of the Past

JOYCE MARCUS

Ruth Tringham (chapter 6) raises issues about archaeology's past and future, among them the role that large-scale excavations play in our understanding of Old World sites and their sociopolitical evolution. To complement her focus on houses and their individual life histories, I have decided to focus on public buildings and monumental structures.

Just as Tringham has questioned various assumptions made by Old World prehistorians about houses and evidence of sociopolitical complexity, I question some of the assumptions often made about monumental structures. Included are the assumptions that (1) monumentality equals power; (2) early states had less power than later states; (3) the bigger the monument, the more powerful the ruler or government that commissioned it; and (4) the most elegant tombs are those of legitimate rulers in the direct line of succession.

Empirical data show that the first and second assumptions are sometimes incompatible. If monumentality equaled power, and if later states were more powerful than early states, one would expect the later states to have constructed the largest public buildings. The opposite is true of many ancient states; for example, the largest pyramids ever constructed in Egypt were built by the Dynasty 4 rulers. Evidence suggests that some early states, still lacking effective institutionalized power, invested heavily in public construction or elaborate tombs precisely because they needed impressive visible symbols to mask that lack of power. In addition, some of the most spectacular tombs and monuments were erected by usurpers who seized power; they were rulers from outside the direct line of succession.

If the four assumptions listed above are too simplistic, why do so many archaeologists continue to treat them as universally valid? One reason is that archaeologists tend to believe that both power and monumentality increase over time. They assume that later states continued to display power by constructing monumental works, when in fact many used labor in ways that earlier states could not. Just as Tringham argues that sites without tells in Europe and the eastern Mediterranean "must indicate not so much a lack of social complexity among their inhabitants, but a very different intention in the production of continuity and a very different use of architecture in the construction of remembered places," so later states devoted their energies to wars of expansion rather than pyramid construction.

A second reason that scholars cling to our four assumptions is that, when an ancient society lacks writing or when relevant texts are unavailable, archaeologists tend to rely too heavily on factors such as the height and volume of a pyramid or the number of luxury items in a tomb, treating these as indicators of power. In cases where texts are abundant and readable, we sometimes find that such factors are unreliable and that rulers sometimes revised and manipulated history.

Finally, a third reason that archaeologists treat our four assumptions as valid is that they are simply impressed by monumentality. Like the subjects of ancient kings, archaeologists accept uncritically the ruler's message: "Gaze on my works, ye mighty, and tremble." As social scientists, however, anthropological archaeologists have an obligation to determine whether claims made by ancient rulers were true or exaggerated.

Power is an admittedly difficult topic for archaeologists because it can only be observed indirectly. We make inferences from pyramids, palaces, tombs, and texts, but we should not treat any of them as objective accounts. Ancient rulers, like all politicians, sought to place themselves in the best light possible (Marcus 1992, 1995). They sometimes claimed descent from rulers to whom they were not related, and they sometimes claimed to be great conquerors when they were not. We will look at several examples suggesting that monumentality is not always a direct reflection of power, and that the motivation for investing in monumentality might be to disguise a non-royal background and hide the lack of effective institutional power.

Egyptian Pyramids

Of the eighty pyramids known from Egypt, the three largest were built at Giza during a period called the Old Kingdom (2650–2150 BC). Today, this period is known as the Pyramid Age, because it witnessed the peak of pyramid construction. Twenty-five dynasties, amounting to hundreds of pharaohs, followed the Old Kingdom, but none of those pharaohs constructed a pyramid as large as that constructed by the Old Kingdom rulers named Khufu

FIGURE 8.1. The Pyramids of el-Geezeh (Giza). Photograph ca. 1857. From Francis Frith, *Lower Egypt, Thebes and the Pyramids*, London 1862. *Getty Research Institute, acc. no. 84-B8850.*

and Khafre. The first of the three monumental works at Giza was Khufu's Great Pyramid. Edwards (1949:85) has called the construction of the Great Pyramid the apogee of pyramid building, both in terms of its size and quality of construction. It was the largest pyramid ever built, over 146 m in height, containing about 2.3 million blocks of stone that are said to weigh on average 2.5 tons (Lehner 1997:108). Khufu's pyramid was surrounded by cemeteries, rows of mastabas containing the bodies of his close relatives and high officials. The second pyramid was built by Khafre, a successor to Khufu. Khafre selected a spot near the Great Pyramid, but on higher ground. His pyramid was almost as tall as Khufu's. It originally rose to 143 m, only 3 m lower than Khufu's pyramid. The third Giza pyramid was Menkaura's, 65 m high, less than half the height reached by Khufu's or Khafre's. No later pyramid built in Egypt approached Khufu's or Khafre's in height and volume (figure 8.1).

Should we conclude from these data that Khufu and Khafre were Egypt's most powerful rulers? Hardly, since later rulers extended their power far beyond the borders of modern Egypt into areas like Nubia and Syria. Gold from Nubia was not mentioned in Old Kingdom texts, but from Middle Kingdom times onward Nubia was mentioned frequently as the major source of gold (Gardiner 1978:134). The principal point here is that powerful rulers in later times chose to use labor in different ways than their Old Kingdom predecessors. They sent larger numbers of men on long-distance trading expeditions to procure diorite, basalt, amethyst, alabaster, wood, and other items; they invested in irrigation works in various parts of Egypt; they built massive fortresses between Elephantine and Semna; they maintained large garrisons at those fortresses; and they dug channels for their ships to prevent the Nubians from expanding north. During the reign of Tutmosis III in New Kingdom times, more than 14 separate military campaigns were conducted in the space of only 15 years to subjugate areas south of Egypt; these wars enabled Egypt to incorporate more than 350 places into their state (Gardiner 1978:193). Thus we see that after Old Kingdom times much more of Egypt's labor force was sent to far-flung territories to trade, conquer, and defend the state's expanding frontiers rather than to build immense pyramids.

Let us now turn to the New World for further insight into the relations between power and monumentality.

Teotihuacan, Mexico

One of Mexico's earliest states arose in the Basin of Mexico in the context of several competing chiefdoms. With the collapse of the chiefdom at Cuicuilco, the chiefdom centered at Teotihuacan took over the entire basin. By 100 BC Teotihuacan was a city of 30,000 people, which constituted 90% of the valley's population; by AD 150, its population was 80,000, and it had emerged as the capital of a state. This explosive growth resulted from Teotihuacan's ability to concentrate most of the basin's population into its urban core. George Cowgill has assessed the actions of the early Teotihuacan state as follows:

> In a sense, the central authority must have had extremely strong power in order to be able to see to it that no secondary or tertiary centers existed for many kilometers around. In another sense, however, intolerance of subsidiary centers may be a sign of weakness or poorly developed statecraft. Perhaps the central authority felt it could not keep control if it delegated any authority to representatives of lower levels of the political hierarchy who were not located immediately at hand within the city itself. (Cowgill 1992:97)

During this early period, Teotihuacan built its two largest public structures, the Pyramid of the Sun and the Pyramid of the Moon (figure 8.2). Unlike the pyramids of Giza, these pyramids were built to support temples rather than to house the tombs of rulers. The Pyramid of the Sun covers an area 220 × 220 m, about the same as the area covered by Khufu's Great Pyramid. The Pyramid of the Sun is only about half as high as Khufu's Great

FIGURE 8.2. The pyramids of Teotihuacan, Mexico. In the foreground is the Pyramid of the Moon; in the background (at left) is the Pyramid of the Sun. In the center is the Street of the Dead, which begins at the Pyramid of the Moon, runs by the Pyramid of the Sun, and continues into the distance.

Pyramid (Cowgill 1992:96), however. The Pyramid of the Moon was smaller, containing only 250,000 m^3 of fill, in contrast to the estimated 1 million m^3 of fill it took to build the Pyramid of the Sun.

By AD 500, Teotihuacan covered at least 20 km^2 and had an urban population of 125,000 to 150,000. Teotihuacan directly controlled at least 25,000 km^2 of central Mexico and had an impact on areas up to 1000 km distant. Never again, however, did Teotihuacan construct public buildings as large as the Pyramids of the Sun and the Moon. Instead, the later Teotihuacan state seems to have used its manpower to conduct long-distance trading expeditions, to establish colonies in other ethnic areas, to increase craft production inside and outside the city, to create areas of intensive agriculture, and to maintain military orders and garrisons that would defend merchants as well as the frontiers of the state.

The Moche State, Peru

Perhaps the earliest of Peru's indigenous states was that of the Moche, which arose sometime around AD 100 (Uceda and Mujica 1994). Originating on Peru's north coast, it eventually grew to include fourteen contiguous valleys, extending 550 km from north to south and covering perhaps 30,000 to 44,000 km^2. This early state built the largest pyramids ever seen in Peru. The largest of all was the Huaca del Sol in the Moche Valley, which required more than 143 million sun-dried mudbricks. It was at least 28 m tall and covered 5 ha at its base. The nearby Huaca de la Luna required 50 million adobes and was more than 20 m high (Hastings and Moseley 1975:196–197; Moore 1996a:54–55).

Like Egyptian pyramids, some Moche pyramids housed the tombs of early rulers. The most famous Moche tombs are those from the site of Sipán in the Lambayeque Valley on Peru's north coast (figure 8.3). One tomb, excavated between 1987 and 1990, occurred below a building that underwent six construction phases between AD 100 and 300 (Alva and Donnan 1993:44). In its earliest phase this building was a low platform; in each of the six phases it was enlarged. During its three final phases, the structure achieved greater height, ultimately resembling a truncated pyramid. Buried 4 m below the top of the pyramid was the skeleton of a 20-year-old man lying on his back, wearing a gilded copper helmet on his head and a copper shield on his right forearm. His feet were missing, suggesting he was a mutilated war captive. In a small niche on the south wall of the tomb chamber, 1 m above the roof beams of the tomb itself, was a seated male buried with his hands on his knees, peering out over the burial chamber. Immediately below the roof beams appeared Tomb 1, a room about 5 m on a side, with solid mudbrick benches on its sides. Niches had been created in these benches, and in them hundreds of ceramic vessels were arranged in groups. The pottery was predominantly mold-made jars in the form of nude prisoners with ropes around their necks, or warriors holding war clubs and shields. In the center of the burial chamber archaeologists found copper straps at the corners of what had been a 2.2 × 1.25 m wooden plank coffin. Alongside the coffin they found a sacrificed llama. The body of a 9-year-old child had been placed at the head of the coffin. Five adults in cane coffins surrounded the plank coffin belonging to the tomb's most important individual.

Inside the plank coffin were the remains of a male covered with elaborate textiles and banners made from sewing sheet-metal figures to cloth. Careful cleaning showed that the sheet metal covering the banners was gilded copper. Moche pottery sometimes depicts elite warriors who hold banners similar to these. The deceased wears exquisite ear ornaments that depict

FIGURE 8.3. Pyramids at Sipán, Peru. *Courtesy of Christopher Donnan.*

men dressed as warriors; hammered sheet gold and turquoise are combined to create these images. A fabulous necklace of gold and silver beads in the shape of peanuts (the longest being 9 cm long) was found, as well as a necklace of sixteen gold disks (each 4.5 cm in diameter). The right hand of the deceased held a gold-and-silver scepter; the top depicts a nude prisoner seated before a warrior who thrusts his war club at the captive's face. Depicted on the scepter's handle were other military elements: a helmet, military headdress, and a shield.

Tomb 2 was found on the south part of the same pyramid at Sipán (Alva and Donnan 1993). As in the case of Tomb 1, a male was lying on his back above Tomb 2, and his feet were missing. Excavators found a plank coffin containing the principal occupant of the tomb: a 35- to 45-year-old male wearing nose and ear ornaments of gold, silver, and turquoise, accompanied by hundreds of copper disks, thousands of shell beads, copper necklaces of human-head beads, and a massive owl headdress of gilded copper.

Tomb 2 also included possible relatives of the central figure (figure 8.4). To his far left in a cane coffin was a male, 14 to 17 years old, buried with two large copper disks. Lying at the feet of the ruler was a cane coffin holding a child 8 to 10 years old, buried with a sacrificed dog and snake. To the ruler's immediate left was a 19- to 25-year-old woman wrapped in a textile with

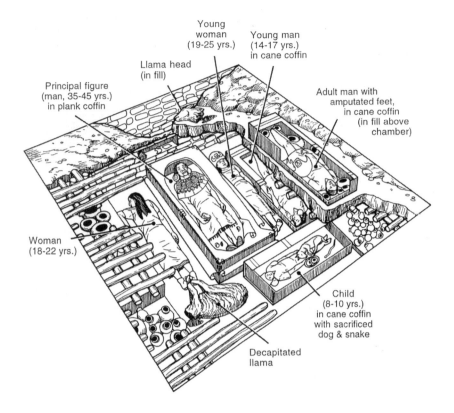

FIGURE 8.4. Tomb 2, Sipán, north coast of Peru, showing a lavish tomb with retainers or relatives of the deceased. *Redrawn from Alva and Donnan 1993 by John Klausmeyer.*

disks of gilded copper sewn to it. To his right lay an 18- to 22-year-old woman sprawled face down with no grave goods; she was perhaps a retainer or servant. Surrounding the tomb were hundreds of pottery vessels and offerings of severed human hands and feet, "quite possibly the trophies taken from sacrificed prisoners whose bodies were dismembered, exactly as shown in Moche art" (Alva and Donnan 1993:165).

Tomb 3 was discovered 5 m below the surface of the pyramid, within the earliest phase of construction. Unlike Tombs 1 and 2, this burial had not been placed in a mudbrick room but was in a simple pit. The principal figure was not in a plank coffin but buried in a sedge mat with textile wrappings. Among the objects found with him was a necklace of ten large gold beads, each depicting a spider with a body in the form of a human head. Also found were a gold scepter and an anthropomorphized crab of gilded copper with claws raised. The crab wears a necklace of owl-head beads and a crescent-shaped headdress with an owl in the center (Alva and Donnan 1993:181).

Before Tombs 1 and 2 of Sipán were excavated, no one had imagined that Moche royalty were buried in room-size chambers surrounded by several individuals. No later Moche tombs had been as rich in gold, copper, and silver jewelry, or in the volume of materials as those included in these earlier tombs.

None of the Peruvian states that followed the Moche expended as much effort in constructing large pyramids. This is not because those later states were smaller or less powerful than the Moche. On the contrary, the capital of the Chimú state, called Chan Chan, reached 20 km² by AD 1100 to 1300. The Chimú state may well have controlled twice as much territory as the Moche state; it extended for 1000 km along the Pacific coast from Tumbes in the north to Chillón in the south. The Inka state of AD 1500 was even larger, stretching 4000 km from Ecuador in the north to Chile and Argentina in the south.

Later Andean states like the Chimú and Inka were larger and more powerful than the Moche. The Inka state chose to invest its manpower in building a vast road system, including bridges and waystations; constructing irrigation canals; manning administrative posts; maintaining armies for reconquest and resettlement of rebellious peoples; and coordinating labor to serve the state through a system of resettling ethnic groups. No Chimú or Inka pyramid or royal tomb compares with those of the flamboyant rulers of the earlier Moche.

Maya Pyramids

Having expressed some doubt that the largest pyramids were always built at the time of a state's greatest power, let us now ask whether the most spectacular royal tombs were always associated with the most powerful rulers. For this I turn to the lowland Maya of Mexico and Guatemala. I suggest that some of the most spectacular temple pyramids and tombs in the Maya region were built by usurpers, rulers who were not in the original line of succession but who seized the throne when conditions allowed. In this I agree with Robert McC. Adams, who wrote the following about the Maya:

> What can be deduced from scale and monumentality is indeed an arresting question that fully deserves a closer, more detailed scrutiny than it has heretofore received. Although the royal lineages [of the Maya] testify to considerable formal continuity, however, they tell us little about the powers rulers actually exercised or about the prevailing pattern of their interrelationships. (Adams 1992:215)

One of the most impressive tomb and pyramid complexes is attributed to a ruler whose hieroglyphic name has been translated as *Pacal* or shield (figure 8.5). Pacal's pyramid supported the Temple of the Inscriptions at Palenque, which he commissioned in AD 675 (figure 8.6). Pacal was considered the founder of a dynasty that lasted from AD 615 to 800. The excavator, Alberto Ruz Lhuillier (1973:216), says that the principal purpose of the pyramid was to house Pacal's tomb, and that its secondary function was to support his temple. Just like the houses discussed by Tringham (chapter 6), the Maya considered their private and public buildings to have a life and life history; thus, these structures experienced dedication and termination rites. From their hieroglyphic texts we know that the Maya gave names to important stone buildings, such as "big white house," "6 sky sacred building," "serpent house," "flower building," "house of the nine bushes," and "his temple, his house" (Schele and Mathews 1998). What we do not yet know is whether the Maya, like the Nahua of Tepoztlan and Amatlan, also named the houses of commoners (Redfield 1930; Sandstrom 1991:106–107).

Pacal's elegant 10 × 4 m tomb, commissioned before his death, had a vaulted ceiling that reached more than 7 m in height. The tomb was reached by a staircase within the pyramid, which descended from the temple above; the ruler's body lay in a mammoth stone sarcophagus. The hieroglyphic text on the sarcophagus lid gives the dates of Pacal's birth (March 23, AD 603) and death (August 28, AD 683); various texts assert that he took office at the age of 12. If these dates are accurate, it would mean that Pacal ruled for almost sixty-eight years and lived to be eighty. Unfortunately, no texts carved during the first thirty-two years of his reign have ever been found (Marcus 1992:346); records exist only for the last thirty or so years of his reign.

The mystery of his early career deepens when we turn to Pacal's predecessors. Pacal claims in his texts that his mother ruled Palenque for three years and that she passed the crown of rulership to him; no records contemporaneous with his mother's reign exist. Did she actually rule, or did her son merely claim that she did so that he could legitimize his right to rule through her? A possible solution to this problem was offered by Heinrich Berlin (1977), who noted that Pacal's alleged grandfather also had a pacal in his hieroglyphic name; Berlin suggested that Pacal incorporated his grandfather's reign into his own, thereby lengthening it considerably. This is possible but cannot be confirmed because no contemporaneous records exist for his grandfather. Pacal mentions his grandfather only retrospectively; therefore, we have no contemporaneous records confirming that Pacal's grandfather or mother ever ruled.

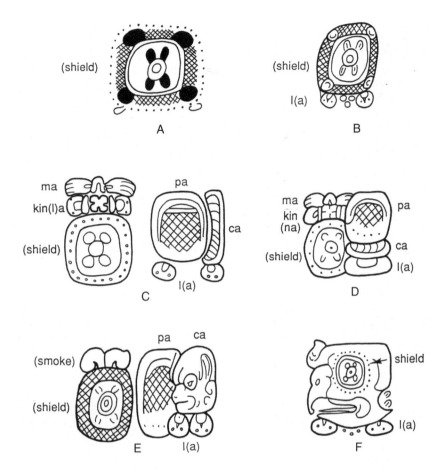

FIGURE 8.5. Six versions of the same name, Pacal, written in Maya hieroglyphs. This Palenque ruler's name could be written using: A, logograms; C-E, syllabic writing; B, F, combined logograms and syllables; or C–E, redundancy. Pacal's body was buried in AD 683 beneath the Temple of the Inscriptions. *Redrawn from Marcus 1992: Fig. 7.17 by John Klausmeyer.*

The lack of independent evidence for Pacal's grandfather and mother may explain why he commissioned such a monumental pyramid, temple, and tomb. It may be that Pacal was, in fact, a usurper who had not been in the direct line to succeed to the throne of Palenque, and that his circumstances forced him to employ several strategies to legitimize himself once he had seized power (Marcus 1992:345–346). One strategy was to commission the carving of a sarcophagus that depicted near and remote royal ancestors; by claiming their existence, Pacal anchored himself in a dynastic line, even

FIGURE 8.6. The pyramid at Palenque, Mexico. Like the three huge pyramids on the Giza Plateau of Egypt, this pyramid contained a royal tomb reached only after walking down a long passageway. Unlike the Giza pyramids, however, this Maya pyramid supported the impressive Temple of the Inscriptions, which stood 25 m above the tomb occupied by the ruler Pacal, who died in AD 683. During the next five years, his son completed the temple and finalized the long texts set within the walls of the temple, referring to building dedications, ancestors, and his own accession to the throne.

though such a line cannot be independently verified by texts carved during the alleged ancestors' lifetimes.

Another of Pacal's strategies was to have his tomb built before his pyramid and temple, thereby ensuring himself a place inside the largest pyramid at Palenque. In the Temple of the Inscriptions crowning that pyramid, he recorded additional information about his mother, Sak K'uk'; and in his nearby palace, he commissioned yet another carved stone that showed her handing him the crown of rulership (figure 8.7). Significantly, all these records were commissioned by Pacal long after he had been inaugurated as ruler.

What do we know of Palenque before Pacal's reign? Enough to make us wonder. For example, the inscriptions left by Pacal and his dynastic successors refer to an early Palenque king who allegedly was born in 993 BC and took office in 967 BC. At that remote time we have no evidence that Palenque was even occupied; in fact, the state had not yet formed anywhere in the Maya region! The next early Palenque ruler mentioned in the inscriptions is a man named Quetzal Jaguar, who allegedly ruled in AD 431, 200 years before Pacal. We do not know whether these early rulers are real or legendary, because no contemporaneous records exist from that early period at

FIGURE 8.7. This carved stone, the Oval Palace Tablet, shows (at left) a woman named Sak K'uk' (her name appears in hieroglyphs above her head) handing the crown to Pacal (whose name is given in the text behind his head). Pacal is shown seated on a throne with two jaguar heads. This transfer of the crown, from mother to son, took place in AD 615, only three years after she took office, according to texts commissioned by Pacal. This monument was set into the wall of Pacal's palace (called the "Big White House") to serve as the back of a throne set against that wall. *Redrawn from Marcus 1992: Fig. 10.23 by John Klausmeyer.*

Palenque. Indeed, it seems unlikely that we will ever find records carved during the reign of an actual Palenque ruler who took office at 967 BC, a period evidencing only simple farming villages in the Palenque region.

One way of interpreting Pacal's behavior is to propose that he was founding a new dynasty without the necessary credentials to rule. His magnificent tomb and pyramid, intended to prove that he was a legitimate and powerful ruler, may therefore imply the very opposite—that he needed to make an exceptional effort to impress his fellow nobles and subjects precisely because he did not have the necessary bloodlines.

Pacal invested more labor in his tomb, sarcophagus, and pyramid than any later ruler at Palenque. Once he had done so, however, his successors were able to claim him as the founder of their dynasty and use him to legiti-mate their own claims to the throne (Marcus 1992:292). Pacal's immediate successor, Kan Balam, was allegedly 48 years old when he took office, 132 days after Pacal's death. After ascending to the throne, Kan Balam commis-sioned stucco modelers to depict him as a child in the arms of Pacal, presum-ably to show that he was in the direct line to accede to the latter's throne.

Kan Balam's "heir designation" rites allegedly took place in AD 641, long before he took office in AD 684. We learn of those rites some fifty years after they supposedly took place. At no time during Pacal's reign does he mention making Kan Balam his successor. Rather, in AD 690 Kan Balam recorded those heir designation rites retrospectively, then went on to commission three temples—each elegant, but much smaller than Pacal's massive Temple of the Inscriptions.

Tikal, Guatemala

A second instructive case is that of the ruler Hasaw Chan K'awiil at Tikal, a major Maya city in Guatemala. His reign followed a period of dynastic tur-moil precipitated by military conflicts with other Maya cities such as Cara-col, Dos Pilas, and Calakmul. Hasaw Chan K'awiil's reign began in AD 682, and one of his goals was to restore Tikal to its position of glory. He immedi-ately began construction of a Twin Pyramid Complex, where the first stone monument of his reign was to be erected. He built Temples 33 and 34 on the North Acropolis, and in them he buried two stone monuments that depict earlier rulers (Jones and Satterthwaite 1982; Marcus 1976). Hasaw Chan K'awiil is also credited with building two huge pyramids, Temples I and II, that face each other across Tikal's Great Plaza and tower above the plaza floor (figure 8.8). The much eroded roof-comb of Temple I displays a seated Hasaw Chan K'awiil.

On a wooden lintel spanning the doorway of Temple I is an inscription claiming that, in AD 695, Hasaw Chan K'awiil had taken prisoner "Jaguar Paw," a ruler of the rival city of Calakmul (figure 8.9). On another building at Tikal (Structure 5D-57), Hasaw Chan K'awiil is shown modeled in plaster on the upper façade. In the latter case, he is shown holding a rope leading to a bound captive identified as a Calakmul noble named Ah Bolon Bakin. The date on this inscription is only thirteen days after Hasaw Chan K'awiil's

FIGURE 8.8. Temple I, a 47-m-high pyramid, at the eastern end of the Great Plaza at Tikal. Along the left side are the stone stelae and altars that depict Tikal's rulers and chronicle political, religious, and dedicatory events. Inside the temple base is the tomb of Hasaw Chan K'awiil, who died in AD 734. Like Pacal's son at Palenque, Hasaw Chan K'awiil's son had the task of finishing a pyramid to house his father's tomb.

alleged capture of Jaguar Paw. It is evident that one of Hasaw Chan K'awiil's strategies was to legitimize himself as a successful military leader by claiming he took important captives from Calakmul (Marcus 1998:63–64).

Hasaw Chan K'awiil died in AD 734 and was buried in a tomb cut into bedrock within the base of the Temple I pyramid. Construction of the tomb was finished during his reign, but the pyramid and temple were finished during the reign of his son (Trik 1963; W. Coe 1990). Hasaw Chan K'awiil's tomb was impressive; he was buried with a jaguar pelt cape, several kilograms

FIGURE 8.9. This text on Lintel 3 of Temple I at Tikal says that Hasaw Chan K'awiil "took the flint + shield of Jaguar Paw, Lord of Calakmul," evidently making the Calakmul ruler his prisoner. This event took place on August 5, AD 695, a date that was carefully selected to coincide with the 260-year anniversary of the death of an early Tikal ruler. *Redrawn from Marcus 1976: Figs. 4.1, 5.2 by John Klausmeyer.*

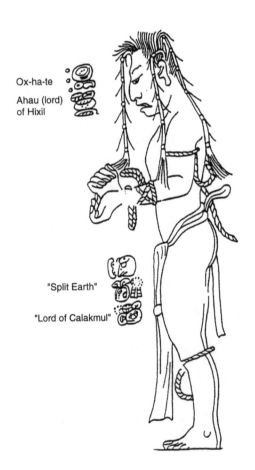

FIGURE 8.10. This prisoner, carved on a bone that had been placed in Hasaw Chan K'awiil's tomb beneath Temple I at Tikal, is shown with rope tied around his arms, wrists, and knees, and wearing only a loincloth. He is apparently a relative of a Calakmul lord named "Split Earth." *Redrawn from Trik 1963: Fig. 9a by Kay Clahassey.*

of jade in the form of beads and other ornaments, and a set of exquisite carved bones with hieroglyphic writing (one of those bones depicts yet a third captive with ties to Calakmul; figure 8.10).

The case of the Tikal ruler Hasaw Chan K'awiil exemplifies the ambiguities of monumentality and power. On one hand, we could interpret his claim of conquest as evidence that he was a very powerful ruler; on the other hand, the text in Temple I might be a posthumous claim commissioned by his son, who acceded to the Tikal throne on December 8, AD 734. On the one hand, we could interpret the construction of Temples 33 and 34 as signs of Hasaw Chan K'awiil's power; on the other hand, his deliberate burial there of the monuments of earlier rulers could be interpreted as an effort to erase the record of even more powerful and important predecessors. It seems clear that Hasaw Chan K'awiil's son was the actual builder of Temple I, since archaeologists excavating there have evidence that Hasaw Chan K'awiil's tomb had been sealed before the temple was built (W. Coe 1990). Hasaw Chan K'awiil's son benefited the most from investing in his father's monumental pyramids and associated texts.

Rulers and Their Descendants: Contemporaneous vs. Posthumous Power

We often assume that royal tombs, like those of the Moche and Maya states, are a direct reflection of their occupants' power. I would like to provide a cautionary note, drawn from the Zapotec civilization of Oaxaca, Mexico.

In the 1980s, a magnificent AD 700 tomb (figure 8.11) was discovered beneath the patio of a palatial residence at Suchilquitongo in the Valley of Oaxaca (Méndez 1988). The layout of the tomb resembles a miniature palace, designed for the afterlife; it consists of a series of small rooms around an interior sunken patio measuring 1.5 × 1.7 m. This tomb was kept open after the first occupant's death and continued to be accessible by means of a stairway that descends from the patio above. For years—perhaps for generations—members of the noble family who lived in the palatial residence above continued to visit the tomb to make new offerings. The "family tomb" was a Zapotec institution of long standing.

Suchilquitongo, a defensible hilltop community, had for centuries been a secondary administrative center below the Zapotec capital, Monte Albán. With the decline of Monte Albán's power after AD 600, Suchilquitongo, like many other major centers in the valley, became a largely autonomous administrative center for its region. During this period of political decentralization and balkanization, the lords of many regional centers began to arrange their own advantageous marriage and military alliances (Marcus 1980, 1983).

FIGURE 8.11. Tomb 5 at Suchilquitongo, found by Enrique Méndez, is one of the most spectacular tombs in the Valley of Oaxaca. Walking through that doorway, flanked by richly carved columns, one enters the burial chamber where the carved genealogical register (figure 8.12) was found.

They also began to commission carved stone monuments to commemorate important marriages. Some of these monuments, called "marriage scenes," show only the noble bride and groom; others, called "genealogical registers," show several generations of a noble family (Marcus 1992:283–285).

One such genealogical register was found near the back wall of the Suchilquitongo funerary chamber (figure 8.12). It appears to have been moved to its final position, and may originally have been set in the antechamber. Here the dead lord is depicted as a venerated ancestor; the hieroglyphic texts not only record his death but also feature his offspring. Such a genealogical record was probably commissioned not by the venerated ancestor but by his descendants, who sought to establish their continuing right to rule. By keeping the family tomb open and accessible below their residence, a noble family could continue to add to the genealogical record, place new offerings,

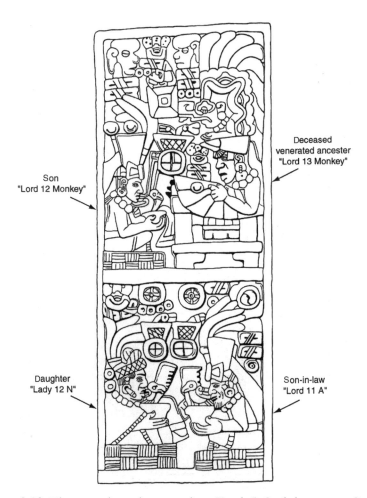

FIGURE 8.12. This genealogical register from Tomb 5, Suchilquitongo, Oaxaca, shows a deceased ancestor (upper right). Sitting in front of him is his son; below are his daughter and son-in-law. Unlike the deceased ancestor who is propped up in a wooden throne, his three relatives sit on mats. Since the death dates of these individuals are recorded on the slab, yet another relative (perhaps a granddaughter or grandson) must have commissioned the carving of this slab. In support of this scenario is the fact that this tomb was reentered twice, evidently to insert this slab into the inner chamber and to repaint portions of the tomb (see Miller 1995:199, 206–207). *Drawing by John Klausmeyer and Kay Clahassey.*

and even repaint the polychrome murals on the walls of the tomb to include new generations of nobles (Marcus 1992:281–287; Miller 1995:206).

The tombs of Zapotec nobles undermine our simplistic notion that the size or magnificence of a tomb directly reflects the power of the ruler. Rather than glorifying one individual, many Zapotec tombs honored an entire noble line. Often, in fact, their final magnificence should be credited not to the original occupant but to the heirs, who added offerings, repainted murals, and commissioned genealogical registers in which they were included (Marcus 1992). Such family tombs became the living records of noble families over multiple generations. In this case, the glorification of a deceased lord was more a reflection of his descendants' need to claim an important ancestor than a record of the deceased's own accomplishments.

In conclusion, I would caution archaeologists not to rely too heavily on the monumentality of pyramids and royal tombs as direct reflections of political power. The Egyptian, Peruvian, Maya, and Zapotec cases we have examined should warn us that the relationship may be complex and indirect. A great deal of symbolism is involved in the construction of tall pyramids and magnificent tombs, and much of that symbolism is political and social propaganda. We should be as skeptical of ancient propaganda as we are when dealing with modern politicians.

Some civilizations that lasted for centuries built their most impressive pyramids early in their history, when the state had only recently formed. Such buildings may symbolize power wished for but not yet fully consolidated. The public works and monuments of early rulers were sometimes destroyed by later usurpers. And those usurpers, precisely because they lacked the genealogical credentials to accede to the throne, often outdid their predecessors in a frenzy of monumental public construction. Their monuments, in turn, made it less important for their heirs to expend as much effort on monumental works. Later rulers were more likely to use their manpower for tasks that were less visible archaeologically but no less important. We sometimes forget that great monuments might be completed or enlarged by a ruler's descendants who had a vested interest in making him look even more powerful than he had been. We also forget that tombs might be repainted and reused, reaching their greatest magnificence long after the death of the original occupant.

PART III

THE RECENT PAST AND THE REMOTE
PAST: REGIONAL SURVEY AND THE
ARCHAEOLOGICAL LANDSCAPE

CHAPTER 9

Archaeology Beyond the Site: Regional Survey and Its Future

JOHN F. CHERRY

Almost two decades ago, I was invited to summarize and respond to some eighty short contributions presented at an international colloquium on "Archaeological Survey in the Mediterranean Region" held in Athens in June 1981 (Keller and Rupp 1983). My paper, "Frogs round the pond" (Cherry 1983)—perhaps because it offered an unapologetically robust defense of survey as an approach to regional research questions, and perhaps also because its publication coincided with the explosive growth of survey work in most of the countries bordering the Mediterranean (see below)—evidently struck a chord; at least, it appears to have been widely read and cited. But that was then, at a time when it was appropriate, in fact necessary, to adopt a strongly evangelical tone about survey. Most of those battles have since been won by deeds rather than words, and in the intervening years a very great deal has been achieved.

Such success is very gratifying, but the sheer volume of fieldwork, analysis, and publication on which it rests also makes it virtually impossible to fulfill satisfactorily my daunting brief from the organizers of the first Cotsen Advanced Seminar—namely, to say something about the past and present state and future scope of regional survey in the Mediterranean, and to do so in a way that might trigger responses from archaeologists working in different parts of the world. What follows has necessarily to be the merest sketch of a few parts of a very large and active field. My focus is mainly on regional surveys in Greece and the Aegean, not only because this is the area I know best, but also in acknowledgment of the primary interests of Lloyd Cotsen in whose honor this seminar was convened. I make some mention of other parts of the Mediterranean and refer to topics and trends that I hope may resonate more widely, but my perspective is deliberately hellenocentric, and inevitably personal.

Past Development

A little historical scene setting is necessary to provide some context for the issues I introduce below. An important initial point to be stressed is that a sustained interest in regional survey in the Mediterranean is a (relatively) recent development: it is certainly a feature of the post-war period and largely of the last twenty-five or thirty years. The validity of such a statement, of course, depends crucially on what one means by "survey," and—as I took pains to point out in my "Frogs" paper (Cherry 1983:380–381)—this English word not only embraces a remarkable variety of styles of prospection but is also one for which there exists no satisfactory corresponding term in several other European languages. In the Classical lands and parts of the Near East, a tradition of topographic antiquarian research can readily be traced back to the Renaissance, if not in fact to antiquity itself. To some extent, landscape reconnaissance has always been part of archaeology, since one has first to find one's site before being able to dig it! But there is a big difference between field prospection treated as a sort of preliminary warm-up before the main bout (that is, excavation) and work that takes a defined region as its research focus and systematic team-based survey as its primary mode of data collection. And it is only in this latter sense that it can fairly be said that Mediterranean survey has "taken off" in the past two or three decades.

This point can be documented quantitatively, with reference to some results of a review of the literature recently carried out for another related paper (Cherry forthcoming). Figure 9.1, for example, shows the pattern for the 33-year-period 1966–1998 of journal articles devoted either to the primary publication of survey data or to other topics directly related to survey. The fifteen journals from which these data were culled provide good coverage of archaeological research in the majority of the circum-Mediterranean countries.[1] While only about 420 (7%) of the 6441 articles consulted dealt with survey, clearly indicating its minority status within archaeological research overall, it is also quite obvious that there has been a marked increase since the late 1970s (and, interestingly, some drop-off in the 1990s). A different perspective, this time focusing on Greece alone, is afforded by figure 9.2. The information here has been culled from the thorough summaries of current fieldwork, entitled "Archaeology in Greece," published annually since 1954 in the journal *Archaeological Reports*—some 2255 printed pages in all. Based on the number of survey projects that find mention in those pages, the picture is again one of sustained and dramatic growth since about 1980. Yet another way of looking at these same data (figure 9.3) is in terms of start-ups of new survey projects in Greece, each year over the past thirty years, where much the same pattern is evident.

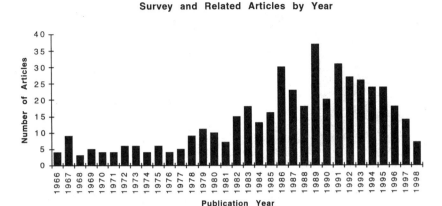

FIGURE 9.1. Numbers of articles devoted to the primary publication of survey data published in fifteen archaeological journals between 1966 and 1998; for the journals consulted for this study, see note 1.

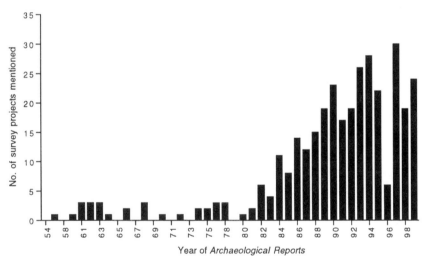

FIGURE 9.2. Numbers of archaeological survey projects in Greece reported annually in *Archaeological Reports* 1954–99.

Now one might suppose that what we are seeing here is a straightforward crossing of what Colin Renfrew (1980; see also Snodgrass 1985) famously dubbed the "Great Divide." In other words, archaeologists working in the Classical lands fell, from the early 1970s, increasingly under the influence of Anglo-American "New Archaeology," with its emphasis on quantification,

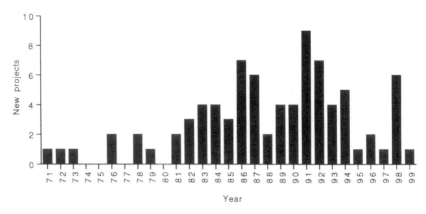

FIGURE 9.3. Annual start-ups for new survey projects in Greece, 1971–99.

sampling, systematic data collection, environmental issues, and a focus on the regional perspective—itself, of course, drawn from a long New World tradition of settlement pattern studies (Billman and Feinman 1999) but given renewed urgency with Lewis Binford's exhortation (1964:426) that archaeological research must involve "the detailed and systematic study of regions that can be expected to have supported cultural systems." It cannot be denied that this was indeed one influential factor, especially on the generation of Mediterranean prehistorians who were graduate students at that time; but matters were actually much more complex and interesting than that. For one thing, among traditionalists (such as Popham 1990) there was stiff resistance to survey on the grounds that either it was a second-rate technique, parasitic upon stratified excavations and beset with inherent shortcomings, or that it was what we had been doing all along anyway—so why the fuss? Consequently, the Mediterranean survey literature of the 1970s and early 1980s is replete with rather self-consciously evangelical apologias. Even as late as 1987, when Anthony Snodgrass published his Sather Lectures at Berkeley as *An Archaeology of Greece: The Present State and Future Scope of a Discipline*, some reviewers felt uneasy about his devoting half the book to landscape studies and regional survey: this somehow was not the proper study of (Classical) mankind.

Yet people have traveled about the Classical lands and many parts of the Levant and Near East looking for ruins and trying to identify them, virtually since they first had Homer in their heads. From Pausanias's second-century AD *Description of Greece*, via a veritable procession of pilgrims, crusaders, merchants, post-Renaissance travelers, young gentlemen on the Grand Tour, the first scientific expeditions to Egypt and Greece, and the antiquaries and early archaeologists of the nineteenth century, we come finally to the sorts of topographic researches that have continued unabated through the twentieth century—associated in Greece with names such as Eugene Vanderpool, Sinclair Hood, Richard Hope Simpson, and especially W. Kendrick Pritchett (1965–91). The so-called New Wave of regional projects of the past quarter-century (for this term see Cherry 1994; Bintliff 1994) stands apart from all the foregoing: what made them so distinctively new and different was their degree of intensity, diachronic focus, interdisciplinarity, and use of the region as the conceptual basis for addressing historical or anthropological questions. But I would also stress that they are lain on top of a vast stock of prior knowledge; indeed, the fact that few surveys in the Mediterranean take place in *terra* that is anything like as *incognita* as that of most New World projects is one of the features that most sharply distinguishes the two traditions.

These topographic researches of earlier generations generally had as their primary purpose the identification of the settlements, sanctuaries, battlefields, and the like mentioned in the Greek and Roman authors, especially Homer. Ironically, the acknowledged mother of all modern-style surveys in Greece—the University of Minnesota Messenia Expedition (UMME)—began in precisely this way. This hugely influential "originary" project had its beginnings in William McDonald's and Richard Hope Simpson's efforts half a century ago to resolve some problems in the Homeric geography of the kingdom of Nestor in the southwestern Peloponnese (McDonald 1942; Hope Simpson 1957, 1966). This soon became a more general search for Mycenaean sites (particularly those mentioned on the Linear B tablets), then a search for sites of all periods, from Neolithic to Medieval. Next came the appreciation that these sites' locational characteristics could not be understood without proper attention to questions of coastal change, alluviation, natural resources, soil fertility, the traditional agricultural economy, and even the social anthropology of local farming communities. By the time of the final monograph (McDonald and Rapp 1972), UMME had bootstrapped itself into a large-scale, multidisciplinary, strongly scientific, survey-based research project covering some 1500 km^2—although one that retained at its center "the reconstruction of a Bronze Age regional environment."

A whole generation of students, newly conversant with mainframe computing and spatial analysis, seized eagerly on its detailed site gazetteer and sets of almost GIS-like transparent map overlays to try out the sorts of ideas they had been reading in David Clarke's *Models in Archaeology*, Lewis Binford's *An Archaeological Perspective*, or Colin Renfrew's *The Emergence of Civilisation*, all also published in that same *annus mirabilis*, 1972. This project, and responses to it, not only kick-started regional studies in Greece, but gave them the strongly prehistoric and Anglo-American bent they have had, at least until recently. Interestingly, UMME's introductory chapter, in narrating the evolution of the project's interdisciplinary methodology and regional approach, explicitly named some of the pioneers of regional exploration projects in the Near East (Robert Braidwood and Robert McC. Adams) and the New World (Gordon Willey, William Sanders, Richard MacNeish, Kent Flannery); but it did so, not so much to acknowledge intellectual debts, as to report, almost with surprise, the seemingly independent existence of "particularly instructive models" in other parts of the world and to discuss points of contrast between them and UMME (McDonald and Rapp 1972:13–17).

Elsewhere in the Mediterranean the picture is by no means the same. Italy, for instance, where useful local studies (often by nonprofessionals) have been under way in some areas since the nineteenth century, nonetheless also has its own first great pioneering survey venture to which nearly all subsequent work seems somehow indebted (much as Willey's Virú Valley project affected settlement pattern studies in the New World). But it arose from an entirely different set of impulses than UMME. John Ward-Perkins, as Director of the British School at Rome after World War II, was struck by the massive damage being done to the rich archaeological landscape of southern Etruria as a result of Rome's postwar northward suburban expansion and by the mechanization of agriculture. His Sunday afternoon sherd-picking outings came gradually to be transformed into a whole series of thoughtful small-scale projects involving systematic surface collection, supplemented in time by a number of excavations on settlements of different periods from the Bronze Age to the Medieval, and by palynology and geomorphology. The late Timothy Potter's 1979 synthesis of all this work, *The Changing Landscape of Southern Etruria*, provided an early and persuasive example of how low-budget but persistent salvage fieldwork, with an interdisciplinary approach, could write the archaeological history of an entire landscape. It set the tone for much that has followed, including current collaborative research activities in much the same area (Patterson and Millett 1998; Patterson et al. 2000). Many Italian surveys have had their strongest emphasis on the Roman and medieval landscape (see, for example, Barker and Lloyd 1991)—or, at any rate, prehistorians have not played so dominant a role as in Greece. A less centralized organizational framework and more flexible archaeological laws than in Greece has made it not only easier to initiate regional projects in Italy, but in some cases to conduct truly multistage and multiscalar research of a kind that has rarely been feasible (and is now essentially impossible) in Greece, at least for the foreign scholar. Another difference, emphasized recently by Barker (1996b:160–162), is that allegiance to the home region rather than to national identity has given a special importance in Italy to the work of amateur enthusiasts with detailed local knowledge.

In a number of other countries, too, one can readily point to individual projects that, while perhaps not "originary" in the above sense, have been influential in demonstrating locally what survey can achieve, thus stimulating the wider growth of regional fieldwork and impacting the directions in which it has developed. Examples would include, in Spain, the surveys of the Guadalquivir Valley (Ponsich 1974–79) and the *Ager Tarraconensis* (Carreté, Keay, and Millett 1995); or Leveau's (1984; see also Leveau, Sillières, and Vallat 1993) study of rural settlement around Caesarea (Cherchel) in Algeria. In general, on the southern side of the Mediterranean basin (as also in parts of the Levant), matters have, however, followed a quite different course, since European colonial agendas have long been the primary factor underlying the principal trends in archaeological research there (van Dommelen 1997; Mattingly 1996b). This, I speculate, partly accounts for the strong impulses in countries such as Cyprus or Tunisia to inventory—that is, to create regional sites-and-monuments registers, and comprehensive archaeological map-sheet series, like the multivolume *Atlas préhistorique de la Tunisie* (for a historical overview of different styles of survey in Tunisia, see Stone 1997). Latterly, the postcolonial agendas of the independent states have been more important. Thus, for instance, one of the more impressive regional projects of recent years, the UNESCO Libyan Valleys Survey, was allowed to proceed in part because of Colonel Gaddafi's interest in the circumstances that made Roman farming practicable in the pre-desert, where agriculture is now nonexistent (Barker 1996a; Mattingly 1996a).

In fact, as one looks around the Mediterranean, one sees wide variation in the extent to which systematic regional surveys have penetrated standard archaeological practice; a detailed study of why this is so, in fact, would make a fascinating contribution to the historiography of the discipline. The underlying factors would turn out not to be purely academic and archaeological, for of course all archaeological practice is politically situated, and in the Mediterranean many governments have viewed archaeology as a tool of national ideology (Silberman 1990; Meskell 1998). This is nowhere more so than in Greece, a country virtually synonymous with archaeology, and one where senior archaeological appointments are generally made along lines of party affiliation. As Kardulias (1994) has described, the 1981 election of the socialist PASOK government led to a distinct hardening of attitudes toward the west and challenges to Eurocentric archaeologies. The 1932 Greek law limiting each foreign school to three excavation permits each year was enforced much more rigorously, and in 1988 was extended to cover surveys, too. It may well be the case that the apparent lessening of survey activity in the last several years (see figures 9.1–9.3) is one consequence of this more restrictive atmosphere.

Some Current Issues

This brings me to the present state of "archaeology beyond the site" and some current trends, issues, and problems. But here, under constraints of space, I must limit the *tour d'horizon* primarily to Greece. Recent work toward an overview of the impact of regional surveys on Aegean prehistory over the past thirty years or so (Cherry forthcoming) has led me to review publications in this field somewhat more systematically than before. Here, then, are some notes on a few of the things that struck me.

One is the quantitative explosion of data now available at the regional level. Greece is a country of modest size, yet many hundreds of professional archaeologists work there, either for the Archaeological Service or under the aegis of the numerous foreign schools and institutes—and an increasing proportion of their efforts has been devoted to survey. Although the earliest systematic projects were British or American, nearly every foreign school in Greece has now become involved in sponsoring surface surveys, as have several Greek universities and other institutions. Understandably, it is a handful of the better organized regional projects that happen to have reached final publication in full that has attracted most attention so far. But there are very many more in press or still in progress: indeed, I am currently aware of at least eighty-five formally constituted surveys in Greece since the 1970s (see figure 9.4, which locates fifty of the more significant of these projects). They vary greatly in duration, manpower, regional scope, field methods, data collection procedures, research objectives, and even their relative degree of optimism about the validity of survey data.

Yet in order to underscore the rich diversity of recent and current work, it needs to be mentioned—albeit parenthetically—that a vast range of other types of noninvasive, nondigging field exploration also exists, often of wide spatial scope yet not quite "survey" (in the sense I have been using the term so far). There are, for instance, regional studies focusing on very specific categories of site, whether it be Classical towers (Dousougli and Morris 1994; Morris 2001), or Dark Age refuge sites (Nowicki 2000), or vernacular architecture (Miller, Alchermes, and Cooper 1992), or Paleolithic remains (Runnels 1988). There are examinations of linear phenomena that traverse regions—for instance, Roman aqueducts (Lolos 1997), or the Late Bronze Age road network around Mycenae (Jansen 1997), or the geophysical investigation of Xerxes' canal built across the Athos peninsula in northern Greece about 480 BC (Sarris and Jones 2000:38–39). There is the careful mapping of land division systems, the cadastral surveys and centuriation patterns, of which Romano's work around ancient Corinth (Romano and Schoenbrun 1993) and Doukellis's (1988) around Nikopolis are the best examplars.

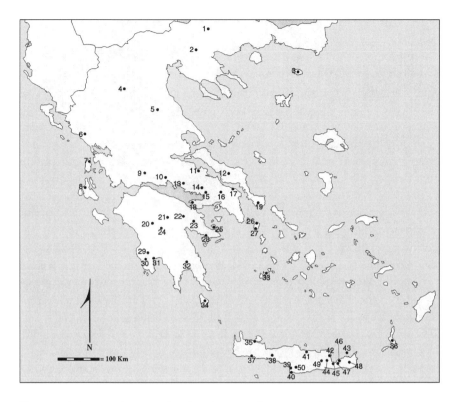

FIGURE 9.4. Map showing the distribution of recent surface surveys in Greece: 1- Serres Basin; 2- Langadas; 3- Samothrace; 4- Grevena; 5- Peneios River; 6- Nikopolis; 7- Lefkas; 8- Kephallinia; 9- Aetolia; 10- Phokis-Doris; 11- Opountian Lokris; 12- Euboea; 13- Eastern Phokis; 14- Boeotia; 15- Khostia; 16- Skourta Plain; 17- Oropos; 18- Perachora; 19- Southern Euboea; 20- Megalopolis; 21- Eastern Arkadia; 22- Nemea; 23- Berbati-Limnes; 24- Asea; 25- Methana; 26- Northern Keos; 27- Southern Keos; 28- Southern Argolid; 29- Messenia (UMME); 30- Messenia (PRAP); 31- Five Rivers; 32- Lakonia; 33- Melos; 34- Kythera; 35- Chania; 36- Kasos-Karpathos; 37- Sphakia; 38- Agios Vassilios; 39- Kommos; 40- Ayiofarango; 41- Knossos; 42- Vrokastro; 43- Pseira; 44- Ziros; 45- Agia Photia; 46- Gournia; 47- Kavousi-Thiphti; 48- Praisos; 49- Lasithi; 50- Western Mesara.

There is an increasing number of instances where the field techniques of intensive survey have been applied to the entire surface of large ancient sites: in Greece, this is known as "urban survey," of which there are now numerous examples (Snodgrass and Bintliff 1988, 1991; Alcock 1991), although one could include here large-scale surveys of nonsettlement sites, such as the obsidian quarries on Melos (Torrence 1982). In at least one case

(Praisos in eastern Crete), what began life as strictly an urban mapping project has transformed itself into a true regional survey (Whitley, Prent, and Thorne 1999). And finally, we ought not to overlook research that comprises a "regional survey" only in the much looser sense of being a drawing together of all known information about sites in a region, but in the absence of systematic new fieldwork explicitly designed to test and establish the full range of the archaeology. I would include here everything from the long-running work of the Athens Center of Ekistics on ancient Greek cities, to standard gazetteers of the Bronze Age sites of the Greek mainland and islands (Hope Simpson and Dickinson 1979) or prehistoric settlements in eastern Thessaly (Gallis 1992), to studies on the territories of Greek cities by a whole school of French scholars (see papers in Blum et al. 1992; Brunet 1999), and to the efforts of many solo historians and archaeologists—Wiseman (1978) on the Corinthia, Sanders (1982) on Roman Crete, Müller (1992) on the Delphi region in the Mycenaean period, or McInerney (1999) on ancient Phokis.

All this is certainly regional work "beyond the site," not involving excavation. But there are often critical weaknesses in its reliability—all too rarely acknowledged—arising from the lack of comparability in data collection and recording, the absence of intensive fieldwork to collect the fullest range of data, and thus uncertainties about the validity of such temporal or spatial patterns as may emerge. This is precisely where the more systematically designed and executed "New Wave" surveys should pay dividends. We have, for instance, witnessed progressive sophistication in devising methods to detect, record, and describe patterns in surface archaeological phenomena at various spatial scales, including the thin and discontinuous carpets of artifacts found in many Mediterranean landscapes (at least when people actually look for them). Some examples from my own projects illustrate the point: in the Melos survey twenty-five years ago, "sites" (never very clearly defined, I admit) were represented simply by undifferentiated dots (Cherry 1982: Figs. 2.1–2.8); by the early 1980s on the Cycladic island of Keos, we were mapping variable artifact densities much more carefully, within a complex mosaic of small survey tracts (Cherry, Davis, and Montzourani 1991: Figs. 3.3, 3.4). A few years later still, the Nemea Valley Archaeological Project was doing much the same kind of thing, but now within a GIS framework and served via the Internet: *http://classics.lsa.umich.edu/NVAP.html*.

Comparable examples from beyond the Aegean are now becoming common. The Segermes survey in northeastern Tunisia, for example, has devised illustrations that show rather clearly how sites emerge from an almost ubiquitous artifactual background (Dietz, Sebaï, and Ben Hassen 1995:134–175; see figure 9.5). Other inventive forms of data display have been tried, as in the Akamas survey in northwestern Cyprus, which uses long linear transects running across the topographic and environmental grain of the landscape, allowing various classes of data to be plotted quantitatively along each transect (Hayes 1995: Figs. 1–6). But intriguing and helpful though these newer forms of graphical illustration may be, they run afoul of the general problem that the description of pattern does not ipso facto tell us about process. Crudely, we can put dots on maps, but we often have little real idea what they represent behaviorally (let alone how such cultural landscapes were conceptualized, experienced, and symbolized).

Just two examples of where more work is needed must suffice. With the more intensive surveys of recent years, isolated small sites (< 0.5 ha) have become recognized as a recurring feature of settlement patterns throughout antiquity; their exact function is not fully clear, but the majority were probably farmsteads of some sort, and they are particularly frequent in the Classical-Hellenistic and late Roman periods. So, are we looking at the residences of a class of free peasant farmers? Probably not (or at least not only that), for

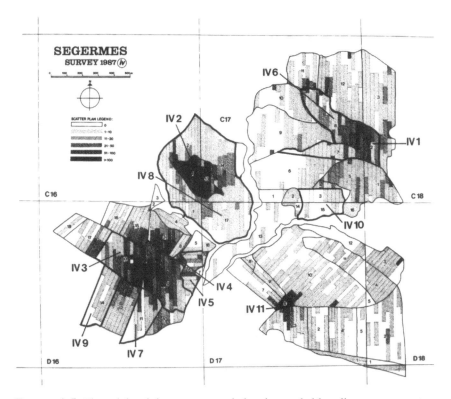

FIGURE 9.5. Plot of sherd densities recorded in linear field-walking transects in Survey Area IV of the Segermes survey in northeastern Tunisia, showing how local high-density foci ("sites") emerge from an almost ubiquitous artifactual "background." *After Dietz, Sebaï, and Ben Hassen 1995:147, Fig. 7.*

the historical evidence strongly suggests that in many Greek city-states a very small percentage of wealthy citizens owned well over half the land, so some of these small sites may represent residences of tenant farmers or estate workers. To make matters even worse, surviving fourth and third century BC lease agreements indicate that, when buildings changed hands, very often not only domestic items such as pottery and tools were removed but even doors and entire roofs (Osborne 1985)—a draconian version of a Schiffer C-transform! In a recent intriguing case study, based on survey data from the peninsula of Methana in southern Greece in the Late Roman period, some of the easily identifiable farmsteads are equipped with relatively expensive industrial equipment for olive processing, probably beyond the means of the average farmer; and yet these sites are at high elevations, in fact well above the altitudinal limit for olives and so seem to represent something other than self-sufficient farms, possibly connected with agricultural estates of landowners who may not even have resided on Methana themselves (Mee and Forbes 1997:77–91, 257–268; see figure 9.6). The general problem at issue here is that of working out the archaeological signature of different forms of land tenure and tenancy (Garnsey 1979; Foxhall 1990).

A second area of fierce debate is the explanation of the "off-site" artifact scatters that are so prominent a feature in many Mediterranean surveys. How, for instance, should one account for a picture such as that of figure 9.5 from Roman Tunisia, where there are evidently significant artifactual foci but also diffuse and discontinuous scatters of material (of similar periods) at various distances from them? The incorporation of domestic refuse in manure applied to the fields has been argued to play a significant role in such cases, but many other factors, such as erosion and the long-term effects of plowing, are also relevant. This turns out to be a complex and intriguing problem (see Wilkinson 1982, 1989; Alcock, Cherry, and Davis 1994) involving nothing less than the taphonomy of a significant proportion of the surviving surface archaeological record. It has been disappointing to see the relevance of this problem challenged and those who have worked on it castigated for "making a mountain out of a manure-hill" (Morris 1995:185) or "wallowing in the dung-heaps of the New Archaeology" (Spivey 1994:11). At the same time, there are those who, while recognizing the importance of such taphonomic factors as these, conclude that surface finds cannot be taken at face value, either because their composition is so dynamic, even over short time periods (Ammerman 1995; compare Davis and Sutton 1995), or that the landscapes of whole epochs are literally hidden from us and are therefore encountered only in a serendipitous manner (Bintliff, Howard, and Snodgrass 1999). Both views contain some truth, but in my view they have been greatly exaggerated.

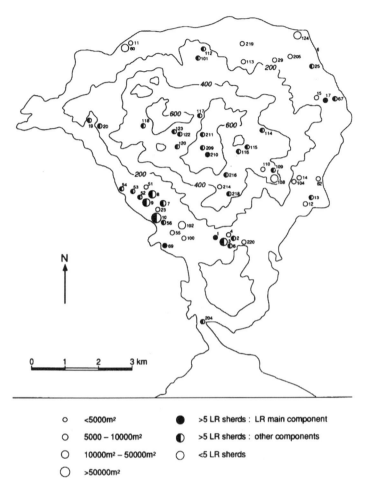

FIGURE 9.6. Sites of the Late Roman period found in the survey of the peninsula of Methana in southern Greece. *After Mee and Forbes 1997: Fig. 8.1.*

Apart from interpretive issues of this sort, another roadblock is increasingly being encountered. Some major incompatibilities between the data sets generated by New Wave surveys are making it problematic to move beyond them to comparatively larger and more useful collective observations. Inevitably, one such difficulty revolves around the very different views of what constitutes a "site," especially in light of what we now know about so-called background noise: thus when one survey project, on the 2 km^2 Cretan island of Pseira (Betancourt and Hope Simpson 1992), reports almost as many "sites" (about 300) as another, namely the entire 2500 km^2 northern Greek province of Grevena (Wilkie 1993), something must surely be amiss.

Likewise, even a problem seemingly so routine as the use of nonequivalent or fuzzily defined chronological phases (for example, what exactly "Early Roman" means) can require some serious "archaeological source criticism," as was the case in Alcock's pioneering attempt, in her book *Graecia capta* (1993:49–53), to use all the then-available regional survey evidence comparatively in studying the Romanization of the Greek landscape.

And yet in my estimation, the advent of comparative regional studies is by far the most exciting current development in Mediterranean survey, and one I have long anticipated (Cherry 1983:405–408; 1994:94–95). It is something that is bound to grow, as more of the New Wave surveys reach full publication and we can begin to set side by side the data from surveys in closely adjacent areas. Greece is environmentally diverse, and has also supported very varied forms of political organization over the millennia, and that diversity seems reflected in regionally based similarities and differences that are now coming into better focus. Just from the past several years I can think of comparative uses of multiple survey data sets from Greece to study: the development of states on the southern Greek mainland in the later Bronze Age (Cavanagh 1995); the apparent north-south divide in Greek prehistory and history (Halstead 1994; Bintliff 1997); long-term patterns in the prehistory of the Peloponnese (Mee 1999); the role of pastoralism in the Greek Neolithic (Cavanagh 1999); the regional context for the emergence of Mycenae (Cherry and Davis 2001); and divergent political hierarchies in different areas of Crete in the Old and New Palace periods (Driessen 2001).

On a substantially larger canvas, there is Blanton's recent attempt (2000) to provide a comparative context for Hellenistic through Byzantine settlement patterns of the coastal area of western Rough Cilicia in Turkey via structured comparison with eighteen other surveys in areas ranging from Spain to Cyprus; or Alcock's study (1994) of the rural settlement patterns of the Hellenistic kingdoms, all the way from Greece to Afghanistan, using evidence from some fifty surveys in a dozen countries; or, as a final example, Wilkinson's review of long-term patterns in environment, urbanism, and demography based on data from forty-two surveys in southeastern Turkey, Syria, and Iraq (Wilkinson 2000). This style of work will assuredly play an increasingly important role in the future of Mediterranean archaeology as ever larger bodies of systematic data from survey begin to accumulate (Alcock and Cherry 2003). Just as the synthetic and comparative analysis of multiple sets of survey results helped rewrite and reorient the archaeology of parts of Mesopotamia (Adams 1981) and Mesoamerica (Blanton et al. 1982) some years ago, so, too, we may now anticipate that the fruits of hundreds of Mediterranean survey projects will begin to have a similarly far-reaching impact.

Looking to the Future

What, if anything, can be said about possible future directions for regional surveys in the Mediterranean? One must be wary of assuming that current "hot-button" issues will remain hot, or that present trends allow reliable prediction of developments in the years to come. This is so not only because of the sheer pace of evolution in the technologies for acquiring, analyzing, and displaying archaeological data at the regional scale, but also because of subtler shifts in the relationship between archaeology as a disciplinary practice and the social and political milieu that provides its relevance and justification. The few thoughts that follow merely highlight five aspects of some conceivable futures for survey—at least, as seen from the perspective of the year 2000:

1. If only because computer chip speeds have, for some years now, been doubling roughly every eighteen months, it can be asserted with absolute confidence that the impact of changes in information technology will be enormous. The point is already painfully obvious to those at or beyond mid-career—the dinosaurs of the Information Age for whom the past quarter-century has been a constant struggle to stay abreast.

   My own experience of using computers in survey-based research is surely not atypical. Following a decade of wrestling with boxes of IBM punch-cards to perform SPSS (Statistical Package for the Social Sciences) analyses on the mainframe computer, I acquired my first desktop machine (a 128K Apple Macintosh) in 1984, among the first at my university to do so; and the ways in which the Mac was assisting our survey work in Greece actually seemed sufficiently novel to be featured in Apple's national advertising campaign in 1985 (figure 9.7, reproduced here as a historical curiosity). The advent of portable computers with adequate memory and storage made feasible their use in the field during our Nemea Valley Archaeological Project (1984–87). My first e-mail message was sent (via Arpanet) in about 1987, although the routine sending and sharing of text, data, and image files did not come until the 1990s; and it was in 1992 that I first accessed archaeological data via the Internet (using the Mosaic browser). Now at work with colleagues on traditional (that is, printed) publications relating to surveys, virtually all of whose primary data have been available on-line for several years and which can now be compared with a good many other Web-based survey "publications," I wonder if we should not simply be writing an e-book or perhaps designing a state-of-the-art Web site.

   Reflecting on such experiences leads, on the one hand, only to the conclusion that we should expect in the future to be blindsided from

FIGURE 9.7. Newspaper advertisement in 1985 for Apple Computer UK Ltd. featuring the use of the Macintosh computer in connection with archaeological survey research in Greece.

unexpected quarters. On the other hand, with fast-growing Internet access to data from so many regional projects, past and present, we already not only have a much better idea of what is happening in the field of Mediterranean survey, but can actually see and share images of sites and artifacts, maps, plots, graphs, GIS analyses, virtual realizations, and so on, all with an unparalleled immediacy. The likely next stage— though it may require some convergence or agreement about standards of data presentation—is the possibility of conducting meta-searches of numerous Web-based survey databases, thus making a reality of the laudable, but largely unfulfilled, vision laid out years ago by, for example, the Southwestern Archaeological Research Group (SARG 1974).

2. Still in the realm of technology, it could fairly be claimed that we are in the midst of a remote-sensing revolution, one with far-reaching implications for research at the regional level. We are all by now very familiar with the types of scenes captured by the Space Shuttle or satellite-based systems (such as Landsat, Corona, and SPOT), designed mainly for large-scale land-surface mapping and monitoring. They have mainly been used by archaeologists for either generic scene setting (see, for an example, Ashton 1995:3) or environmental classification and site prediction prior to survey (for a general overview, see Ebert 1988). But the past year or two have witnessed the emergence of the first truly high-resolution, commercially available images of the earth from space as the result in part of the declassification of military images and in part from the launch of a new generation of earth-imaging satellites.

The IKONOS satellite launched in September 1999, for example, collects panchromatic (gray-scale) data to 1 m resolution and multispectral (color) data to 4 m resolution, with imagery stored in a digital archive designed to service quickly the needs of commercial clients. The extraordinary clarity and resolution with which objects on the ground as small as 1 m can be distinguished from 680 km above the earth is dramatically illustrated in this image of the Washington Monument in Washington, DC (figure 9.8). More generally, there now exist airborne and satellite sensors providing far higher spectral resolution than hitherto; much greater bandwidth; various advanced types of sensing systems; enormously faster computers for processing, calibrating, and enhancing this imagery; greater cross-platform compatibility, allowing (for example) easier integration with GIS systems; and, importantly, Web-based delivery systems (Rees 1999 offers a convenient index to many of these developments; see also El-Baz 1997). At a rather different scale, geophysical prospection has made rapid and very substantial advances in the past decade, particularly with regard to systems such as

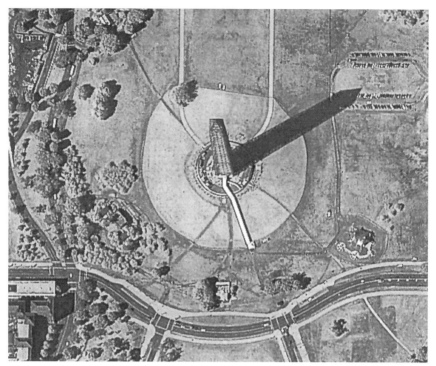

FIGURE 9.8. The first high-resolution image from the IKONOS satellite, taken in 1999, of the Washington Monument in Washington, DC, as seen from 680 km above the earth. *From* www.spaceimaging.com.

ground penetrating radar; this, however, is a field about which no more need be said here in light of the recent publication of a thorough over-view of geophysical work with special reference to survey in the Medi-terranean region (Sarris and Jones 2000).

Without exaggeration, it may fairly be claimed that we stand at an important juncture. These technologies may partly replace, and will cer-tainly improve, traditional pedestrian autopsy methods at the regional level as a result of enhanced predictive modeling. One area where major improvements may be expected is in image classification techniques to identify discrete multispectral signatures of archaeological interest. Recent work in Greece has met with some success in isolating spectral emission characteristics that indicate, for instance, the exposed Plio-Pleistocene sediments often associated with Paleolithic cultural materi-als, ancient clay beds and marble quarries, abandoned water channels, ancient architecture totally hidden by dense brush, and so on (Stein and Cullen 1994; Wiseman 1996). These efforts, while promising, remain somewhat crude and labor intensive; so I anticipate substantial advances as a direct result of greater spatial resolution and spectral range in the available space imagery. The larger point here, as Wilkinson (2000:255) put it, is that "archaeological site survey is not the only way of conducting research at a regional scale."

3. According to a recent study (Inglis 2000), one in every eight or nine people worldwide now travels to another country each year; in the Mediterranean, the permanent population of about 130 million balloons seasonally to something close to 260 million. One has only to cross from Greece into Albania—politically isolated for decades under Enver Hoxha, but broadly comparable in climate and environment—to appreciate just how radically the Greek landscape has been transformed by the tourist industry, by urban in-migration and rural abandonment, and by the depredations of the bulldozer and the deep plow, often in direct response to financial incentives provided by the European Union's agricultural policies (Sutton 2000; compare Barker 1995:300–307 for southern Italy).

At a time when the understaffed Greek Archaeological service is locked in a losing battle with these inexorable pressures of development, one would suppose that the masses of new information gathered by regional surveys all over the country would play an ever more central role in developing sensible schemes for the protection and management of cultural resources. This has not been the case. Local superintendents of antiquities, already with more than enough on their plates, are generally not thrilled to learn that some research project—probably one conducted by non-Greek academic archaeologists during university vacation time and supported by significant research funds—has brought to light dozens, sometimes hundreds, of new sites in their area. The irony is that such information, presented in an appropriate form, could help them make informed decisions about critical daily threats to the very antiquities for which they are legally responsible. I found it dispiriting, a few years ago, to watch helplessly as the new National Highway leading from Corinth into the central Peloponnese was blasted right through the region northwest of Mycenae that we were at the selfsame time intensively surveying (Wright et al. 1990; Cherry et al. n.d.). It obliterated Neolithic sites, Classical towers, segments of Roman aqueduct, indeed all that lay in its path, without much (if any) prior investigation and despite our detailed reports to the relevant local authorities. A pertinent observation in this regard is that, in Greece, there exists no equivalent of the county records or state archives of western and central Europe or North America to which all legitimate parties have access and can contribute.

At the root of these problems are Greece's unreformed nineteenth-century antiquities laws, the confusing and generally inefficient organization of its Archaeological Service, and the long-running rivalries and resentments among the Service, universities, private entities such as the Archaeological Society of Athens, and the numerous foreign archaeological schools (Zois 1990).

4. There is, perhaps, an even more fundamental issue that the regional projects of recent years have brought to a head. All the organizations just mentioned, and the legislation under which they are obliged to operate (see Kardulias 1994), have worked on the assumption that archaeological remains are concentrated in a finite number of locations (sites), with a consequent emphasis on excavation, especially the "big dig" at major sites, many subsequently protected and developed as tourist attractions. Systematic surveys, however, not only in Greece but Mediterranean wide, have demonstrated that the surface archaeological record is, in fact, much more interesting and complex than this. Given the vast number and greater variety of sites of which we now know, yet faced with still decidedly finite resources for their curation, it seems to me obvious that strategic, informed decisions will increasingly need to be made—not so much about which sites to sample by excavation before they are gone for good, as about what parts of whole archaeological landscapes to defend and preserve, and which simply to let go. Either way, regional studies projects surely should play a central role. In areas where economic development makes it inevitable that archaeological remains cannot survive, careful surveys to document cultural resources in advance of their destruction, not just the piecemeal excavation of bits of a few sites, seem the natural solution.

To the oft-voiced objection that there are insufficient resources for such undertakings, one response is that even a modest relaxation of current permit restrictions would unlock huge reserves of money, manpower, and expertise from the many foreign scholars who would leap at the chance to become involved in this way. Certain other countries—Syria, Turkey, Cyprus, or Italy, for instance—have generally been receptive to such initiatives. Yet in Greece, oddly, I can call to mind only a single such multinational CRM-type collaborative venture: the surveys and test excavations conducted in the late 1960s ahead of the barrage dam on the Peneios River in the western Peloponnese. The resistance to such cooperative ventures involving Greek and non-Greek archaeologists is understandable in a country with so long a cultural memory of political and cultural domination by outsiders, and in which national identity is so intimately entwined with cultural patrimony and heritage.

This is an ironic, modern-day inversion of *timeo Danaos et dona ferentes*, but not one that makes sense in the context of the escalating pace at which the archaeological record is being degraded.

Yet, if we were to move more toward the notion of preserving cultural resources at the landscape level, regional survey would again be a critical element. Heritage management beyond the level of the individual site, however, has yet to get off the ground in Greece. There do exist, to be sure, a few archaeological set-asides (Rhamnous in Attica, Messene in the Peloponnese, Kommos in Crete), but these "parks" simply protect the local hinterlands of major excavated sites, and none is more than a few dozen hectares in extent. There is nothing akin to the Italian state's preservation of the supra-regional network of ancient pastoral *tratturi* or drove-roads (Barker 1995:34–35, Figs. 16, 17) or the current plans to establish an archaeological park covering the ancient Greek colonial city of Chersonesos and much of its *chora* on the Heraclean Peninsula in the Ukrainian Crimea (Carter 1998:35–38, Fig. 37).

Several respondents to the oral version of this paper rightly commented that, as a profession, we archaeologists are not sufficiently aware of how our own current work is situated in relation to the time dimension of the likely near-total annihilation of the archaeological record everywhere over the period from about 1950 to 2050. Even a simple linear extrapolation of present rates of population growth, global economic development, and destruction of cultural resources suggests that this record will soon be a poor thing of shreds and patches. By some estimates, if current trends continue, as much as 98% of all archaeological sites will be destroyed by the mid-twenty-first century (Knudson 1989; Cameron 1994); in some cases—as, for example, the Classic Mimbres sites of the American Southwest, 90% of which have now been looted or destroyed—such dire predictions have already come to pass (for many additional examples, see Renfrew and Bahn 2000:533–564). If we are the last generation, or nearly so, to have access to a still moderately intact archaeological record, then it follows that we have certain important obligations to the future, and the data we produce now will constitute an archive of exceptional importance. Cultural resource management strategies and priorities, as we know them now, may not be up to the task of coping with this final tidal wave of data. A corollary issue, of course, is the long-term preservation and curation of such data archives, when the technologies and media for data storage are themselves being replaced on ever shorter time scales.

5. This is the segue to my final topic. Commenting on heritage management issues a few years ago, Kristian Kristiansen wrote:

The archaeological heritage contributes to the historical identity of nations, people, and local communities. . . . It represents an irreplaceable contribution to what has been termed the collective memory of mankind. This memory is stored mostly in the landscape. It is in the landscape that the heritage should be protected, and only as a last resort, after excavation, in museums. (1989:27)

There is a growing sense, I believe, that however cooperative the natives may have been, many of our surveys have been rather crudely colonialist in character, a coarse tension between insiders and outsiders, privileging the imperatives of science over responsibility and sensitivity to local inhabitants' economic concerns, to their cultural identities, to the ways in which those identities are expressed through attachment to landscapes, and to the sorts of alternative narratives they bring to bear. Even the regions we study have tended to be defined more in terms of abstract research goals than as units of local geohistoric significance. As Fotiadis (1993, 1995, 1997), Sutton (2000:1–24), and a number of others have recently shown, to devastating effect, most of the writings by anthropologists attached to regional projects about the supposed timelessness of Mediterranean peasant farmers can be exposed for the orientalist, nationalist, romanticized, touristic, and urban-based motivations that underlie them.

These points are significant, because they relate to a divergence that has developed in recent years, one that sets up a "Great Divide" of another sort. Most of the Mediterranean regional survey projects mentioned in this paper could be said to have followed a broadly processual approach: their primary focus, at least, has been the coevolution of human settlement and landscape over long periods, and the methodologies employed in pursuit of this goal have been strongly scientific, quantitative, and environmental in character. Now "landscape" is a capacious mansion with many rooms, and rightly so. Yet such work seems decidedly out of step with the postmodern "archaeologies of landscape" that have emerged in recent years (see, for example, some of the papers in Ashmore and Knapp 1999; Ucko and Layton 1999), most prominently in the writings of certain British prehistorians (Bender 1993; Bradley 1993, 1998; Tilley 1994; Edmonds 1999). These foreground experiential and phenomenological approaches focus on human perception and symbolic ordering of space. For them, the overworked metaphor of "landscape as palimpsest" means much more than merely a confusing overlay of temporal snapshots: the emphasis, rather, is on the process of reinterpretation and reworking of dynamic landscapes whose changing appearance communicates cultural values and is charged with meaning. Past landscapes are historically contingent entities; they are active sites of memory, of associations, even of morality (Basso 1996); a "sense of place" (Tilley 1999) can generate sacred or ritual landscapes (Alcock and Osborne 1994), but also symbolic materializations that were open to conflicting perceptions and to contestation, and thus "landscapes of resistance" (Alcock 2002).

Bringing these two broad approaches into closer dialogue is both desirable and necessary, not merely for intellectual or disciplinary reasons but also to enhance the relevance of our work to the present-day occupants of the lands we survey and to help build a less appropriating Mediterranean archaeology for the future. Among all the possible futures I have sketched in this section, this seems at once the most exciting and the most important.

Acknowledgments

The first Cotsen Advanced Seminar was a memorable occasion. I am very grateful to Richard Leventhal and John Papadopoulos for inviting me to Southern California during the Michigan winter and for their challenge to say something worthwhile about Mediterranean survey's past, present, and future in thirty minutes! As co-recipient a decade ago of the first Cotsen Prize, which honored the publication of our survey work on Keos (Lloyd Cotsen's own turf), it was gratifying to have the opportunity to speak about survey in his presence—all the more so on an occasion celebrating Lloyd's continued extraordinary generosity to our field.

Note

1. The journals consulted for this literature review are *American Journal of Archaeology, Anatolian Studies, Antiquités Africaines, Annual of the British School at Athens, Bulletin of the American Schools of Oriental Research, Hesperia, Israel Exploration Journal, Journal of the American Research Center in Egypt, Journal of Egyptian Archaeology, Journal of Mediterranean Archaeology, Journal of Roman Archaeology, Levant, Libyan Studies, Papers of the British School at Rome,* and *Report of the Department of Antiquities of Cyprus.* My thanks to Bryan Burns and Geoff Compton for their assistance with this study.

CHAPTER 10

A Brief Americanist Perspective on Settlement Archaeology

CHARLES STANISH

As a settlement archaeologist who has worked in the Americas for more than twenty years, I was fascinated by a number of issues raised by the participants of the symposium. It is clear that the Mediterranean is an area of the world with a very different research tradition than my own vis à vis settlement archaeology. In particular, I was struck by some comments about the role of settlement archaeology in the Mediterranean. Several participants implied that archaeological survey did not enjoy the same status as large-site excavations conducted by Mediterranean archaeologists. There appears to be a greater split between settlement archaeology and large-site excavations in the Mediterranean than in the Americas.

This view is curiously different from that expressed in the Americas where settlement studies and excavations are usually integrated in single-project research designs. In the Americas it is much easier to conduct large-scale excavations in conjunction with survey. It is rare, in fact, when major multiyear research projects do not include a regional settlement survey along with excavations. In some areas of the Americas where surface preservation is excellent, settlement archaeology often defines the theoretical issues that guide both excavation and regional research.

I wish to briefly explore this theme in this paper: the difference in the practice of settlement archaeology in the Old World and the Americas from the point of view of the latter. I would like to make two points that I believe offer some insight into this difference. First, settlement archaeology is not solely confined to surface collections as is sometimes assumed. Rather, settlement archaeology is a distinct methodological approach in contemporary Americanist archaeology. Surface survey is one component of a regional research methodology that almost always includes excavations and other techniques to obtain archaeological data.

Second, the development of settlement archaeology in the Americas was intimately tied to the emergence of cultural ecological theory associated with the New Archaeology a generation ago. The development of a very distinct field methodology that is specifically tied to a new theoretical framework is a rare phenomenon in the intellectual history of archaeology. This linkage has not been adequately explored, but it has greatly affected the practice of archaeology in the Americas. In short, the development of regional approaches in Americanist archaeology is directly tied to the adoption of a new theoretical framework. As such, this development partially explains the strong degree to which settlement archaeology in the Americas is integrated with excavation programs.

Methods and Theories

The strong intellectual and professional bonds of archaeology and anthropology in the Americas fostered a rare linkage between a new method and a new theory in the 1950s and 1960s. It was at this time that cultural ecology emerged as the dominant framework for studying prehistory. The story of the emergence of cultural ecology and the New Archaeology in this period is well known.[1] Given the dominance of cultural history paradigms in the pre-World War II era, cultural ecology emerged as a scientific (that is, comparative and processual) alternative to the historicist traditions of the past. Earlier models of cultural evolution (the unilinealism of White and his nineteenth-century predecessors, for instance) required certain kinds of databases. Likewise, the cultural historical paradigm required a different kind of database. Cultural ecology was no different. The kind of data that cultural ecology required was, however, new in the field. It required a regional data set that included not only large sites but all types of sites, particularly the smaller settlements that represented the bulk of the population of the period under study.

Modern settlement archaeology was initiated, in large part, by Gordon Willey and his colleagues during the 1940s in the Virú Valley of the northern coast of Peru. Willey emphasized that his work began at the suggestion of Julian Steward, an anthropologist and one of the pioneers of cultural ecology (Willey 1999). This association is not coincidental. Settlement methodologies have become a staple of comparative processual archaeology in general and cultural ecological theory in particular. In the intellectual history of the discipline, settlement archaeology represents a methodology that closely developed in tandem with a new theoretical orientation.

Of course, archaeological survey has a very long history in the western world. From the catalogs of antiquities in colonized countries to the many archaeological societies in Britain and Europe, the comprehensive location of ancient settlements is a long and distinguished tradition. In the Americas as well, archaeologists had cataloged sites for decades. Numerous naturalists of the nineteenth century explored the length and breadth of Central America, Mexico, the Andes, and other regions documenting the antiquities. By the immediate post–World War II era, huge inventories of sites from around the world had been cataloged.

Prior to Willey's work in Virú, however, most surveys or catalogs around the world were designed to discover "sites in order to select a 'good one' for excavation," as Charles Redman (1982:375) points out. These early surveys were conceived of as simply the expansion of single-site methodologies over a large area. In other words, there was no conceptual difference between finding sites in a particular area and conducting settlement survey. Without any theoretical framework to guide the discovery of sites, settlement survey was nothing more than an exercise in creating site catalogs of any particular region. The discovery of one site, or hundreds of sites, had no real impact on interpretation except insofar as the larger number of sites provided more cultural historical data.

This view of settlement survey changed in the 1950s and early 1960s. The adoption of cultural ecological theory required a focus not just on the large sites and major population centers but on the entire settlement system in any area. This focus occurred because a basic tenet of cultural ecology was that culture was humanity's "superorganic means of adaptation" to the physical and social environment (see Steward 1973 [originally published in 1955]: 30–39). In this view, it was necessary to understand the entire population of individuals in any place and time in order to understand their adaptation to a particular environment. Large centers were important but could not be understood without controlling for the rest of the settlements in any social system. For cultural ecologists the sum total of all the humble agriculturalists who spread over and exploited a landscape was more important than the temples and palaces of the elite found in the major centers.[2] It was, after all, the peasant farmers who provided the vast bulk of subsistence goods for the society. Subsistence was at the "core" of the human adaptation, while the art and architecture of the centers were viewed as largely epiphenomenal. The subsistence strategies, in turn, were determined to a large extent by the physical environment in which they operated. In short, it was considered impossible to understand the evolution of culture without controlling for the entire range of human land use in a region and controlling the environmental context in which they lived.

FIGURE 10.1. Relic *chinampa* in the Xochimilco survey, Mexico, conducted by Jeffrey Parsons and his associates, 1972.

Gordon Willey continued his settlement work in Mesoamerica in the 1960s and 1970s, and survey came to dominate many areas of New World archaeology. A number of scholars conducted huge surveys in Oaxaca and the Basin of Mexico (Parsons 1971; Parsons et al. 1982; Sanders, Parsons, and Santley 1979; Nichols 1995). The central Mexico surveys focused on the habitation and specialized production sites. They also collected data on a variety of features, including the large *chinampas* or raised fields of the area. Figure 10.1 shows a relict chinampa in the Xochimilco survey by Parsons and his associates. Figure 10.2 is from the Tenango region, an area in which crews conducted surveys of the entire landscape. The focus not just on archaeological habitation sites but actual landscapes in the Americas can reasonably be said to have begun in the central Basin of Mexico.

In this intellectual context, the contributions of Robert McC. Adams in the other hemisphere cannot be overstated. He conducted the first systematic and intensive settlement research in Mesopotamia, work that led to a qualitatively new understanding of the cultural dynamics of that region. Figures 10.3 through 10.6 show Adams, a scholar who contributed so much to archaeological survey in both the Old World and the New World, at work at a number of sites in Mesopotamia. Adams pioneered one kind of full-regional coverage survey. He located ancient canals and correlated the distribution of sites along these features. His work illustrated the dynamic nature of settlement shifts in the region and correlated them to different political and economic landscapes through time. One could argue without much exaggeration that he set the standard for using regional data to define the evolution of political organization of complex societies.

FIGURE 10.2. Surveying the landscape of the Tenango region, Mexico, 1972, by Jeffrey Parsons and his associates.

FIGURE 10.3. Robert McC. Adams in the field, 1957.

Figure 10.4. Robert McC. Adams and Hans Nissen inaugurating use of a "Jalbert Parafoil" (high-tech kite) for low-level remote sensing at Uruk/Warka, February 1967.

Adams's work defined a whole new paradigm in archaeological regional studies. It is curious that his influence on archaeological methodology had perhaps as great an effect in the Americas as in the Old World. Adams's work, cited as a model for settlement archaeology in North and Middle America, contributed to the methodological canon of anthropological archaeology during this formative period in the discipline. Again, we see the influence of theory on method in settlement archaeology. Adams adopted a cultural ecological framework with certain modifications, and his methodology was ideally suited to his theoretical goals. In spite of the fact that his work was conducted in Mesopotamia, he contributed to the consolidation of settlement survey and anthropological theory in the Americanist literature throughout the 1960s and 1970s.

FIGURE 10.5. Robert McC. Adams and Elizabeth Skinner in the sherd yard at the Abu Sarifa excavations, January 1969.

While Willey may have been correct to state in 1956 that "there [was] no settlement pattern approach to archaeology" (Willey 1956:1), by 1972 Parsons (1972:134) could properly speak of a distinctive New World "tradition of settlement pattern archaeology" that was developing out of Americanist roots reaching back generations. Regional research is a distinctive methodology that acquires qualitatively different data and can ask qualitatively different questions than large-site excavations alone.

This tradition continues unabated in the Americas. In particular, there has been a major influx of Mesoamerican-trained archaeologists who moved into the Andes in the 1980s (Stanish 2001). Over the years, settlement pattern survey has been used by archaeologists utilizing a variety of theoretical frameworks, not just cultural ecology (for example, see the volume edited by Billman and Feinman 1999). From this perspective, settlement archaeology is more than a means of recovering surface archaeological data from a large area. It is a methodology associated with comparative approaches in the discipline to address certain kinds of regional problems of anthropological interest. This is the primary defining characteristic of settlement archaeology: it is regional in scope and utilizes models that must be formulated and tested with data from a large area.

FIGURE 10.6. Transportation problems near Habis el-Gharbi, February 1957.

In fact, the term "settlement archaeology" is often implicitly used as a shorthand for "regional approaches in anthropological archaeology." A regional approach relies on several kinds of surface survey methodologies, as well as excavations, air photograph analysis, and the use of other geographical data. I cannot emphasize sufficiently that regional approaches recover data that are qualitatively different from those collected with single-site or community-focused methodologies. The regional approach inherent in settlement archaeology allows us to formulate research questions at a level not available by intensive work at one or a few sites alone (Ammerman 1981). This qualitative distinction is based upon the contextual information that can be derived from regional data. A key point is that, by controlling for context, the whole of the information collected from a region is greater than the sum of the individual observations. For instance, the discovery of an isolated ancient agricultural canal and a contemporary habitation site are two valuable sets of data in and of themselves. But when these data are placed in context—the habitation site is demonstrated to be functionally and temporally connected with the canal—the amount of information is greater than the sum of the data from each site alone.

The association and contextual relationship between the two sites represents a third kind of "data" that would not be recoverable if the canal and habitation site were analyzed in isolation from each other. Likewise, regional research designs provide perspective on the long-term diachronic patterns of land use and landscape alteration through time. Comparing settlement patterns from different periods provides qualitatively different data than that which can be obtained from the analysis of just a few sites.

A regional methodology can be executed at several levels of intensity. "Intensity" is defined as the total amount of resources committed to a particular area of landscape (Plog, Plog, and Wait 1978:389). Reconnaissance is the least intensive kind of survey methodology. Reconnaissance methodologies simply involve the cataloging of sites in any region, either on foot or through the analysis of air photographs. It is not intended to provide a precise model of the archaeological materials in the region but seeks a more general characterization of the nature and range of materials in any area.

Reconnaissance is particularly useful in areas where little work has been conducted. It is a very cost-effective means of characterizing the broad outlines of the cultural history in a region, and permits the development of models that can be tested with more intensive survey methodologies. It is also useful to recognize nonsystematic reconnaissance as a bona fide methodology, because it incorporates the work of earlier scholars who made great contributions without explicitly utilizing scientific research designs. In the Americas we recognize that many of the early Spanish historians who traveled the countryside and reported on the ruins they encountered in effect represent some of the first archaeologists of the New World. In the same way, the millennia of historical reporting on ancient ruins in the Old World, and the attendant speculation about what they were, represent some of the first survey reports of archaeology.

Systematic reconnaissance is more intensive. It involves the sampling of locations in a region based upon a set of consistently used criteria. John Hyslop, for instance, systematically reconnoitered the western Titicaca Basin of highland Peru looking for sites described in sixteenth-century texts (Hyslop 1976). His purpose was to test the reliability of these historical documents as well as to define the nature of the fifteenth and sixteenth century AD occupation in the region. Other criteria might be ecological (sampling only early Holocene riverbanks), topographical (all hilltops), or cultural (all walled sites). Systematic reconnaissance permits one to control biases better, but it still does not provide a precise characterization of the settlement pattern from a region.

Surveys differ from reconnaissance in that they seek to provide a precise characterization of the extant surface (and possibly subsurface) of archaeological materials of a region. The most intensive kind of survey is referred to as "full-coverage regional survey" (Fish and Kowalewski 1990). This technique ideally covers 100% of an area. Full-coverage surveys are preferred by most settlement archaeologists in the Andes and Mesoamerica because they eliminate any random omission of surface sites. Given the arid environment of much of these regions, full coverage of large areas is a feasible goal. Less intensive surveys use sampling techniques that, at least in theory, provide data that permit inferences concerning the nature of the entire region tested. The idea here is to use a sampling method that permits a statistically valid characterization of the entire region.

One of the major methodological issues that has received some attention is the question of the problems associated with the definition of a site (see Lesure chapter 14). As in the Americas, there is an ongoing critique of the site concept in Mediterranean archaeology. John Cherry touched on this issue on several occasions in his paper. His work in northern Keos (Cherry, Davis, and Mantzourani 1991) illustrates the problems associated with the conception of a site as a discrete scatter of artifacts on the surface. As Cherry, Davis, and Mantzourani (1991:21) note, considerable information among the discrete sites is lost using a traditional settlement pattern methodology.

From this perspective, the emergence of "landscape archaeology" is a welcome trend in the discipline. Definitions of landscape archaeology differ among scholars, of course. Most definitions center, however, on the goal of viewing a region as a palimpsest of settlements in their physical and social context, and not just defining discrete sites in place and time. Settlement archaeology also is theoretically connected to the "New Geography" that emphasizes the active role that humans play in shaping their environment, both physical and social (Erickson 2000). As such, landscape archaeology represents a different way of looking at ancient settlements. As opposed to a somewhat static view of a series of sites connected by political, economic, social, and ideological linkages at a particular moment in time, landscape archaeology forces us to view history as a changing set of human interactions that leave a continuous stream of material remains.

As mentioned, a common misunderstanding is that settlement archaeology methodologies do not include excavations. This is certainly not the case in the Americas. In most circumstances excavations following survey are an essential component of a properly executed regional research design. Certain kinds of data, such as botanical, faunal, and mortuary, are rarely available from the surface. Geomorphological processes can also systematically skew surface data and complicate interpretations. Regional studies require small but numerous test excavations in many sites to define the chronology, even in the best of environmental circumstances for collecting surface data. An appropriate regional research design therefore includes both surface and sub-surface data to control for natural and cultural skewing of the surface archaeological record.

Regional approaches in archaeology add a qualitatively new means of understanding the past around the world. The current debates on a number of issues surrounding regional research have improved our ability to construct superior research designs and interpret data from around the world. It is obviously desirable that Americanists and Old World archaeologists work together to refine these methodologies and concepts even more. This symposium is a fine example of such collaboration, and we all look forward to more such interaction in the future.

Notes

1. The link between cultural ecology and the New Archaeology is strong but not completely overlapping. In general, almost all archaeologists who adopted a cultural ecological framework were part of the New Archaeology. The converse—that almost all New Archaeologists were cultural ecologists—is not necessarily true, however.
2. This also coincided with a dramatic expansion in the number of Americanist archaeologists and a broad-based "democratization" of the profession in the 1960s. While this is not the place to examine this interesting issue, it is no coincidence that the so-called bottom-up approaches that emphasized the role of everyday people emerged in this political environment.

CHAPTER 11

Settlement and Survey Archaeology: A View from a "Periphery"

STEVEN A. ROSEN

Compare and contrast the rise of survey or settlement archaeology in different areas. Include in your answer origins in the search for a mythological past, the shift to systematic methodologies and multidisciplinary approaches, and directions for the future. Comment on cross-regional influences.

The above would serve as a nice exam question for a graduate course in archaeological methods (depending on how one defines "nice"). In fact, I cannot remember such issues being addressed, except perhaps in informal forums. John Papadopoulos's invitation to me to respond to the papers on survey by John Cherry and Charles Stanish from my own perspectives from the Levant and the Negev provides an opportunity to think about these issues in a somewhat more than informal fashion, hopefully on a level beyond that of our hypothetical graduate students being examined above.

Like the Greek case outlined by Cherry (chapter 9) vis à vis Homer, after an initial stage of explorers, adventurers, and spies in the early nineteenth century, survey archaeology in the Levant developed in the late nineteenth and early twentieth centuries as part of the quest to identify legendary or mythological sites, in this case, those associated with the Bible (for example, Robinson and Smith 1841; Palmer 1872; Besant 1895; see also Silberman 1982, especially for continuing ties to military intelligence). In a real sense, the subsequent divergence of the two regional archaeologies, which seemingly ought to have developed in parallel, can be seen as a consequence of a difference in initial conditions, the different texts. The deep symbolic power of the Bible as the source text for fundamentalist Christianity (for example, Dowley 1986) and nationalist Zionism (for example, Brilliant 1970:139–140; also for archaeology, Elon 1971:280–288) is maintained to this day. Thus, beyond the crude "archaeology confirms biblical account" stories that still appear occasionally, even avowedly secular leading archaeologists seem to define themselves and the research agendas of the region to a great extent as a stance against the biblical narrative as opposed to independence of it. This is true for both sides of the Arab-Israeli conflict, with the dispute over the Bible dominating much discussion. In contrast, as Cherry indicates, even when research in Greece focuses on the Bronze Age, it is no longer overly preoccupied by the questions raised by reading Homer.

The American case stands in contrast. Stanish indicates that settlement archaeology seems to have jumped directly from the explorers and adventurers cataloging exotic sites to a universalist theoretical paradigm, cultural ecology, not based on a particularistic text whose symbols demanded ground truth legitimization. Willey's (1953) work in the Virú Valley, combined with Steward's (1955) anthropological framework, gave impetus and explanatory power to what amounted to an entirely new research agenda.

Put another way, the cultural milieu of the early survey archaeologists working in the classical world and in the Near East related to these areas as of intrinsic ancestral interest. In a very real sense, these scholars felt they were investigating their own past, not someone else's. This is clearly not the case for the New World, at least until recently with the increasing involvement of Native American archaeologists in Canada and the United States, and local cadres of archaeologists in Latin America.

The next stage in the general development of survey archaeology in Greece is defined, according to Cherry, by what Renfrew called "The Great Divide." One cannot fail to agree with Cherry's assessment that the Great Divide, the seemingly overnight adoption of the goals and methods of "New Archaeology," was, in fact, made possible only by the long accumulation of background data. In a sense, we are seeing as much a threshold as a divide.

From the outside, one can perhaps detect a parallel between the University of Minnesota Messenia Expedition and the Virú Valley Project. Both seem to have been watershed investigations that set the basic tenor of research for generations of later work. In a real sense, both established the value of systematic survey and settlement archaeology for their respective regions.

The lag time between publication of these two surveys, 1953 for the Virú Valley versus 1972 for the UMME, begs for comment. Given the difference of almost twenty years, one is tempted to assign some priority or influence to Willey's project. This would be a misunderstanding of two issues, however. First, the archaeologies of Greece and the New World, and for that matter the Near East as well, operated at that time as virtually discrete disciplines. This is readily evident even today in the near absence of overlapping bibliography in Cherry's and Stanish's papers. It is simply difficult to detect influence from Willey's work in the operation of the UMME project. Second, to assign some priority to the Virú Valley project is to ignore the long evolution of the Messenia expedition. Both projects were, in fact, initiated in the 1940s.

The lag time is, nonetheless, real. The Virú Valley project did crystallize as a "modern" survey two decades before Messenia, which in terms of disciplinary development is no mean span. Before attempting some explanation of this lag time, however, it may be instructive to look at the Levantine situation as an added case study.

Nelson Glueck (for example, 1945, 1959), working in the desert regions of the southern Levant from the 1930s and later, was undoubtedly the pioneer of survey archaeology in the Levant. Although such projects as the Palestine Exploration Fund Survey of Western Palestine (Conder and Kitchener 1881–85) had cataloged vast numbers of sites, theirs was a topographic survey. It even predates the use of ceramics to date sites and of course related only to large and named features. Although, for example, Woolley and Lawrence (1914) had the use of ceramic chronologies, they concentrated almost exclusively on the largest sites. Glueck registered all the sites he found, regardless of size or identity (figure 11.1), placing them in a culture historical sequence fixed on one hand by excavations such as those of

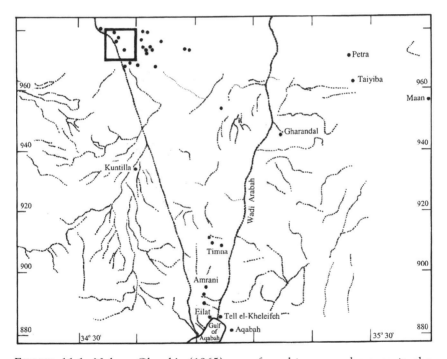

FIGURE 11.1. Nelson Glueck's (1965) map from his renewed survey in the Negev. None of the unnamed sites can be associated with any special historical place or event. The square toward the left (representing 100 km^2) should be compared to figure 11.2. *Drawing by Patrick Finnerty after Glueck 1965.*

Albright at Tel Beit Mirsim (Albright 1936–37) and on the other by the biblical narrative. There is, of course, a certain naivete in the work. No mention is made of field coverage methods, site definition criteria, or collection methods. Interpretation was very much based on historical assumptions derived from the Bible. The large quantity of materials provided grist for later evaluations, however, with conclusions derived from other theoretical frameworks like culture ecology (for example, Baron 1978), as well as inspiration for more fieldwork.

Glueck's successors in the 1950s and 1960s, especially Aharoni (for example, 1967:91–93; also see Geva 1992), maintained this basic culture historic/biblical mode. This is evident as well in the surveys conducted immediately following the 1967 Arab-Israeli War, both on the West Bank (for example, Zertal 1988, 1992; Dar 1982, 1986) and in Sinai (for example, Meshel and Finkelstein 1980; Oren 1973). Although numerous sites were registered and documented, survey was ad hoc, with a sense of urgency about it. Later analyses of the survey materials well reflect their theoretical connection to biblical history (for example, Zertal 1988, 1992).

It is difficult to pinpoint a watershed project or date for some transition to landscape or settlement archaeology, as opposed to a culture historical one, and it is clear that the picture is actually more complex than outlined so briefly above. For example, Higgs's work (1972) around Nahal Oren and Gezer had a clear influence on research frameworks for prehistoric archaeology (and to a lesser extent on historic-period archaeology), as did the researches conducted in Egypt by the foreign teams on the Aswan Dam-related projects. Prehistoric surveys by Bar-Yosef and Phillips (1977; also see Bar-Yosef and Goren 1980) in North Sinai, and Marks (1976–83) in the Negev, were clearly multidisciplinary, incorporating basic culture history, as well as social, economic, and ecological perspectives, into their conception and analyses (also Goring-Morris 1987). Rothenberg (1972), working in the southern Negev and South Sinai, deliberately eschewed standard periodization schemes (for example, Rothenberg and Glass 1992), claiming they were misleading for desert societies whose basic continuities were of a different order than in the settled zone.

By the 1980s surveys were more systematic and more rigorous than ever before. This is reflected especially in the Negev Emergency Survey (figure 11.2; see, for example, S. Rosen 1994:11–14; Haiman 1986:12–14; Avni 1992:11–13), but can be seen elsewhere in the ever greater attention paid to issues such as site visibility and formation, site definition criteria, field coverage and sampling, land use patterns, environmental reconstruction (for example, Portugali 1982; Gibson 1995; Finkelstein 1988; Finkelstein, Lederman, and Bunimovitz 1997; Levy 1983; A. Rosen 1986), and theoretical issues such

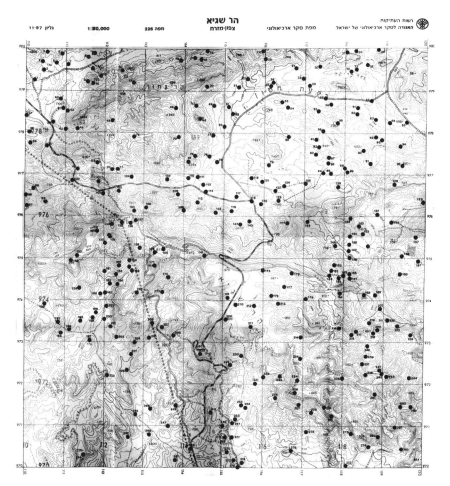

FIGURE 11.2. Archaeological Survey of Israel/Negev Emergency Survey Map of Har Saggi Northeast (Avni 1992). Comparing this survey with Glueck's pioneering work (figure 11.1) well reflects the development of survey methods over thirty years, from the 1950s–1960s to the 1980s–1990s.

as those surrounding the feasibility of an archaeology of pastoral nomadism (for example, S. Rosen 1992). By this period the foreign projects, especially those in Jordan, were working well within settlement archaeology paradigms (for example, Betts 1998; Garrard et al. 1985; Macdonald 1992; Henry 1995). Even in the peripheral regions, however, the biblical account continued to play a significant, if reduced, role in analysis (for example, Anati 1986).

Given the above outline, the development of survey and settlement archaeology in the three areas can be compared. Clearly, the general adoption of settlement archaeology as a theoretical approach, independent of some specific culture history, occurred latest in the Levant.

At first glance, the primary variable that seems to affect the lag in adoption of settlement archaeology as a primary archaeological research theme is texts. The more powerful the mythological narrative in its particular cultural and political milieu, the more archaeological energy is devoted to engaging it. Thus, in the absence of engaged texts in America (as least insofar as European archaeologists were concerned), the adoption of settlement archaeology is early. In Greece, with Homer, it is somewhat later, and in the "Land of the Bible" it is later still. It is significant in this context to note the developing schism in Maya archaeology between the newly emerging text-based archaeology and the more traditional nontext-derived framework. For an anthropological archaeologist working in Israel, there is a strange irony in viewing nontext-based archaeology as traditional and as part of the "establishment," manning the barricades against an "upstart" archaeology driven by the newly deciphered Maya political-historical narratives (for example, Coe 1992:271–274, but see Fash and Sharer 1991 for a less extreme perspective).

Texts are not the entire story, so to speak. The differing roles of foreign (nonlocal) and Paleolithic and Neolithic archaeology have also affected the adoption of settlement archaeology as a theoretical framework. The archaeologies described by both Cherry and Stanish are foreign archaeologies. The fieldwork and publications were the products of expeditions whose conceptions derive from Western European and North American academia. As such they are divorced from the concerns of local culture and reflect agendas not necessarily germane or relevant to local needs or historical perceptions. This is not necessarily a bad thing (unless there is a serious conflict with local needs), but it does constitute a difference.

The Israeli case is different. From the 1950s archaeology in Israel has been dominated by a local cadre of archaeologists whose research agenda was dictated by the needs and concerns of a larger society, in essence those of building a national identity (for example, Zerubavel 1995). This is hardly an unusual situation, but it stands in some contrast to the agendas set by foreign expeditions. The transition to larger theoretical perspectives, including those incorporating settlement archaeology, were embedded in the maturation of Israeli academia, part and parcel of the transformations of Israeli society from a developing nation to a developed one. It is beyond the scope of this paper (not to mention the author's competence) to delve into the nature of these transformations, but it is clear that the cultural symbol systems transformed as well. The role of the Bible and biblical archaeology in defining national identity is no longer pervasive, and hence the rise of new theoretical paradigms. The increasing integration of Israeli academia into a larger world provides a primary source for these new frameworks.

The role of Paleolithic and Neolithic archaeology is significant as well. In the absence of texts, Stone Age archaeology in the Old World developed a set of theoretical frameworks more universalist than Near Eastern and Classical archaeology, in this sense more similar to archaeology in the New World. This universalism, essentially variations on evolutionary themes, fostered greater cross-regional comparison than that evident in the historical archaeologies. In turn, the integration of prehistoric and historic archaeologies in Israeli departments of archaeology, and the maturation of a generation of prehistorians, especially in the 1980s, has effected the adoption of some of the methods and goals of prehistoric archaeology into the study of later periods (for example, Levy 1995).

Having achieved some "modern" status for survey and settlement archaeology, the issue of future directions has both its technical and social aspects. The ever increasing sophistication of our technologies, from GIS and computer applications to remote sensing methods, has resulted in an ever increasing demand for both fine-grained data and more extensive coverage (that is, larger samples). The technical improvements have been, and will continue to be, accompanied by new theoretical directions. In a sense, these kinds of advances are to be expected.

Moreover, we can anticipate major changes in the social aspects of settlement and survey archaeology. A trend toward increasing local roles in survey archaeology is not only inevitable but ought to be actively encouraged by foreign projects. The ability of local archaeologists to immerse themselves in the data sets, including the "gray literature," and the ease of access to the landscape are significant advantages enjoyed by "natives." The integration of local perspectives and sensibilities into theoretical frameworks ought to increase our range of theoretical tools. Partnerships, joint projects, and the integration of local students and volunteers cannot but be profitable for all involved, both economically and in terms of the substance of the research.

CHAPTER 12

The History and Future Prospects of Paleolithic Archaeology in Greece

CURTIS RUNNELS

Introduction

This essay discusses the history and current state of Paleolithic archaeology in Greece and attempts to assess its future prospects. The exploration of the Greek Paleolithic was hindered in the beginning by an outmoded research model that focused on caves and gave little attention to open-air sites. This model was largely abandoned in the 1980s for a new paradigm of regional survey and land-use studies based loosely on the catchment analysis of Eric Higgs and Claudio Vita-Finzi, which put open-air sites and regional settlement patterns at the center of analysis. The new research model is severely limited, however, by antiquities laws based on the nineteenth-century practice of excavating individual cave sites.

The systematic investigation of the early Stone Age in the Aegean, which began in the 1930s, is of comparatively recent origin. The origins of early Stone Age archaeology in Europe, however, can be dated from the publication in 1865 of Sir John Lubbock's *Pre-Historic Times* (Lubbock 1865), which synthesized the findings of the earliest generation of prehistoric archaeologists and, among other innovations, introduced the terms "Paleolithic" and "Neolithic" to the literature. Paleolithic archaeology spread quickly, with excavations first in Western Europe (France, Germany, Great Britain) and then in the Iberian peninsula, Italy, the Balkans, North Africa, and the Near East. It is a curious fact of history that Greece was almost entirely neglected during this early period. The earliest reference to the existence of a Stone Age in Greece of which I am aware is a pamphlet published in Athens by the historian George Finlay (Finlay 1869), a copy of which is in my possession. In this small work Finlay described and illustrated

ΠΑΡΑΤΗΡΗΣΕΙΣ

ΕΠΙ ΤΗΣ ΕΝ

ΕΛΒΕΤΙΑ, ΚΑΙ ΕΛΛΑΔΙ

ΠΡΟΪΣΤΟΡΙΚΗΣ ΑΡΧΑΙΟΛΟΓΙΑΣ

ΥΠΟ

ΓΕΩΡΓΙΟΥ ΦΙΝΛΑΫ.

EN AΘHNAIΣ.

ΤΥΠΟΙΣ ΛΑΚΩΝΙΑΣ

1869.

FIGURE 12.1. Title page of George Finlay's pamphlet *Observations on Prehistoric Archaeology in Switzerland and Greece* published in Athens in 1869, a groundbreaking article marking the beginning of research on the Stone Age in Greece.

celts and flaked stone tools from his own collections, some of which were gathered as early as 1836 from Attica, Euboea, the Cyclades, and the Peloponnese (figure 12.1). The ground stone celts and the flaked stone artifacts illustrated in this work include types that are clearly Neolithic (figures 12.2 through 12.5). This pamphlet is likely to be unfamiliar to most readers. I have been unable to locate any reference to this work in the writings of prehistorians, either Greeks or foreigners, and a search of the National Union Catalogue located only three copies of the pamphlet in major research libraries in the United States. Given its rarity, it is perhaps not out of place in this introduction to say something about the content of this pioneering work.

By way of introduction, Finlay discusses the references to prehistoric artifacts found in the writings of early travelers and antiquarians such as Colonel William Leake. An example of the artifacts noted by these travelers

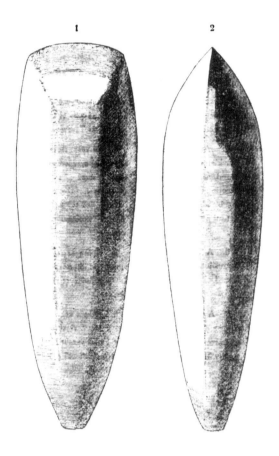

FIGURE 12.2. Drawings of a Neolithic celt (ground stone axe) from Finlay's 1869 pamphlet. It is perhaps the first illustration of a pre-Bronze Age lithic artifact of this type from Greece.

are the obsidian pieces picked up on the tumulus at Marathon and interpreted as the arrowheads of "Ethiopian stone" which Herodotus said were used by some contingents of the Persian army in the fifth century BC. After this introduction, Finlay turns to the recent excavation by Ferdinand Keller of the famous Swiss Neolithic lake dwellings. At the time the Swiss Neolithic sites were the most famous Stone Age sites next to the Paleolithic sites of the Dordogne Valley in France. Finlay describes the Swiss lake dwellings in some detail in order to establish the general character of the Swiss Neolithic material culture. After describing the principal characteristics of the Neolithic culture, he turns to the ground and flaked stone tools from his own collection. He describes the celts and the flaked stone artifacts and notes their evident similarity to the artifacts from the Swiss Neolithic sites. Based on this comparison he concludes, "Oudemia amphivolia, oti kai en

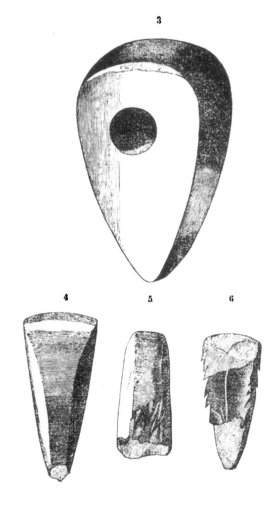

FIGURE 12.3. Drawings of celts from Finlay's 1869 pamphlet. The lithic artifacts illustrated here were evidently collected by Finlay himself from sites in central Greece and Attica. The shaft-hole axe (no. 3) is a Middle Bronze Age type, which Finlay could not distinguish from the earlier Neolithic specimens at this early stage of research.

Elladi uperxe lithine periodos" ([There is] no doubt, that a stone age also existed in Greece) (Finlay 1869:17).

Finlay includes a list of sites where he believes prehistoric remains may be found in Greece, based partly on the discovery of actual artifacts and partly on the occurrence of certain sites in myth and ancient texts (for example, Homer and Herodotus). He astutely observes that numerous and substantial mounds of earth are to be found in Greece and Macedonia (meaning the modern Greek province), and he predicts that they would produce further evidence of the Stone Age if excavated (Finlay 1869:19). Although Finlay was concerned only with the Neolithic in this tract, the pamphlet should have alerted archaeologists to the potential of finding evidence of the Paleolithic in Greece.

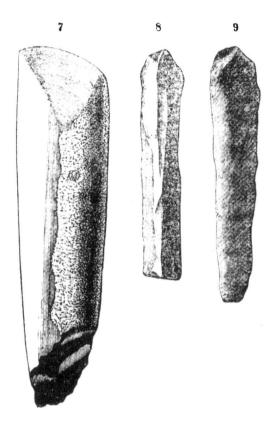

FIGURE 12.4.
Drawings of a
Neolithic celt and
obsidian blades from
Finlay's 1869
pamphlet. Finlay
based his attribution of
these artifacts to a pre-
Classical Stone Age
on the basis of their
similarity with lithics
excavated by Keller in
the Neolithic lake
dwellings in
Switzerland.

It is hard to explain, therefore, the considerable gap that exists between the beginning of prehistoric archaeology in Europe in the 1860s and the beginning of Paleolithic archaeology in Greece in the 1960s. It should have been evident to Finlay's contemporaries, at least those familiar with the new field of archaeology in Europe, that his finds were definite evidence of prehistoric cultures existing in Greece. It is difficult to determine why this information was not acted upon, and why a long interval of time was to pass before the systematic and scientific study of the Stone Age in Greece got under way. That this pamphlet was published in Greek and not widely distributed among European scholars certainly lessened its effectiveness in attracting scholarly attention to these finds, but this is not a sufficient explanation for the slow start of Stone Age archaeology in Greece. More than thirty years elapsed before there was an excavation of a Neolithic site, and another thirty years before the first excavation of a Paleolithic site.

This surprising gap in archaeological activity does not refer, of course, to the considerable level of activity in the field of Bronze Age archaeology that followed Schliemann's initial discoveries at Mycenae, Tiryns, Orchomenos, and elsewhere. The success in the exploration of the Greek Bronze Age was due to archaeologists trained in classics and art history, who belonged to the emerging field of Classical archaeology, itself derived from a tradition different from the prehistoric archaeology of the European Stone Age (for example, Dyson 1998:1–21). It is generally acknowledged that prehistoric archaeology emerged in Europe from an entirely different historical tradition based on Quaternary geology (Daniel 1963:38–59; Trigger 1989:87–102; Schnapp 1996:275–289), which for the purposes of the current argument is considered a distinct tradition with aims different from those of Aegean prehistory as it is usually regarded, viz. as being chiefly concerned with the Bronze Age. In this essay, the prehistoric archaeology being discussed is the archaeology of the early Stone Age (that is, the Paleolithic, which, for the sake of economy in this essay, includes the Mesolithic).

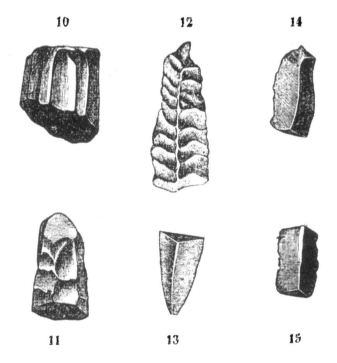

FIGURE 12.5. Drawings of Neolithic (or perhaps Early Bronze Age) obsidian artifacts from Finlay's 1869 pamphlet. The artifacts illustrated include blade cores (nos. 10, 11), a crested blade (lame à crête, no. 12), and fragments of blades (nos. 13–15). The lithics shown in figures 12.4 and 12.5 are perhaps the first flaked stone artifacts from Greece to be recognized as such and accurately illustrated in a scientific publication.

Noting the different historical traditions of Paleolithic and Bronze Age archaeology does not provide a sufficient explanation for the evident neglect of the Greek Stone Age from 1869 to 1962 when the first archaeological project aimed specifically at the investigation of the Greek Paleolithic was initiated by Eric Higgs of the University of Cambridge (G. Bailey 1992; Runnels 1995). Higgs was evidently the first archaeologist trained in the European tradition of Paleolithic archaeology to choose Greece for investigation. Why was Higgs the first? Almost every neighboring country was the object of Paleolithic research before Greece, and I am unaware of any political, economic, or scientific reason why Greece was overlooked. One can argue, as I have done (Runnels 1995), that the rich Classical record somehow played a part in drawing attention away from the Paleolithic, but the same could be said for Italy, where the tradition of Paleolithic research was nevertheless established much earlier (Peet 1909). Perhaps the effect of the nineteenth-century model of Paleolithic research was a factor. This model targeted caves for excavation because they were thought to preserve datable stratification. Open-air sites were regarded as too disturbed by postdepositional factors to be of much use (Sackett 2000). As Greece has few caves or rock shelters, it would have been an unattractive area for fieldwork from the point of view of archaeologists used to the riches of the French Paleolithic cave sites. Perhaps these considerations also affected the research conducted by Greek archaeologists. Further research may throw light on this matter, but for the present it is safest to say that explanations for the delayed beginning of Paleolithic studies in Greece still elude us.

Of the two divisions of the Stone Age identified by Lubbock, only the Paleolithic had a slow start in Greece. The Neolithic was not neglected. Some thirty years after Finlay, from 1901 to 1906, B. Stais and Christos Tsountas carried out systematic excavations of Neolithic sites in Thessaly at Dimini and Sesklo (Gallis 1979), and the publication of these excavations by Tsountas in 1908 marks an important moment in Greek prehistory. The pioneering work of Stais and Tsountas has been carried on in a more or less uninterrupted fashion to the present day and has entered a mature phase of research, with numerous ongoing surveys, excavations, individual studies, detailed catalogs of sites, and full reviews of the period (for example, Andreou, Fotiadis, and Kotsakis 1996; Demoule and Perlès 1993; Gallis 1992; Papathanassopoulos 1996).

The Discovery of the Paleolithic in Greece

The recognition and investigation of the Paleolithic (and Mesolithic) lagged far behind that of the Neolithic. The first excavations of Paleolithic sites of which we have definite knowledge were carried out by the speleologist Adalbert Markovits at Zaimis Cave (Corinthia) and Ulbrich Cave (Argolid) in the 1930s and by R. Stampfuss at Seidi Cave (Boeotia) in the 1940s (Kourtessi-Philappakis 1986; Perlès 1987:202–229; Runnels 1995). Their work, however, was ignored and all but forgotten for thirty years, perhaps because Markovits published his finds in Greek in regional speleological journals, and Stampfuss was an officer in a wartime army of occupation. Although the Seidi report was published in a German periodical, the finds were removed from Greece, and the entire episode was forgotten in the troubled aftermath of World War II. The research of Markovits and Stampfuss was recalled and these facts made known only in the 1960s when the modern period of Paleolithic research began (Runnels 1995; Weinberg 1970). The first large project, and the most significant undertaking from the point of view of the scope of the project and the scale of the surveys and excavations, was the work in Epirus by Eric Higgs beginning in 1962 (G. Bailey 1992).

Higgs's excavations at Kokkinopilos, Asprochaliko, and Kastritsa were followed in the mid-1960s by detailed and pathbreaking reports published in international journals and widely circulated. Higgs's work in Epirus, particularly his innovative collaboration with the geologist Claudio Vita-Finzi, introduced to Greece the concepts of site catchment analysis and the study of settlement patterns and human land use on a regional scale. These approaches have been very influential, especially when combined with cultural ecology in anthropology, and are arguably the basis for much of the regional survey work that took place in the 1970s to the 1990s (Cherry 1994; Jameson, Runnels, and van Andel 1994:1–12; Runnels 2000).

New projects followed quickly or, in some cases, coincided with Higgs's work. First came the chance discoveries of Paleolithic artifacts in Thessaly, the Argolid, Elis, and Corfu (G. Bailey 1992; Runnels 1995), discoveries that were given a major fillip by the publication of a fossilized hominid cranium from Petralona in the Chalkidiki in 1960. Excavations followed in the 1960s and 1970s (see G. Bailey 1992, Runnels 1995, and Weinberg 1970 for summaries and references). Jameson and Bialor investigated a number of rock shelters and caves in the Argolid. Ludwig Reisch conducted salvage excavations at the deeply stratified cave at Kephalari, and Augustus Sordinas explored the Upper Paleolithic Grava Cave in Corfu. In Boeotia, G. Freund reinvestigated the Seidi Cave. The most significant project, however, and the longest running, was the excavation of Franchthi Cave in the Argolid, which began in 1967 under the direction of T. W. Jacobsen and continued until 1979. Finally, in the same year that the Franchthi project was drawing to a close, a team led by G. N. Bailey returned to Epirus to resume the research program begun by Higgs, which had lapsed in the late 1960s. The new

Paleolithic research in Epirus concentrated on the restudy of Higgs's excavation materials, combined with new surveys and the excavation of the Upper Paleolithic rock shelter at Klithi (G. Bailey 1992, 1997).

Regional Surveys and Interdisciplinary Research in the Paleolithic

The first phase of Paleolithic research in the 1960s focused on the excavation of caves and rock shelters along the lines familiar from nineteenth-century practice. In recent decades, new methods have had a profound effect on Paleolithic research. Since 1970 excavations in most regions of Greece have been supplemented by intensive regional survey. The research design behind most of these surveys calls for a diachronic approach to the study of human settlement and land use, and as a consequence, the search for Paleolithic and Mesolithic sites was usually included, at least theoretically, in the goals of most surveys. Search teams are usually instructed to look for lithic artifacts as they would Greek or Roman sherds (for an early example, see Jameson, Runnels, and van Andel 1994:214–224, 326–340). While this is a step in the right direction, this method is impractical. Paleolithic and Mesolithic sites are very rarely discovered in surveys employing the technique of field walking, with groups of people walking between tightly spaced lines. Early prehistoric sites are widely scattered over vast tracts of landscape as a consequence of the large catchment areas required by foragers. Early sites are also disproportionately affected by postdepositional site formation processes, such as erosion and burial, that tend to make their discovery very difficult (G. Bailey 1992; Runnels and van Andel 1993; Runnels et al. 1999). By the mid-1980s, it was apparent that search techniques would have to be modified in order to detect Paleolithic and Mesolithic sites. New techniques were especially necessary if open-air sites, as opposed to caves and rock shelters, were to be discovered and inventoried. Caves are rare in Greece, and were occupied mostly in the Upper Paleolithic during the last glacial maximum (ca. 20,000 to 18,000 years ago). The study of the Paleolithic, therefore, required a research design that would maximize the identification of small open-air sites, findspots, and scatters, usually marked by small numbers of stone tools and often highly disturbed by postdepositional formation processes.

The new techniques developed in the 1980s (for example, Pope, Runnels, and Ku 1984; Runnels 1988; Runnels and van Andel 1993) focused on the Paleolithic and Mesolithic and required close consultation among archaeologists familiar with the archaeological artifacts and geomorphologists who interpreted the landforms to be searched with a view to identifying the areas most likely to preserve early sites. This approach attempted to maximize the probability of finding early sites by identifying locations or features of the landscape (such as redbeds or river terraces) where early sites were most likely to be preserved. In this way the new technique resembled the topographic survey methods used before 1970 that focused attention on "hot spots," such as hilltops, in the search for Bronze Age remains. The new Paleolithic surveys were often carried out as part of other regional survey projects but differed from them in the way that prior knowledge of the special circumstances surrounding the preservation and discovery of early sites was used to modify search strategies. As a result of these changes, specialized surveys were extremely productive in the 1980s and 1990s in bringing to light large numbers of Paleolithic open-air sites and vastly enriching the available database (G. Bailey et al. 1999; Runnels 1995). The importance of open-air sites for interpreting the past has been systematically underrated by a prejudice for the stratified sequences to be found in caves and rock shelters. This is an unrealistic holdover from the nineteenth century when the emphasis in Paleolithic archaeology was on the discovery and excavation of such sites, a research design inherited from Quaternary geology (Sackett 2000). In those parts of Europe affected by glaciation, caves were thought to preserve the intact stratification essential in the days when typological series and stratigraphic position were the only available techniques for organizing and dating Paleolithic materials. Open-air sites were thought to be too disturbed by intractable taphonomic processes, such as solifluction and cryoturbation, to be of any use.

The focus on caves eventually gave way in the relatively stable and arid Mediterranean lands (including southern France), which are rich in open-air sites with well-preserved, stratified, and datable Paleolithic deposits. The interest in surface sites as major sources of evidence about the past gained ground partly as the result of research on open-air sites in Africa, where they provide the only evidence for the early Paleolithic (Klein 2000). Early Paleolithic open-air sites in Africa have major taphonomic problems like their European counterparts which had to be solved before the sites could be used to interpret the past. In the absence of rich cave deposits, archaeologists set about solving many of these taphonomic problems (Schick and Toth 1993: 187–224). The progress in taphonomy was helped along by the development of a new interest in recent (that is, Quaternary) geologic processes such as erosion and soil formation (Jameson, Runnels, and van Andel 1994:149–213; Runnels 2000) and the development of dating techniques such as radiocarbon, uranium series, and thermoluminescence. As a result of these studies, open-air sites have become the main source of data for understanding the early Paleolithic in many parts of the world.

In Greece, open-air Paleolithic sites are important for investigating human activity and are vital components in studying prehistoric land use on a regional scale. Breakthroughs in understanding site formation processes, stratification, and the technology of dating open-air sites have greatly enhanced their importance for prehistorians (Pope, Runnels, and Ku 1984; Runnels et al. 1999). Some archaeologists remain unconvinced that open-air sites and surface scatters can be studied with profit, but this is simply the result of the dominance of an obsolete nineteenth-century paradigm. For understanding the Paleolithic, particularly the Lower and Middle Paleolithic, open-air sites present perhaps the most important body of evidence available to prehistorians. The new research model requires access to large geographic areas and new techniques for locating and investigating open-air sites, and consequently a change in the education and training of archaeologists. If the excavation of rock shelters and caves was the focus of Greek Paleolithic archaeology from roughly 1930 (Markovits) to 1979 (the end of the Franchthi Cave excavation), the 1980s and 1990s were dominated by the exploration of open-air sites, although caves would, and will, continue to be studied, as can be seen by a perusal of the papers from a 1994 conference in Ioannina on the Paleolithic (G. Bailey et al. 1999) and other sources. The number of caves studied after 1980 is about 8 in my admittedly rough computation, while more than 15 survey projects have brought to light over 150 Paleolithic and Mesolithic open-air sites. These numbers support the hypothesis that Paleolithic archaeology in Greece has undergone a major shift in research strategy in the last twenty years, marking a sharp and irreversible break with the nineteenth-century paradigm of Paleolithic archaeology.

Future Prospects

It is clear from what has been said that the forty years from 1960 to 2000 have seen much progress in the area of Paleolithic and Mesolithic studies. Paleolithic sites of all periods have been identified from Thrace in the north to the Mani in the south and on some of the major islands such as Corfu and Kefallinia. Mesolithic sites have been excavated at Franchthi Cave, Sidari, and Theopetra Cave, and new sites have been identified in the Argolid and Epirus. Major excavation reports on Franchthi Cave (Jacobsen and Farrand 1987; van Andel and Sutton 1987; Perlès 1987, 1990; Shackleton 1988; Wilkinson and Duhon 1990; Hansen 1991; Talalay 1993; Vitelli 1993, 1999; Farrand 2000) and Klithi Cave (G. Bailey 1997) have done much to establish the stratigraphy, typology, and chronology of the Upper Paleolithic and Mesolithic. These reports outline the methodological approach to the study of these periods while providing a foundation for future excavation work.

Regional surveys and the study of open-air Paleolithic and Mesolithic sites grew rapidly from 1980 to the present. Paradoxically, while demonstrably very successful, this research has an uncertain future. The reasons for this are no doubt very complex, but some of the possible factors at work can be identified. It is my prediction that, unless some way is found to bring about a solution to these problems, Paleolithic research in Greece is likely to be unproductive.

The most important problem facing the field is the lack of jobs for qualified specialists in Paleolithic archaeology in Greece and abroad. In Greece there are no positions for Paleolithic archaeologists in the universities, and laboratory and museum positions for specialists in lithic and faunal analysis are few and far between, whether in the universities or the Archaeological Service. This problem affects prehistoric research in almost every country, but in Greece the design most needed for Paleolithic research also runs counter to prevailing antiquities laws. These laws, originally drafted in 1834, were based on Italian legislation concerning Rome. They were revised in 1899 and again in 1932, but the 1932 code is still in force and is chiefly a "codification of miscellaneous pre-existing legislative texts" (Dimacopoulou and Lapourtas 1995:319). The existing Greek antiquities laws reflect the concern of early archaeologists for the protection of individual sites and the control of antiquities exportation (Kardulias 1994). I believe that the restrictions these laws impose on foreign archaeologists and members of the Archaeological Service of the Greek Ministry of Culture prevent any significant reorientation of research in Paleolithic archaeology.

The future direction of this discipline calls for research designs focusing on the study of human settlement and land use within large regions by interdisciplinary groups of archaeologists, geomorphologists, and other specialists. The sort of regional projects required to study open-air sites should have several levels of analysis that include, at a minimum, survey, surface collection, sample extraction from large numbers of sites and findspots for dating and soil analyses, and remote sensing work at multiple localities. Augering, shovel testing, and test excavation of many small sites is especially desirable. The research projects allowed by the current antiquities laws, with their emphasis on excavations at individual sites rather than the study of regions, make such projects very difficult or impossible to carry out. In the absence of significant new legislation designed to permit research projects using the new research paradigm, with large numbers of scholars carrying out multidisciplinary projects with different levels of research involving numerous sites, significant progress cannot be expected.

The organization of the Greek Archaeological Service in the Ministry of Culture also presents a problem, particularly in the overlapping jurisdictions of the supervising authorities (*ephoreia* in Greek). The archaeological ephoreias overlap the boundaries of the administrative prefectures of regional

governments and are themselves overlapped by other archaeological entities (Kardulias 1994). The so-called super ephoreias, such as the Ephoreia of
Caves and Paleoanthropology, cut across the boundaries of all other ephoreias responsible for prehistoric, classical, and Byzantine archaeology, and they
create wasteful overlap, confusion, and sometimes interdepartmental jealou-
sies that conflict with strictly scientific goals. Any significant reform of the
antiquities laws must also embrace the structure of the Antiquities Service
that administers these laws. Finally, there are historical rivalries in Greece
among the members of the foreign archaeological missions, universities,
Archaeological Service, and private institutions, such as the Archaeological
Society of Athens, that only add to the confusion.

Conclusion

Research on the early Stone Age prehistory of Greece began late when compared with similar studies elsewhere in Europe, owing at least partly to the
prevalence of an old research design directed toward the study of single
caves. Prehistoric research changed after 1980, largely as a result of the
expansion of regional surveys and the study of open-air sites which extended
the range and depth of prehistoric studies and led to the abandonment of the
nineteenth-century model of cave research. Much progress was made in the
decades after 1960, but research in the 1990s has slowed to a crawl. The ris-
ing interest in Paleolithic archaeology in Greece among archaeologists both
at home and abroad has not been matched by changes in the systems of education, legislation, or administration of archaeology by the government. I am
forced to conclude that if the antiquities legislation of 1932, which is itself a
product of nineteenth-century thinking, is not redrafted with twenty-first-
century scientific research methods and goals in mind, future progress in
Paleolithic archaeology in the short term is doubtful.

Acknowledgments

I wish to thank the organizers of the Cotsen Seminar, particularly John Papadopoulos, Richard Leventhal, and Sarah Morris, for the invitation to participate in the conference and to submit this essay for inclusion in the
conference proceedings. It is also a pleasure to thank Daniel Pullen for bringing the pamphlet by George Finlay to my attention in 1991, Ricardo Elia for
advice on the references, and Priscilla Murray for reading an early draft of
the essay.

CHAPTER 13

Exploring the Paleolithic in the Open Air: A View from the Perigord

JAMES R. SACKETT

I applaud the impressive efforts of Curtis Runnels to recover open-air sites dating to Old Stone Age times in Greece. Cave sites (most of which in fact are rock shelters) have always been favored by Paleolithic specialists because they often incorporate multiple and stratigraphically well-segregated artifactual horizons, because their deposits can preserve organic remains such as hearth debris and butchered animal bones, and because their archaeology comes neatly packaged by nature itself. But the so-called cave people of the Old Stone Age, like everybody else since, spent most of their time in the open air. As a consequence, the thousand or two generations of Paleolithic folk who lived in what we now call Greece presumably left an archaeological record outside the caves whose bulk exceeds by several orders of magnitude that which is to be found inside them.

Yet, while that record may be nearly ubiquitous to the landscape in which he works, the challenge Runnels faces in getting at it is, as he well knows, not one that can be met satisfactorily by the methods field archaeologists conventionally employ in exploring later, more accessible periods of culture history. The reasons are due to the empirical makeup of the Paleolithic open-air record itself, matters of a concrete and practical kind that must, I think, be wrestled with successfully before there is much profit in attacking such questions as the nature of Stone Age demography, economics, or social organization.

My own experience with the Paleolithic in the open air took place in a rather different, and undoubtedly more user-friendly, archaeological environment than the one in which Runnels labors. This is a large and varied group of open sites in the Neuvic sector of the Perigord in southwestern France whose exploration was pioneered by the eminent amateur prehistorian Jean

Gaussen (see Gaussen 1980; Sackett 1988, 1999). Many of the conclusions I came to about Paleolithic research in the open air as a result of this experience are probably relevant to Runnels's field situation, and, indeed, they seem to confirm most of the ones he himself has drawn. Here is what came to mind as I reviewed his most informative contribution to the session.

The Paleolithic dates back to Pleistocene times, the geological epoch that immediately precedes our own. Its open-air sites therefore are ordinarily found in a reasonably intact and undisturbed condition only where they happen to lie beneath what may loosely be referred to as the "topsoil" that has been formed during modern post-Pleistocene times in all but the deserty areas of the Old World. Thus any sites in such areas whose artifactual contents are visible at the surface of the ground, that is, on or in the topsoil, are sites that have largely been destroyed either by natural agencies such as erosion, cultural agencies such as farming, or by some combination of the two. Their scientific value is compromised because they have probably lost whatever horizontal organization they once possessed, along with, thanks to curious passersby, a good part of their more distinctive, and hence diagnostic, artifactual content.

Furthermore, even when their industrial (or "cultural") affiliations can be identified, surface sites still fail to constitute a representative sampling of the nature and variety of industrial phases actually represented in the archaeological record of any given region. Among other reasons, this is because the older archaeological horizons are simply less likely to have become incorporated into the topsoil, in part by virtue of their priority in the depositional sequence and in part because they tend to be associated with topographic situations (for example, the banks of streams that subsequently changed their course) that now lie buried under the modern landscape.

To be sure, the disturbed sites one encounters during the course of a walking survey deserve to be mapped, sampled, and recorded. But the field worker's ultimate goal, and much greater challenge, must be to find the intact sites that lie hidden beneath the surface, that is, sites of the kind that will fill out our knowledge of the regional industrial sequence and, even more importantly, provide a worthwhile subject for enlightened archaeological investigation of Paleolithic lifeways. How are these to be found? To my knowledge, unless and until some breakthrough is achieved in remote sensing technology, we have but three methods at our disposal, all of which are pretty hit-or-miss.

The first is to conduct test excavations from a surface that already contains a destroyed site, on the assumption that a locality we know to have been occupied at one particular time was likely to have been favored for occupation at some earlier particular time or times. Usually the attempt fails, more often than not because the topsoil itself simply constitutes a reworking of all that remains, thanks to erosion or cultivation or whatever, of what were once the Pleistocene soils of that locality. But occasionally the results can be fairly spectacular, as we had the luck to find at the Neuvic group site appropriately named Solvieux. Here there exists a Pleistocene colluvium that can extend to a depth of up to 3 m below the surface and which in many localities incorporates a multileveled archaeological deposit rivaling that of most rock shelters in its wealth and variety.

The second method is to put down deep test excavations at a locality that appears to be artifactually sterile at the surface but which, nonetheless, the researcher's cultivated knowledge of the archaeological landscape leads him or her to believe warrants a shot-in-the-dark testing effort. Initially, this method may have a lower success rate than the first, but it does pay off occasionally and, of course, holds out greater promise as the researcher progressively cultivates an intuitive sense of archaeological place.

Let it be stressed that the demands made by both of these methods far exceed those of the conventional field-walking survey. As Runnels's own work illustrates so well, below-the-surface investigation requires a solid working knowledge of local geomorphology. It also requires, as our work in the Neuvic sector illustrates, a major commitment to excavation. The probing, auguring, shovel sampling, and other quick-and-dirty methods advocated by archaeologists who work in Neolithic and Bronze Age deposits are entirely inadequate for the job. Due to the nature of the deposits involved and the sampling problems that attend them, the task calls for labor-intensive and technologically demanding archaeological exploration that must be conducted at several different points over a locality before one can make reasonably trustworthy claims about what does, or does not, lie deeper down (see Sackett 1999:1–45, 313–316 for a detailed discussion). In such cases, "testing" is only a euphemism for what is in fact a demanding and areally extensive business of vertical stratigraphic profiling that often necessitates the controlled excavation of tens of cubic meters of deposit, and sometimes more.

The third method for discovering intact open-air deposits may sound in theory like a compromise between the first two, but in practice it is altogether different. It entails finding at the surface only very minor evidences of "fresh" stone artifacts (that is, flints whose patination and lack of plow-marks and other signs of bruising show they have only recently been brought to light) whose presence hints that a substantial archaeological deposit may lie buried, still intact, in the immediate vicinity. For example, recent plowing of a hillside may bring to light fresh artifacts downslope but not upslope, suggesting the existence of an archaeological horizon bedded at such an angle that it remains well below the surface, and hence undisturbed, in the higher reaches of the locality. Or a new roadcut may expose a hitherto hidden deposit, as may digging a house foundation, an irrigation ditch, or a latrine. The surface hint may involve no more than a single piece of flint brought up in the bowl of a tree uprooted by the wind, which is precisely how the Neuvic group's most striking and distinctive open station, Le Cerisier, came to light (Gaussen 1980:103–126).

Now, it was by means of this third method, if it can be called such, that most of the important Neuvic sector open-air stations were discovered. But it bears stressing that these are exactly the kinds of discoveries that are unlikely to be made during the course of field-walking surveys like those designed and conducted by archaeologists working in post-Paleolithic periods. For they are a matter of serendipity, opportunity, an intimate and day-to-day familiarity with the landscape and the people who work it, freedom of entry to private property, and, to be sure, a cultivated eye for the odd flint. We are referring, of course, to the métier of the local amateur prehistorian whose knowledge of, and access to, what happens on the ground over the hundred or so square kilometers that make up his or her own domain can never be equaled by a professional archaeologist housed elsewhere in some university, museum, or research facility. Such people play a key role in French Paleolithic research (as they do as well, of course, in much of the rest of Europe), since what their avocation actually amounts to is a kind of ongoing, year-round archaeological survey by those who happen to know the landscape best. They, and not some more formal kind of organized survey, are the professional's best link to the archaeological record.

All this seems to bring us to some rather sobering conclusions. It takes much more than the conventional sort of walking survey to explore an open-air Paleolithic landscape in a part of the world that is covered by post-Pleistocene topsoil. The job cannot really be done adequately without intensive test excavation pursued in the light of intelligence gathered from archaeologically knowledgeable people already on the ground. When viewed in this perspective, what Runnels is attempting to do nearly verges on the heroic. For he finds himself in a topsoil landscape, but apparently has neither the right to dig, at least in any systematic fashion, nor anyone to talk to, at least in the sense of an in-place cadre of local archaeological informants. (Indeed, it seems that Greece lacks even the critical mass of professional Paleolithic specialists that would be needed to elicit the interest of, and in turn train, such a cadre.) Runnels has chosen the path of a pioneer, laboring to explore a territory that does much to hinder, and little to help, his efforts. His achievement is certainly to be admired, but his task is not to be envied.

CHAPTER 14

Archaeologists and "The Site"

RICHARD G. LESURE

Curtis Runnels's innovative survey strategies have helped reinvigorate Paleolithic and Mesolithic research in Greece and serve as a model for other
regions as well. Much of his description of the state of the discipline in
Greece mirrors the situation of preceramic archaeology in Mexico, where I
work. Despite the major interdisciplinary projects led by MacNeish (1981,
1992) in Tehuacan and Flannery (1968, 1986) in Oaxaca, both of which
devoted considerable resources to the preceramic period and the origins of
agriculture, work on these topics has languished during the last two decades.
Runnels's comments on the failure of standard field-walking survey techniques for recovering Pleistocene or early Holocene sites resonate with the
Mexican case. The highland valleys of Mexico can be thought of as center-
pieces for the success of full-coverage survey in contemporary archaeology,
but these surveys have identified very few preceramic sites. Despite a recent
spate of publications on the origins of agriculture in Mexico, there has been
little new fieldwork on the preceramic (Stark 2000 provides an up-to-date
overview). Most recent publications have a botanical focus, involving
genetic and distributional studies of modern plants or the reanalysis of
archaeological specimens from decades-old excavations. The kinds of specially designed surveys Runnels describes for Greece are only just beginning
in Mexico (for example, Voorhies and Kennett 1995).

An extended commentary on the Paleoindian and Archaic periods of
Mexico is not appropriate here; indeed, it is not the field of my direct interests, which lap up against rather than subsume the preceramic epoch. What I
have chosen to do instead is to select a theme upon which Runnels ends his
discussion—the fetters placed on innovative Paleolithic research by Greek
antiquities laws—and turn the charge back on archaeologists themselves.

My goal is to highlight both some divisions within contemporary archaeology and the value of talking across those divisions.

Greek antiquities laws appear to reify and even fetishize "The Site." Yet archaeologists are guilty of the same sin. That issue was raised by implication in the ironic title for the session in which Runnels's paper and these comments were originally presented: "Below the Site." Is it not laughable to place a Paleolithic locale in the same conceptual category as a Knossos?

Something of a schism between the archaeology of mobile and sedentary peoples is apparent in the divergent demands on and uses made of the concept of site. Certainly, the spaces we live in today are full of fixed boundaries: cities have limits, plots of land are bought and sold. It is hardly surprising that contemporary property relations infuse the treatment of archaeological remains. Site managers want something specific to manage, conservators something definitive to conserve.

The kinds of links we experience today between physical and social boundaries undoubtedly also existed in the ancient past. Cities had walls; rights to property were jealously guarded. This, we might argue, is not a modern conceit but a fundamental feature of settled life. When we pursue the archaeology of settled peoples, it is not completely unreasonable to leave undertheorized the relationship between the site as identified by archaeologists and the town as experienced by ancient inhabitants. Those of us who study sedentary peoples are often casual about using "site" interchangeably to refer either to a set of ancient remains in the present or to a community of people in the past.

For archaeologists studying mobile peoples, such carelessness is completely unacceptable. Sites are palimpsests of repeated short-term occupations, no one of which can ever be isolated. Olorgesaile, with its acres of hand axes that most certainly do not represent an Acheulean metropolis, is an obvious example. An archaeology of mobile peoples has wrestled for several decades with the exceedingly complex relationship among the "sites" it views archaeologically and the social phenomena it seeks to study (Dunnell and Dancy 1983; Foley 1981; Thomas 1975).

What kinds of archaeological approaches are appropriate for the study of mobile peoples who did not identify particular points as homes but instead maintained a generalized relationship with a wider landscape? Our immediate answer might well be: regional survey!—and certainly a regional perspective is fundamental. It is worth recalling, however, Runnels's point about the failure of standard field walking for the recovery of Pleistocene and early Holocene sites, a failure we have seen as well in Mexico, where some of the pioneering efforts at full-coverage regional surveys were undertaken.

Runnels proposes instead the development of specialized survey techniques based on close consultation between archaeologists and geomorphologists. A great variety of such creative interdisciplinary endeavors have become fundamental to archaeological analyses of mobile peoples of the Pleistocene and early Holocene. "Creative" is a key term here. Somehow we need to wring all the social information we can from the fragmentary scraps left to us from these epochs.

But the challenges that lie before a regional archaeology of mobile peoples are surely as much theoretical as methodological. Could it be, for instance, that archaeologists working on mobile hunter-gatherers conceptualize social landscapes—and therefore regional archaeology—in ways fundamentally different from scholars studying agriculturalists (Bettinger 1999: 42–43)? A conceptual framework appropriate for an archaeology of mobile peoples and free from the fetters of The Site may be formulated in a variety of ways (compare Binford 1992 and Dunnell 1992). A useful current in social archaeology has not sought to produce a new theory of the site but has turned instead to the general problem of human mobility. A major dimension of such a theory is, of course, the relationship between mobility patterns and their material traces. In the two decades since Lewis Binford's (1980) important article on collecting and foraging as alternative strategies of mobility, a voluminous literature has accumulated on this topic. In the New World, this growing body of theory has been most extensively applied in North America, but work on preceramic times in Mexico has increasingly referenced this literature as well.

Is there anything that an archaeology of sedentism can draw from current trends in the study of mobile peoples? It is first important to point out that there are major divergences between these two archaeologies, divergences that seem likely to grow. Apparent points of convergence can become arenas of contention. One example is the widely shared recent interest in agency where a divide between what might be called "evolutionary" and "practice" approaches loosely reflects the mobile/sedentary distinction (see Dobres and Robb 2000). The first approach excites the most interest among archaeologists working on more ancient, more mobile peoples, traced across long periods of time; the second tends to appeal to those studying more recent, more sedentary cases, resolvable at shorter time scales (but see Gamble 1998 for an inspiring exception). As each approach increasingly develops its own specialized vocabulary, the two seem likely to drift toward mutual unintelligibility.

Fully acknowledging such inherent theoretical divergences, it nevertheless seems possible to find inspiration for the study of settled life in an increasingly sophisticated archaeology of mobility. First, of course, theories of mobility may be directly relevant to the study of "sedentary" epochs. Even people who had permanent houses crammed with objects may have been more mobile than the archaeological record leads us to assume. Of relevance in the current volume is Whittle's (1996) argument for persistent mobility in Neolithic societies of southeastern Europe. Second, archaeological work on mobility may be of more generalized interest to the study of sedentary peoples as an instance of creative thought beyond the conceptual bounds of The Site. A unifying theme in archaeology is surely the attempt to think creatively beyond the apparently obvious material facts we recover. Successful theoretical specialties are typically founded on some innovative way of thinking about the material record, and the attempt by an archaeology of mobility to think beyond The Site is a good example. The core insights of such specialties can prove refreshing and inspirational to other perspectives in the field, even when they are not of direct substantive relevance. Runnels's work would appear to have this potential for the archaeology of settled life in the Mediterranean. Indeed, I would suggest that Runnels (chapter 12) and, for instance, Palyvou (chapter 15), different as their papers appear, are united in stretching archaeological thinking about The Site in surprising and productive ways.

PART IV

ARCHAEOLOGY AND ARCHITECTURE

CHAPTER 15

Architecture and Archaeology: The Minoan Palaces in the Twenty-First Century

CLAIRY PALYVOU

"Architecture *after* archaeology"—as was the suggested initial title of the paper—is a rather odd statement, for the word "after" seems to imply that there is an end to the task of archaeology and a beginning to that of architecture. Yet the two disciplines go side by side, and the aim of this paper is to discuss architects and archaeologists at work and follow the history of their common involvement.[1] Knossos may serve as an excellent case study, for the 100 years of history of the site reflect the spectacular developments of the twentieth century.

The year 2000 has been a year of celebrations for the centenary of work at Knossos. A celebration of this sort is a ritual in its own right; it is the occasion to reflect on the work of all those people—foremost the pioneers—who devoted their lives to digging and studying so that we today may teach our children at school the early history of the Aegean civilization, and indeed, as Arthur Evans conceived of it, "European" civilization for that matter. Because monuments link us to the past as much as to the future, it is also the occasion to contemplate what we bequeath to those who follow in this perpetual relay race for knowledge.

The Interpretation Process in Archaeology: The Architect's Contribution

Architecture and archaeology are two disciplines quite distinct from each other. They have different tools of thought, different goals, and a very different practice. The work of the architect is literally to construct the future, whereas the work of the archaeologist is to reconstruct, metaphorically, the past.

205

FIGURE 15.1. Archaeologists and architects at work: a, Theodore Fyfe (*after Farnoux 1993:40*); b, Christian Doll (*after Brown 1983:100–101, Plate 54b*); c, Piet de Jong (*after R. Hood 1998:263*); d, Duncan Mackenzie (*after Momigliano 1999:147, Fig. 39*); e, Arthur Evans (*after Farnoux 1993:51*).

When and where do they meet then? They meet halfway at the present, as they bend over a monument with the curiosity of the scholar and the responsibility of the professional (figure 15.1). They meet when the archaeologist starts thinking of the past in terms of the future—how to preserve—and the architect looks back into the past for knowledge and inspiration. But foremost they meet at the common effort to understand the past, in other words to interpret the material remains of a culture and reach out to the human mind and feelings that produced and used this material.

Interpretation is a key word in archaeology (figure 15.2); it is present even before the dig as the reasoning for selecting a place to excavate and throughout

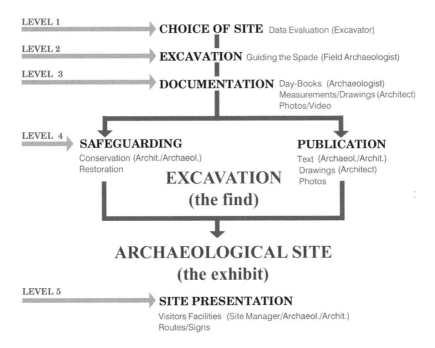

ARCHAEOLOGY
An Interpretation Process

LEVEL 1 → **CHOICE OF SITE** Data Evaluation (Excavator)

LEVEL 2 → **EXCAVATION** Guiding the Spade (Field Archaeologist)

LEVEL 3 → **DOCUMENTATION** Day-Books (Archaeologist)
Measurements/Drawings (Architect)
Photos/Video

LEVEL 4 → **SAFEGUARDING**   **PUBLICATION**
Conservation (Archit./Archaeol.)   Text (Archaeol./Archit.)
Restoration   Drawings (Architect)
EXCAVATION   Photos
(the find)

ARCHAEOLOGICAL SITE
(the exhibit)

LEVEL 5 → **SITE PRESENTATION**
Visitors Facilities (Site Manager/Archaeol./Archit.)
Routes/Signs

FIGURE 15.2. Archaeology: an interpretation process, by C. Palyvou.

the dig in guiding the process of excavation. Interpretation is predominant during the documentation of the dig. And this is usually where the architect comes into the picture. Documentation is the task of the field archaeologist and the architect. Their tools are the daybooks and the drawings, respectively, and they are both equally anxious to record as faithfully as possible what they see. But what one sees is quite subjective and depends largely on how much one knows and therefore can recognize and understand. It is not uncommon for an architect to go back to an early drawing to add or change some details that he/she became aware of, and was subsequently able to see, only after a long acquaintance with the monument. It is also not uncommon, however, for an architect to be summoned only after the dig is over.

Daybooks and drawings are but a third level of interpretation; there are fourth and fifth levels involving preservation and finally publication. This is where it often ends. Site presentation, where applied, is the ultimate interpretation, however. It is the crystallization of all previous levels of scholarly work into a message that has to be passed on to the public. Site presentation is what transforms the dig into an archaeological site—the archaeological find into an exhibit. Yet, in many cases the dig is handed over to the public exactly as the excavator left it—an excavator whose interest in the place may end when he or she reaches bedrock. Trenches are left wide open, heaps of debris are lying around, and of course, there are no signs or other means of guidance whatsoever. A fence and an entrance fee make the difference.[2]

Arthur Evans and His Architects

Evans's (figure 15.1e) work at Knossos was different (the bibliography on Evans's work at Knossos is extensive: see, among others, J. Evans 1943; Brown 1983; Zois 1995; MacEnroe 1995; and Papadopoulos 1997). His approach to interpretation started the other way round, so to speak. Site presentation became important to him soon after he began the dig; this is actually surprising for it was not the norm or even the trend of his time. It is a concept he advanced on his own, primarily as a consequence of his efforts to preserve information about the upper stories he was witnessing as he was digging through the thick layers of debris, and also to protect the ruins from weathering. The idea of site presentation may have derived from the communication flair he developed as a journalist and his socializing nature, and it was surely accentuated by the publicity his finds received from the start.

Evans was a pioneer in more ways than one: he set the foundations for the study of one branch of Aegean prehistory, and he used the most up-to-date technology of the time to preserve the material remains of the culture he was excavating at Knossos. He was also ahead of his time in that, from the very beginning, he called upon the services of competent professionals of various disciplines, particularly architects. "He was one of the first excavators to have a trained architect always on the site" (J. Evans 1943:338)—hardly the case with many digs today.[3] Duncan Mackenzie (figure 15.1d) may have played a role in this. In a letter to Evans, as early as 1902, Mackenzie, the so-called cautious canny highlander (Momigliano 1999), asked that a full-size tracing of architect Theodore Fyfe's plan of the excavation be sent to him, for it would be "very helpful," and he took the opportunity to evoke the importance of working side by side with an architect. Mackenzie wrote:

> From my experience of the architects at Phylakopi, . . . I have long ago come to realize how harmful it is to one's work to be left without this help.

My experience of architects, by-the-bye, is not a small one, during my connection with the British School at Athens I had to do with four of the craft. (Momigliano 1999:161–162)

Theodore Fyfe (1875–1945) was Evans's first architect (figure 15.1a). He was an architectural student with the British School at Athens in 1900. At the School he met David Hogarth, who recommended him to Evans, and soon after he was employed to prepare "architectural plans and drawings" (Evans 1900–1901:1; restoration work is not mentioned as a task). He worked with Evans for five years and in 1905 returned to England to work as an architect. In 1907 he was elected a fellow of the Royal Institute of British Architects, and in 1922 he became director of the newly formed School of Architecture at Cambridge University. He came back to Crete several times, and in 1926 he stayed for a month to help with the drawings.[4]

Fyfe was followed by Christian Doll, also a student of the British School (figure 15.1b). Doll spent five years at Knossos working on architectural plans and drawings, as Fyfe had done, but was also responsible for building the Villa Ariadne for Evans, as well as supervising restoration work. On top of that he had daily administrative work and was also asked regularly to show visitors around the site. The latter included friends, guests, and acquaintances of Evans, as well as other archaeologists (Brown 1983:30–31).

Piet de Jong (1887–1967) was appointed architect in 1922 and worked with Evans until 1932. He remained involved with Knossos to his death, serving as a curator of Knossos for the period 1947–1952 (figure 15.1c). Most of the restoration work took place during his tenure at Knossos (R. Hood 1998; Alexiou 1965:301–302).

F. G. Newton (1878–1924), who had been working as an architect at Ur, visited Knossos briefly and offered his services to Evans for three successive seasons until his premature death while digging at Tell el Amarna in 1924 (A. Evans 1928:158, n. 3). Newton arrived at Knossos coming from Egypt, and it may be no coincidence that Evans "became actively interested in the South road to Egypt" that very year (quoted from a letter by de Jong sent to John Myres dated 1941, in Momigliano 1999:208). Mackenzie had known Newton for a long time. They had worked together in Italy, and later on it was at his suggestion that Newton was appointed architect of the Palestine Exploration Fund (Momigliano 1999:82, 91).

All of these architects have hardly published anything regarding their work at Knossos, and with the exception of Piet de Jong, there is very little written about them.[5] It is basically through the drawings they left behind that we can assess their contribution to Minoan archaeology. Since these drawings have been in constant use for a century by all scholars working on Knossos, it would be useful to evaluate their significance per se. Just as with the writings of archaeologists, the drawings of the architects are, after all, interpretations that are influenced by many factors, foremost of which is the cultural context of the time in which they were produced.

The Drawings

The drawings produced by the four architects, with few exceptions, have been published in *The Palace of Minos* volumes and the Provisional Reports for the years 1900–05 in the *Annual of the British School at Athens*. In Hood and Taylor (1981:13), there is a brief account of these drawings. They are of two main categories: (1) general drawings of the overall excavated area prepared at the end of each season and (2) detailed drawings of special areas and surrounding houses. (The sketches they made for their diaries are not taken into account in this study because, technically speaking, they are not architectural drawings.)

The general drawings are basically versions of the plan of the palace drawn at large scales (1:500 and 1:800 by Fyfe, and 1:250 by Fyfe and Doll). Fyfe also measured and drew in pencil general sections through the site, but these versions were never completed as presentation drawings. Mackenzie praises Fyfe to Evans, in a letter dating to 1902, telling him how absorbed Fyfe became while working with a section looking west, calling the drawing "a monument of work" (Momigliano 1999:164). These sections were published in 1990 by Driessen, and the use he makes of them clearly shows how important they remain (Driessen 1990:10–12).

Evans did not use Fyfe's sections, nor did he ask Doll or de Jong for more sections of this kind. This seems rather odd, for you cannot read space on paper unless you have all three dimensions.[6] Evans's architects of course knew that and drew many sections of various individual parts of the palace, but there is no one general or overall section, to my knowledge, from these early years (for new sections through the site, see Hood and Taylor 1981).

The detailed drawings are plans and sections, as well as isometric drawings, prepared at small scales: 1:20 and 1:10. (I am grateful to Mrs. Vasso Fotou for information about the scales of the original drawings.) The majority of these drawings were published by Evans in the provisional reports and in *The Palace of Minos* volumes. Finally, there are several sketches and the well-known perspectives in color showing restored views of parts of the palace.[7]

Drawings are based on measurements taken in situ. Taking measurements is a difficult task in its own right and determines to a large extent the credibility of a drawing. It is interesting to note that, among the very first tasks before the dig commenced, was the establishment of a proper grid system covering the Kephala hill; soon after, "the first real floor level was discovered and this served as datum point" (Driessen 1990:10).

Doll wrote in his diary that he was worried because his measurements did not always agree with Fyfe's (Brown 1983:30). Though it is not clear what exactly he was referring to, I would say that this was almost to be expected in the sense that there is no objective and absolute way of taking measurements, especially when dealing with the amorphous ruins of a structure that was not designed with precision and accuracy in the first place (unlike the monuments of the Classical period). The discrepancies between Fyfe's and Doll's drawings are not necessarily the result of good and bad work; they are most probably due to the vagueness of the ruins themselves and the interpretation process that interferes while taking the measurements.

Interpretation Drawings One Step Ahead

A basic observation regarding these drawings, especially those at scales of 1:10 and 1:20, is their technical nature: they are linear drawings, with measurements, symbols, commentaries, and hatches that indicate materials. This is not so much the case with the general plans, which, on account of their scale, are understandably "somewhat schematic," as Hood comments (Hood and Taylor 1981:13). They are reminiscent of the kind of drawings an architect would prepare to implement his work and to guide the masons at work. Such guidance could well have been a goal of these drawings for the restoration work that was going full speed at that time.

These interpretation drawings represent one step ahead in the process. What seems to be missing is the meticulous depiction of the ruins "as found."[8] In *The Palace of Minos* several perspectives show an area before excavation, but informative as they may be, they cannot be treated as architectural documentation per se (see, for example, A. Evans 1928: Figs. 32, 38, 173). One of these, a watercolor of the Grand Staircase by Fyfe, bears the explicit title "Sketched in Course of Excavation and Before Re-Supporting of Upper Flights" (figure 15.3; A. Evans 1921:324, Fig. 237).

Why is this so? Most probably because that is what Evans asked for. And why did he not ask for drawings of the actual state of the ruins as they were revealed through excavation, stone by stone? Was the pressure of the dig and the restoration work so great that there was no time for this kind of work? It is surely not due to lack of interest in recording the finds as best as possible. This interest is well attested in the daybooks of Evans and Mackenzie and in the meticulous photography of the excavation (they even built a tower for this purpose). Perhaps it just did not occur to Evans that his architects should make such drawings.

FIGURE 15.3. Watercolor entitled "Sketched in Course of Excavation and Before Re-Supporting of Upper Flights" by Theodore Fyfe (A. *Evans 1921:324, Fig. 237*).

From the architects' point of view it is difficult to tell; their task in the field, after all, was defined not by the norms of their own discipline but by those of archaeology. The profession of field archaeologist was just beginning to develop, with Mackenzie one of the first of the kind (Momigliano 1999: 5). The profession of the architect, however, was well established but had to be readjusted to serve the needs of archaeology.

At this point, it would be interesting to see the kind of education and training these architects had acquired, their views on the main trends of their time, and their conception of archaeology. From the little that is known

FIGURE 15.4. "The Propylaia" by Prosper Desbuisson, 1848 (*Hellman, Fraisse, and Jacques 1983*).

it is clear that their education had been in the classical tradition. Fyfe, New-ton, and de Jong (there is, to my knowledge, no information on Doll) had expressed a strong interest in the history of architecture, as is evident by the fact that all three spent considerable time in their youth traveling in Italy and the Mediterranean, sketching, measuring, and drawing monuments of architecture of various periods, especially the Renaissance.[9] Fyfe, in particu-lar, followed an academic career in the history of architecture, and though he wrote very little on Minoan architecture he published extensively—articles and books—on the architecture of the Classical period (Fyfe 1914, 1920, 1936, 1942).

At about the same time that Fyfe, Doll, Newton, and de Jong were work-ing for Evans—broadly speaking the first three decades of the twentieth cen-tury—the prestigious École des Beaux-Arts in Paris was conducting its "Missions to Rome" and later to Greece; these were widely publicized and influential events (figure 15.4). It is quite conceivable that the elaborate work of the young architects of the École des Beaux-Arts, especially the win-ners of the Grand Prix de Rome, influenced Evans's architects, particularly their perception of ancient architecture; their travels and their work in Italy are suggestive of this. There seems, in fact, to have been something of a feedback process in this correlation, for some of the École des Beaux-Arts students became highly interested in the newly discovered "creto-mycenien" architecture. This is attested in the choice of Tiryns and Knossos, respectively, as themes for the 1924 and 1929 entries for the Rome Award.[10]

The work of the École des Beaux-Arts architects, however, was different from that of an architect following an excavation process: they were not recording the gradual revelation of a ruin through excavation but rather the extant remains of a monument with the ultimate goal—according to the specifications of their school—to learn from the fine architecture of classical antiquity (see Hellman, Fraisse, and Jacques 1983). For this reason, their work emphasized reconstruction drawings (figure 15.4), that is, their own interpretations of what the ruins originally looked like based upon meticulous measurements and carefully collected data.

The early drawings of Knossos are reminiscent of this kind of approach: they are reconstructions based most certainly upon meticulous measurements and first-hand observations. They remain, nevertheless, subjective interpretations, and the absence of the "as found" documentation upon which they were based will always impede reinterpretation. But, to be fair, the concept of detailed drawings of the architectural remains as found is hardly applied to all excavations even nowadays, and it is not always the work of an architect. Strange though it may seem, graphic documentation of a monument is a vague task, largely relying on the individual who has undertaken it. Although handbooks and guidelines do exist, we are still lacking a well-established and widely accepted methodology. A quick overview of the drawings published in archaeological reports suffices to show the great range of presentation modes and the common deficiencies (architectural sections, for example, are rarely included and plans float in the blank space of the paper with no indication of the contours of the ground or the relationship of the edifice to its surroundings). This is a serious matter and an underestimated handicap in the interpretation process of archaeology.

At Knossos, the "interpretation" drawings were made while restoration work was in progress. This association has been rather overlooked; we turn to the drawings for their archaeological value, to understand Minoan architecture, yet they are equally important as documentation drawings for the restoration work at the site. Most "restored views" can almost be identified with the way the monument looks today: Grand Staircase, Queen's Megaron, Little Palace, Caravanserai, North Entrance, East Bastion, and so on. Of these, I illustrate only a drawing and photograph of the East Bastion (figure 15.5). How do these drawings relate to the restoration work? Restoration at Knossos, after all, was such a large-scale and demanding operation that it could hardly be carried out without a drawing. Evans, referring to "re-supporting"

FIGURE 15.5. East Bastion, Knossos: a, isometric drawing by Piet de Jong (A. Evans 1930:237, Fig. 166); b, restored East Bastion (A. Evans 1930:238, Fig. 167).

a

b

and restoration, wrote that: "Many drawings for this work have been gradually executed by competent artists like Monsieur E. Gilliéron and his son, Mr. Halvor Bagge, and Mr. E. J. Lambert" (here Evans is referring, however, to color perspectives, that is, artistic renderings rather than technical drawings; see A. Evans 1921:vii). Joan Evans (1943:338) commented that "with Fyfe as part of the team reconstruction could be carried out almost *pari passu* with the excavation."

It seems, therefore, that the drawings had to play a triple role:

- To record the original parts of the monument as best as possible

- To interpret them by presenting a restored view of the missing parts

- To guide the restoration work

Reading Structure, Form, and Function through a Drawing

The exquisite drawings made by Fyfe, Doll, Newton, de Jong, and the Gilliérons are an interpretation of Minoan architecture in their own right. Yet, how does one (or can one) read architecture through a drawing alone? The question is too complex and generic to be approached in this paper, but we may attempt some answers concerning issues related to the specific draw-ings. To facilitate the approach, I will examine architecture in its three basic constituents: structure, form, and function.

As mentioned above, most of the drawings are, foremost, technical descriptions: they present a crystal clear picture of the structural aspect of Minoan architecture. It is obvious that the architects who drew them were pri-marily interested in understanding the building technology of the Minoans. Even the scales they chose to use (1:20 and 1:10) are indicative of their inten-tion to provide detailed accounts of this technology, for the scale of a drawing defines to a large extent the quantity and quality of information it can carry.

This interest is absolutely understandable, for the technical achieve-ments of Minoan architects are very impressive, even by modern standards. The kind of half-timber technology they used in multistory architecture, where mass and void interchange freely from one story to the other, is breath-taking in its boldness and exhibits unique mastery of building materials and techniques. All of this is well documented in the drawings of Evans's archi-tects, and I can almost identify with them in their exhilaration when this technical knowledge was revealed to them through the archaeological finds.

Their technical interests are also explicit in their scarce writings: Doll's brief comment, in the discussion following Evans's paper delivered in 1926 (A. Evans 1927:267), is all about the dimensions of staircases, proportions, and mathematics, and Fyfe praises Minoan materials and techniques in his brief account of his visit to Knossos, eighteen years after he originally worked there, and in his article on architectural depictions in Minoan art (Fyfe 1903, 1926).

Form is better described by the graphic restorations the architects pro-duced and through the actual restoration work. Form is the prevailing ele-ment at the site itself, because the structural had to be faked (fake structure, however, cannot but produce fake form as well; cement instead of wood makes all the difference). Form has been largely deduced from contemporary (Bronze Age) art depictions. These depictions were treated almost as "architectural drawings" that the Minoans left behind, to such an extent that they were literally applied on the monument in some cases.[11] Needless to say, these Bronze Age representations are far from true; or to say the very least, they cannot be taken for granted.

Three years after he began working at Knossos, Fyfe wrote a paper "at Dr. Evans's request," as he explains, on "Painted plaster decoration at Knossos with special reference to the architectural schemes." This paper includes interesting remarks about the decoration and form of Minoan architecture, yet its primary purpose seems to have been to prepare the ground for the extensive reconstructions, based chiefly on art, that were to commence soon after. One of the sections of the paper has the explicit title "Some probable restorations of the palace—based chiefly on the miniature frescoe" (Fyfe 1903).

Evans and his architects became gradually convinced of the "polychrome style" (Fyfe 1914:489) of Minoan architecture, as depicted in art, and passed it on to the otherwise colorless remnants of this architecture (figure 15.6).[12] Fyfe was more reserved in his earlier writings—"colours may be conventional"

FIGURE 15.6. Polychrome style of Minoan art: a, watercolor of Queen's Megaron by Piet de Jong (A. Evans 1930: Plate XXVI, frontispiece); b, later watercolor in the Herakleion museum; c, restored Queen's Megaron.

a   b

FIGURE 15.7. Black column shafts: a, as depicted in the miniature fresco (A. Evans 1930: Plate XVI); b, as restored in the light well over the Throne Room.

(Fyfe 1903:114)—and suggested that black may stand for old and seasoned wood and red/yellow for new. Yet black, red, and yellow were the very colors used in the restoration work (figure 15.7): the signifier, in other words, became the significant!

The bold use of color may have been further encouraged by the work of the architects of the École des Beaux Arts (figure 15.8) and the rigorous discussions concerning the polychromy of the architecture of the Greek Classical period, which dates back at least as early as 1820. These discussions, while primarily concerned with archaeological issues, were also paving the way for the use of color in contemporary architecture (Kruft 1994:278–279). Evans's architects, therefore, had two good reasons to use color.

In some of the (re)constructions that the architects supervised at Knossos, one can detect the formal qualities of the contemporary architecture of Art Deco (Laroche 1996; Farnoux 1996:110–111; Papadopoulos 1997:110). This suggests a modern architect at work, which, in fact, is not far from reality, for

a   b

FIGURE 15.8. Color in ancient architecture: a, hypothetical detail from Delos by Henri Paul Nénot *(Hellman, Fraisse, and Jacques 1983)*; b, restored north Lustral Basin at Knossos.

in many cases they were actually "building" something altogether new. Just as with the technology they were using (Christian Doll applied the same materials and techniques to build the Villa Ariadne and the upper floors of the Domestic Quarters at the palace of Knossos), the morphology of their constructions also reflects the trends of their time.

The modern-looking reconstructions must have been facilitated by the fact that Minoan art and architecture appealed to contemporary ideas of modernism. As early as 1902 the *Times* and *Guardian* newspapers published the faience plaques of the Town Mosaic, and Evans himself pointed out how "surprisingly modern" they were. During the 1920s and 1930s architectural journals closely followed the new discoveries of the Minoan and Mycenaean world, and several architects of the time were inspired by these remote, yet so familiar, cultures (Laroche 1996:194–199), not to mention the almost authentic copies of Minoan villas in Crete and even Athens (figure 15.9). To quote Farnoux: "Evans's restoration belongs to the architectural legacy of the turn of the century. . . . Its continuing restoration . . . will have to take this dual artistic heritage into account" (Farnoux 1996:111), and indeed it does.

Function, finally, is not self-evident in a drawing. It is certain that Evans discussed such matters with his colleagues, and we know how important Mackenzie's contribution was, but the basic interpretation of function was mostly his own intellectual work. Fyfe speaks of the bifurcated main staircase of the Royal Villa in two lines as "securing a certain privacy and an additional reason for considering that the villa was a place of some distinction"

FIGURE 15.9. A "Minoan" villa at Philothei, Athens, built in the 1930s by architect Zoumboulides. The white columns were later painted in Minoan colors. *Courtesy of M. Papaioannou, Syllogos Prostasias Perivallontos Philothei [Society for the Protection of the Environment of Philothei].*

(Fyfe 1926:479). This weak remark shows perhaps how little there was in terms of methodology to guide their thoughts.

Evans projected the Victorian mode of life, among other models, in interpreting function in Minoan architecture, and he has been strongly criticized for that (see, for example, Zois 1995 and MacEnroe 1995). A general problem was perhaps the lack, at the time, of a methodology for interpreting architecture—the lack of a theoretical background in general. This was a time when archaeology was beginning its development as an independent discipline and "very little was written—and even less published—about theories, methods, and techniques," as Nicoletta Momigliano cogently noted in the preface of her book about Mackenzie (Momigliano 1999:xiv–xv). Architecture, although as a practice is among the oldest in the world, is still struggling to find a theoretical standpoint (see especially Kruft 1994 and see further below).

The Technical Aspect of the Architect's Work: Restoration and Reconstitution

Evans's architects approached Minoan architecture in the way a practicing architect would, as opposed to an historian, theoretician, or critic of architecture. Fyfe's brief comment on the columns in Minoan art, as expressing the "Mycenean order" (Fyfe 1903:113, Fig. 3), and his comparisons with the architecture of the Classical period in discussing triglyphs and half rosettes

(A. Evans 1928:605–606) vaguely echo an historian's approach, yet it is not taken much further (as he has done in his writings on the architecture of the Classical period, for example). The structural aspect of Minoan architecture remains his primary concern; perhaps it had to be so, for restoration work was proceeding at full speed, and no restoration can be carried out unless there is good knowledge of the building technology with which one is dealing.

The architects were asked to provide what was expected of them as professionals, that is, their technical assistance—assistance urgently needed in the case of Knossos since much of the restoration work was a very demanding construction project. The Grand Staircase, for example, was a most difficult case, involving careful calculations of the loads to be transferred to the ground through a set of superimposed columns, and Evans comments that "this taxed all the resources of our architect, Mr. Christian Doll" (A. Evans 1927:261).

Once, when facing a particularly difficult situation, Evans wrote: "Professional guidance ceased at this point but, as the case seems desperate, I took upon myself the responsibility of what might be thought a very risky operation" (A. Evans 1927:261–262). This interesting remark shows that the work at Knossos went beyond technical professionalism, to enter the initiative realm of one man's vision.

Evans was very interested in technical matters and did not hesitate to dismantle and rebuild his earlier structures so as to use a more up-to-date building technology if such technology would ensure longer duration (see Evans's own remark: "Knossos . . . has passed through three 'periods' of conservation" [A. Evans 1927:262]). His architects surely helped him in this direction. But it seems that he often took initiatives of a technical nature on his own. Piet de Jong gives a lively account of Sir Arthur's impatience. In his letter to Myres in 1941, he wrote: "Sir Arthur as you know always liked to have things go quickly and be done immediately; he could not wait for preliminaries," and he gives the example of the restoration of the *taverna* done by Evans himself, "illustrating the desired changes with the aid of his walking stick." He also added that "the impatience of Sir Arthur and my expressed annoyance with him never impaired our friendship. I think, on the contrary, it cemented it" (Momigliano 1999:208–210).

Another kind of cement, reinforced concrete, was to change the situation dramatically. Concrete was a true breakthrough in building technology and extremely influential in the development of architecture on the whole. It is no surprise, therefore, that it soon invaded archaeology as well. Evans was a pioneer once more, and many have followed his footsteps since. Cement is relatively cheap and fast to produce, easily adjustable to any form, and easy to construct in situ by local technicians. No wonder it became a panacea, and not only at Knossos (cement was used at Pompeii at approximately the same time, perhaps following the Knossian example, as Evans [1927:258] believed). Evans, however, got carried away with the potential of the new technology. Far beyond the essential needs of preservation, he copied in concrete "for explanatory purposes" door jambs, columns, ashlar walls, and so on.[13] What started as preservation evolved rapidly into didactic restoration, with emphasis on the formal interpretation of Minoan architecture.

During the period 1922–30 Evans made extensive use of reinforced concrete in his restorations, under the supervision of Piet de Jong. "The new facilities afforded by the use of R.C.," writes Evans in 1926, "made it possible not only to renew in a more substantial form the supports of upper elements . . . but to profit by a better knowledge of the meaning of existing remains" (A. Evans 1927:264). The first part of this comment—more substantial—implies less reversibility; the last part of the comment, however, is less clear in its meaning: it may imply the easiness of extending the work of reconstruction.

A rather bizarre use of reinforced concrete, relevant to the above, is worth mentioning. In constructing the upper floor of the House of the High Priest, instead of pouring the cement so as to obtain a monolithic structure, he built in concrete three independent elements (a pillar, a beam, and a slab) resting one upon the other in an effort to imitate the structural concept of the original load-bearing wooden elements (compare Karetsou 1997:19) (figure 15.10). This must have been his own idea—as a kind of experiment perhaps—for an architect could hardly think of distorting the logic of a technology in such a way.

The Knossos Evans and His Architects Left Behind

Evans's long discussions with Mackenzie concerning various archaeological issues are well attested in their diaries. Their arguments had little direct impact on the monument itself, for both sides could retain their views in writing. But when it came to restoration there could be only one outcome: how much of this is Evans's and how much his architects'—or Mackenzie's—we cannot tell in the absence of written records. The form of the columns, for which there is some written information, is indicative of a case where there was no consensus: Doll's reservations as to the tapering of the column shaft were settled by Evans, who ordered tapering shafts for the actual construction; Doll was allowed to retain the uniform column shaft in his drawings. Doll's disagreement is mentioned in a footnote, whereas Evans's arguments are explained at great length.[14]

FIGURE 15.10. House of the High Priest: a bizarre use of reinforced concrete. *Photo by John Papadopoulos.*

Evans is surely not the only one responsible for what we see today at Knossos. His architects must have played a very important role in this, not only from the technical point of view—a contribution that Evans generously acknowledges—but also from the "interpretive" point of view as well; the drawings and the Art Deco touch speak of this contribution. They were surely following Evans's instructions, but Evans, too, was relying very much on their understanding of Minoan building technology. Strangely enough, however, this contribution has not been properly evaluated, and their names are hardly ever mentioned in most major analyses and critiques of the work at Knossos. Like Mackenzie (Momigliano 1999:xiii), Fyfe, Doll, de Jong, and Newton were destined to remain in the background.

So Evans and his architects presented their interpretations of Minoan architecture through their writings and their drawings as much as through their work on the monument itself. The paperwork—writings and lately drawings, too (see, for example, Hiller 1980:216–232, where he compares Fyfe's plans drawn in 1900–01 and in 1903 to determine elements that were completed in the second version)—has been analyzed, scrutinized, and criticized exhaustively. There is hardly a term left that has not been debated and a graphic restoration that has not been challenged. Such words as "palace," "king," "queen," and the like have been banned by some scholars or denuded from their meaning, and suspicion lingers over "lustral basins," "peak sanctuaries" "villas," and most other terms.

The kind of interpretation of Minoan architecture that Evans and his team left behind at the site may be analyzed and criticized, but it can hardly be changed. The various versions of what the ruins at Knossos ought to look like (no one has actually attempted such a drawing) will never be realized in situ. The reason is not only the amount of new material that has been mixed with the original and the inadequate knowledge of the original state of preservation. It is also the nature of the architecture of these structures. Stone buildings made of well-cut blocks fitted together with no mortar can be dismantled time and again and rearranged if necessary, as is done with the monuments of the Athenian Acropolis (Economakis 1994). But buildings made of loose stones, earth, and gaps where wood once stood, once consolidated into a certain form are almost impossible to undo. Moreover, Evans stressed that the conditions were very different from the "mighty stone buildings of Egypt, or the massive brick structures of Mesopotamia or those of Classical Greek and Roman sites" (A. Evans 1927:258). This is very true, and I would join my voice with those who emphasize the difficulties of preserving a place like Knossos (see A. Evans 1927:266–267; Platon 1961:106). What is questionable, however, is the constructions that were added for didactic purposes alone, for they freeze didactic values to Evans's time.

Knossos stands out as a warning for those responsible for the future of any monument. Preservation is not only about the material aspect of a monument but foremost about its historical value. All actions of protection, conservation, restoration, integration, and the like should therefore be carefully considered, for they all put authenticity at stake. "A little more" in this case, may end up with "much less."

Architecture and Archaeology in the Twenty-First Century

The architects' contribution to archaeology became increasingly appreciated through time. When Piet de Jong went to Crete for the first time in 1922 it was with a recommendation from Wace with whom he had worked at Mycenae. As Rachel Hood writes, "Piet was soon to become almost a bone of contention between Wace and Evans" because they both wanted eagerly his services. Hood goes on to give a further account of the importance of having an architect's services through Wace's letters dating soon after World War II (R. Hood 1998:246–247).

From that point onward things changed, and a gradually increasing number of architects (still relatively small, however) became involved in archaeology (Lloyd Cotsen, himself, was among the first of this "new era").

Computer technology has taken over, and the techniques for measuring and drawing have improved. Computers, however, do not efface subjectivity; measuring and drawing are still an interpretation process, even if one is working with an electronic theodolite and a mouse instead of a measuring tape and a pencil. What is more, computer technology is interfering with the process of interpretation in other, more subtle ways. Speed, for one, is not necessarily a benefit; safe judgment presupposes time to absorb the information and process it. The rigidity of a computer drawing, unpleasant as it is, is even more foreign to prehistoric architecture, and though we are well aware of this situation, it may nevertheless affect our perception in a latent way.

Technical assistance is not asked from the architect alone. Restoration work is now an interdisciplinary matter with emphasis on the analysis and study of ancient materials, incorporating the aid of the new field of archaeometry, and a dozen international charters to guide our decisions. Unlike the situation in Evans's time, the materials preferred today for restoration are low tech and as compatible as possible with the building technology of the Minoans. High tech has to be used to restore Evans's restorations with reinforced concrete.

Architects, finally, are now using the pencil—or the mouse—to express themselves in writing, as well as through drawings. It is interesting to see that more and more publications of archaeological sites include architects in the team of authors. This scholarly indulgence is creating a new type of architect who goes beyond understanding structure and form through his or her drawings and seeks to find ways of using the theoretical tools of his or her discipline to address the more pressing questions of archaeological discourse: human behavior and culture change (see, for example, Preziosi 1983).

Understanding Minoan Architecture: What Is New about It?

In terms of understanding Minoan architecture we have gone a long way since Evans, thanks to a large number of new excavations all over Crete and the Aegean islands, and also because of the hard work of an ever enlarging group of scholars. Our knowledge now extends beyond the palaces and beyond Crete itself, as well as beyond the time limits of the palace periods. There are new palaces coming up, the most recent being very close to Knossos, at Galatas, and there is Knossian presence as far as the Nile Delta (Tell el Dab'a). There are numerous towns all over Crete but also in Thera and the Dodekanese, as well as rural installations of great wealth. There are large-scale civil engineering works—roads, bridges, dams—and metallurgical kilns going as far back as the Early Bronze Age (for example, Chryssokamino). There is also new knowledge deriving from fields of research less known to

Evans, such as the environmental sciences. The great advantage of the accu-
mulating material is that it provides more balanced information concerning
the Aegean Bronze Age culture, both in terms of place and time.

This is the new raw material of our research, but what is also new is the
way we look at it, the way we approach the past. The hundred years that
have elapsed since Evans set foot at Knossos were years of overwhelming
change in this respect. Various movements have replaced one another, and
archaeological thought has gone through intensive elaboration; Bruce Trigger's *History of Archaeological Thought* (1989) gives an excellent account of
this evolution.

As far as architectural thought is concerned, however, all movements
seem to hold tight to the triadic basis of structure-form-function (*firmitas,
utilitas, venustas*, to go as far back as Vitruvius). In the last few decades these
three constituents have been simply changing position of priority according
to the movement employing them (for example, neo-realism, neo-rational-
ism, high-tech, postmodernism, deconstructivism [see the comments of
Tanoulas in Economakis 1994:187–189, and for a detailed account of the
developments in architectural theory, see Kruft 1994]).

Of the three constituents of architecture, structure is perhaps the easiest
to assess, form is deceptively easy to speak about, and function is the most
elusive of them all. The structural aspect of Minoan architecture is quite well
understood today thanks to detailed and systematic studies, such as Shaw's
(1973) comprehensive work. More recently, the finds at Akrotiri, Thera,
have added valuable information—to give just one example: openings above
the doors of a polythyron did exist, as Evans had assumed, yet only where
necessary to allow light and air into an adjacent room with no windows
(Palyvou 1999:356–359, Fig. 194). The well-preserved architecture of Thera
has given ample evidence of the abundant and sophisticated use of timber in
Bronze Age building technology. The significance of wood in Minoan architecture was emphasized by Evans and his architects. Evans speaks of a half-
timber technique and goes as far as commenting that "the expectation of
earthquakes may have influenced the style of building in Crete" (A. Evans
1927:266–267). This is quite true, and it is important that disciplines such as
that of the civil engineer are now joining forces in studying the use of timber
and the development of a sophisticated seismic resistant technology as early
as the Bronze Age (see Tsakanida forthcoming).

Although dealt with by Graham (1972) in his pioneering work on
Minoan architecture, *The Palaces of Crete*, the morphological aspect of
Minoan architecture is still not fully studied (for more recent work on the
subject, see Palyvou 1995b, 2000). The depictions of architecture in Bronze
Age art remain a basic source of information in this respect. To these past

pictures of the Minoan world we respond with our own versions of artistic depictions of a hypothetical reality, blending actual evidence, pictorial evidence, and contemporary aesthetics, and sometimes too much imagination. These graphic reconstructions are not meant as a study of the morphology of Minoan architecture per se (usually they are working tools to understand the archaeological remains), but the "virtual reality" effect they produce unavoidably refers to form and aesthetics (see Klynne 1998 and Driessen's [1999] response).

Sometime within the 1950s Nikolaos Platon, then director of the Herakleion Museum, commissioned several large watercolors from Piet de Jong, now hanging in the Herakleion Museum. These drawings were executed long after the restoration work was finished, and when compared with his earlier drawings of the same area (the Queen's Megaron, for example) it is clear that they were adjusted so as to conform to the actual state after the reconstruction (figure 15.6). The new representation—meant to be a restored view—is almost a true illustration of the room as seen today. The restoration work, in other words, had produced a life-size model of the Queen's Megaron "as it might have been in Minoan times."

Thirty years after Evans's work at Knossos, Platon conducted extensive restoration work at the site (Platon 1955, 1956, 1957, 1958, 1959, 1960). It is interesting to note that during this work he decided to change some of the colors that Evans and his architects had used in their restorations; they were thought to be too dominant, especially the yellow marking the wooden elements, which were repainted in a somewhat lighter tone, imitating the texture of wood (Platon 1961:111). This decision does not reflect a new understanding of Minoan architecture but rather the preferences of the time. The third generation of interventions at Knossos, which has been taking place during the past few years, chose to deal with the colors in a purist way, as part of the history of the monument. The cement elements of the South House were repainted, after the restoration work was over, just as they were before.

Coming finally to function, there is trouble in the air: a quick glance at the proceedings of the Symposium on The Function of the Minoan Villa suffices to show the controversies over terminology, methodology, and interpretation (Hägg 1997b). Function in architecture, from the archaeological point of view, needs to be redefined, or refined, for it has no clear meaning, and it is even doubtful whether we all mean the same thing. How do we deal with, for example, the discrepancies between function as the needs of the client (the user) expressed in the building program prior to construction, and function as the numerous potentials of use that a built space can offer? And this refers not only to the "initial" building program but to all subsequent

FIGURE 15.11. A single-room house from Rhodes. *After Philippides 1984: Fig. 62.*

ones, for every single modification, adjustment, or addition that may occur to a building through time, any act of building, has a design concept (a building program) behind it. In this consumer-producer-consumer cycle, values and significance may diverge significantly.

Time is an important variable of function. Within the same room, and by the same people, different activities may take place in different times— times of the day or seasons of the year. The full range of activities of a life-time may find shelter in one and the same room in certain cases (figure 15.11). Moreover, time is not significant to an architect in the same way it is to an archaeologist, for time in architecture is not a determinative "linear" factor as in archaeology. Which function are we looking for then? How can we deduce functions from the empty shell of a room? How much can we rely on the movable findings? The questions are endless, and though we are all quite aware of the circumstances of this "function hunting," our need to envisage people using this architecture is imperative, and for the time being we have no alternatives to propose.

Problems of this sort are not generated by the archaeological motivation to define function—that is, human behavior—through architecture. They are inherent in architecture itself, as is evident in the agonizing efforts of the theoreticians to understand how architecture is produced and what its meanings are (see, for example, Kruft 1994; Nesbitt 1996). They dwell in the divergence between architectural theory and practice. As with the other sciences that archaeology has been flirting with, architecture brings to archaeology its own innate problems of interpretation.

A most powerful dogma of our time has been the fundamental axiom of the modern movement, expressed in the 1920s by Sullivan (a student of the École des Beaux Arts himself during the years 1874–1875): *"form follows function"* (first published in the *Journal of the American Institute of Architects* 10/11, 1922–23; see Kruft 1994:355–363). The statement was inspired largely by the study of vernacular architecture and was believed to apply to primitive cultures in general. The modern movement saw function as rational and scientific, and assumed that form in architecture is *transparent to function*, implying that there can be a direct correspondence between specific forms and specific functions. Yet, "this correspondence requires codes to create meaning, since meaning is not inherent in the forms, but is culturally constructed" (Nesbitt 1996:45). The postmodernists challenged these ideas: they reversed the axiom to "function follows form" and tried to deassociate function from form, only to produce exaggerations such as "form-follows-fiasco" (Blake 1977) and "form follows fiction."

Whatever the case, the basic correlation between form and function is well established in our minds when dealing with architecture from the archaeological point of view. Form is what we believe we have in our archaeological records, and function is what we think it should be pointing at. But form is not what we have—that, too, is deduced to a large extent—and form does not lead to function. Structure, however, has been underestimated as a key to understanding both form and function. In a way, the form follows function idea has retained in archaeology the "romantic and thoroughly American" concept that Sullivan's axiom enclosed: that architectural forms should express human functions and needs, not structural laws (Kruft 1994: 357).

From Interpretation to Optimization: Site Presentation

A final question is: How do our changing interpretations of Minoan architecture affect site presentation? The question has two sides: the message and the recipient. In Evans's work the picturesque effect lingers in the half-restored areas, while a chaotic aspect with an underlying idea of a labyrinth was passed on to the casual early visitor by the sole fact that his or her movements around this extensive building complex were unrestricted—not only in the sense of being free to roam around, but also in being given no clues as to what his or her movements meant. The message that Evans's work evoked was the majestic palace, isolated from the modern world by a natural barrier of trees, denoting literally what his half-sister Joan Evans described as "a world which seemed to isolate him from a world in which he had found no place" (J. Evans 1943:350). The recipients in Evans's time were not visitors; they were mainly guests who were specially taken care of and even entertained by Evans himself or his collaborators according to their status, or simply intruders (Brown 1983:18).

The situation is dramatically different today. The recipient is a heterogeneous hoard of people who visit the place briefly. More than just visitors, they are the new users of the place, and their presence has an enormous impact on the site. Their needs have to be counterbalanced with those of the monument, and the outcome of this optimization should be clearly articulated on the site itself.

The message is twofold. The visitor is gaining a fuller understanding of the site as a town within which is the multifunctional complex, conventionally called a palace. The other side of the message is more subtle and has to do with the attitude that visitors adopt toward history, for their physical position defines their disposition toward the monument.

People are not free to move around anymore; their circulatory paths have been defined (Palyvou 1995a; Papadopoulos 1997). For safety reasons the kind of circulation that has been imposed is highly restricted. It may be argued that this kind of circulation does not allow the visitor to experience the intricate circulatory pattern that characterizes Minoan architecture. A basic feature of Minoan architectural design is indeed the amazing flexibility of circulation: all major buildings have two and three stories and an astonishing number of doors, corridors, and staircases combined in the most imaginative ways. The resulting circulation, however, is neither arbitrary nor chaotic; it was wisely designed to perform in a multifunctional manner. It is a circulatory pattern that offers multiplicity of choice and not complexity; this is the message that has to be passed on to the visitors.

A relevant dilemma is authenticity versus experience. The closer you get to the authentic parts, the more you need to protect them; and effective protection will unavoidably lead to large-scale interventions and extensive covering, so that finally there will be no authenticity left to be seen. This was the case with the Grand Staircase leading down to the Domestic Quarters at Knossos. The question was to decide between the kind of experience one should offer to the visitor: active or passive. The former would be actually using the staircase but not appreciating its superb appearance, since it would have to be covered over entirely—not only the steps, but the fragile sidewalls as well. And passive would be to look at the authentic staircase and admire its beauty from a small distance (from the light well). The latter was unanimously chosen, and circulation was diverted to other staircases. The basic argument was that more authenticity means more respect to the monument, and respect to the monument reflects respect to the visitor as well. Moreover, the coexistence of so many staircases in this area provides clues as to the hierarchy of circulation. If properly presented to the public, the experience of using a secondary staircase may even enrich their understanding and enhance the importance of the Grand Staircase.

Final Remarks

Our understanding of Minoan architecture is steadily improving thanks to the common efforts of archaeologists, architects, and other professionals. The meticulous work on the original material and first-hand information, as well as the reexamination of earlier material (as, for example, Fotou's meticulous work at the Ashmolean), is adding valuable pieces to the puzzle and is clearing up misconceptions and mistakes of the past. This fundamental work is of utmost value, for no matter how brilliant and effective the theoretical models are, they are worthless if applied to a "contaminated" material. As for the theoretical models, these will always be temporal—the way of thinking cannot be anything else but time and culture specific.

The scholarly work that each generation leaves behind will add "new" raw material for future students, alongside the new findings. The trend of our time to analyze the social context of each generation's work—the historiography of scholarship, as Palaima described it—will become even more important in the future, with questions such as "how do computers and the kind of virtual reality they produce influence our interpretations of the past?" This perpetual chase for interpretation may suggest that certainty, as envisaged by positivism, cannot be obtained (Trigger 1989:340), but the quest for "certainty" is a powerful intellectual drive in its own right.

Paperwork and digital work can be revised forever, for interpretations are not enacted once and for all. But what each generation leaves behind on the site itself will only enhance the notion of "a highly biased palimpsest of the past" (Bintliff 1984:33). Reading monuments as palimpsests may even become a field of archaeology. So things are changing, but change is a process of adaptation to alterations, and there is good reason to believe that we are adapting well. Archaeology may no longer be one man's vision; the polyphony of an interdisciplinary collective work, however, will need even stronger individual visions to succeed.

Notes

1. An involvement most eloquently expressed by the life and the work of the architect Lloyd Cotsen in honor of whom this workshop was held.

2. As of September 2000, according to the Ministry of Culture, among at least 500 excavations there are 71 archaeological sites in Greece with an entrance fee. Very few have been organized according to a specifically designed site presentation project. Knossos was one of the first, followed be Eleusis, Messene, and others. See also the ongoing project for the Unification of the Archaeological Sites of Athens. This, of course, does not mean that all the other sites are necessarily in a bad state; several archaeological sites are very well presented and maintained thanks to the efforts of the local authorities or simply of the guard who lives there, such as the example of Perachora near Loutraki.

3. Brown (1983:30) refers to the architects as "somewhat of a novelty." Yet, the Germans had set the example; the excavations at Olympia, begun in 1875, had a field team led by one art historian, one archaeologist, and two architects (Friedrich Adler and Wilhelm Dorpfeld).

4. I am most grateful to Lilah Clarke (née Forester, daughter of Anne Fyfe, daughter of Theodore Fyfe) for providing information on Fyfe's career and for her efforts to preserve Fyfe's drawings. I also wish to express my warmest thanks to Martin Goalen, MA DipArch RIBA Architect, for his help in providing information from the RIBA archives (of the architects employed by Evans, only Fyfe became a member of the RIBA); to Vasso Fotou for her most valuable help and her insight into the Ashmolean Archives; and to Nicoletta Momigliano for our discussions.

5. See Fyfe 1903 and 1926. Lilah Clarke, Fyfe's granddaughter, also comments on the absence of any writings from Fyfe's time at Knossos. In the five volumes of *The Palace of Minos*, only one contribution is signed by Fyfe, on triglyphs and half rosettes (see A. Evans 1928:605–606), and there are very few references to the architects in the index (mostly to their drawings). In the Ashmolean Museum there are four notebooks containing sketches and plans by Fyfe, 1900–04, and two daybooks by Doll, 1906–07 (Momigliano 1999:42). For published information on the lives and careers of these architects see, for Fyfe: Momigliano 1999; Brown 1983:15–31; *Royal Institute of British Architects (RIBA) Journal* 1945; and two obituaries published in *The Times* (5 January 1945) and the *Builder* (January 1945). For Doll: Momigliano 1999 and Brown 1983. For de Jong: Alexiou 1965 (obituary) and R. Hood 1998:223–270. For F. G. Newton: obituary in *Journal of Egyptian Archaeology* 11 (1925):70–71; Momigliano 1999; and Brown 1983.

6. There is a general tendency to omit architectural sections in archaeological publications. The low height of preservation of most architectural remains may discourage archaeologists from presenting such drawings (they do not reproduce well in print when reduced in size). Yet, understanding a structure by reading a plan alone is impossible or—what is worse—very misleading.

7. A point should be made about isometric drawings versus perspectives: the former are important technical drawings that help you check the structure in all three dimensions simultaneously. It is through isometric drawings that you

sometimes come to understand the full meaning of certain details or you realize that you have been missing important details. Evans's architects were aware of the value of such drawings. Isometric drawings are not "artistic" representations of the same ambiguous value as perspectives. The latter simulate reality and cannot be treated as technical drawings; they are useful, however, for understanding formal qualities.

8. Mrs. Fotou kindly informed me of the existence of one such drawing in the Ashmolean Museum. Made by Fyfe, it depicts the pavement of the Queen's Megaron on a scale of 1:10.

9. Fyfe had spent a year (1899) traveling in Italy on an Architectural Association Travel Studentship, just before he came to Greece (RIBA Journal 1945); Newton had worked with Duncan Mackenzie in Italy (Momigliano 1999:82, n. 119); and de Jong spent a year in Italy (1912), having won a prize from the RIBA (R. Hood 1998:228–235).

10. The architects were Roux-Spitz: État actuel du palais du Tyrinthe, in 1924, and Audoul: Palais mycénien de Tyrinthe et palais de Cnossos, in 1929 (see Hellman, Fraisse, and Jacques 1983).

11. The form of the column (shaft and capital) is such an example. See Evans's arguments (A. Evans 1921:342) based on a wall painting.

12. Color plays a significant role in Minoan architecture, as is evident from the sophisticated use of the multicolored building materials, but these are the only colors about which we can be certain (Graham 1972:199–209; Palyvou 1999:433–440). Wall paintings, of course, also added to the polychrome aspect of Minoan architecture.

13. See the chapter entitled "New Era in Reconstitution Due to Use of Ferro-Concrete" in A. Evans 1928:288–290. On the use of concrete, see also A. Evans, Knossos Summaries, *Journal of Hellenic Studies* 1928:186–187; 1929:226–227.

14. A. Evans 1921:342, n.1, Fig. 247 (Doll's reservation and drawing) and 342–343 (Evans's arguments). Doll's unpublished diaries, kept in the Ashmolean, may include more thoughts on the matter.

CHAPTER 16

Archaeology in Search of Architecture

JERRY D. MOORE

Clairy Palyvou's discussion of the artistic renderings of Knossos raises the matter of how archaeologists understand and document ancient architecture. As a New World archaeologist with an interest in architecture, I found Palyvou's presentation interesting, convincing, and one to which I had little to add. So in the following, I examine a different, but related, set of problems. I contend that the objectives and methods of archaeology and architecture are fundamentally divergent. Architecture and archaeology become slightly tangent when they approach ancient buildings but are largely distinct from each other. Prior to my own study on prehispanic Andean architecture (Moore 1996a), I conducted a reading survey of major architectural theorists. While specific ideas and techniques were relevant and much of the literature was interesting, I became convinced that architecture and archaeology were so fundamentally different that we archaeologists need to develop our own approaches to understanding ancient constructions. This is not meant as a criticism; it is simply true. Neither should architects adopt archaeologists' objectives—any more than one would contend that archaeologists should (or could) drop their trowels and start building houses.

Nothing in the following should be misconstrued. I am not suggesting that archaeologists can learn nothing from architects or that collaborative projects are without value. I do insist, however, that archaeologists should devise robust approaches to the built environment, approaches rooted in anthropological holism and attentive to the multiple decision domains involved in the cultural creation of architectural space.

There is a temptation among archaeologists to borrow indiscriminately the ideas and terminology used by architects, architectural historians, and architectural critics. I argue that this is a flawed strategy that ignores the two fields' very different agendas. I contend that archaeologists should invest in the creation of an anthropologically informed, holistic approach to the built landscape, with the central objective of how past societies shaped and were shaped by their culturally constructed environments. That objective, I believe, is profoundly distinct from the goals of architecture.

Architecture is an extraordinarily fragmented, deeply divided field into which archaeologists venture at their own risk. Paul Shepheard (1994:25) writes in *What Is Architecture?*: "Going into the book stacks in pursuit of architecture is like looking in a butcher's shop for a sheep; it's there, all right, but laid out in a rather particular way." And although architecture may be divided among the bookshelves, one can establish a minimal thematic unity: architecture's arenas of practice and critique are architectural creation and the appreciation of architects' accomplishments.

For many architectural theorists, the process of "analysis" is essentially critical and normative; it is a convincing manifesto about the way things should be. Palyvou (chapter 15) expressed a cautious annoyance with the "powerful dogma of the modern movement 'form follows function.'" Louis Sullivan's famous dictum has been so integrated into architectural thinking that we overlook what Sullivan actually said: "Form *should* follow function." Sullivan's statement was a normative declaration, and the fact that Sullivan felt compelled to say it implies that form does not always or necessarily follow function. Architects can accept this dictum if they want—although Gaudi ignored it with marvelous results—but it is not a cross-cultural law true for all creations in the human-constructed landscape.

Architects' creations are viewed as fine art. "The business of architecture," Le Corbusier (1946:10) wrote, "is to establish emotional relationships by means of raw materials." In this view, the architect is an artist, architecture is art, and architectural criticism is a variant of art criticism. Master architects like Le Corbusier, Louis Sullivan, and Frank Lloyd Wright were true artists and perceived themselves as such. "I was a real Leonardo da Vinci when I built that building," Wright said of his Larkin Building, "everything in it was my invention" (Cronon 1994). Similarly, Le Corbusier (1946:2) in his manifesto *Vers Une Architecture* argued:

> The Architect, by his arrangement of forms, realizes an order which is a pure creation of his spirit; by forms and shapes he affects our sense to an acute degree and provokes plastic emotions; by the relationships which he creates he wakes profound echoes in us, he gives us the measure of an order which we feel to be in accordance with that of our world, he determines the various movements of our heart and of our understanding; it is then that we experience the sense of beauty. (Le Corbusier 1946:2)

More recently Alberto Pérez-Gómez has written in a similar vein:

> The traditional mission of the arts has been to make explicit the ideal and
> eternal through an interpretation of the given in the specificity of percep-
> tion, providing humanity with a sense of belonging to a meaningful col-
> lective realm, transcending our limitations as finite and corruptible
> individuals. In this most profound sense, regardless of the secondary func-
> tional utility (or uselessness) or artifacts, art has always been a primary
> form of knowledge. Humans could thus orient themselves in the world
> and perceive the meaning of existence, otherwise confused in the contin-
> uously mutable reality of everyday life. The painter, sculptor, or architect
> has been concerned with the revelation of the truth of reality, with the
> stabilization of meaning. (Pérez-Gómez 1997:1)

If the architect creates art, then the building is a subject for admiration
and discussion, and writing about architecture is architectural criticism or art
history. Architectural critics, like Charles Jencks, Ada Louise Huxtable, Paul
Goldberger, or Nicolai Ouroussoff, present an informed aesthetic response to
a larger audience, one often composed of individuals who have not viewed
the building first hand. Like other critical writing, architectural criticism is
designed to highlight or illuminate specific aspects of a creation, in this case
the built environment. By turns instructive or entertaining, good critical
writing draws attention to previously unnoticed patterned relationships, historical connections, artistic intentions, and abject failures. At its worst,
architectural criticism may descend into an exercise in obscurantism as a
quick examination of some articles in the infelicitously named *Cloud-
Cuckoo-Land: An International Journal of Architectural Theory and Criticism*
will indicate.[1]

Even at its best, architectural criticism employs an impressionistic
vocabulary, as Bruno Zevi complained decades ago:

> The average reader, leafing through books on the aesthetics and criticism
> of architecture, is horrified by the vagueness of the terms: *truth, movement,*
> *force, vitality, sense of outline, harmony, grace, breadth, scale, balance, pro-*
> *portion, light and shade, eurhythmics, solids and voids, symmetry, rhythm,*
> *mass, volume, emphasis, character, personality, analogy.* These are attributes
> of architecture which various authors use as classifications without speci-
> fying what they refer to. (Zevi 1957:21, original emphasis)

If architects have difficulty describing modern architecture, they experience greater problems writing about and envisioning the past. For example,
Joseph Rykwert's fascinating book, *On Adam's House in Paradise: The Idea of
the Primitive Hut in Architectural History*, provides an historical overview of

how architects have construed the origins of architecture as exemplified by
the "hut." Such musings about "the hut" go back to Vitruvius, whose first-
century BC writings contain the earliest preserved architectural criticism.
Vitruvius contended that human social life began after an enormous wind-
storm whipped tree trunks together until the friction caused them to burst
into flames. Humans first fled but then were attracted to the resulting fire and
there learned the pleasures of group life. After this social transformation, the
first architecture was created in imitation of nature: screens of boughs as patterned on leafy trees, man-made caves dug out in hillsides, and wattle constructions modeled after bird nests (Rykwert 1972:105). Rykwert argues that
Vitruvius's ideas were probably derived from earlier, now lost sources:

> The account is elliptical, and references are made to various other writ-
> ings. The outline of the account, from the trauma of fire to the invention
> of language and of the arts as a social activity, the close developments of
> the techniques from the fragments of sensory impression, and the succes-
> sion of logical steps which the impressions prompt in primitive man, until
> they achieve mastery of the environment by observing external nature
> and by "realizing" their own bodies: all this smacks of Stoic doctrine
> tinged by peripatetic empiricism. (Rykwert 1972:110)

Two millennia later an equally "fabulized prehistory"—in Rykwert's fine
phrase—was outlined by Frank Lloyd Wright in his 1945 book, *The Living
City*:

> Go back far enough in time, mankind was divided into cave-dwelling
> agrarians and wandering tribes of hunter-warriors; and we might find the
> wanderer swinging from branch to branch in the leafy bower of the tree,
> insured by the curl at the end of his tail [!], while the more stolid lover of
> the wall lurked, for safety, hidden in some hole in the ground or in a
> cave. . . . The cave dweller became the cliff dweller. He began to build cit-
> ies. . . . (Wright 1945:23–24)

A significantly less egregious, but still cautionary, example comes from
one of the great architectural historians, Vincent Scully, who has made in-
depth studies of Native American architecture, as well as written about
everything from ancient Greek temples to the Shingle Style. And yet even
Scully (1991) in his *Architecture: The Natural and the Manmade* slips, presenting the native Southwestern and Central Mexican architectural styles as representing a "pre-Hellenistic attitude" in which the built landscapes reflect

> . . . the imitation of natural forms by human beings who seek thereby to
> fit themselves safely into nature's order. When the resources of large

populations made it possible to build monumental architectural forms of communal function and at the landscape's scale, exactly the same principle was brought to bear. We can see it at work at Teotihuacan, which was in all likelihood the most important ceremonial center the North American continent ever produced. (Scully 1991:5–6)

As buildings "echo and clarify" mountains in such disparate places as Taos Pueblo, Teotihuacan, Tikal, and the ziggurat of Ur, Scully argues, then perhaps this reflects "a common, world-wide development." And if these sacred places reflect some vestiges of a deep *ur*-religion, then Scully (1991: 36) can state that the buffalo dances of Puye Pueblo and the charging bull depicted in the north entrance of Knossos, although "Far apart in time and place, their rituals are clearly celebrating much the same moment of human consciousness."

Further examples are unnecessary. Specific domains of architectural criticism and history are clearly informative for prehistoric archaeology, but the point at which architecture and archaeology diverge is precisely at the central archaeological question: How can we understand the past? I think that archaeologists must fall back on their own creativity and develop a robust archaeological approach to ancient building and the constructed landscape.

Pivotal to that endeavor is the question: How was prehistoric architecture experienced? I think this issue is pivotal because it leads us back to a well-established body of anthropological theory from which we still have much to gain—namely anthropological holism—and forwards to a body of analytical techniques whose full potentials we have yet to explore—specifically, virtual reality and computer reconstructions. And it also, I believe, can contribute to what Colin Renfrew described (in comments in a precirculated paper at the workshop) as "the aspirations for a generalizing approach, which seeks to look at the full range of human experience, and to do so through systematic comparison. . . ."

Toward an Anthropological Archaeology of Architecture

I have argued that archaeological approaches to architecture should be rooted in anthropological holism (Moore 1996a:10–15). I believe anthropology's holistic concerns are specifically illuminating when applied to architecture and the built environment, if for no other reason than constructions are always concrete compromises between different decision domains. More than thirty years ago in his book *House Form and Culture*, architect-anthropologist Amos Rapoport (1969) listed some of the different domains shaping dwellings, including technology, construction, economics, defense, siting, and religion, among others. In a fundamental way, structures are holistic enterprises. In a later work, Rapoport (1982) outlined what he called "The Choice Model of Design":

> The organization of the environment is, therefore, the result of the application of sets of rules that reflect differing concepts of environmental quality. Design can hence be seen as an attempt to give form of expression to some image of an ideal environment, to make actual and ideal environments congruent. *This involves ideas of environmental quality which are extremely complex and variable and cannot be assumed a priori but need to be discovered* [emphasis added]. (Rapoport 1982:15)

Rapoport (1982:15) further observed that constructed environments are "the result of a series of choices among various alternatives. All man-made environments are designed in the sense that they employ human decisions and choices and specific ways of resolving the many conflicts implicit in all decision-making." (Anyone who has been involved in a construction project—as designer, builder or owner—immediately recognizes the pragmatic truth of Rapoport's observation.) Finally, Rapoport concludes:

> What all this activity has in common is that it represents a choice among many alternatives. The specific nature of the choices made tend to be lawful, to reflect sets of rules, so that one way of looking at culture is in terms of the most common choices made. . . . This consistent set of choices also affects many aspects of human behavior and symbolic meaning—the way people interact, their proxemic distances, how they structure space, whether they use streets for interaction and so on. (Rapoport 1982:15)

Modern architects have failed when they have emphasized a single decision domain over all others. One thinks of Philip Johnson's elegant icon of modernism, his 1949 Glass House, a crystalline box of plate glass and steel that lacks a broom closet. Interestingly, the New Urbanism, a planning movement attempting to remedy the flaws of previous urban designs, explicitly adopts a holistic perspective, contending "that the city, its suburbs and their natural environment should be treated as a whole—socially, economically, and ecologically. Treating them separately is endemic to many of the problems we now face. . . ." (Calthorpe 1994:xi).

I advocate a holistic approach to understanding architecture, not because "holistic" is a long-cherished concept in American cultural anthropology but because architecture and the built environment are inherently multidimensional. No building ever created has solely reflected "function," "style," "engineering," "energetics," "ideology," or "gender" to the exclusion of all other decision domains. And, just as obviously, not all decision domains are weighted equally, but determining their relative significance is, as Rapoport points out, an empirical process grounded in specific analytical cases, a process to which anthropological archaeologists can contribute.

This said, an anthropologically informed, holistic approach to architecture is necessarily a collective enterprise. No single study will equally explore all the decision domains relevant to understanding a particular prehistoric built environment. While we may emphasize specific dimensions and ignore others in a given study, we should make our objectives and analyses transparent. An anthropologist may examine a single causal thread but should not mistake it for the entire cultural fabric.

Further, different theoretical sets are relevant to different decision domains. For example, cost-benefit models (for example, Abrams 1994) may best illuminate construction processes, while house forms may restate cosmologies (Blier 1987). Frankly, I doubt that there is an overarching "theory" of archaeological approaches to architecture—except one that recognizes the different domains of architecture and their associated theoretical modules. My suspicion is that these individual theoretical modules are stubbornly irreducible.

For example, my own interest in architecture developed out of a broader concern with the organization of power relations in ancient Andean societies, initially focused on the Chimú Empire (AD 900–1470) of the North Coast of Peru (for example, Moore 1981, 1985, 1989, 1995). The towering walls and labyrinthine corridors of the royal compounds (*ciudadelas*) of the Chimú capital of Chan Chan had been interpreted as reflecting a Chimú obsession with access control. An initial study applied techniques drawn from network graphing to ciudadela plans, allowing for the test of specific hypotheses regarding movement and control within the structures (Moore 1992). This preliminary study was incorporated into a trio of analyses—on the architecture of social control, the architecture of ritual, and the architecture of monuments—that I explored with a larger body of Andean architectural data from sites dating from 2200 BC to AD 1470. I argued that significant shifts in different architectural dimensions reflected changes in the organization of power in the development of ancient Andean societies (Moore 1996a).

A more recent work has examined the ritual landscapes of the dead created by two prehispanic Andean societies, the Chimú and the Inka (Moore 2002). In trying to understand these differences, I have employed Mary Douglas's concepts of grid and group. Douglas discusses how material dimensions, including buildings, funerary structures, and landscapes, can restate different social conceptions and relations. This theory stretches back to Durkheim's notions of collective representations, but Douglas's ideas make a specific link between the built environment and the social domain. "Group is obvious," Douglas (1970:viii) writes, "the experience of a bounded social unit. Grid refers to the rules which relate one person to another on an ego centered basis." Group/grid analysis

> . . . is a method of identifying cultural bias, of finding an array of beliefs locked together into relational patterns. The beliefs must be treated as part of the action, and not separated from it as in so many theories of social action. The action or social context is placed on a two-dimensional map with moral judgments, excuses, complaints and shifts of interest reckoned as the spoken justifications by individuals of the action they feel required to take. As their subjective perception of the scene and its moral implications emanates from each of them individually, it constitutes a collective moral consciousness about man and his place in the universe. (Douglas 1982b:199–200)

Douglas outlines a series of explicit, testable hypotheses linking social order and symbolic statements, such as the economic and political expressions of differing social contexts, symbolic structures relating to the human body and society, and cosmological statements regarding nature, time, human nature, and social behavior (Douglas 1970, 1982a, 1982b). And these ideas are relevant for understanding at least some domains of the built environment—in this specific application, the funerary landscapes of two Andean societies.

The Inka and the Chimú created very different forms of funerary architecture; to oversimplify, the Inka buried their dead in crypts and architecturally modified caves from which the dead could be removed, feted, and honored. The Chimú buried their dead in sealed tombs that ranged from massive burial mounds to unmarked pits in cemeteries, but the Chimú dead could not be removed and displayed as the dead were in Inka society. Further, there is a stark division among burial treatments in Chimú sites that undeniably reflects the division of the dead into discrete social classes. These differences in funerary architecture reflect differing social matrices, the Inka emphasizing lineal descent and the connections between the living and the dead, while the Chimú emphasized class differences in their funerary architecture, as well as in the architecture of the living.

Different architectural studies necessarily employ distinct sets of relevant theory. The control of access in the Chimú ciudadelas and the varying material restatements of social order reflected by Chimú and Inka funerary landscapes are related issues at a general level: both problems concern how constructed environments reflect and shape social order, but they are more brightly illuminated by bodies of theory proximate to the matter at hand.

New Methods for the Study of Architecture: Virtual Reality or Distorted Reality?

If the built environment involves different decision domains and it is the task of a holistic approach to understand those domains, then it follows that no single analytical method will be sufficient for understanding ancient architecture. Archaeologists employ a shockingly narrow set of methods for studying ancient architecture. Despite all the efforts invested in excavating and mapping ancient buildings, fewer analytical techniques are applied to architecture than are used in the analysis of ceramics, lithics, or even coprolites. Archaeologists most commonly approach architecture from one of three analytical directions: as a reflection of style, as a material index of social labor, or as a passive backdrop to human activities reconstructed from other artifactual sets. The "analytical methods" usually employed involve nonsystematic inferences derived from visual inspection of two-dimensional plans. Obviously, much more can be done.

In attempting to understand prehistoric architecture, it is useful to ask how an ancient society may have experienced a built landscape. This is not an attempt to mysteriously penetrate the ancient psyche. Rather, it is an effort to understand the prehistoric experience of the built landscape based on scientific data regarding human sensory perception and applying them to reconstructions of ancient constructions. One can pose questions such as: How was this building or constructed landscape experienced? Who could see what from where? What modes of human interaction could occur in this space? Is access restricted or open or interconnected? and so on, and then pose additional questions like: What kinds of social intentions motivated such a built environment?

Investigations like this have already begun. For example, Christopher Tilley's (1994) work on landscape has stimulated an interest and associated controversy in developing new archaeological methods. Bender, Hamilton, and Tilley (1997) examined the "nested landscapes" surrounding the Bronze Age settlement of Leskernik, Cornwall, by literally building a portable "door frame," placing it at the entrances of each of some fifty huts and then determining each hut's viewshed. Recently, Bender et al. have been criticized for ignoring paleoenvironmental data indicating that the Leskernik viewsheds would have been blocked by a thick mantle of oak-hazel scrub (Chapman and Gearey 2000), but provocative analyses are improved by healthy debate. Another study (Watson and Keating 1999) has investigated the acoustic properties of two sites in Scotland, discovering that the megalithic stone circle of Easter Aquorthies and the burial mound of Camster Round had distinct sound properties. I have analyzed Chiripa/Pukara/Tiwanaku, Chimú, and Inka plazas, arguing that, given the very different sizes of these plazas and human sensory thresholds, three traditions of Andean plazas existed, each employing distinct modes of communication in pre-Hispanic public rituals (Moore 1996b). Each of these studies employs new analytical methods for studying ancient architecture.

One of the most exciting methodological arenas involves virtual reality (VR) and computer-based reconstructions. A number of examples of this work are viewable on the World Wide Web, enough examples to suggest the problems and potentials. One pitfall is to use the Web as an elaborate medium for displaying postcard images. For example, the Daedelus Group in Athens and the Hellenic Ministry of Culture have Web sites on Knossos, but the pictures are static, small, and noninteractive.[2] Some of the best examples of integrating VR and archaeology are presented by the Foundation of the Hellenic World, which blend VR, film, and other media into archaeological reconstructions.[3] At this Web site, for example, one can view a three-dimensional reconstruction of the Theater of Epidaurus and listen to a brief extract from Aristophanes' comedy "Peace." Perhaps the best example is presented by Alan Chalmers and other colleagues at Bristol whose visual reconstruction of underground burial complexes in Malta, dating to ca. 3000–2500 BC, allow for testing alternative hypotheses about intervisibility and spatial interaction between priests and audience involved in prehistoric rituals.[4]

Palyvou posed the question: Computer technology—does it interfere with the process of interpretation? This is an interesting issue, one understood by scholars working with computer reconstructions. For example, Chalmers et al. (1996) write:

> Three dimensional computer reconstructions of archaeological sites have existed for a number of years. These computer reconstructions may be viewed either as a series of static images, or as a precomputed video walkthrough, possibly within a multi-media presentation package. The user is thus presented with a fait accompli representation of a site. This single representation may impose a "true" vision of the past on the viewer creating a misleading impression of accuracy.

VR is seductive and potentially misleading. And yet all systems of representation—verbal descriptions, blueprints, elevations, models, watercolors, and photographs—necessarily shape and potentially distort one's interpretation of an architectural space. For example, one of the most famous images of any archaeological site in the Andes or elsewhere is a classic view of Machu Picchu (figure 16.1). The stone ruins stretch along what Pablo Neruda called "the high reef of the human dawn" (Felstiner 1980:215) with the mountain peak of Huayna Picchu in the background. This beautiful vista is repeatedly

FIGURE 16.1. A "biased" view of Machu Picchu.

photographed, partly because it is the only point of view that crops out the large and architecturally uninspiring Hotel de Turistas located just behind the photographer. This famous photograph is a distortion, yet one would never suggest that we not use cameras to document archaeological sites.

Rather than ignore a powerful technology, we need to learn to "read" VR images and computer reconstructions just as we archaeologists have learned to read stratigraphic sections, Harris matrices, or contour maps. Further, VR and computer reconstructions are potentially interactive. If the problem of interactivity can be solved, then these reconstructions' potential for alternative rendering confers real advantages—if informed by a robust body of theory that leads to testing multiple hypotheses about the experience of architecture. If theory and hypothesis testing do not inform such reconstructions, then they are merely video games—and not particularly exciting ones.

Summary

I have attempted to make several points. First, I contend that architecture and archaeology have significantly distinct objectives and intents. Archaeology's principal aim—understanding past human societies—is not one that architecture broadly shares, and therefore architecture provides a narrow set of ideas and techniques of use to the archaeologist. Conversely, archaeology provides little of interest to the architect. These are simply two different fields, tangent only at a limited number of points.

Second, archaeologists need to develop a more robust approach to ancient architecture. I argue that this approach should be rooted in anthropological holism because every construction entails multiple decision domains. Defining and ranking these different decision domains is an empirical matter based on specific cases. One cannot argue that any one decision domain—energy or ideology or whatever—is always the dominant concern in the built environment. An immediately relevant body of theory, rather than some overarching "theory of architecture," best illuminates each of these decision domains.

Finally, archaeologists need to develop new methods for understanding architecture. I have cited several examples of methods informed by a "phenomenological" approach to the built environment, all directed to the question: How was this constructed landscape experienced? Other questions will lead to other methods, but we need to solve these methodological problems creatively. There is an essential synergy among theory, method, and data in archaeology, and there is a clear need for archaeologists to develop new approaches to ancient architecture.

Notes

1. At *www.mcgill.ca/wolke*; the name, which may sound better in German or Russian, is derived from Aristophanes' *Birds*.
2. At *www.daedelus.gr*.
3. At *www.fhw.org*.
4. At *www.cs.bris.ac.uk/~alan/Arch/INSITE/research/comvis/insite2.htm*.

CHAPTER 17

Architecture and Archaeology:
A View from China

LOTHAR VON FALKENHAUSEN

Architecture, with all of its messy complexities, is notoriously resistant to explanation, hostile to revelation.

Rem Koolhaas in Koolhaas and Mau 1995:1

At the outset, I would like to signal polite disagreement with Jerry Moore's (chapter 16) strong-worded insistence that archaeologists have no intellectual common ground with architects. Moore perceives correctly that architecture is an art, but it is also, like archaeology, a craft as well as a science. By engaging with the excavated remains of ancient buildings—drawing their plans, reconstructing their building techniques and structural principles, and recreating their ancient appearance—its practitioners can, in a very real sense, commune with their professional colleagues in the remote past. Their activity, as part of archaeological teams, recovers information—indeed potentially entire bodies of knowledge—essential to the archaeological enterprise and without which the "anthropologically informed, holistic approach to the built landscape with the central objective of how past societies shaped and were shaped by their culturally constructed environments" that Moore is calling for would not be practicable.

Moore fails to appreciate that the "built landscape" of early humanity was fashioned not by impersonal, quasi-mystical abstractions such as "culture" or "social intentions" but by individuals pursuing specific creative goals and possessing specific skills. Its analysis today by persons trained to design and build buildings offers unique opportunities to find out about the thought processes that went into the planning, and into the iterative refashioning over time, of such an environment. In stating this, I am not advocating that every ancient structure be interpreted as the manifestation of an artistic

247

genius (or as the work of a secretive Masons-style professional group of initiates); nor do I wish to limit the analysis of buildings to formal features immanent to the architectural realm, disregarding their sociocultural context. I would, however, insist that the decisions that went into the construction of any building were taken by real-life human beings consciously working to meet certain well-defined needs, and that the physical remains of any ancient building embody its builders' conscious intentions in ways that are at least partially verifiable. To be sure, the realization of these intentions was always limited by the technology and materials available, by the structural and stylistic habits accumulated during previous generations, and—perhaps most importantly—by the topographic constraints of the building site. It goes without saying that such factors must be understood in their specific context by anyone undertaking to interpret an ancient building.

Moore's rejection of the impressionistic vocabulary in certain works of traditional architectural criticism is well taken, but the passages he quotes, rather than being typical for the disciplinary discourse of architecture, seem to reflect the adoption, by non-anthropologists, of some exceedingly obsolete anthropological ideas. Such ideas should not detract from the fact that architecture and archaeology stand to profit a great deal from serious interdisciplinary cooperation. Clairy Palyvou's thoughtful essay (chapter 15) describes an early example of one such collaboration in the Aegean realm, pointing out pitfalls to be avoided in future work along those lines. She reminds us that modern architects studying ancient buildings must be aware of their own aesthetic biases lest those biases be allowed to color, however unconsciously, their reconstructions; when this is not done, the consequences can range into the humorous. Of course, as Collingwood (1946), building on Hegel, has compellingly theorized, no modern scholar—no architect, but no archaeologist either—can escape the imprint of his own knowledge base and life experience onto his or her perception of the past. This inescapable predicament is not necessarily all bad in its consequences, however. For instance, since modern architects are trained in a far wider panoply of different building techniques and styles than their predecessors in antiquity, they are better able to classify what they observe, and they can judge the specific qualities of a building through comparison with others that could not have been known to its builders. The architects' empathy with their professional colleagues of the past is thus sublated and brought into a much more comprehensive panorama, one that is fit to serve the needs of modern scholarship.

Anthropological archaeologists should appreciate that the architect's work is not mere guesswork or nonscholarly intuition but an application of rigorous science. Like Moore's quest for the experience of the consumers of ancient architecture, the "thinking along with the ancients" modern architects can engage in in no way constitutes "an attempt to mysteriously penetrate the ancient psyche" (see chapter 16). (My main quibble here is with the word "mysteriously"; just like a responsible and methodologically aware anthropologist, an architect approaching an ancient building from the perspective of his or her craft will penetrate rationally into aspects of the psyche of certain persons of antiquity. This is very much of the essence of anthropology as well: that discipline would be an impossibility without its underlying working assumption of the psychic unity of humankind.)

I hasten to add that the thought processes recoverable through the study of ancient buildings often undoubtedly involved other persons besides the builders. Every building is the outcome of negotiations between different participants in the surrounding culture—a dialogue that by no means terminated with a building's construction, as shown by its often complex history of reconstruction and reuse. Ruth Tringham's proposal (chapter 6) to study the "life histories" of buildings through time points toward a useful methodology aiming to do justice to such realities. She commendably insists that, aside from a building's plan, configuration, construction, and ornamentation, its furnishings and contents must also be incorporated into these histories; if this is done, the view of a building as it develops in time will be more fully contextualized than the rather aseptic reconstructions of successive building stages that tend to result from architects' work on excavated buildings. Even though Tringham herself is concerned with Neolithic dwellings, which are small in scale and both simple and relatively standardized in their form, features, and functions, her approach seems particularly promising when dealing with complex, multifunctional, monumental structures that are to a much greater extent unique cultural statements, such as the élite settlement ("Palace") at Knossos treated by Palyvou.

It stands to reason that such a Palace exerted a dominant impact on the surrounding landscape and that it conditioned the local inhabitants' spatial experience in fundamental ways. But in order to understand how this happened, it helps to perceive the Palace not as a passive foil for such experience, but as an active statement by specific human beings—a work of architecture built by those who were, presumably, the most outstanding masters of that craft in their day. The builders were, to be sure, following guidelines set for them by patrons, and both these guidelines and their own responses to them were no doubt socioculturally conditioned. But Moore errs in assuming that "social intentions" were all that mattered to "motivate" a built environment (see chapter 16). We owe to recent art historical interest in artist-patron relationships the insight—which is fully applicable to the analysis of any building of some complexity—that the guidelines could cover only certain general aspects of a building's plan and layout; there always remains an irreducible gap between the intentions of a patron and what the artisan can or will produce. In some respects, even a successfully executed commission will fall short of its patron's goals; in others, it may well transcend these goals in ways that the patron may not realize or appreciate. Anyhow, for reasons of expediency, the professionally relevant details of construction have to be left to the expert to deal with. And it is these professionally relevant details that are most immediately recoverable through archaeological excavation. Only after they are thoroughly accounted for can there be any hope of grasping the patrons' guidelines and, possibly, the even more general "social intentions" behind them. This is perhaps the most important reason why any archaeologist excavating an ancient building, especially a monumental building, needs an architect on site.

In reconstructing the life histories of ancient buildings, one must thus start by asking those questions that are most immediately pertinent to the physical task of construction: What were the technical difficulties involved in enclosing a space of a given size? How was it lit and aired? What were the implications of locating the doorways where they are? How do the location and shape of a room make sense in terms of the building plan as a whole? How was each room accessed, and what "accessibility patterns" emerge? In addressing such questions, the professional skills of the architect are invaluable. As Palyvou points out (chapter 15), architects are likely to perceive things differently from field archaeologists, not only because their training conditions them to consider, first of all, the technical possibilities and constraints on the builder, but also, I suspect, because their perspective on the remains of an ancient building tends to be a synthetizing one, differing from the primarily analytic perspective of the field archaeologist. To some extent, thus, the methodological justification for including an architect as part of an archaeological team is the same as that for ethnoarchaeological research and experimental archaeology (Hodder 1986): collaboration with an architect yields insights into ancient buildings that are of the same order as the insights into ceramics obtained by a professional potter inspecting or recreating them, or those into lithic tools obtained through flint knapping. In a wider perspective, however, the importance to the archaeological enterprise of the professional opinions of architects on ancient buildings arguably far exceeds anything that can be gained from those other kinds of collaboration. This is due chiefly to two reasons.

First, buildings are by definition immobile and must be perceived in situ. They constitute part of the site matrix that is destroyed in the process of excavation (even when efforts are made, as they were at Knossos, to excavate a site in such a way as to preserve and even highlight the building remains, this almost inevitably involves a decision as to the construction stage chosen for presentation—and such a decision is typically taken retrospectively, involving reconstruction of portions already dismantled during excavation). It follows that—unlike ceramics and lithics which are portable and can still be studied by experts at some later stage—the study of buildings must proceed in tandem with the excavation.

Second, buildings are—if not always, then most of the time—infinitely more complex, culturally important, and potentially informative about a society than sundry artifacts such as tools and vessels. This is due less to their larger size than to the considerable investment of labor that goes into their construction and upkeep. Their life histories are consequently far more complex and multifaceted, and they involve far more deliberate decision making than the production and use-life of most other human-made objects. This seems to be true cross culturally, especially in those cultures that have traditionally placed a high value on architecture, such as those of Europe, the ancient Near East, and the circum-Mediterranean world.

* * * * *

In China, architecture has not historically been regarded as an art (Ledderose 2000:187–194), and until quite recently ancient buildings were not considered worth preserving. The first scholarly studies of Chinese architecture were undertaken in the early twentieth century by European and Japanese scholars (Boerschmann 1911, 1925; Tokiwa and Sekino 1926–29; Sirén 1929; Prip-Møller 1937). It was only during the 1930s that Chinese intellectuals became aware of the value of buildings as historical monuments and as objects of aesthetic value. Key figures in introducing this new awareness were the remarkable husband-and-wife team of Liang Sicheng (1901–72) and Lin Huiyin (1904–55), both trained as architects at the University of Pennsylvania, very much in the aesthetic and artisanal mold of the École des Beaux-Arts. Together with a small group of like-minded friends, they established the discipline of architectural history in China (Fairbank 1994). Working under the auspices of the privately funded Society for the Study of Chinese Architecture (*Yingzao xueshe*), they combined textual scholarship and fieldwork. They produced a new commented edition of the canon of architectural theory, the *Yingzao fashi* by Li Jie (d. 1110) (see Liang Sicheng 1984b), as well as braving difficult and often dangerous journeys to identify, measure, and record ancient buildings that were still extant. To this day, Liang Sicheng remains the single towering figure in the discipline, and all ongoing work in architectural history in China still follows his methodology (Liang Sicheng 1982–86 [1984a]).

Throughout the twentieth century, wars, revolutions, and economic modernization combined to decimate China's architectural patrimony drastically. After 1949, the government of the People's Republic of China took steps to protect the country's most important remaining historical buildings (Fresnais 2001). The first list of 180 national-level Cultural-Relics Protection Units (*Guojia zhongdian baohudanwei*), promulgated in 1961, comprised 77 ancient buildings, built structures (such as bridges), and architectural complexes. Inclusion in that list meant that central government funds could be expended in their upkeep, and guardians on government salaries were retained to protect them. Almost all of these monuments were saved from destruction during the Cultural Revolution (legend has it that Premier Zhou Enlai personally dispatched troops to guard them against the marauding Red Guards). Three additional national-level lists have been promulgated during the last quarter-century (in 1982, 1988, and 1996), raising the number of protected architectural monuments to 326. In addition, mirroring China's tiered administrative structure, many historic buildings and architectural ensembles are now being listed at the provincial and county (or city) levels. A fair number of archaeological sites with building remains are also accorded protection under this system.

Addressing the history of preservation efforts in Western countries, Stanley-Price (chapter 18) describes the historical shift in focus from individual monuments to urban contexts and, finally, landscape environments. Implementation of the latter two levels of protection is still in its infancy in China, though the third and fourth lists of national-level monuments do include some urban environments, and some of China's most spectacular landscapes (as well as such monuments as the Forbidden City and the Dunhuang Caves) have been designated UNESCO World Heritage sites. Currently, a debate is afoot in China as to whether the principles of the Venice Charter are applicable to Chinese conditions, or whether they should be replaced with a more culturally specific set of rules. A long-term cooperation project financed by the Getty Conservation Institute is now attempting to define, very gradually, a set of basic conservation principles acceptable to Chinese sensibilities (Agnew and Demas, eds. 2002). Some of the currently observable differences in opinion arise from the historical differences between China and many European countries concerning the way in which architecture has been culturally positioned in the past.

In traditional China, built structures were appreciated principally for their functionality. They were not the focus of major aesthetic elaboration or technological experimentation, and the task of constructing them fell to relatively lowly craftsmen who, with very few exceptions, have remained anonymous. This situation is linked, no doubt, to the impermanence of traditional

Chinese architecture in which wood-framed halls standing atop stamped-earth platforms constitute the predominant building type. Such buildings are almost invariably rectangular in shape and aligned to the cardinal directions; regularly spaced wooden pillars support the roof structure. Walls of wood, earth, or wattle-and-daub can be inserted into the intercolumnar spaces to form rooms; alternatively, they can be left open. The uncanny similarity of the underlying structural principles to those of modern steel-frame construction has been pointed out (Needham 1971:97, 103–104). On the Chinese mainland, this building type can be traced back to the fourth millennium BC, and it endured with only insignificant modifications (such as the introduction of tiled instead of thatched roofs around 850 BC; placement of major buildings on towering, pyramid-like platforms ca. 500–150 BC; and building platforms faced with bricks after ca. 250 BC) until the introduction of Western architecture brought about major changes in the nineteenth and twentieth centuries.

The genius of this type of architecture lies in its extraordinary versatility. Highly standardized in layout and built from modular parts (Ledderose 2000:103–137), the wooden structures can be built at almost any scale and are adaptable with very few modifications to virtually any kind of natural environment (Falkenhausen 1986:132–133). Combined into ensembles, buildings of identical types can fulfill all manner of different functions conceivable. While other types of construction (for example, using brick and stone) were known in traditional China, they were used only exceptionally, as for pagodas. Compared to Europe or the Mediterranean world, traditional Chinese urban ensembles consequently feature a high degree of visual uniformity, with monumental differing from vernacular buildings mostly in size and proportions but not in shape, technique, or materials of construction.

The distribution of ancient buildings in China is much less dense than in European countries or in Japan. This is due both to tremendous losses in recent history and a cultural penchant for rebuilding rather than repairing. The earliest preserved wooden structure dates to the late eighth century AD, and there are now but a small handful of buildings or complexes predating AD 1400. For the earlier stages of Chinese architectural history, one must therefore rely on a small number of depictions and, mainly, on archaeological excavation.

The excavation of traditional Chinese architecture poses major challenges to the archaeologist. Most of the time, all that is left are the foundation platform with post holes and/or foundation stones indicating the location of the pillars. Distinguishing different stages of stamped-earth construction and separating out different stages of construction from interspersed sets of post holes of different dates are daunting tasks. Even when they can be successfully completed, much less of a building usually survives than is the case with brick or stone masonry constructions in Europe and the circum-Mediterranean world. Another difference vis-à-vis Western architecture, broadly speaking, is that comparatively little stylistic change is observable over the millennia; and, frustrating though this may be to the archaeologist, those aspects of Chinese buildings that are prone to show temporal specificity, such as the wooden bracketing system (*dou gong*) below the eaves, are typically invisible in excavated remains. Even though representations of buildings on pictorial bronze vessels (sixth–fifth centuries BC), as pottery models made for funerary purposes (first century BC–second century AD), on wall paintings in tombs (second century BC–thirteenth century AD), on carved stone reliefs (first–second centuries AD), and on Buddhist cave temple decoration (fifth–tenth centuries AD) can convey some idea of what these structures might have looked like (see *Zhongguo gudai jianzhu jishushi* 1985:59–67), depictions in these various media are usually schematic and fail to render details of technical interest (figure 17.1).[1] Many facets of Chinese architectural history during its early phases of development are lost beyond any hope of recovery.

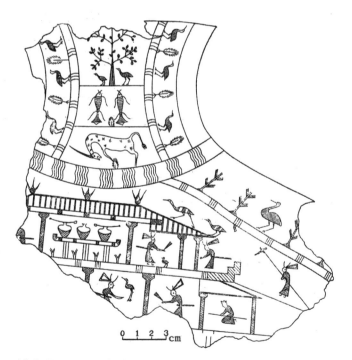

FIGURE 17.1. Fragment of a bronze pouring vessel (*yi*) excavated in 1953–54 from tomb no. 12 at Fenshuiling, Changzhi (Shanxi); late fifth century BC. *From* Kaogu xuebao (Journal of Archaeology) *1957 (1):109, Fig. 2.*

In spite of these difficulties, the study of traditional Chinese architecture has progressed immensely over the course of the last half-century. Much of the credit for the new insights gained must go to new archaeological discoveries that have greatly extended the chronological depth of Chinese architectural history. Numerous reconstructions of early buildings have been published which are based on their archaeologically recovered foundations. Since, in many cases, these reconstruction drawings are the only attempts at visualization of buildings from otherwise undocumented epochs, they have been quickly incorporated into the canon of Chinese architectural history (for example, *Zhongguo gudai jianzhu jishushi* 1985; Yang Hongxun 2001), gaining wide currency. For the above-ground portions of the buildings, their creators usually cannot do any better than to extrapolate based on later material; this is always risky. In a number of cases, divergent reconstructions have been proposed for the same building. One case in point are the buildings on the mounded tombs of the late fourth-century BC kings of Zhongshan (figures 17.2, 17.3), where the reconstruction proposed by Fu Xinian (1998:64–81 [originally published in 1978]) differs from that by Yang Hongxun (1987:120–142 [originally published in 1980]) in its smaller angle of incline of the mound, by the addition of corner turrets on each story, and by many other details (for an extensive critique, see Klose 1985).

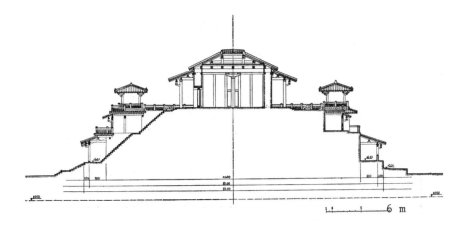

FIGURE 17.2. Reconstruction of the mounded tomb of king Cuo of Zhongshan (d. 309 BC) seen in profile, according to Fu Xinian. *From* Kaogu xuebao (Journal of Archaeology) *1980 (1):112, Fig. 12.*

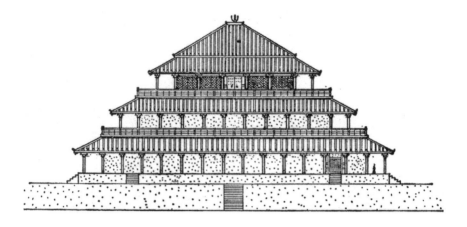

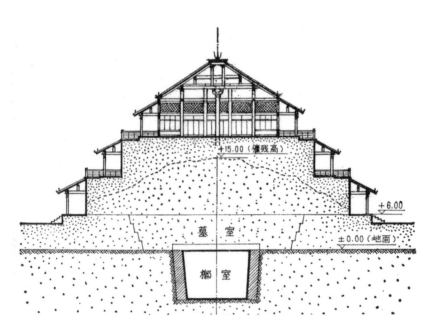

FIGURE 17.3. Profile and frontal view of the same structure as reconstructed by Yang Hongxun. *From* Kaogu xuebao (Journal of Archaeology) *1980 (1):123, Fig.*

*   *   *   *   *   *

As far as I know, Yang Hongxun (b. 1931) is China's only full-time specialist in architectural archaeology so far. Like all Chinese architectural historians of his generation, he was trained as an architect at Qinghua University in Beijing, where, after his graduation in 1955, he served for a time as research assistant to Liang Sicheng, as secretary of the Department of Architectural History and Theory, and as head of the Garden History Study Group. At the initiative of Xia Nai (1910–85), for many years the paramount leader of Chinese archaeology, Yang entered the Institute of Archaeology of the Chinese Academy of Social Sciences in 1973. This affiliation has given him unparalleled access to some of the most important archaeological sites in China as they were being excavated. His main task has been to provide reconstruction drawings for the buildings or building complexes of all periods, the remains of which have been excavated by the Institute. Over the years, he has produced a distinguished body of publications (collected in Yang Hongxun 1987; see also Yang Hongxun 2001).

In December 2001 I was privileged to observe Professor Yang in action at Anyang (Henan province). He had come to inspect a large Shang-period (ca. 1550–1046 BC) palace building foundation—the largest such foundation so far excavated in China—that had been excavated during the fall season within the recently discovered walled capital (Huanbei gucheng) to the north of the Huan River. Yang's three-day visit was treated as an affair of great importance. The site had been cleaned over several days in preparation for his arrival. While he was there, the director of the Anyang excavations, Tang Jigen, and his assistant, Yue Hongbin, were always at his side to answer any questions, and excavation personnel were on hand to clean a detail or to scrape down a profile whenever needed. Yang had been provided with the plan of the excavations (drawn at the scale of 1:50), which he compared, detail by detail, with the situation observable in the field. His many questions triggered extensive discussions about fine points of stratigraphy and site formation (figure 17.4). As he familiarized himself with the site, he took copious notes and photographs, as well as additional measurements of his own.

Very much the artist in both dress and demeanor, Yang was visibly in a state of great excitement. As he moved about the site he was taking in everything with an enhanced sensitivity and concentration, allowing the site, as it were, to inspire him. At night in his room at the Anyang Work Station of the Institute of Archaeology, he would write up his notes and synthesize his impressions of the monument. Before he left he handed excavation director Tang a highly detailed sketch, drawn freehand with a ballpoint pen, which rendered his vision of the lost building that had once graced the foundation Tang had excavated. Unlike his published reconstruction drawings, it bore a multitude of explanatory labels, demonstrating how every detail of the reconstruction could be justified either by reference to the situation on the ground or to the formal canon of traditional architecture. This sketch drawing (or another similar one Yang might have retained for himself) would become the

FIGURE 17.4. Professor Yang Hongxun (left) in the field (with Excavation Director Tang Jigen at Anyang, December 2001). *Photograph by Lothar von Falkenhausen.*

basis for a more formal, ruler-aided reconstruction drawing that would be published with an article by Yang at the same time as the preliminary report on the excavation. Eventually, that article might also be appended to the final excavation report.

Unlike his counterparts in the Aegean sphere, Yang does not normally follow the excavation of a building from beginning to end. Instead, he usually spends several days at the site when the foundation—invariably the only recoverable portion of the building—has been fully exposed. This limited presence on site is his own choice; his Institute would allow him to participate in the entire season, and he has done so on occasion. Queried by me about the issue, he replied that, for the kinds of architectural remains at hand, he considered his mode of operation sufficient, as well as most efficient.

Perhaps the most important practical difference between Yang's approach and that of architects working with archaeologists in the Aegean sphere is that the building plans are drawn, not by an architect, but by the excavating archaeologists. Since the latter have no architectural training, this method potentially introduces simplifications and distortions, though in practice, at least at sites excavated by the Institute of Archaeology, the plans are usually highly accurate. It goes without saying that these plans have a crucial impact on the practice of architectural history: not only does Yang Hongxun himself use them as a blueprint, but other prominent specialists who lack Yang's direct access to the sites, such as his estranged former class-mate Fu Xinian (b. 1933), are prone to prepare reconstructions of excavated buildings based entirely on their published floor plans.

Rather than being a fully integrated member of the excavation team, the architectural archaeologist in China tends to be, then, mainly a procurer of architectural reconstructions. The appearance and "style" of these recon-structions is influenced primarily by their creators' intensive exposure to tra-ditional Chinese buildings. Long seasons of fieldwork involving the close study and measuring of extant buildings constitute a core component of the curriculum in architectural history at Qinghua and all other leading institu-tions in China. Ultimately, of course, this particular pedagogical approach derives from Western practice, in particular that of the École des Beaux-Arts during the late nineteenth century. Fieldwork is complemented by intensive study of the *Yingzao fashi* and other textual sources relating to building tech-nique. Even though neither Yang Hongxun nor Fu Xinian are, normally, practicing architects, they have learned to construct traditional buildings and are sometimes called upon to do so (see below). Their reconstructions, like those of their colleagues in the Aegean, thus may be said to derive from architectural practice. The degree of empathy into the thought processes of ancient builders is difficult to judge; if such empathy were directly correlated with the amount of time spent in the field, one might suspect that it is signif-icantly less in the Chinese case than in the Aegean, but such an inference may not be entirely appropriate given the more standardized nature of Chi-nese architecture.

The contribution of the work done by Yang and his colleagues, seminal though it is to the study of art and architectural history, is still regarded as somewhat marginal in Chinese archaeological circles. Aside from the objec-tive limitations on the evidence, this situation may still reflect the tradi-tional low regard for architecture in Chinese culture, but it may also have to do with the fact that archaeological practice in China is still predominantly concerned with the recovery of artifacts and issues of dating rather than with excavating sites and interpreting their sociopolitical contexts. As research orientations are gradually changing, one may expect that more attention will be paid to the built environment, and one hopes that the role of architects in excavation teams will be enhanced. While the accuracy of reconstructions may not necessarily increase in the future, one may expect the development of a more sophisticated understanding of the cultural context and signifi-cance of excavated buildings as larger surfaces are uncovered and complexes of buildings rather than individual structures are excavated.

*   *   *   *   *

. . . non seulement vous ne démolirez pas, vous préserverez et conserverez.
Mais vous ne restaurerez pas, ce qui de toutes formes du vandalisme, est d'ordi-
naire la pire.

From a letter by Auguste Barth, member of the Institute, to Louis Finot,
first director of the École française d'Extrême-Orient
(*Clémentin-Ohja and Manguin 2001:18*)

The need to weigh the concerns of national education against those of tourism arises in Chinese archaeology as it does in the circum-Mediterranean sphere, and it is safe to predict that this issue will be discussed even more in future years. Different from the US (see Gamble chapter 19), the modern inhabitants of China do not have any problem in identifying with the creators of the country's archaeological past. Instead, the main impediments to effective protection of China's ancient heritage are the low level of education in the countryside and, above all, poverty. In international comparison, the amount of resources poured into archaeological excavation and heritage preservation from the 1950s through the mid-1980s was admirable for a developing country. At that time archaeology was used as a vehicle for educating the masses, a source of material proof for the validity of Marxist historiography. Large numbers of citizens visited archaeological exhibits and museums, and there was considerable popular interest in archaeology.

In recent years, with the advent of Western-style consumer culture and the shift in emphasis in scholastic curricula from Marxism to the natural sciences, this interest in archaeology has largely waned. Ironically, moreover, as China has become vastly more prosperous, government involvement in archaeology and preservation has slackened considerably. Research-driven excavation has almost come to a standstill, though international collaboration ventures, permitted since the mid-1990s, have opened new opportunities. The main justification for archaeology and preservation these days lies in their exploitability for touristic purposes—more specifically for purposes of foreign tourism. This emphasis has engendered specific styles of presentation of the Chinese past that are geared to foreigners, and which tend to be entertainment-oriented rather than educational, simplified and prone to exaggeration in their coverage of history, as well as gaudy, prettified, dumbed down, exoticizing, and (sometimes) mildly erotic. Whether the rise in Chinese tourism in recent years will modify this self-orientalizing caricature of Chinese civilization remains to be seen.

Different from practices in places like Cyprus, described by Nicholas Stanley-Price (chapter 18), archaeological sites in China are always reburied after excavation. The excavation protocol promulgated by the State Bureau of Cultural Relics (Wenwuju) demands this, and funds are allocated for this purpose in excavation budgets. The underlying rationale is, no doubt, to ensure that precious land is returned to agricultural use after excavation. As a result, there is rarely anything for the visiting public to see. This is true even at the few exceptionally important sites that are set aside for preservation. Sometimes the outlines of building foundations and the foundation stones of the wooden pillars are made visible above ground, but the original floor surfaces are covered by protective layers of sands and grass; otherwise, they would disappear within a very short time.

Only very rarely are the excavations (or portions thereof) roofed over and made accessible as site museums. Most museums are at cemeteries and tombs, and only a minority are at settlement sites featuring architectural remains. At the Neolithic villages at Banpo (in Xi'an city, Shaanxi province) and Dahecun (in Zhengzhou city, Henan province), the remains of original buildings are preserved as excavated (figure 17.5), and full-scale reconstructions are erected elsewhere on the museum grounds to help visitors visualize what they have seen (figure 17.6).

There have been a few attempts to reconstruct buildings to full scale based on the reconstruction drawings. An archaeologically informed, full-

FIGURE 17.5. Neolithic site of Dahecun, Zhengzhou (Henan): lower portions of wattle-and-daub built structures preserved at the site museum; fifth millennium BC. *Photograph by Albert E. Dien.*

FIGURE 17.6. Reconstructed building on the grounds of the site museum in Dahecun. The statue in the foreground shows a Neolithic woman. *Photograph by Lothar von Falkenhausen.*

FIGURE 17.7. Replica of the First Emperor's palace at the Xi'an Film Studios. *Photograph by Lothar von Falkenhausen.*

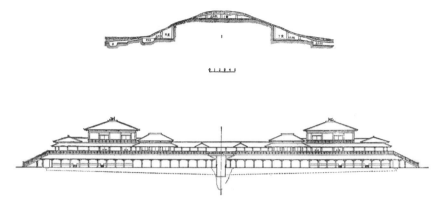

FIGURE 17.8. Section drawing and Yang Hongxun's reconstruction of a large earthen platform at the site of the First Emperor's palace at Xianyang; late third century BC. *From* Wenwu (Cultural Relics) *1976 (11):5, Fig. 4; 33, Fig. 2.*

scale model of the palace of the First Emperor of Qin, constructed for a major film epic in the mid-1980s, can still be visited at the Xi'an Film Studios (figure 17.7), but it is neither particularly exact (for instance, it is a multistoried building rather than consisting, as did the original, of concentric layers of single-storied construction around a pyramidal earthen core; compare figure 17.8), nor is it located anywhere near the actual site. Different is the case of the reconstructed temple/palace buildings at the Late Shang–period capital near Anyang (Henan province); here in 1987 structures that had been excavated between 1928 and 1937 were reconstructed on the original foundations as part of an effort to turn the site into a park for tourists. Apparently, the foundations were not reexcavated for the purpose.

The reconstructed buildings (figure 17.9) were designed by none other than Yang Hongxun. They differ quite radically from the cautious and somewhat schematic reconstruction drawings published by the original excavator, Shi Zhangru (1954, 1970, 1976) (figure 17.10). For one thing, Yang holds, somewhat controversially, that ancient builders extended the eaves over and beyond the stamped-earth platform to protect the platform from the rain, and he reconstructs a row of *chiyanzhu* (eaves-upholding pillars) surrounding the platform. Moreover, all wooden members of the building are embellished with carved and lacquered motifs similar to those seen on Shang ritual bronzes; even though the chambers of the royal Shang tombs are known to have been fitted with large-scale, ornamented lacquered wood panels, the use of such lacquered decoration is so far undocumented in the excavated remains of standing architecture. The specific execution of the wooden

FIGURE 17.9. Reconstructed palace building designed by Yang Hongxun at the Anyang Archaeological Park, 1987. *Photograph by Lothar von Falkenhausen.*

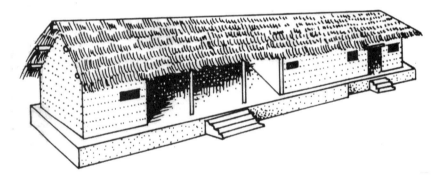

FIGURE 17.10. Proposed reconstruction by Shi Zhangru of Late Shang (fourteenth–eleventh centuries BC) ceremonial building no. I.4 at Yinxu, Anyang (Henan). *From Shi Zhangru 1954: unnumbered illustration.*

crests gracing the building's hipped thatched roof is based on the decoration of *fangyi* (casket-shaped wine vessels) from the Shang dynasty (figure 17.11); it is quite uncertain whether these vessels were really meant to look "architectural" rather than, for instance, rendering the shape of a casket-like piece of furniture.

Since no actual Shang buildings, or even depictions thereof, are now extant, the mixture of fact and informed fantasy reflected in such recon-

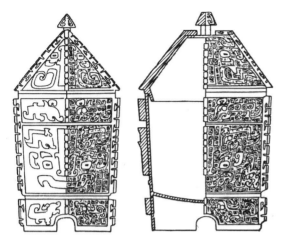

FIGURE 17.11. *Fangyi* vessel from tomb no. 238 at Yinxu, Anyang (Henan); Late Shang period. *From* Yinxu de faxian yu yanjiu (Discoveries and research at the last Shang capital) *1994: 286, Fig. 155.3.*

structions is inevitable. Unlike such bizarre aberrations as the adjacent Forest of Oracle-Bone Writing Stelae—inscribed standing stones in the shape of over-dimensioned Shang oracle bones—the reconstructed buildings do have some educational value, helping the general public to envision the Shang architectural environment. Even so, one may well remain ambivalent as to the wisdom of constructing such ersatz monuments at the very place that, for three millennia, had been the proverbial epitome of the utter physical annihilation that will follow the fall of a dynasty.

* * * * *

Acknowledgments

This article grew from my discussant's comments at the workshop on archaeology in the Mediterranean in honor of Lloyd E. Cotsen at UCLA on March 23–25, 2000. Many thanks to Lloyd E. Cotsen and the organizers of the conference for instigating a great deal of stimulating discussion, to the editors of this volume for their invitation to contribute, and to Professor Yang Hongxun for allowing me to interview him in the course of preparing this article.

Note

1. The pictorial décor on vessels like this one contains the earliest, very schematic depictions of buildings in the history of Chinese art. In keeping with the vessel's decorative program, these are sizable temple/palace structures within which ritual activities are being performed on two tiers; the top of one pillar of a third tier below is visible on the lower right. Rather than multistoried construction, this design is believed to represent a single-storied building placed concentrically on different levels of a large earthen platform like that seen in figures 17.2, 17.3, and 17.8.

PART V

SITE PRESERVATION, CONSERVATION, AND ARCHAEOLOGICAL ETHICS

CHAPTER 18

Site Preservation and Archaeology in the Mediterranean Region

NICHOLAS STANLEY-PRICE

Introduction

In the long history of archaeological excavation in the Mediterranean region, issues such as site preservation, presentation to the public, and management have tended to be addressed after the fieldwork has been finished. By contrast, contemporary thinking would stress that they need to be considered in advance of any fieldwork, and especially in advance of the use of any destructive technique such as excavation.

On this view, archaeology in the sense of field research is but one of many components in an overall policy of heritage management. A strategy for archaeological investigation is as necessary as strategies for site conservation, public presentation, and tourism. To put it provocatively, we could say that, from the viewpoint of the heritage manager, archaeological sites are too important to be left to the archaeologist. They have many potential uses. In fact, management of the archaeological heritage has to reconcile three potentially conflicting goals, namely, research, long-term preservation, and public access and interpretation.

The practice of archaeological heritage management is not new, of course. It consists of all those responsibilities that have always been entrusted to national antiquities authorities or archaeological services. But it has changed in recent years in two important ways. One has been the greater pressure from national tourism offices to promote tourism to heritage sites. The other lies in the steadily increasing number of known sites, particularly excavated sites, that require protection. Staff and budgetary resources are no longer adequate, if they ever were, to respond to these trends. In the absence of greatly increased budgets, one response by heritage authorities has been to require archaeologists who are given fieldwork permits to share the responsibilities of site conservation and protection.

These developments are evident in Mediterranean countries, though they are not unique to that part of the world. In fact, some of the impetus behind these trends in the Mediterranean region must be due to the growing international consensus with regard to the practice of archaeological heritage management. This is reflected in international charters, recommendations, and codes of ethics. Ironically, most of those documents have their origins in the countries of classical civilization. The initial need for them arose from the problems of protecting and restoring the monuments of the ancient world.

This paper therefore begins by reviewing the historical development of policies for archaeology in the Mediterranean world. It then considers current issues in site preservation, which, in turn, point to possible future trends.

Development of Policy Toward the Archaeological Heritage

The foundations of national policies for archaeology in the Mediterranean region lie in the work of the League of Nations following the First World War. In 1920 the League had been responsible for approving the mandate agreements for the countries of the Middle East following the defeat of the Ottoman Empire. The agreements included articles to ensure equal treatment for all member states of the League of Nations as far as archaeological research was concerned. In reaction to the competition among the imperial powers of the pre-war period, efforts were made to guarantee access to sites by archaeologists of all nationalities (O'Keefe and Prott 1984:45, 74). This principle was adopted in drawing up the national legislations of Iraq, Syria, Lebanon, and Palestine, which were enacted in the 1920s and 1930s. Some of this legislation is still in force—for instance, the Règlement sur les Antiquités of 1933 in Lebanon.

By the 1930s a consensus was emerging in this part of the world about the principles of archaeological practice. Especially influential was the International Conference on Excavations organized in 1937 by the Egyptian Government and the International Museums Office (O'Keefe and Prott 1984: 237–238). Almost all the Mediterranean countries were represented at this landmark event. The Cairo Conference had two important outcomes: the publication of a *Manual on the Technique of Archaeological Excavations*, and a series of recommendations for the conduct of excavations and international collaboration (International Museums Office 1940:211–225).

The recommendations of the Cairo Conference were duly recognized by the League of Nations. Following this endorsement, the "Final Act" of the Cairo Conference was described by its secretary-general as "a veritable international charter of antiquities and excavations" (Foundoukidis 1940:213).

But because of the deteriorating international situation in the years 1938–39, the recommendations were not widely disseminated, although a number of countries did enact or amend their national legislations.

In fact, between 1937 and 1939, thirteen countries submitted commentaries on the Cairo recommendations to the League of Nations (UNESCO 1955:7–9). Eight of these were European, the others being Turkey, Iraq, Guatemala, Chile, and the Union of South Africa. Following the war, UNESCO again requested the comments of member countries. In their replies, Poland before the war and Belgium and the Union of South Africa after the war commented on the geographical bias of the Cairo Conference and the need to consider the rest of the world (UNESCO 1955:10).

It was not that national legislation regarding archaeology was lacking in other continents, nor attempts to bring some uniformity to archaeological policies. For instance, as early as 1910, the Congreso Científico Internacional Americano, meeting in Buenos Aires, approved a proposal from Peru for a "Proyecto de reglamentacíon pertinente a la conservacíon y explotacíon de los yacimientos y monumentos arqueológicos americanos" (Endere and Podgorny 1997:57).

Thus, what was needed in the post-World War II era was a single document providing principles that were truly valid internationally. Very soon after its founding in 1945, UNESCO pursued this goal as a priority. At its first session in 1946, the General Conference decided to seek expert advice on freedom of access to sites of historical and artistic interest. At its second session held in Mexico City in 1947, a resolution was passed concerning measures to secure every possible access by archaeologists of all countries to archaeological sites (UNESCO 1955:7). This initiative culminated in 1956 in the adoption of its "Recommendation to Member States on International Principles Applicable to Archaeological Excavations." (The text is reproduced in UNESCO 1983 and Stanley-Price 1995:145-149, and at *www. unesco.org/general/eng/legal.convent.html.*)

The main aim of the recommendation was to guide states in drafting national archaeological legislation. Indeed, many national legislations now in force do echo the principles of the 1956 UNESCO document (see O'Keefe and Prott 1984). It has also remained the benchmark to which later charters refer when dealing with the conduct of archaeological research. Thus Article 15 of the influential Charter of Venice (text reproduced in Jokilehto 1998 and at *www.international.icomos.org/icomos/e_charte.htm*) states that excavations should be carried out in accordance with scientific standards and the 1956 recommendation.

As recently as 1990, although the field of site conservation had by then advanced significantly since the 1950s, the Charter for the Protection and

Management of the Archaeological Heritage adopted by the International Council on Monuments and Sites (ICOMOS) still referred to the 1956 UNESCO recommendation for guidance regarding the principles of site conservation. The relevant paragraph (21) of the 1956 document, under the heading "Preservation of archaeological remains," states:

> The deed of concession should define the obligations of the excavator during and on completion of his work. The deed should, in particular, provide for guarding, maintenance, and restoration of the site together with the conservation, during and on completion of his work, of objects and monuments uncovered. The deed should moreover indicate what help if any the excavator might expect from the conceding country in the discharge of his obligations should these prove too onerous.

In practice, in most countries the national authorities have tended to retain responsibility for guarding, protecting, or restoring archaeological sites. Exceptions include Turkey, which requires excavators to be responsible for the guarding, maintenance, and restoration of the sites they excavate; and Afghanistan during the 1970s when, for a foreign excavator to secure an excavation permit, he or she also had to agree to undertake the restoration of a historic building. These have been exceptions to the general rule, but the rule is now changing, with a greater contribution—sometimes literally in the form of a percentage of the project budget—being required from the excavator for site conservation. In reality, this shift is tantamount to reverting to the principles advocated in the 1956 recommendation.

The UNESCO recommendations have also dealt with salvage archaeology. The 1956 recommendation was used as the basis for drawing up contracts with the foreign teams that took part in the Nubia salvage campaigns in the 1960s (UNESCO 1978:2). A similar model was used in the 1970s, with the foreign teams taking part in the international Save Carthage campaign. For the Carthage campaign, postexcavation policy followed the 1956 recommendation: each director had to agree to plan and pay for the costs of the mise-en-valeur of the sites that he or she excavated (Greene 1999:46). In Nubia, of course, the excavated sites were due to be inundated and no mise-en-valeur was possible, except through the drastic action of relocating monuments outside the area to be flooded.

The loss of monuments in Nubia represented a landmark in the evolution of attitudes toward the preservation of outstanding sites. In 1964 UNESCO launched an International Campaign for Monuments "with a view to protecting the monuments that are mankind's heritage and enhancing their impact" (Säve-Söderbergh 1972:140). This line of thought eventually led to the drafting of the World Heritage Convention that UNESCO adopted in 1972.

The other significant agreement resulting from the Nubian salvage campaigns was UNESCO's 1968 Recommendation Concerning the Preservation of Cultural Property Endangered by Public or Private Works. This document was drawn up because of the dispute at the time of the Nubia campaigns as to who should fund the salvage excavations (Säve-Söderbergh 1972). The 1968 recommendation clearly states that the costs of financing salvage projects should be met by national or local heritage authorities, or that they should be borne by the developer or by a combination of the two.

This was in 1968, but it took many years before the principle of developer funding was adopted in Mediterranean countries. The ICOMOS Charter of 1990 (referred to above) and the European Convention on the Protection of the Archaeological Heritage of 1992 reaffirmed the principle that the polluter should pay. Typical of the philosophies underlying these and other recent charters are recommendations that excavation should be undertaken only when unavoidable; that preservation in situ is the preferable course of action; and that reconstruction of sites should be undertaken with caution and preferably not on top of the excavated remains. The extent to which these principles have been incorporated into practice varies widely from country to country, but they illustrate the direction in which thinking about archaeological heritage management is evolving.

This historical review provides some background to what amounts to a broad international consensus on principles. I now consider key issues concerning the practice of site conservation and presentation in the Mediterranean region.

Site Conservation

The classic problem facing antiquities authorities is what to do with exposed excavated remains. Given that they are bound to continue to deteriorate if left exposed and that conservation and maintenance cost money, why not rebury them after excavation? There has, in fact, been increasing interest in the techniques of reburial—a much less glamorous field than restoration and reconstruction but an essential one, nevertheless, if one is to be responsible about the archaeological record (Dowdy and Taylor 1993; Corfield et al. 1998; Podany, Agnew, and Demas 1993).

But the solution of reburial comes up against numerous difficulties—legal, ethical, and practical. For example, if land has been expropriated for an excavation to take place, the evidence of the excavated remains is often needed to justify the act of expropriation. In a country such as Cyprus, backfilling an excavation is the exception, and special permission to do so is needed from the Department of Antiquities. The fieldwork of archaeologists is more difficult to justify to local communities if it is covered over again after excavation. Are the finds important or not? If they are, should they not remain visible and be actively displayed?

So, probably the majority of excavations at Classical-period sites in the Mediterranean region remain open following excavation. Whatever the logic of selective reburial, attitudes do not seem to have changed much with regard to this problem, despite the insistence of the international recommendations and charters stating that excavated remains should not be left exposed unless maintenance and protection can be guaranteed.

Faced with the protection of exposed archaeological sites, how have archaeological authorities tackled this problem? Most solutions have fallen into one of two traditions. The first has been conservation, with the aim of preserving the remains as they are excavated. The second has been restoration and reconstruction, which also has a didactic and interpretative goal. The work of Evans at Knossos exemplifies the reconstruction tradition (A. Evans 1927; Papadopoulos 1997; Palyvou chapter 15).

The Venice Charter of 1964 (Article 15) ruled out all reconstruction, permitting only *anastylosis* or the reassembly of existing but dismembered parts. The principles of the charter are still observed in many reconstruction or reerection projects on Classical sites of the Mediterranean region (see Nohlen 1999 for a recent example). Other projects, though, have interpreted the principles liberally or else ignored them, sometimes due to the pressure from national tourism authorities to produce substantial buildings from surviving ruins. Ancient theaters and other places of performance have been particularly susceptible to such pressures of reuse for staging contemporary events. In response, the Verona Charter (1997) on the Use of Ancient Places of Performance has attempted to lay down principles agreed to by archaeological and theatrical interest groups. Significantly, the charter requires that any restoration work at ancient theatres incorporate the principles of the earlier Venice Charter (*The Verona Charter [1997] on the Use of Ancient Places of Performance 1999*).

To return to the less interventive policy of conservation, perhaps the most important innovation in the postwar years was the development of modern synthetic materials. These have been widely used in two ways: as synthetic consolidants and protective coatings applied to exposed stone and mudbrick surfaces, and as sheeting or panels to cover exposed archaeological remains.

The earlier faith placed in synthetic consolidants and protective coatings for treating exposed archaeological remains now appears to have been premature. Experience has shown that caution is needed in their use, and more rigorous approaches to their long-term evaluation must be developed (Price 1996; Tiano et al. 1996). Generally speaking, wider use is made nowadays of natural materials such as lime-based mortars and grouts than of synthetic consolidants such as the polyvinyl acetates and acrylics of earlier days. Cost has also been an important consideration. Treating an outstanding painting or sculpture with a synthetic consolidant can perhaps be afforded. But earlier hopes that cheap synthetic products would be identified for application to large areas of exposed stone or mudbrick have proved to be overly optimistic.

Today, there is much more emphasis on reducing the rate of deterioration of excavated remains by using preventive measures such as shading and controlled drying (for example, Costanzi Cobau 1985). Such preventive approaches, in turn, affect the method and rate of excavation. But, as all conservation measures ought, they lead to a greater retrieval of information for the archaeologist.

As with synthetic consolidants, ideas have changed with regard to plastic sheeting or panels. The polyethylene sheets well known to archaeologists are still widely used despite the damage they often cause to sensitive surfaces. Modern permeable synthetics such as geotextiles now seem promising—for instance, as a component of reburial fills (Demas et al. 1993). Caution is needed, however; if the history of synthetic materials used on archaeological sites teaches us nothing else, it is that each generation believes it has found an appropriate solution. For instance, sheeting made of plastic materials was used extensively as part of the protective measures for the sites of Piazza Armerina (figure 18.1), and Heraclea Minoa and Gela (figure 18.2) in Sicily

Figure 18.1. Protective enclosure of sheet glass and Perspex/Plexiglas, from the west, at the Roman villa site of Piazza Armerina, Sicily, 1984.

FIGURE 18.2. Protective panels of Perspex/Plexiglas bolted to the ancient mud brick walls at Gela city-state, 1984. Note the development of plant growth between the panel and wall surfaces.

(Minissi 1978). Forty years later, its removal at all three sites has already taken place or is actively under discussion because of the damage it has caused to the archaeological remains (Stanley-Price 1997; Alaimo et al. 1996; Chiari, personal communication).

Although high-tech approaches still exist, there has been a return to more traditional methods of protection. For instance, there has been renewed interest in the design of protective roofs and shelters. Experience over more than one hundred years (for instance, at sites such as Pompeii) helps to identify successful examples of shelter design. In a project drawing upon this experience, a prototype shelter for possible application worldwide was developed and tested at Paphos in Cyprus (figure 18.3) and in the USA (Agnew and Coffman 1991; Agnew et al. 1996). The aim was to develop an inexpensive modular design constructed of lightweight materials, easily transported and erected, and requiring no penetration of the subsoil. The cost of the materials for the Paphos shelter was $12,000 (Stanley-Price 1991:66-67), a figure that can be compared with those for other recent shelter designs. The protective structure over the Neolithic site of Kalavasos-Tenta, also in Cyprus, cost about $340,000 and the much more extensive shelters at Mallia in Crete cost over half a million dollars (Schmid 1998).

The work of some architects in developing new shelter designs is complementary to the work of others on restoration and reconstruction projects.

FIGURE 18.3. Protective "hexashelter" over Orpheus mosaic at the House of Theseus, Paphos, Cyprus, 1990.

In much of the world there has been a reaction against ambitious on-site reconstructions (see the comments on the Charter of Venice above). Some earlier reconstructions have been shown to be erroneous and have actually misled later scholars (Molina Montes 1982). But the reaction against reconstruction can also be attributed generally to the growth of a critical approach toward the concept of heritage and to the realization that many reconstruction projects have had a strongly political and nationalist motivation. The discovery that some reconstructions owe more to faith than to evidence has, in turn, reinforced interest in the documentation of original material.

Documentation and Publication

In going back to reassess earlier restoration work and to recover the original evidence, the records are often found to be inadequate or entirely lacking. Archives such as those that exist for Evans's work at Knossos are unusual. Even nowadays, much conservation and restoration work is inadequately documented. The number of excavation reports that include relevant information about conservation treatments is growing but is still far from impressive.

If a published record of conservation on excavations is rare, publication of the excavations themselves is still very uneven. If, in 1937, there was held the International Conference on Excavations referred to earlier, in 1999 an International Conference on Unpublished Excavations was organized by the Department of Antiquities of Cyprus and the Anastasios G. Leventis Foundation (the conference papers are due to be published). Herzog (1996) had already graphically illustrated the scale of the problem by examining the publication record of 100 years of research excavations in Palestine and Israel. He studied the records of 146 excavations, which together had required over 800 different field campaigns. Only 27% of the excavation projects had been the object of published final reports.

Herzog's analysis included only research excavations. One wonders what a similar analysis of salvage excavations would reveal. Salvage archaeology operates on a quite different scale than research excavation (Greene 1999). In addition to infrastructure development, illicit excavation to feed the antiquities market remains a major contributor to site destruction. But the scale of site loss is perhaps appreciated most dramatically in the case of the construction of large dams. To take one country only, according to statistics compiled by Özdogan (2000), the total number of dams in Turkey either completed or under construction is 298. Of these, sufficient archaeological surveys have been carried out in only about 25 reservoir areas (that is, less than 10%). Organized extensive rescue work was undertaken in only five cases. In all the other areas, there is no idea of what has been lost. In all cases except the Keban project, existing monuments have been left to be inundated by the new reservoir lakes.

The loss of archaeological sites in Turkey (along with others in Syria and Iraq) is sobering, despite the salvage archaeology programs organized in advance of dam construction. Portugal, however, provides an exception to the rule of extensive site loss, with the abandonment of the hydroelectric dam construction project on the Côa River as a result of popular protest (Zilhão 1998). But the Côa controversy has not led to the abandonment of large dam construction projects in Portugal. The lessons, both positive and negative, learned from the Côa controversy are now being applied to the mitigation project for the huge Alqueva hydroelectric scheme in the Alentejo in southern Portugal. The scheme foresees the inundation of an area of about 250 km^2, 30 of them actually in Spain, and is due to form one of the largest man-made lakes in Europe. A large-scale salvage project well funded by the state is under way (Silva 1999, personal communication).

From Sites to Landscapes

Salvage archaeology epitomizes many fundamental issues in preservation of the archaeological record. Because it requires making decisions about comparative significance, it also helps direct emphasis away from individual sites toward groups of sites and even landscapes. Several current approaches to archaeological site management in the Mediterranean region go beyond the single site and treat whole landscapes. They also move away from the traditional model of sole management by an overextended department of antiquities or archaeological service. Typically, they use models that involve a number of interest groups, including the statutory authority, academic specialists, professional planners, tourism promoters, and local communities. There are both rural and urban examples of such approaches, which perhaps give an indication of future trends in this field.

Rural examples would include the Parco della Roca di San Silvestro in Tuscany (Francovich and Buchanan 1995) and the Côa Valley in Portugal (figures 18.4, 18.5), already mentioned (Zilhâo 1998). The Côa Valley is in an area of traditional agricultural landscape, much of which has been progressively abandoned in recent years. Incentives are needed to encourage the population not to migrate. The Park authorities are investigating ways of subsidizing traditional land management practices while also providing employment. It is diversifying the attractions offered to visitors—for instance, through recreation opportunities and ecotourism (figure 18.5). The evolution of management structures is also significant. The original salvage program was established by Portugal's Instituto Português do Património Arquitectónico e Arqueológico, of which one section was responsible for archaeology in the country. Following the dam controversy, a new Portu-

FIGURE 18.4. Côa Valley, northeast Portugal, from the east.

FIGURE 18.5. Guide and visitor inspecting a Paleolithic rock engraving in the Côa Valley, site of Canada do Inferno.

guese Institute of Archaeology was founded as an agency within the Ministry of Culture, with the archaeological park being created as a department of the Institute. Thus, the controversy in Portugal over the importance of archaeological sites in the face of development, and the public debate that it provoked, has acted as a catalyst in the complete reorganization of archaeology in the country.

A rather different model, one of public-private cooperation, is being applied at Butrint in Albania (Butrint Foundation 2000) (figure 18.6). This important Classical site is situated in an unusual rural landscape, the product of the agricultural policies of the previous Albanian regime and the lack of the industrialization and tourism development along most northern Mediterranean coastlines. The Butrint project is establishing not only a national park that protects the city site but also a much larger area that is as important for its natural values as for its cultural history. The city site covers an area of some 16 ha, but a much larger protected zone of 184 ha was declared last year. This zone includes a substantial stretch of the coastline that had already been bought up by tourism speculators. A management plan is now being developed that integrates research, preservation, and public access while promoting economic development through controlled tourism. As with the example of the Côa Valley in Portugal, the Butrint project has led

FIGURE 18.6. Roman theater, Butrint, Albania. Note the high water table.

to new mechanisms of heritage management in Albania, with a separate office being established in 1999 by the Albanian Ministry of Culture to oversee the daily management of this World Heritage site and to coordinate the development of the national park.

If pressures on rural sites such as Butrint are intense, they may nevertheless seem minor compared with the complexity of urban sites. The reconciliation of urban development with heritage preservation continues to be controversial in such capital cities as Athens and Rome. Both cities have had long-standing plans to protect the archaeological remains in their historic centers as parks. In Athens the first proposals go back to S. Kleanthes and E. Schaubert in 1833, shortly after Independence (Papageorgiou 2000). In Rome the idea of an archaeological park extending out from the Roman Forum to the Appian Way was initiated by G. Baccelli in 1887 (Jokilehto 1999:208). In both cities, current projects are realizing long-standing goals: in Athens with the plan for the Unification of Archaeological Sites, and in Rome with the Progetto Fori Imperiali, both designed to facilitate pedestrian access to continuous archaeological zones in areas of intense vehicular traffic use.

Despite the models of Athens and Rome, in other Mediterranean urban centers archaeological heritage still has to fight for full legal protection. In the 1970s, the international salvage campaign in Carthage was prompted by the threats of uncontrolled urbanization in the area of the ancient city. Despite the success of the archaeological campaign, the promised Archaeological Park of Carthage–Sidi Bou Said has still not been formally approved. A 600 ha zone was declared in 1985 in which most construction was banned, but major encroachments on this zone have been tolerated and formal designation of the park is still awaited.

The case of Beirut (figure 18.7) also exemplifies the difficulties of securing adequate investigation and preservation of the archaeological heritage of

FIGURE 18.7. Middle Bronze Age glacis found in the salvage excavation of the ancient Tell of Beirut, Lebanon.

a city in the face of intense redevelopment pressures (Seeden 2000). Among the sites excavated is the Zone des Eglises, which from the start was isolated as an archaeological park that would remain free of redevelopment. A recent initiative that is now being implemented following an international design competition is to create a Garden of Forgiveness around the excavated remains as a symbol of reconciliation among the different communities of Lebanon. Significantly, the proposal came from a concerned individual and not from the developers or the national antiquities authority.

The proposal for a Garden of Forgiveness recalls not only the proliferation nowadays of peace museums (in contrast to the war museums of an earlier generation) but other designs for peace parks centered around monuments. Another example is the proposed International Peace Park straddling the Dardanelles in Turkey, linking the existing Gallipoli National Park to the north with the protected area around the site of Troy on the southern side of the channel. The deliberate association of monuments of the past with contemporary aspirations for peace is not new, of course. But it is salutary to recall that heritage sites have multiple uses rather than solely the promotion of tourism or other economic benefit.

Acknowledgments

I am grateful to Dr. Mehmet Özdogan for allowing me to refer to his unpublished paper, and to Dr. Antonio Silva for information concerning the Alqueva dam in Portugal. This paper has not been updated since its original presentation at the seminar in 2000.

CHAPTER 19

Obstacles to Site Preservation in the United States

LYNN H. GAMBLE

The practice of cultural resource preservation in the United States is markedly different from that found in most countries in the Mediterranean region. Three major obstacles in the history of the United States have affected the conservation and preservation of archaeological heritage, particularly American Indian heritage. The first, and perhaps the most significant of these, is that the United States is a colonial nation with a tragic history of either overlooking, pushing aside, or decimating the first inhabitants of the nation, the American Indians. The colonial backdrop of United States history is pervasive in the nation's heritage management legislation and can readily be observed today in what is considered worthy of preservation. Scholars such as Ferguson (1996), McGuire (1992), Trigger (1980), and Thomas (2000) have noted that America's colonial foundations have affected the entire practice, theories, and teaching of archaeology in the United States. Clear examples of biases in the interpretation of archaeological remains were most apparent in the 1800s when many scholars believed that the large earthen mounds scattered throughout the eastern United States could not have been built by American Indians because the Indians were incapable of such architectural sophistication. In tandem with these beliefs, American Indian skulls were actively collected in an attempt to prove that American Indians were racially inferior (Bieder 1992). Although some would say that these biases have receded, they have existed up to the present in various forms. This history has created a situation of distrust of archaeologists by many American Indians.

a

b

FIGURE 19.1. Cahokia mound sites: a, view of Monk's Mound, Cahokia, in the early 1990s, with a road in the foreground; b, reconstruction of mounds at Cahokia, ca. AD 1150.

The second major obstacle affecting historic preservation in the United States is that cultural resources are protected differentially based on the type of landownership (Elia 1993:427). In the United States, legal ownership of land overrides the significance of heritage sites. Private property owners are afforded considerable rights that are not seen in many other parts of the world, with a distinctive set of rules applying to federal lands that are not applicable to privately owned lands.

The third obstacle is the limited number of sites with architectural features. At least some of the public is familiar with the mound sites in the central and southeastern United States, such as Cahokia, IL (figures 19.1a, b), or the cliff dwellings in the southwestern United States, such as Mesa Verde. Unfortunately, however, prehistoric sites with clear architectural features are relatively rare in the United States. Given the relative dearth of sites with monumental architecture, or any architecture at all, preservationists must overcome great barriers to convince the public that sites with more subtle significance are worthy of preservation. Moreover, because architectural remains are limited in many parts of the United States, conservation issues surrounding the preservation of exposed excavated features are not as pervasive a problem as in the Mediterranean.

The Effects of National Legislation on the Protection of Cultural Resources

The imbalance between the preservation of non-native sites and native sites can be seen in the history of US legislation. In contrast, more recent legislation of relevance to cultural resource heritage reflects a shift in perspective in an attempt to recognize the significance of American Indian heritage sites and to correct the injustices American Indians have experienced. The Antiquities Act of 1906 (16 USC. 431–433) represents the first general law in the United States to provide protection for cultural resources on lands owned or controlled by the federal government. Under this law, an antiquities permit was required for scientific study of sites, artifacts, human remains, or structures on federal properties. Certainly, this law was significant in that, at a relatively early date, archaeological resources were recognized as valuable assets. Nevertheless, the act lacked clarity and did not stipulate the need for permits on any other than federally owned property.

By the 1970s, the law was declared "unconstitutionally vague" and viewed as inadequate (King 1998:197). To strengthen the Antiquities Act of 1906, the Archaeological Resources Protection Act was enacted in 1979. This legislation states that archaeological resources that are at least 100 years old are an irreplaceable part of the American heritage. Furthermore, the law requires a permit to excavate or remove archaeological resources from federal or Indian lands. As with the Antiquities Act, sites on private properties are not entitled to the same protection.

Although other congressional acts that emerged during the twentieth century were significant in the preservation of national heritage, they continued to emphasize the conservation of archaeological resources on federal lands, while protection of similar resources on private property was primarily left to state and local agencies. Ten years after the Antiquities Act, the National Park Service (NPS) was established. The NPS was the first United States agency to focus on the conservation of natural and cultural resources (King 1998:13). The role of the NPS has evolved over the years. In 1966 the NPS was authorized, as a result of the National Historic Preservation Act (NHPA), to develop and maintain a National Register of Historic Places. This act declared a national policy of historic preservation that includes conservation of structures, sites, and cultural objects, and has been responsible for much of the research that archaeologists conduct on Native American sites in the United States (Ferguson 1996:67). This legislation called for the creation of the President's Advisory Council on Historic Preservation to oversee the review of projects under Section 106 of the law. Amendments approved in 1992 include the formal recognition of "traditional cultural properties" as being eligible for the National Register. These properties include such cultural landscapes as oak groves, fishing spots, traditional gathering areas, and traditional religious areas and sites. Although these types of resources were always eligible for the National Register, many professionals had overlooked them when determining eligibility (King 1998:98).

NHPA represents a significant step in the preservation of historic resources, although it is debatable how effective a listing on the National Register is as protection for a property (King 1998:93–94). Moreover, most of the properties listed on the National Register of Historic Places are historic buildings, some of which are not particularly old. Very few archaeological sites have been determined eligible for the Register, in part because the criteria used to determine eligibility make it easier to recognize historic properties and not archaeological sites. The law (36 CFR 60.4) identifies four criteria for evaluation:

> The quality of significance in American history, architecture, archeology, engineering, and culture is present in districts, sites, buildings, structures and objects that possess integrity of location, design, setting, materials, workmanship, feeling, and association.

> A) That are associated with events that have made a significant contribution to the broad patterns of our history; or

B) That are associated with the lives of persons significant in our past; or

C) That embody the distinctive characteristics of a type, period, or method of construction, or that represent the work of a master, or that possess high artistic values, or that represent a significant or distinguishable entity whose components may lack individual distinction; or

D) That have yielded, or may be likely to yield, information important in prehistory or history

Generally, properties that are less than fifty years old are not considered eligible for the National Register. There are, however, exceptions for unusual circumstances. Only one criterion is necessary to determine eligibility for any given property. Criterion D is obviously the one most often used to nominate archaeological resources to the Register. Properties listed in the National Register reflect a bias in the United States for recognizing non-Indian sites. For example, of the 2102 sites in California listed in the National Register as of July 2000, only 137, or 6.6%, are significant because they are American Indian archaeological sites, and most of these are recorded in rural counties in the state. Los Angeles County has only four Indian sites in the National Register. Properties that do appear in the National Register for Los Angeles County include a diversity of buildings, including numerous banks, churches, oil wells, and even a Ralph's grocery store on Westwood Boulevard in West Los Angeles. Historic organizations interested in recognizing and preserving buildings and other landmarks in the United States appear to have succeeded in their goals. In contrast, archaeologists have been less successful in recognizing archaeological resources as significant properties in the National Register.

Another policy act of the 1960s that is of particular significance to the preservation of cultural (and natural) resources in the United States is the National Environmental Policy Act of 1969. This act requires agencies to consider environmental impacts on federal projects. At its best, it has the potential to be an open and honest analysis of impacts that balance cultural resource protection with other public issues (King 1998:269). As a result of this act, environmental impact statements are required for any projects that may adversely affect the environment. Cultural resources probably have the highest chance of being protected under this law, but again the law refers only to federal projects, leaving the bulk of projects that may adversely affect archaeological sites under local legislation.

The most recent legislation in the United States that has affected preservation of cultural resources is the widely publicized Native American

Graves Protection and Repatriation Act (NAGPRA) of 1990. The law represents a compromise between American Indian concerns and those of archaeologists and museums. It has provided ownership rights of human remains, grave goods, and items of cultural patrimony to Native Americans—in other words, "awards an equal protection of property rights already extended to other Americans" (Thomas 2000:214). Much of the law is focused on the rights of Native Americans to reclaim ancestral remains that have been stored in museums and academic repositories throughout the country for decades. Museums and agencies that receive federal funds must adhere to the law; therefore, the majority of collections throughout the United States are affected. The law also regulates the excavation of human remains and associated cultural items on federal or Indian land (King 1998:273). Similar to other legislation in the United States, the law has no effect on the excavation of such remains on private lands unless federal oversight is required. Despite its limitations, the law has empowered American Indians to make decisions about their ancestral and cultural remains, a right they had not previously been afforded.

Even though recent legislation has been at least partially successful in providing protection for American Indian ancestral sites on federal lands, approximately two-thirds of all lands in the United States are not protected by federal legislation. This leaves the protection of cultural resources on private properties to local agencies that are usually subject to state laws. These laws vary considerably from state to state and jurisdiction to jurisdiction. A paradoxical situation has arisen in California where state laws provide some of the strongest protection of sites in the nation, but because of corruption within the system, optimal protection is often not afforded (Glassow 1990). In most counties in California, for example, the developer chooses the archaeological consultant. Developers quickly learn and share information concerning which contract archaeologists will provide determination of significance in their favor.

Few jurisdictions have professional archaeologists on their planning staffs. Furthermore, there is no legal system in place that requires archaeologists in the United States to become certified. In some jurisdictions, anyone can hang up a shingle. Underbidding your competition has become commonplace, and, of course, the more limited the excavation and analysis, the more likely that a site will be determined insignificant. This situation has been accurately characterized by Elia (1993) who compared cultural resource management in the United States with the International Committee on Archaeological Heritage Management Charter of 1990. Elia clearly identified underbidding as a problem in contract work and suggested that training at the graduate level be prioritized. Unfortunately, as a result of unscrupulous archaeologists, research and preservation have been severely hindered, particularly on private properties. Differential preservation of cultural resources according to land status has a long history in the United States that can be seen in the strong principles of private property rights (Elia 1993:426–427).

Private Property Rights and Cultural Resources in the United States

Private property owners in the United States are granted legal rights over archaeological resources that far exceed rights in the Mediterranean and in most regions in the world. Approximately 31% of the 2.3 billion acres in the United States are owned or held in trust by the federal government. State and local governments own 9% of lands. This leaves the majority of property, 60%, privately owned (Wiebe, Tegene, and Kuhn 1998:79) and not subject to federal legislation relevant to cultural resources. Furthermore, private property law contains a clear bias toward development uses that has been built into legislation since the nineteenth century. "This bias is so deeply ingrained in the United States legal culture that it presents itself as a law of nature: the fundamental liberty of private owners to develop their property as they please is the cornerstone of American civil and economic freedom . . ." (McEvoy 1998:94). Concepts of private property rights can be seen in the Fifth and Fourteenth Amendments of the US Constitution. Basically, private property owners are granted ownership rights to all objects embedded in the land, including artifacts and other cultural resources (Price 1991:23). In some jurisdictions, Indian burials are protected by law, but this is not true for all areas. In jurisdictions that do not recognize or protect Indian or unmarked graves, property owners have ownership rights over them. In other words, archaeological resources on private property in some jurisdictions in the United States have not been granted basic protection, even when burials have been encountered.

Probably the most infamous case of looting on private property in the past twenty years occurred at the Slack Farm site in Kentucky, where the property owner leased plots of land for $10,000 each to looters to dig between the fall harvest and spring planting (Arden 1989). The scale of looting at Slack Farm, a late Mississippian settlement, brought the site to the attention of the Kentucky State Police, who visited the site after receiving a complaint. Unfortunately, this complaint came after two months of destructive digging on the part of the pothunters (Fagan 1988:15). Upon police arrival, looters claimed that no human bones had been encountered. The detective who visited the site observed a very different and disturbing picture. Broken human skeletons were scattered across the farm which now resembled a lunar landscape because of the hundreds of recently excavated pits. Ten men were charged that day under a state law that made desecrating a venerated object a misdemeanor punishable by a maximum fine of $500 and as much as a year in jail. Four of the men were from Illinois and Indiana and could not be extradited for a misdemeanor (Arden 1989). The public outcry and media condemnation over the desecration at Slack Farm, where more than 600 graves were disturbed, brought the site to national attention. By March 1988, the Kentucky Legislature unanimously made desecration of graves a felony (Arden 1989; Fagan 1988).

In the eastern United States where federal land is particularly limited, many states have followed suit in strengthening existing legislation or enacting new laws that protect unmarked graves (H. Davis 1998). Unfortunately, though, in the Slack Farm case, charges were dropped against the ten men caught looting. The judge placed them on one-year probation and warned that, if they were caught grave robbing again, they would stand trial on their Slack Farm actions (Scot Free! 1990:14). A Cherokee Indian living in the area remarked that the court's action "just shows the bureaucracy of the white government. It's not what would have happened if it had been a white graveyard" (Scot Free! 1990:15).

Despite recent legislation providing Indian burials the protection that has been afforded non-native burials for hundreds of years, the United States still lags behind most nations in terms of protecting cultural resources on private property. Developing countries in the New World such as Mexico and Peru, at least in theory, offer legal protection of cultural resources whether they are on private or public lands. Part of the problem is that the non-Indian public does not identify with prehistoric Indian sites (Fagan 1988: 16). This situation brings us to the third major obstacle of site preservation in the United States: their low visibility.

How Do You Save a Site When No One Knows It Exists?

Most archaeological sites in the United States lack monumental architecture. Even the larger sites in the southwestern and eastern United States are unfamiliar to much of the public. Lesser-known sites are even more problematic because of their obscurity. Most people are unaware that archaeological sites exist throughout the United States, often within a few miles of where they live. To further complicate efforts to inform the public, archaeologists in the United States have an ethical responsibility not to inform the public of the locations of archaeological sites because of the fear that they will be looted. The State Historic Preservation Officer (SHPO) oversees archaeological site records for each state. In California, twelve regional Information

Centers maintain the site records for the SHPO. Access to these records is restricted to professional archaeologists and landowners. When professional archaeologists want to look at the site records, they must sign an agreement of confidentiality stating they will not disclose information regarding the location of the sites or other sensitive data. Because of this agreement, it can be very difficult for archaeologists to heighten public awareness about sites that are threatened by destruction.

Unfortunately, the vast majority of sites in the United States lack features that the public can readily see. Instead, these sites are marked by small, broken pieces of bone, shell, ceramics, and lithic debitage. In many regions of the United States, including most of California, ceramics were not even used. Most of these sites are, therefore, invisible to the public. Because the archaeologist is required to maintain the confidentiality of site locations, they cannot even heighten public awareness by leading or encouraging site visits. This situation promotes the obscurity of archaeological sites, making it even more difficult to gain public support for the protection of threatened remains. Furthermore, these measures have not been fully successful in curtailing looting, which continues to flourish in many regions of the United States. Any serious looter generally knows the locations of sites and has a library that may rival that of some archaeologists.

It is not just the small hunter-gatherer campsites that are difficult to preserve. One of the most spectacular rock art sites in the United States is Painted Rock (CA-SLO-79) in the Carrizo Plain of central California (D. Whitley 1996:165). The site consists of a massive sandstone outcrop in the shape of a horseshoe situated on the flat plain in eastern San Luis Obispo County. Prior to extensive vandalism, hundreds of painted images covered the interior and exterior walls of the boulder that rises approximately 183 m above the plain (Grant 1993:90). The most extensive paintings were inside the horseshoe that forms a type of natural amphitheater. The site was recognized early on by many, including its Spanish discoverers, who named it La Piedra Pintada, or Painted Rock (Angel 1979). The earliest photographs of this impressive site were taken in 1876. In 1910, Myron Angel wrote a legendary narrative of the rock art site that he called "a temple of the sun-worshipers" (Angel 1979:17). Angel compared the site to the sphinx of Egypt because of its magnitude and significance. In 1967, rock art specialist Campbell Grant wrote:

> Today the site is a complete shambles. Beer cans and empty rifle cartridges litter the ground, and the paintings that survived the gunfire are painted over or carved with names and dates. What was the finest rock-painting site in the United States has been completely ruined by senseless vandalism. (Grant 1967:74)

FIGURE 19.2. Photograph, probably from the late nineteenth century, of the main panel at Painted Rock. *From the Santa Barbara Museum of Natural History.*

Although graffiti can be seen in the earliest photographs (figure 19.2), apparently most of the damage occurred during the oil explorations of the 1920s (Hyder personal communication). Grant (1993: Plates 4, 5) reconstructed some of the rock art based on early photographs and remnants of the paintings that he saw in the mid-1900s (figure 19.3a, b). Monochrome and polychrome pictographs include red, black, and white pigments (Grant 1993: Plate 4). The main panel, over 122 m long (Grant 1993:98), consisted of anthropomorphic and zoomorphic figures, in addition to many other intricately painted images, both abstract and representational. Most of this is now destroyed. Grant (1993:90) suggests that the amphitheater could have easily held hundreds of people. In addition to the main panel, forty-two other painted panels have been recorded on the outcrop, many of which are also quite large. Other features have also been recorded, including twenty-one bedrock mortars and numerous other ground cupules. Surrounding the tremendous rock outcrop is a midden deposit with a wide range of artifacts, including beads, projectile points, stone tools, groundstone, and other artifacts indicating substantial occupation (Johnson, Osland, and Rudolph 1985). A rock art site of this magnitude should have been preserved as a national treasure, but instead is seriously damaged, if not destroyed (figure 19.4). This tragic situation occurred in part because archaeologists have not trusted the public to help with preservation. Until archaeologists educate the public about the significance of a variety of archaeological sites in the

United States, citizens do not even know that we are losing this nonrenewable resource at a rapid pace due to looting and development.

a

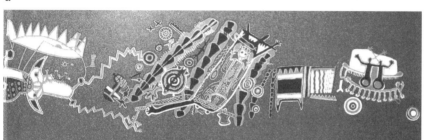

b

FIGURE 19.3. Reconstruction of the main panel at Painted Rock: a, left half; b, right half. *After Grant 1993.*

FIGURE 19.4. Photograph of the main panel at Painted Rock, 1995. The large white patches represent damage.

The Future of Conservation in the United States

Although the United States is the wealthiest nation in the world, it has fallen behind many countries in the Mediterranean and elsewhere in the preservation of cultural resources. Biases concerning what is recognized and preserved in the US clearly exist. Most schoolchildren have heard of such colonial American sites as Jamestown and Williamsburg or mission sites in California and the Southwest. Civil War battlegrounds such as Gettysburg are visited by thousands of schoolchildren. But mention almost any Native American site, even one as imposing as Cahokia, to a grammar school child or their parents, and you probably will get a blank stare in return.

Recent legislation in the United States, such as NAGPRA, has attempted to recognize the significance of American Indian resources and the impact of the destruction of these resources on the American Indian. The loss of resources to the public, however, has not been emphasized. The Sierra Club and other nonprofit organizations have been successful in gaining public support in the preservation of renewable resources. Animal rights activists are frequently in the news in their attempts to subvert indignities against animals. Students in my archaeology classes at San Diego State University are much more likely to speak out against the recent revival of whaling by the Makah Indians than to be concerned about the bulldozing of an archaeological site.

Nevertheless, in the last decade a shift within the archaeological community in the United States can be seen. With the passing of NAGPRA, archaeologists have become aware that they have not taken the time to educate the public effectively about their point of view. The Public Education Committee of the Society for American Archaeology (SAA) was formed in 1990 with a goal to "promote understanding of and respect for other cultures and encourage preservation of heritage resources" (*http://www.saa.org/ Pubedu/index.html*). To meet this goal, the SAA prints a newsletter entitled *Archaeology and the Public* that is intended for a wide audience, including educators. A similar emphasis is seen within regional archaeological societies, as well as national preservation groups, that have prioritized public education. The Archaeological Conservancy, the only nonprofit organization in the United States that acquires and preserves archaeological sites in the nation, has bought more than 195 sites. In 1996 the Conservancy printed the first issue of *American Archaeology*, a popular magazine that focuses on significant archaeological sites in the Americas, especially North America. The editors state that the purpose of the magazine is to "help readers appreciate and understand the archaeological wonders available to them, and to raise their awareness of the destruction of our archaeological heritage" (The Role of the Magazine 2000:4).

A recent poll regarding the public's knowledge of archaeology reflects the effects of these efforts (Mulvany 2000:9). The poll was commissioned by the Archaeological Conservancy, Archaeological Institute of America, Bureau of Land Management, Fish and Wildlife Service, US Forest Service, SAA, and Society for Historical Archaeology. The research company, Harris Interactive Inc., randomly selected 1016 adults across the continental United States for questioning. Results of the poll (Ramos and Duganne 2000) indicated that most respondents believe archaeology is important to today's society. Moreover, 99% of the respondents stated that archaeological sites have educational and scientific value, and 96% believed that archaeological resources should be legally protected (Ramos and Duganne 2000:25–26). Those respondents who believed that there should be laws to protect sites were asked additional questions. A majority (85%) thought that there should be laws to prevent the general public from building on a prehistoric Indian village. Finally, about 67% stated that there should be laws preventing the general public from digging up arrowheads or pottery on their own property (Ramos and Duganne 2000:27).

The results of the poll are very promising and indicate that archaeologists and the media have been relatively successful in educating the public about the value of archaeological sites. The archaeological community now needs to provide tools to help the public become advocates of preservation, just as they are for natural resources. More effective protection of cultural resources on private properties will never advance unless there is strong backing among the public. The public is now demanding more professional archaeological reporting and needs tools to determine whether archaeological reporting is adequate. Otherwise, substandard reporting will likely continue to flourish in some areas of the United States. Archaeologists, the public, and American Indians share the common concern that archaeological sites need to be protected. If these groups work together, with professionals providing the legal knowledge on how to attain this goal, we hopefully can curtail the destruction of archaeological sites from development, vandalism, and looting.

CHAPTER 20

Archaeology, Conservation, and the Ethics of Sustainability

CLAIRE L. LYONS

A fundamental sea change in archaeology is the deepening respect for the physical and social consequences of field excavation. Years of ever more refined subject specialization, technological innovation, and theoretical rigor have brought the field to a healthy and indispensable sense of introspection and self-reflection. Looking back at recent accomplishments and forward to the challenges to come, we are now witnessing a renewed focus on the conduct of the profession: our obligations to the research enterprise, to the public, and most of all, to the unique and fragile sites we excavate. If these concerns have sharpened in recent years, it is no doubt due to reminders that the past is an endangered and contested commodity. Much more than the sum of ancient artworks, artifacts, and ruins, the past that archaeologists seek is firmly embedded in society's current needs and its future aspirations. Framed in terms of an inclusive notion of cultural heritage, archaeology's mission goes well beyond rediscovery and interpretation. It aims to reconcile three goals that often stand at odds: scientific research, public access, and long-term preservation. This mission is now conducted on a public stage before audiences whose demands can be inconsistent or even incompatible.

The field of conservation has followed a path similar to that of archaeology, from the treatment of deteriorating objects and structures to sophisticated research in materials science and environmental conditions. Realizing that the life and meanings of objects in their care are not frozen in time, conservation professionals have played a lead role in shaping policies that take contemporary values into account. Archaeological sites are microcosms that are intimately linked to surrounding cultural and natural landscapes. Their destiny is part and parcel of the process of valuing the world's heritage, which is an essential anchor for a thoughtful and grounded society. Thinking about how best to protect, manage, and learn from the legacies of the past has led to tremendous progress in conservation and promises to transform the ways in which archaeology and conservation are conducted in the years to come.

The two chapters by Nicholas Stanley-Price and Lynn Gamble examine some of the serious challenges that face archaeological heritage and describe strategies that are being pursued. Their presentations look at two regions, the classical Mediterranean and the United States. Despite obvious differences in history and approach, the traditional boundaries that divided excavators from "restorers" and the branches of archaeology from one another are being breached. An interdisciplinary, multilateral environment is emerging that will have lasting consequences for how we conduct our work. Several observations are immediately obvious. For those most closely involved in the study and care of the physical remains, there is an ethical responsibility to preserve these remains in all their dimensions. This obligation is perhaps best framed as respecting and liberating the many values that communities invest in heritage. Heritage is a common good, but in a world of fast-paced globalization and interactivity, it is progressively coming under siege by those who negate, disregard, or cherish it as symbolic (and actual) capital. Archaeologists and conservators must, therefore, take a stronger advocacy role in public policy discussions about the importance of history and heritage in society. To do this effectively, they must not only collaborate more closely and share expertise on artifacts and monuments, but—above all—synthesize their knowledge to institute new paradigms for a sustainable "conservation archaeology."

The impetus for redefining goals and practices is grounded in the ethical dimensions of the two professions. Over the past three decades, codes of ethics adopted by the major archaeological organizations recommend ideal standards in fieldwork and scholarship. Rather than prescribing a set of mandates, they point to the relationships among objects, practitioners, managers, descendant populations, and consumers of ancient heritage. Such standards are important not only for the principles they articulate, but especially because they are generated from a reflexive process of critical dialogue and consensus building. Codes of ethics are naturally evolutionary and form a platform upon which changes in philosophy and field practices can be regularly reviewed.

Principles of preservation have been embedded in archaeological codes of ethics from the outset and over time have assumed more prominent stature. The 1990 Code of Ethics of the Archaeological Institute of America (AIA) asserts the dedication of its membership, the largest in North America, to "the protection and preservation of the world's archaeological resources." The Society for American Archaeology (SAA) established stewardship as the paramount responsibility of archaeologists who "work for the long-term conservation and protection of the archaeological record." Similarly, the Society for Historical Archaeology emphasizes curation as a professional and ethical responsibility (Rotroff 2001). Just how closely interconnected archaeology and preservation are becoming is clear in the AIA's recent formulation of its core mission and values in which conservation is identified as one of three primary goals. Such an awareness is laudable. As often as not, however, preservation principles have not been effectively implemented in the planning, funding, conduct, or aftermath of excavation.

The momentum of ethical consciousness was propelled by one threat to archaeological heritage above all: looting and the illicit traffic in antiquities. Both the AIA and SAA recognized early on that the field's traditional roots in art history and its routine symbiosis with collectors and dealers were taking a serious toll on the integrity of the discipline as a primarily scientific exercise. Since the 1970s when the antiquities market was promoted as an affordable investment opportunity, the plundering of sites has spiraled out of control. Many types of artifacts have come to be privileged as artworks, with the result that sites and monuments are vandalized, the information from original contexts is fragmented or lost entirely, and perhaps most seriously, scholarship is reduced to a circular, backward looking rehearsal of past knowledge and dated ideas. The impact is most keenly felt when trade-inspired tastes for exotica incite plundering in lands whose ancient history has barely been written, such as Central and Southeast Asia and sub-Saharan Africa, to name but the worst cases (Brodie, Doole, and Renfrew 2001; Renfrew 2000).

It is some comfort that the actions of cultural authorities and archaeologists in a number of source countries have put stronger legal sanctions and international cultural property conventions into force. The downside, however, is that traffickers relocate to areas where protective legislation is weak and the risks are negligible. Nevertheless, the movement against "illicit antiquities" has reaped success on several fronts. Regular media coverage is bringing the scope of the loss to the attention of a broad and largely sympathetic public. Countries in which stolen artifacts originate, such as Turkey, Italy, Greece, China, and Mexico, are actively seeking restitution or repatriation of important works from museums and private collectors. Prosecuting the dealers in stolen cultural artifacts is a boon for consciousness raising and recuperation. Most significantly, aggressive advocacy is slowly accomplishing a series of legal precedents that establish mutual respect for national patrimony laws both within and among countries.

Archaeologists on the front lines of professional ethics have helped to change the mentality of the profession itself, which is no small undertaking. They represent a minority, however, not the least because participating in legal cases, lobbying for legislation, and educating policy-makers can balloon into a full-time occupation. Conservators and archaeometry laboratories need to strengthen their ethical guidelines concerning the treatment and authentication of undocumented antiquities, because this practice indirectly support the illicit traffic by adding aesthetic and monetary value to single objects as opposed to safeguarding their original contexts. With few exceptions, major museums continue to lag behind on the issue of acquiring undocumented ancient art, and in the current climate of claiming and reclaiming culture, polarizing politics overshadow constructive, cooperative tactics.

When it comes to its own "best practices," archaeology still has some way to go. The extent to which archaeologists and conservators must rethink and integrate their approaches to material history is implicit in the overviews that Nicholas Stanley-Price and Lynn Gamble offer here. The Mediterranean and North America developed divergent approaches to excavation and preservation. In the Classical lands, state authorities invested heavily in preserving the abundance of historic structures, prehistoric sites, and monumental architectural complexes built by cultures that were seen to stand at the roots of Western civilization and national identity. In North America, by contrast, archaeological exploration is a more recent phenomenon. The more modest remains of precolonial native cultures have not been such a focal point of the image we have of ourselves as a nation. The tendency to give short shrift to post-antique levels in the classical and Near Eastern worlds (that is, to "dig through") is reversed in North America, where according to Lynn Gamble, dismissive attitudes toward Native American heritage and a lack of prominent architecture mean that colonial sites and later historical monuments win a greater share of attention and funding.

Old World and New World archaeology actually have as much in common as not. Preservation faces greater and more intractable threats than looting. Agriculture, development, tourism, hydroelectric dams, environmental degradation, ethnic conflict, religious iconoclasm, and plain neglect contribute to the inexorable decay and disappearance of monuments and sites throughout the world. As the legislation and international agreements reviewed in these papers show, awareness of the dangers is hardly a novel phenomenon. In spite of an admirable range of laws, conventions, directives, and protocols to safeguard cultural property in general, the situation appears increasingly dire. The inescapable fact is that political and economic forces arrayed on a global scale demand new approaches to archaeological research. Codes of ethics must reflect the reality that excavation is a privilege and that communities have vital concerns in the outcome of archaeologists' work. So long as we think of excavators and conservators as partners in the introspective project of "archaeology as usual," the two professions will fail to make a real difference outside their own spheres (Federspiel 2001).

A model for future archaeological investigation can be found in the way cultural resource management invites participation from community interests at all levels. Sites and monuments are endowed with values and meaning by groups of stakeholders: national antiquities authorities, politicians, tourism offices, urban planners, developers, and museums, among many other specialists. Of central importance are local residents near heritage places, indigenous peoples, and descendant groups that are directly impacted but commonly sidelined by those who control and manage sites. The benefits are not only scientific but also recreational, educational, spiritual, and aesthetic. Identifying stakeholder interests and devising feasible plans to accommodate research agendas and public expectations within economic constraints is an exercise in compromise. It compels us to reflect on how and on whose behalf we are acting (*cui bono?*) and apply our theory to practical programs (Skeates 2000).

Engaging in dialogue with stakeholders acknowledges that the very concept of archaeological patrimony means different things to different people. A paradox exists in the fact that, while its meanings are inevitably local, heritage is often posited as a universal or common good. Universal heritage, however, is not a transparent notion. On the one hand, it is necessary to posit the uniquely meaningful qualities of humankind's cultural achievements in order to build an international consensus for its protection. The effect, on the other hand, can be the opposite of the aim. In classic economic terms, the "tragedy of the commons" occurs when resources are treated as common goods, which in the normal course of events can lead to their extinction. Universality also implies a transcendent view of material culture as an intrinsically significant class of immutable objects or sites rather than products that are embedded in a nested set of discourses: academic, political, religious, and psychological. The act of preservation is thus not a simple scientific intervention but an interpretive act. Legitimizing the values that are invested in a site or monument at any given time by recognizing interested communities can achieve a viable long-term method for dealing with patrimony in the midst of social transformation (Avrami, Mason, and de la Torre 2000, see especially Values Bibliography 73–96).

I do not mean to gloss over the fact that stakeholder dialogue can be a tricky, exquisitely frustrating business—to wit, consider the case of Stonehenge and the intense debates over access to the megaliths and their surrounding landscape. Even fundamental assumptions concerning the decision to preserve can come into conflict with belief systems that would allow buildings and other remains to decay and be reabsorbed into the earth, as in the case of some Native American groups. Engaging stakeholders is a course of action that validates archaeology and conservation as culturally creative acts, where processes of negotiation and management are just as important as the actual conduct of excavation and treatment.

Several promising models of public-private cooperation that have leveraged significant funding and political support suggest future directions for archaeology and archaeological conservation. Nicholas Stanley-Price cites the case of the Parque Arqueológico do Vale Côa in Portugal, where controversy over the negative impacts of dam construction catalyzed the creation of an archaeological park and a diversified plan for rural development and ecotourism. The Butrint Foundation frames its concerns for the Classical remains near a popular stretch of southern Albanian coastline in terms of preserving the site and surrounding woodland through training and managed development. Given that tourism is an inevitable fact and that local authorities are looking to sites to generate rather than siphon off revenue, plans that attempt to harmonize the needs of the archaeological heritage and its users are more likely to benefit from long-term support. Other good examples of this sort of approach can be found at Çatalhöyük in Turkey (Tringham chapter 6), where an international team is applying integrated planning to the remains of one of the world's earliest urban settlements and its spectacular wall paintings and sculptures. Smaller sites in the US are being rescued, as Gamble notes, through purchase by nonprofit organizations like the Archaeological Conservancy, which puts such sites out of the reach of encroaching development.

Managing the archaeological landscape in rural regions is comparatively easy. Large urban projects, such as that undertaken by the city of Rome for the 2000 Jubilee, become mired in political and economic pressures. Extensive plans to unify archaeological sites in the historic center of Athens, for example, are confronting complex challenges in anticipation of waves of tourists for the 2004 Olympic Games.

Innovative approaches to historical monuments in an urban setting are being applied at the National Preserve of Tauric Chersonesos, a site located in Sebastopol on the Black Sea. Known as the "Ukrainian Pompeii," Chersonesos represents the world's best-preserved ancient Greek landscape and a nearly intact Byzantine city. Three times it has made the World Monuments Watch 2002 List of Most Endangered Monuments. Archaeological reconnaissance there is taking place in the ancient city, formerly a restricted military zone and now a beachfront recreational area, and in the surrounding agricultural territory. To harmonize the scientific, religious, and touristic potential of the site, a conservation master plan envisions training, creation of laboratory and storage space, inventory of museum collections, establishment of a heritage management organization, and restoration of a historic monastery. Despite the uncertainties of Ukrainian politics, the master plan aims to position Chersonesos as the anchor for regional economic renewal via tourists drawn to the unspoiled coastline and numerous historic monuments (Carter 2001). Efforts such as these demonstrate that archaeologists have a major contribution to make to public policy, one that will ultimately benefit the field, the objects of its study, and especially its audience.

Changes in archaeology's field of operation mean change within the discipline's ethics and practice. What would a new paradigm of conservation archaeology entail? As noted above, such a paradigm needs to move beyond collaboration among insider specialists toward a synthesis with the preservationist spirit of the cultural and natural heritage movements. A fundamental assumption is that archaeological heritage is nonrenewable. Maximizing the potential of all the data during the dismantling process that is excavation is normally a one-time chance. Borrowing a page from environmentalists, we must judge our practices on the basis of sustainability (Mason and Avrami 2002). Sustainability involves satisfying the needs of the present without rendering those of the future impossible. Among the guiding principles are several that are not radically new concepts, addressing all too well known but often ignored problems:

- *Caution.* Codes of ethics and international charters stress that excavation should be undertaken only as a last resort and not solely as a means to satisfy curiosity or train students. Because archaeological investigation is irreversible, in situ preservation takes precedence. Excavation should be undertaken only when it advances knowledge or preservation in demonstrably significant ways. When it is obvious that techniques on the ground and in the laboratory can only improve in the future, more sites should be left undug until we are better equipped to explore all their ramifications. Greater efforts could instead be made on regional survey and landscape studies employing non-invasive technologies. Diachronic field survey, such as that undertaken in the territory of Morgantina in central Sicily, can revise the way primary sites are interpreted and open the door for comprehensive understanding of historical landscapes.

- *Utilizing resources carefully.* Closely following the precautionary principle is the wise use of existing resources, in this case the known sites themselves. As the recommendation from Monuments at Risk in England shows, an average of one recorded monument has been destroyed each day since the end of World War II (Wainwright 2000). Census taking, monitoring, and preventive care of existing remains are daunting undertakings. Because the rate of loss and degree of change over time is so high, such undertakings are an investment that must be made. This investment is likely to entail a shift of resources away from the "big dig" and toward more diversified field projects.

- *Leveraging existing data.* An enormous bank of previously excavated data awaits analysis in storerooms throughout the world. There is enough material to nourish research subjects for decades. Retrospective publication was urgently recommended at the 1999 International Conference on Unpublished Excavations in Nicosia (Hadjisavvas and Karageorghis 2000). Backing up this duty by precluding permission to excavate new sites and other professional perquisites was one of the conclusions reached and is starting to be enforced. It is likewise incumbent upon the directors of national archaeological services and museums to make materials more widely accessible and to discourage scholars from the practice of "staking out" long unpublished excavations and objects. This practice, by some accounts, has left in limbo some 80% of stored archaeological materials in Italy (Stoddart and Malone 2001). On a positive note, the 2001 Memorandum of Understanding concluded between the US and the Republic of Italy contains provisions for making long-term loans of archaeological objects for study, conservation, and publication. These exchanges will be a great boon for graduate programs and museums.

- *Documentation.* Standards of documentation are scarce, and there are great disparities in how field records are maintained. Inventorying and disseminating the primary evidence contained in computer files, notes, drawings, photographs, and historical archives of the discipline requires a serious investment to create the necessary databases. Upgrading computer databases and Web sites so that they are compatible with evolving standards looms as a costly challenge. The suggestion made above to slow excavation is counterintuitive in the face of threats posed by construction, road building, and deep plowing. For this reason, an all-out effort to document essential fieldwork generously and to open data sets to the scrutiny of colleagues in a timely manner must be made. Records of salvage and contract archaeology will eventually prove to be a vital source of primary information that up to now has only occasionally been published.

- *Equity.* The planning and conduct of archaeological excavation and conservation projects are most viable when there is equitable benefit sharing among the various stakeholder groups. Because the costs involved in such projects are substantial, a full range of social and economic benefits should be aimed for. The principles of caution and wise use also result in equitable consideration of future generations who are the beneficiaries of our work. Their ability to carry forward the enterprises of scientific and historical research is dependent upon decisions made today.

- *Planning for diversity.* Biodiversity and cultural diversity promise healthy, thriving natural and social environments, and offer good models for archaeology. The extent to which research and conservation interventions contribute to greater diversity of the archaeological heritage should be a guiding principle. More stringent review procedures of project design and management plans for all phases of fieldwork would help to prioritize which projects are justified and which can wait. Funding agencies and academic sponsors share in the responsibility for establishing criteria and ensuring that benchmarks are met.

- *Education.* Graduate curricula generally do not reflect the new realms in which archaeologists and conservators are operating. Many of the perspectives that Gamble and Stanley-Price discuss, in fact, are probably not well understood outside a small circle of archaeological patrimony "policy wonks." Yet thinking about the past in contemporary contexts demands a much broader grounding in the relevant aspects of international heritage policy, cultural properties law, curation, site management, ethics, and (for want of a better term) studies in cultural values. Exposing archaeology students to the principles of conservation—and conservation students to the theory and methods of archaeology—is an important first step in bridging the gap between these two increasingly entwined fields.

These recommendations are remedial steps that underscore the greater responsibility to redirect our ethical ideals. A sustainable archaeology is one that attends to "conservative" principles of cautious intervention, stewardship, and the preservation of as much diversity of evidence as possible. By all rights, the strengths of the environmental movement should be matched in the sector of cultural heritage. The two sectors are natural allies and are naturally interdependent. By applying their expertise in cultural geography, urban development, resource exploitation, and the experienced landscape, archaeologists have a vital critical perspective on questions that increasingly affect the quality of life. While many archaeologists are rightly focused on intellectual parameters of their own humanistic discipline, they also need to look outward. By recognizing that ancient artifacts, works of art, and architecture hold multiple legitimate values for numerous communities and by approaching this legacy holistically, we may embrace two final elements of sustainability: the interdependence and relevance of heritage. Demonstrating its essential contributions to issues that society will face in the next millennium will be conservation archaeology's core mission and greatest challenge.

RETROSPECT AND PROSPECT

CHAPTER 21

Retrospect and Prospect: Mediterranean Archaeology in a New Millennium

COLIN RENFREW

Beyond the Polarities

To sit down toward the end of the passing century and of the millennium in contemplation of the recent and in anticipation of the new is a somewhat disconcerting experience. The vehemence of the theoretical approaches that characterized the 1960s and 1970s (the "processual era" of theoretical debate) and then the 1980s and early 1990s (the "post-processual" or "interpretive" era) has diminished. Clearly, many commentators have wearied somewhat of the polemic. As a Scandinavian archaeologist observed to me at a recent meeting in Oxford of the Theoretical Archaeology Group with reference to the polemics of the past two decades: "Not many souls have been saved." Or as John Papadopoulos remarked at our meeting: "Processual and post-processual are irrelevant terms: we are all culture historians and all processualists and post-processualists."

Yet there are some differences to be observed between such a retrospective (and prospective) overview held today and one held a couple of decades ago. Above all, there is a much greater awareness of the social context in which we work. This is not simply a matter of the scale of funding and the sources of funding for the work we are undertaking. The question "whose archaeology?" is now much more widely asked. It is asked, very properly, in relation to minorities whose interests may have been overlooked in earlier research strategies. It is asked in relation to former colonial countries, where historic and prehistoric studies remain unbalanced in the wake of the dominant but now sometimes irrelevant research interests of an earlier era. And it is asked in relation to the wider public in almost every advanced country, where the political necessity of demonstrating the value of the wider interests

311

underlying the concerns of professional archaeologists has generally come to the fore. The responsibilities of ensuring site conservation, public access, and general education are perhaps still not felt keenly enough among professionals who sometimes fail to communicate the wider significance of their work to the public at large.

What has also become apparent is that the pace of the destruction of archaeological sites in the Mediterranean, as no doubt elsewhere, has advanced so markedly that the assumptions that underlay site surveys in mid-century can now be questioned. The opportunity is now past in some areas for conducting the systematic surveys in open country, which seemed in some ways an obvious and not especially urgent task just forty years ago. With the "new wave" survey, about which John Cherry (chapter 9) spoke so clearly, has come the realization that a survey undertaken today cannot simply be regarded as an assessment in the "archaeological present" of a settlement pattern in some specific period in the past. In that sense there is no generalizable archaeological present. It is now very clear that the present of 2001 is not that of 1995: the present is changing more rapidly than it used to. The past as a vanishing resource is now a more evident reality, and those of us who have experience of two or three decades of fieldwork are very much aware that the opportunities of yesterday, which seemed at the time unproblematic, are already in many cases opportunities that exist no longer. This, although a somewhat dispiriting awareness, is nonetheless realistic. It is a necessary one if there is to be a firm foundation for action in the new century.

The Tyranny (and Opportunity) of Technique

It was Lloyd Cotsen who spoke at our meeting of the "tyranny of technique," suggesting that to accept existing systems, for instance of classification, is to permit the ossification of thought. And clearly there is a certain inevitability: when new techniques become available, they will be applied to archaeology (as to other things). The drive to gather new data comes often as much from the new potential availability of those data as from any fresh sense that it would be profitable or germane to any current question or concern to gather them.

Yet while that is sometimes true, the opportunities for using new techniques to carve out entire new fields of knowledge are always there. It is not an exaggeration to say that, for most fields of archaeology, the potentialities were transformed by the application of radiocarbon dating just half a century ago. If this transformation was less marked in the field of Aegean archaeology than in most research areas, that is partly because, from the end of the

Neolithic, traditional methods of cross-dating will already give some sort of answer within a century or two. We are fortunate, too, that the hope of a secure tree ring chronology stretching right back to early prehistoric times is always inherent in the work of Peter Kuniholm and his colleagues (see the annual progress reports of the Malcolm and Carolyn Wiener Laboratory for Aegean and Near Eastern Dendrochronology). But, of course, there are gaps that will take many years to bridge, especially since good-sized lumps of usable wood or charcoal are of rare occurrence in much of the Mediterranean.

Fortunately, new techniques are becoming available all the time. For nearly forty years we have seen how the potential of trace element studies for the characterization of materials and therefore the understanding of exchange relationships might be fulfilled. And there are signs that the techniques of ceramic studies (including the microscopic examination of thin sections) are now beginning to offer some of the insights that have been sought for so long. In a similar way, the early applications of molecular genetics to human populations (mainly living populations) are now being superseded by more coherent programs. It is only in the next decade or so that we shall see fulfilled some of the potentialities that mitochondrial DNA and Y-chromosome studies have for the reconstruction of male and female lineage histories (see Renfrew and Boyle 2000). New techniques do offer new opportunities.

Survey as a Data Source

The most prolific and widely used means of generating new data in the field of archaeology is now survey (see Alcock, Cherry, and Davis 1994). Cherry gave a very good overview of the range of current and recent projects in his useful paper at our meeting (chapter 9). What is much less clear, however, is how the new data are to be brought together for any more synoptic understanding.

There is, in the first place, the almost inevitable delay in the full publication of the results. That, obviously, is a perennial problem in archaeology, not restricted to the Aegean or the Mediterranean. But while the traditional conventions of publication of an excavation entail the lavish illustration of a wide range of material, and hence considerable delay, this is not necessarily so for survey. Although it is desirable that the materials gathered during area survey should be so curated and so published that the conclusions derived from them can be subject to scrutiny, at least it is not expected that a very great quantity of finds will be comprehensively illustrated. But even accepting this, few surveys undertaken over the past thirty years can yet be considered completely published (even in terms of the initial expectations of their own project leaders).

Of course, the hope is that from site density data can come information on population densities, and that these can be followed through time so as to give insight into demographic processes. But the problem seems to be that there are some periods for which surface finds can be exceedingly sparse. The paucity of the data does not necessarily present a fair indication of the population density: it may be the product of differing formation processes as much as of population decline.

The result seems to be that population figures from area and site survey are rarely so robust as to sustain arguments for culture change made on the basis of estimates of changing populations. This means that, while increasing or decreasing population density may well in principle have had a causative role in many of the changes that occurred, it is in practice far from easy to make a persuasive case for it from the survey data. Perhaps here the very concept of the archaeological "site" is a restrictive one, as Richard Lesure (chapter 14) suggested. The notion of "site" is indeed somewhat undertheorized, relying as it does on notions of sedentary occupation and thus sometimes undervaluing the presence of mobile economies. Indeed, the notion of the site may come to be seen as one of those tyrannical classificatory concepts of whose restrictive consequences Cotsen warned us.

Yet there ought be grounds for some optimism in relation to the future, given the vastly more advanced techniques for data storage and data handling now available. It is clear that effective site survey in a defined and localized area is so labor intensive that any wider and more comprehensive overview must be the product of the comparison and evaluation of the results for many different areas accomplished by a number of different teams. The key issue that soon emerges is that of the standardization of methods and techniques, as well as the classificatory categories in use by the various teams. Lloyd Cotsen's remarks about the tyranny of classification of course have their relevance here also, but it may be that some form of standardized classification is indispensable for data sets that are intended to be intercomparable yet which are produced by different research teams.

Better Descriptions and Matching Realities

One area of real progress is well illustrated in a recent monograph of the Cotsen Institute (Galaty and Parkinson 1999) devoted to the Mycenaean palaces. This advance is represented by the much fuller data now available in well-published form for a number of sites. Comparable observations could certainly be made for Minoan Crete. And the steady progress of the Akrotiri project on Thera, together with the growing number of detailed published studies relating to that site, are giving the promise that this settlement will become one of the best understood of the Bronze Age Aegean. The Aegean Bronze Age must now be one of the most intensively researched fields in world archaeology.

What is particularly encouraging also is that the field of Mycenaean epigraphy, as admirably indicated at our symposium by Thomas Palaima (chapter 3), has now advanced to such a point that interpretations are emerging from the study of the Linear B tablets in the field of material culture that can be shown to have a certain internal coherence before they are set against the archaeological data. For among such comparisons there is always the risk of rather piecemeal juxtaposition of atomic facts from the two fields of archaeology and epigraphy, a procedure that is rarely satisfactory. It is gratifying, therefore, to see how far matters have advanced. Of course there were early indications, notably in the work of John Killen, that coherent economic sense could be made from the palace records, and this is clearly true in an increasing range of domains (see Halstead 1999c). For instance, the seemingly rather disparate insights offered by the Linear B tablets pertaining to religious ritual and dedicatory offerings are now sufficiently numerous that they begin to constitute a substantial body of evidence. While a synthesis of the epigraphic data pertaining to religion could not yet be said to make sense or integrate well in relation to the purely archaeological evidence becoming available from the increasing number of excavations of sites of ritual importance, at least there now exist structures of inference in each field, based on quite a wide range of data. This is progress.

The Decline in Comparative Studies

One of the less positive features of Mediterranean archaeology of the past couple of decades, however, is that the increase in available data has not been accompanied by any very great increase in comparative insights. Although at our workshop Richard Leventhal (chapter 4) referred to parallels with Mycenaean political organization, which might be offered by the Maya, the comparative approach, as Charles Stanish (chapter 10) observed, was otherwise not much in evidence. That this is so may well be one of the consequences of emphasizing the richness of the individual context, as recently stressed by the advocates of interpretive archaeologies and their insistence that such specificities militate against any cross-cultural generalizations.

The sad consequence in the field of Aegean or indeed Mediterranean studies is that we have no comparative works to set alongside, let alone supersede, Robert McC. Adams's now classic juxtaposition of the Mesopotamian and Mesoamerican paths toward statehood (Adams 1966). That this should be so may in part be the consequence of a decline in confidence concerning the sort of typology that speaks in terms of "state" societies, as if "the state" were a problem-free concept. Again, we are warned of the tyranny of classification. But the only alternative to the use of some kind of categories and of categorization is the recognition that everything is in its own way unique. While this is no doubt in several senses true, and is indeed one of the central tenets of post-processual or interpretive archaeology, it does not offer any strategy for apprehending the world other than to admire its dazzling variety and multiplicity.

The purpose of this observation is not the reopening of now quiescent debates, against which John Papadopoulos warned us (chapter 1), but simply to point out that the lack of any useful comparative framework has made the quality of theory in our field rather poorer recently than it was thirty-five years ago, at the time of Adams's provoking study. Americanist archaeologists seem rather more adventurous in this respect, as Earle (1997), for instance, or Flannery (1999) demonstrate. In the Mediterranean we have little that is comparably robust since the work of Braudel (1972), other than the recent and ambitious *Corrupting Sea* of Horden and Purcell (2000), although the "island archaeology" approach of Cherry (1981, 1990) and of Broodbank (2000) offers a refreshing exception. Interestingly and perhaps significantly these great syntheses were both works of history, although they also draw upon archaeology. It is notable that the "deep time" perspective for which archaeology is so often praised should be so lacking in the field of Mediterranean archaeology. Intellectual particularism is not a monopoly of post-processual archaeology.

While in this somewhat critical mode, one may observe that it is rare that the field of Mediterranean archaeology should be treated as a whole, in a way that succeeds in regarding the Mediterranean as a unity. Certainly, our own symposium, despite its original title, made no such effort. For "Archaeology in the Mediterranean" one might well have read "Archaeology in the Aegean" or even "The archaeology of the Aegean Bronze Age." The interesting paper on Çatalhöyük (which does not fall precisely in either region) by Ruth Tringham (chapter 6) was a notable exception. In recent years there has been published at least one archaeological monograph claimed as "Mediterranean" in its scope (Mathers and Stoddart 1994). But in reality each of the papers within it was much more local in compass, other than a brave essay by Sherratt (1994) seeking to impose the now ubiquitous "world systems" model of Wallerstein upon the troubled waters of Our Sea.

It is indeed strange that the particularizing tendency in Aegean archaeology should be so marked as normally to preclude general studies carrying a comparative perspective, and to exclude altogether treatments that compare the prehistory and archeology of the Aegean with the west Mediterranean.

The Divide in Aegean Studies: Between Prehistory and History at the Turn of a New Millennium

Many years ago I wrote of the "Great Divide" in Aegean studies (Renfrew 1980), alluding of course to the very different traditions of scholarship operating within the separate and very different fields of Classical studies and anthropological archaeology. I do not seek here to reopen that well-debated theme. Instead, I wish to highlight the related but less explicable polarity between studies of the archaeology of Greece, from the earliest settlement down to about 1000 BC, on the one hand, and those dealing with the time after that arbitrary point in the so-called "Dark Age" period, on the other. We are therefore speaking of an earlier "new millennium," beginning precisely 3000 years before our own most recent æonial transformation. Fortunately, we now have scholars, such as Ian Morris (1987) and James Whitley (1991), whose work does bestride that chronological divide. They have taken inspiration notably from the studies by Anthony Snodgrass (for example, 1971), which, while principally treating the period following the inception of the new millennium, do have a clear perspective on what has gone before (though see Papadopoulos 1993).

It is a curious and notable feature of the archaeological and historical literature relating to the Aegean that, while there are several detailed studies relating to Aegean prehistory, and likewise many volumes offering authoritative accounts of Greek history and archaeology of the Classical era which begin their discussion early in the first millennium BC, it is difficult to think of any substantial and authoritative treatment that covers the whole span and in doing so transcends the millennial divide. One reason for this is, of course, the two traditions of scholarship—the scholarly Great Divide—each operating on its side of the chronological division. In relation to the earlier period, one may certainly imagine comparative or generalizing treatments of the emergence during the Bronze Age of state society in the Aegean; indeed, an important early paper by Cherry (1984) offers a good example, as to some extent does the more recent paper by Wright (1995b). But where do we look for a comparative or generalizing treatment of the origins of the state societies of Greece during the Aegean Iron Age? As noted earlier, such an approach would not be alien to the work of Snodgrass, Morris, or Whitley. But so far as I am aware no such comparative study has been undertaken.

The obvious reason, of course, is indeed the generally perceived uniqueness of the "Greek experience." This phenomenon does indeed see the development and use of alphabetic writing, the inception of new branches of literature (including theater), the development of speculative philosophy as well as of mathematics, and the production of an art style which, via the Renaissance, underlies that of the Western world today: it is an achievement that is understandably felt to defy generalization. And in a sense it is perfectly correct that the unique, in its uniqueness, can defy generalization. But then, as I recalled at the outset, everything in the real world is in its own way unique, at least if we ascend above the level of the atoms and the subatomic particles. Maya civilization was unique, as were the chiefdoms of Polynesia or the city-states of Mesopotamia. Yet that has not in itself in the past proved an obstacle to a comparative or generalizing approach for these societies.

Certainly, it remains to be seen whether a comparative or generalizing approach would offer deep insights into those features of Classical Greek civilization that were indeed unique and without parallel. But I would suggest that such insights might well be available for other aspects of Aegean life and society in the first millennium BC, which may well find appropriate and instructive analogies elsewhere.

This separatist or segregated approach to the study of the Iron Age Aegean carries with it some serious limiting features. For it entails that the processes that led to the inception of state society in the Aegean in the first millennium BC have never been analyzed on an equal footing with those that brought about the (very different) inception of state societies in the Aegean in the second millennium BC. This, the most obvious comparison for any generalizing treatment, has never, so far as I am aware, been undertaken on any detailed level of analysis. Yet it is a task that cries out for experiment and exploration. It is understood that Oliver Dickinson, whose study of the Bronze Age Aegean is a standard work of reference (Dickinson 1994), is undertaking a comparable volume for the Aegean Iron Age. This pair of studies may constitute the first serious treatment that, in a measured and standardized way, sets out to place the two processes side by side and allows one to embark upon a systematic comparison of them. Of course, that will prove an ambitious task, since the fields of Aegean prehistory and of Classical studies have developed as effectively separate disciplines, as noted earlier. But this promises at least to be a beginning.

For how else shall we come better to appreciate the uniqueness of the "Greek experience" other than by understanding what the processes involved had in common with those of other instances of state formation, not least those operating in the Aegean a millennium earlier?

Bibliography

Abrams, E.
1994   *How the Maya built their world: Energetics and ancient architecture.* Austin: University of Texas Press.

Adams, R. McC.
1966   *The evolution of urban society: Early Mesopotamia and pre-Hispanic Mexico.* Chicago and London: Aldine; Weidenfeld and Nicolson.

1981   *Heartland of cities: Surveys of ancient settlement and land use on the central floodplain of the Euphrates.* Chicago: University of Chicago Press.

1992   Ideologies: Unity and diversity. In *Ideology and pre-Columbian civilization*, edited by A.A. Demarest and G.W. Conrad, 205–221. School of American Research Advanced Seminar Series. Santa Fe: School of American Research Press.

Addison, A.
2000   Emerging trends in virtual heritage. *IEEE Multimedia* 7(2):22–25.

Addison, A., and M. Gaiani
2000   Virtualized architectural heritage: New tools and techniques. *IEEE Multimedia* 7(2):26–31.

Agnew, N. and M. Demas, eds.
2002   *Principles for the conservation of heritage sites in China: English language translation, with Chinese text, of the document issued by China ICOMOS.* Los Angeles: Getty Conservation Institute.

Agnew, N., and R. Coffman
1991   Development and evaluation of the hexashelter. In *Conservation of the Orpheus mosaic at Paphos, Cyprus*, edited by N. Stanley-Price, 36–41. Los Angeles: Getty Conservation Institute.

Agnew, N., S. Maekawa, R. Coffman, and J. Meyer
1996   Evaluation of the performance of a lightweight modular site shelter: Quantitative meteorological data and protective indices for the "hexashelter." *Conservation and management of archaeological sites* 1(3):139–150.

319

Aharoni, Y.
1967   *The land of the Bible*. Philadelphia: Westminster Press.
Alaimo, R., R. Giarrusso, L. Lazzarini, F. Mannuccia, and P. Meli
1996   The conservation problems of the theatre of Eraclea Minoa (Sicily). *Proceedings of the 9th International Congress on Deterioration of Stone, Berlin, Germany, 30.9–4.10* (1996) 2:1085–1089. Berlin.
Albright, W.F.
1936–37 *The excavation of Tell Beit Mirsim*. Annual of the American Schools of Oriental Research 17 (monograph). New Haven: Yale University Press.
Alcock, S.E.
1991   Urban survey and the polis of Phlius. *Hesperia* 60:421–463.
1993   *Graecia Capta: The landscapes of Roman Greece*. Cambridge: Cambridge University Press.
1994   Breaking up the Hellenistic world: Survey and society. In *Classical Greece: Ancient histories and modern archaeologies*, edited by I. Morris, 171–190. Cambridge: Cambridge University Press.
2002   *Archaeologies of the Greek past: Landscapes, monuments and memories*. Cambridge: Cambridge University Press.
Alcock, S.E., and J.F. Cherry, eds.
2003   *Side-by-side survey: Comparative regional studies in the Mediterranean region*. Oxford: Oxbow Books.
Alcock, S.E., J.F. Cherry, and J.L. Davis
1994   Intensive survey, agricultural practice and the classical landscape of Greece. In *Classical Greece: Ancient histories and modern archaeologies*, edited by I. Morris, 137–170. Cambridge: Cambridge University Press.
Alcock, S.E., and R. Osborne, eds.
1994   *Placing the gods: Sanctuaries and sacred places in ancient Greece*. Oxford: Clarendon Press.
Alexiou, S.
1965   Piet de Jong. Obituary. *Kretika Chronika* 19:301–302.
Allen, K.M.S., S.W. Green, and E.B. Zubrow, eds.
1990   *Interpreting space: GIS and archaeology*. London: Taylor and Francis.
Alva, W., and C.B. Donnan
1993   *Royal tombs of Sipan*. Los Angeles: Fowler Museum of Cultural History, University of California, Los Angeles.
Ammerman, A.J.
1981   Surveys and archaeological research. *Annual Review of Anthropology* 10:63–88.
1995   The dynamics of modern land use and the Acconia Survey. *Journal of Mediterranean Archaeology* 8:77–92.

Anati, E.
1986   *The mountain of God.* New York: Rizzoli.
Andren, A.
1998   *Between artifacts and texts: Historical archaeology in global perspective.* New York: Plenum.
Andreou, S., M. Fotiadis, and K. Kotsakis
1996   The Neolithic and Bronze Age of northern Greece. *American Journal of Archaeology* 100:537–597.
Angel, M.
1979   *The painted rock of California (La Piedra Pintada): A legend.* San Luis Obispo, CA: Padre Productions. Reprinted from the original, 1910, Los Angeles: Grafton Publishing Co.
Arden, H.
1989   An Indian cemetery desecrated. Who owns our past? *National Geographic* 175(3):376–393.
Ashmore, W., and A.B. Knapp, eds.
1999   *Archaeologies of landscape: Contemporary perspectives.* Oxford: Blackwell.
Ashton, N.G.
1995   *Ancient Megisti: The forgotten Kastellorizo.* Nedlands: University of Western Australia Press.
Aura Jorro, F.
1985   *Diccionario Micénico.* Vol. 1. Madrid: Consejo Superior de Investigaciones Científicas.
1993   *Diccionario Micénico.* Vol. 2. Madrid: Consejo Superior de Investigaciones Científicas.
Avery, T., and T.R. Lyons
1981   *Remote sensing: Aerial and terrestrial photography for archaeologists.* National Park Service, supplement 7. Washington, DC: Cultural Resource Management Division, National Parks Service, US Department of the Interior.
Avni, G.
1992   Archaeological survey of Israel map of Har Saggi northeast (225). Jerusalem: Israel Antiquities Authority.
Avrami, E., R. Mason, and M. de la Torre
2000   *Values and heritage conservation.* Los Angeles: Getty Conservation Institute.
Bailey, D.
1990   The living house: Signifying continuity. In *The social archaeology of houses,* edited by R. Samson, 19–48. Edinburgh: Edinburgh University Press.
1993   The looting of Bulgaria. *Archaeology* 46(2):26–27.

1996   The life, times and works of House 59 from the Ovcharovo tell, Bulgaria. In *Neolithic houses in northwest Europe and beyond*, edited by T. Darvill and J. Thomas, 143–156. Oxford: Oxbow.

1998   Archaeology as socio-politics: Practice and ideology in Bulgaria. In *Archaeology under fire: Nationalism, politics and heritage in the eastern Mediterranean and Middle East*, edited by L. Meskell, 87–110. London: Routledge.

1999   What is a tell? Spatial, temporal and social parameters. In *Making places in the prehistoric world*, edited by J. Bruck and M. Goodman, 94–111. London: UCL Press.

2000   *Balkan prehistory: Exclusion, incorporation and identity*. London: Routledge.

Bailey, D., R. Tringham, J. Bass, M. Stevanovic, M. Hamilton, H. Neumann, I. Angelova, and A. Raduncheva

1998   Expanding the dimensions of early agricultural tells: The Podgoritsa Archaeological Project, Bulgaria. *Journal of Field Archaeology* 25(4):373–396.

Bailey, G.

1992   The Palaeolithic of Klithi in its wider context. *Annual of the British School at Athens* 87:1–28.

Bailey, G., ed.

1997   *Klithi: Palaeolithic settlement and quaternary landscapes in northwest Greece*. Cambridge: McDonald Institute for Archaeological Research.

Bailey, G.N., E. Adam, E. Panagopoulou, C. Perlès, and K. Zachos, eds.

1999   *The Palaeolithic archaeology of Greece and adjacent areas*. London: British School at Athens.

Bar-Yosef, O., and N. Goren

1980   Afterthoughts following prehistoric surveys in the Levant. *Israel Exploration Journal* 30:1–16.

Bar-Yosef, O., and J.L. Phillips, eds.

1977   *Prehistoric investigations in Gebel Maghara, northern Sinai*. Qedem 7. Monographs of the Institute of Archaeology. Jerusalem: Hebrew University.

Barber, E.J.W.

1974   *Archaeological decipherment: A handbook*. Princeton: Princeton University Press.

Barker, G.

1995   *A Mediterranean valley: Landscape archaeology and Annales history in the Biferno Valley*. London: Leicester University Press.

1996a   *Farming the desert: The UNESCO Libyan Valleys Archaeological Survey*. Vol. 1: *Synthesis*, edited by G. Barber. Paris: UNESCO.

1996b   Regional archaeological projects: Trends and traditions in Mediterranean Europe. *Archaeological Dialogues* 3(2):160–175.

Barker, G., and J.A. Lloyd, eds.

1991   *Roman landscapes: Archaeological survey in the Mediterranean region.* BSR Archaeological Monographs 2. London: British School at Rome.

Baron, A.G.

1978   The Glueck survey: Issues and problems in the archaeology of the Negev. Ph.D. dissertation, University of California, Riverside.

Bartu, A.

2000   Where is Çatalhöyük? Multiple sites in the construction of an archaeological site. In *Towards reflexive method in archaeology: The example at Çatalhöyük by members of the Çatalhöyük teams*, edited by I. Hodder, 101–110. Cambridge: McDonald Institute of Archaeology and BIAA.

Basso, K.H.

1996   *Wisdom sits in places: Landscape and language among the western Apache.* Albuquerque: University of New Mexico Press.

Beattie, A.J.

1962   Aegean languages of the heroic age. In *A companion to Homer*, edited by A.J.B. Wace and F.H. Stubbings, 311–324. New York: MacMillan.

Bender, B., ed.

1993   *Landscape: Politics and perspectives.* Oxford: Berg.

Bender, B., S. Hamilton, and C. Tilley

1997   Leskernick, stone worlds: Alternative narratives, nested landscapes. *Proceedings of the Prehistoric Society* 63:147–178.

Bennet, J.

1985   The structure of the Linear B administration at Knossos. *American Journal of Archaeology* 89:231–249.

1988   Approaches to the problem of combining textual data and archaeological data in the LBA Aegean. In *Problems in Greek prehistory*, edited by E.B. French and K. Wardle, 509–518. Bristol: Bristol Classical Press.

1990   Knossos in context: Comparative perspectives on the Linear B administration of LM II–III Crete. *American Journal of Archaeology* 94:193–211.

1997   Homer and the Bronze Age. In *A new companion to Homer*, edited by I. Morris and B. Powell, 511–533. Leiden, New York, and Cologne: Brill.

1998a   The Linear B archives and the kingdom of Nestor. In *Sandy Pylos: An archaeological history from Nestor to Navarino*, edited by J.L. Davis, 111–133. Austin: University of Texas Press.

1998b   The PRAP survey's contribution. In *Sandy Pylos: An archaeological history from Nestor to Navarino*, edited by J.L. Davis, 134–138. Austin: University of Texas Press.

Bennett, E.L., Jr.

1947   The Minoan linear script from Pylos. Ph.D. dissertation, University of Cincinnati.

1950   Fractional quantities in Minoan bookkeeping. *American Journal of Archaeology* 54:204–222.

1951   *The Pylos tablets. A preliminary transcription.* Princeton: Princeton University Press.

1953   *A Minoan Linear B index.* New Haven: Yale University Press.

1959   Tentative identification of the hands of the scribes of the Pylos tablets. *Athenaeum* 46, n.s., 36:328–331.

1989   Michael Ventris and the Pelasgian solution. In *Problems in decipherment*, edited by Y. Duhoux, T.G. Palaima, and J. Bennet, 9–23. Bibliothèque des Cahiers de l'Institut de Linguistique de Louvain 49. Louvain-la-Neuve: Peeters.

Benveniste, É.

1969   *Le vocabulaire des institutions indo-européennes.* 2 vols. Paris: Les Éditions de Minuit.

Berlin, H.

1977   *Signos y significados en las inscripciones Mayas.* Guatemala City: Instituto Nacional del Patrimonio Cultural de Guatemala.

Bernabé, A., D. Hitos, J.I. Juanes, E.-R. Luján, J.A. Negrete, J.G. Rubio, and T. Souto

1990–91   Estudios sobre el vocabulario micénico 1: Términos referidos a las ruedas. *Minos* 25/26:133–173.

Bernabé, A., J.L. Alonso, L.M. Benito, R. Cantarero, A. Leal, M.L. Marín, S. Moncó, P. Pérez, and P. Rodríguez

1992–93   Estudios sobre el vocabulario micénico 2: Términos referidos a los carros. *Minos* 27/28:125–166.

Besant, W.

1895   *Thirty years' work in the Holy Land.* London: Palestine Exploration Fund.

Betancourt, P.P., and R. Hope Simpson

1992   The agricultural system of Bronze Age Pseira. *Cretan Studies* 3:47–54.

Bettinger, R.L.

1999   From traveler to processor: Regional trajectories of hunter-gatherer sedentism in the Inyo-Mono region, California. In *Settlement pattern studies in the Americas: Fifty years since Virú*, edited by B.R. Billman and G.M. Feinman, 39–55. Washington, DC: Smithsonian Institution Press.

Betts, A.V.G.
1998   *The Harran and the Hamad*. Sheffield Archaeological Monographs 9. Sheffield: Sheffield Academic Press.

Bieder, R.E.
1992   The collecting of bones for anthropological narratives. *American Indian Culture and Research Journal* 16(2):21–35.

Billman, B.R., and G.M. Feinman, eds.
1999   *Settlement pattern studies in the Americas: Fifty years since Virú*. Washington, DC: Smithsonian Institution Press.

Binford, L.R.
1964   A consideration of archaeological research design. *American Antiquity* 29:425–441.

1972   *An archaeological perspective*. New York: Academic Press.

1980   Willow smoke and dogs' tails: Hunter-gatherer settlement systems and archaeological site formation. *American Antiquity* 45:4–20.

1992   Seeing the present and interpreting the past—and keeping things straight. In *Space, time, and archaeological landscapes*, edited by J. Rossignol and L.A. Wandsnider, 43–59. New York: Plenum Press.

Bintliff, J.L.
1977   *Mycenaean geography*, edited by J.L. Bintliff. Cambridge: British Association for Mycenaean Studies.

1984   Structuralism and myth in Minoan studies. *Antiquity* 58:33–38.

1994   The history of the Greek countryside: As the wave breaks, prospects for future research. In *Structures rurales et sociétés antiques*, edited by P.N. Doukellis and L.G. Mendoni, 7–15. Paris: Les Belles Lettres.

1997   Regional survey, demography, and the rise of complex societies in the ancient Aegean: Core-periphery, neo-Malthusian, and other interpretive models. *Journal of Field Archaeology* 24:1–38.

Bintliff, J.L., P. Howard, and A.M. Snodgrass
1999   The hidden landscape of prehistoric Greece. *Journal of Mediterranean Archaeology* 12:139–168.

Blake, P.
1977   *Form follows fiasco: Why modern architecture hasn't worked*. Boston and Toronto: Little, Brown.

Blanton, R.E.
2000   *Hellenistic, Roman and Byzantine settlement patterns of the coast lands of western Rough Cilicia*. BAR International Series 879. Oxford: Archaeopress.

Blanton, R.E., S.A. Kowalewski, G.A. Feinman, and J. Appel
1982   *Ancient Mesoamerica: A comparison of change in three regions.* Cambridge: Cambridge University Press.

Blegen, C.W.
1939   The great discovery in "Nestor's Palace" at Pylos: The first tablets with Minoan writing found on the Greek mainland. *Illustrated London News*, June 3:980.
1955   The Palace of Nestor excavations of 1954. *American Journal of Archaeology* 59:31–37.
1962   Pylos. In *A companion to Homer*, edited by A.J.B. Wace and F.H. Stubbings, 422-429. New York: MacMillan.

Blegen, C.W., and K. Kourouniotis
1939   Excavations at Pylos, 1939. *American Journal of Archaeology* 43:537–576.

Blegen, C.W., and M. Rawson
1966   *The Palace of Nestor at Pylos in western Messenia.* Vol. 1: *The buildings and their contents.* Princeton: Princeton University Press.
1967   *A guide to the Palace of Nestor.* Excavations of the University of Cincinnati Guide Book no. 1. Cincinnati: University of Cincinnati.

Blier, S.P.
1987   *The anatomy of architecture: Ontology and metaphor in Batammaliba architectural expression.* Cambridge: Cambridge University Press.

Blum, I., L. Darmezin, J.-C. Decourt, B. Helly, and G. Lucas
1992   *Topographie antique et géographie historique en pays grec.* Paris: Centre National de la Recherche Scientifique (Centre de Recherches Archéologiques).

Boerschmann, E.
1911   *Die Baukunst und religiöse Kultur der Chinesen.* 2 vols. Berlin: Reiner.
1925   *Chinesische Architektur.* 2 vols. Berlin: Wasmuth.

Boone, E.H., and W.D. Mignolo, eds.
1994   *Writing without words: Alternative literacies in Mesoamerica and the Andes.* Durham and London: Duke University Press.

Bourdieu, P.
1977   *Outline of a theory of practice.* Cambridge: Cambridge University Press.

Bowra, C.M.
1934   Homeric words in Cyprus. *Journal of Hellenic Studies* 54:54–74.

Bradley, R.
1993   *Altering the earth: The origins of monuments in Britain and continental Europe.* Edinburgh: Society of Antiquaries of Scotland.
1998   *The significance of monuments.* London: Routledge.

Braidwood, R.J.
1974   The Iraq Jarmo project. In *Archaeological researches in retrospect,* edited by G. Willey, 59–83. Cambridge, MA: Winthrop Press.

Braidwood, R.J., H. Cambel, B. Lawrence, C.L. Redman, and R. Stewart
1974   Beginnings of village-farming communities in southwestern Turkey: 1972. *Proceedings of the National Academy of Sciences* 71(2): 568–572.

Braudel, F.
1966   *La Méditerranée et le monde méditerranéen à l'époque de Philippe II.* 2d ed. Paris: A. Colin.
1972   *The Mediterranean and the Mediterranean world in the Age of Philip II.* Vol. 1. London: Collins.

Brill, D.
2000   Video-recording as part of the critical archaeological process. In *Towards reflexive method in archaeology: The example at Çatalhöyük by members of the Çatalhöyük teams,* edited by I. Hodder, 229–234. Cambridge: McDonald Institute for Archaeological Research and BIAA.

Brilliant, M.
1970   *Portrait of Israel.* New York: American Heritage Press.

Brodie, N., J. Doole, and C. Renfrew, eds.
2001   *Trade in illicit antiquities: The destruction of the world's archaeological heritage.* Cambridge: McDonald Institute for Archaeological Research.

Broodbank, C.
2000   *An island archaeology of the early Cyclades.* Cambridge: Cambridge University Press.

Brown, A.
1983   *Arthur Evans and the Palace of Minos.* Oxford: Ashmolean Museum.

Brunet, M., ed.
1999   *Territoires des cités grecques. Bulletin de correspondance hellénique,* Supplément 34. Paris: De Boccard.

Brunner-Traut, E.
1984   Jean-François Champollion: 'Ein grosser Mann in einer grossen vielbewegten Zeit' (Eduard Meyer). *Saeculum* 35:306–325.

Burkert, W.
1985   *Greek religion,* translated by J. Raffan. Cambridge, MA: Harvard University Press.
1997   From epiphany to cult statue: Early Greek *theos.* In *What is a god?,* edited by A.B. Lloyd, 15–34. London: Duckworth.

Butrint Foundation
2000   Web site: *www.butrintfound.dial.pipex.com.*

Calder, W.M. III, ed.

1991   *The Cambridge ritualists reconsidered: Proceedings of the First Oldfather Conference, University of Illinois at Urbana-Champaign, April 27–30, 1989.* Atlanta: Scholars Press.

Calthorpe, P.

1994   The region. In *The new urbanism: Toward an architecture of community,* edited by Peter Katz, xi–xvi. New York: McGraw-Hill.

Cameron, C.M.

1994   The destruction of the past: Nonrenewable cultural resources. *Nonrenewable Resources* 3(1):6–24.

Carreté, J.-M., S. Keay, and M. Millett

1995   *A Roman provincial capital and its hinterland: The survey of the territory of Tarragona, Spain, 1985–1990.* JRA Supplementary Vol. 15. Ann Arbor: Journal of Roman Archaeology.

Carter, J.C.

1998   The chora of Chersonesos on the Black Sea: The 1998 campaign. Privately circulated report. Austin: The Institute of Classical Archaeology, University of Texas at Austin; Sevastopol: The National Preserve of Tauric Chersonesos.

2001   *The study of ancient territories: Chersonesos and Metaponto.* Austin: The Institute of Classical Archaeology, University of Texas at Austin.

Caskey, J.L.

1956   Excavations at Lerna, 1955. *Hesperia* 25:147–173.

Cavanagh, W.G.

1995   Development of the Mycenaean state in Laconia: Evidence from the Laconia survey. In *Politeia: Society and state in the Aegean Bronze Age,* edited by R. Laffineur and W.-D. Niemeier, 81–87. Aegaeum 12. Liège: Université de Liège, Histoire de l'art et archéologie de la Grèce antique.

1999   Revenons à nos moutons: Surface survey and the Peloponnese in the Late and Final Neolithic. In *Le Peloponnèse: Archéologie et histoire,* edited by J. Renard, 31–65. Rennes: Les Presses Universitaires.

Chadwick, J.

1963   The two provinces of Pylos. *Minos* 7:125–141.

1972   The Mycenaean documents. In *The Minnesota Messenia expedition: Reconstructing a Bronze Age regional environment,* edited by W.A. McDonald and G.R. Rapp, 100–116. Minneapolis: University of Minnesota Press.

1976a   Who were the Dorians? *Parola del Passato* 31:112–114.

1976b   *The Mycenaean world.* Cambridge: Cambridge University Press.

1999   Linear B: Past, present and future. In *Floreant studia mycenaea*, edited by S. Deger-Jalkotzy, S. Hiller, and O. Panagl, 1:29–38. Österreichische Akademie der Wissenschaften Philosophisch-Historische Klasse Denkschriften Band 274. Vienna: Verlag der Österreichischen Akademie der Wissenschaften.

Chalmers, A., S. Stoddart, M. Belcher, and M. Day

1996   An interactive photo-realistic visualisation system for archaeological sites. Web site: *www.cs.bris.ac.uk/~alan/Arch/INSITE/research/comvis/insite2.htm*.

Chambers, M.

1991   Cornford's *Thucydides Mythistoricus*. In *The Cambridge ritualists reconsidered*, edited by W.M. Calder III, 61–77. Atlanta: Scholars Press.

Champion, T.

1990   Medieval archaeology and the tyranny of the historical record. In *From the Baltic to the Black Sea: Studies in medieval archaeology*, edited by D. Austin and L. Alcock, 79–95. London: Unwin Hyman.

Chapman, H., and B. Gearey

2000   Palaeoecology and the perception of prehistoric landscapes: Some comments on visual approaches to phenomenology. *Antiquity* 74:316–319.

Chapman, J.

1981   *The Vinca culture*. BAR International Series 117. Oxford: British Archaeological Reports.

Cherry, J.F.

1981   Pattern and process in the earliest colonization of the Mediterranean islands. *Proceedings of the Prehistoric Society* 47:41–68.

1982   A preliminary definition of site distribution on Melos. In *An island polity: The archaeology of exploitation on Melos*, edited by C. Renfrew and J.M. Wagstaff, 10–23. Cambridge: Cambridge University Press.

1983   Frogs round the pond: Perspectives on current archaeological survey projects in the Mediterranean region. In *Archaeological survey in the Mediterranean region*, edited by D.R. Keller and D.W. Rupp, 375–415. BAR International Series 155. Oxford: British Archaeological Reports.

1984   The emergence of the state in the prehistoric Aegean. *Proceedings of the Cambridge Philological Society* 30:18–48.

1990   The first colonization of the Mediterranean islands: A review of recent research. *Journal of Mediterranean Archaeology* 3:145–221.

1994   Regional survey in the Aegean: The 'New Wave' (and after). In *Beyond the site: Regional studies in the Aegean area*, edited by P.N. Kardulias, 91–112. Lanham: University Press of America.

N.D.   The impact of regional survey on Aegean prehistory, ca. 1970–2000. *Hesperia*. Forthcoming.

Cherry, J.F., and J.L. Davis

1999   An archaeological homily. In *Rethinking Mycenaean palaces: New interpretations of an old idea*, edited by M.L. Galaty and W.A. Parkinson, 91–98. Los Angeles: The Cotsen Institute of Archaeology at UCLA.

2001   "Under the sceptre of Agamemnon": The view from the hinterlands of Mycenae. In *Urbanism in the Aegean Bronze Age*, edited by K. Branigan, 141–159. Studies in Aegean Archaeology 4. Sheffield: Sheffield Academic Press.

Cherry, J.F., J.L. Davis, and E. Mantzourani

1991   *Landscape archaeology as long-term history: Northern Keos in the Cycladic Islands from earliest settlement until modern times.* Monumenta Archaeologica 16. Los Angeles: Institute of Archaeology, University of California, Los Angeles.

N.D.   The Nemea Valley Archaeological Project Archaeological Survey: Web site: *http://classics.lsa.umich.edu/NVAP.html*.

Chippindale, C.

1995   This ancient stuff (a review of Dark, K.R., *Theoretical archaeology* [London 1995] and Ucko, P.J., *Theory in archaeology: A world perspective* [London 1995]). *Times Literary Supplement*, October 20, p. 11–12.

Chippindale, C., P. Devereux, P. Fowler, R. Jones, and T. Sebastian

1990   *Who owns Stonehenge?* London: B.T. Batsford.

Clark, A.

1990   *Seeing beneath the soil: Prospecting methods in archaeology.* London: B.T. Batsford.

Clarke, D.L., ed.

1972   *Models in archaeology.* London: Methuen.

Clayton, P.A.

1982   *The rediscovery of ancient Egypt: Artists and travellers in the 19th century.* London: Thames and Hudson.

Clémentin-Ohja, C., and P.-Y. Manguin

2001   *Un siècle pour l'Asie: L'École française d' Extrême-Orient, 1898–2000.* Paris: Les Éditions du Pacifique, École française d'Extrême-Orient.

Coe, M.D.

1973   *The Maya scribe and his world.* New York: Grolier Club.

1992 *Breaking the Maya code.* London and New York: Thames and Hudson.

Coe, W.R.
1990 *Excavation in the North Acropolis, North Terrace, and Great Plaza of Tikal.* Museum Monograph 61, Tikal Report 14. Philadelphia: University of Pennsylvania Museum.

Collingwood, R.G.
1946 *The Idea of history.* Oxford: Oxford University Press.

Conder, C.R., and H.H. Kitchener
1881-85 *The survey of western Palestine: Memoirs of the topography, orography, hydrography, and archaeology.* London: Palestine Exploration Fund.

Cook, E., and T.G. Palaima
N.D. Sacrifice and society in the *Odyssey.* Paper presented at the annual joint meeting of the American Philological Association and the Archaeological Institute of America, San Diego, CA, January 5–9, 2001.

Corfield, M., P. Hinton, T. Nixon, and M. Pollard, eds.
1998 Preserving archaeological remains in situ. *Proceedings of the Conference of 1st–3rd April 1996.* London: Museum of London Archaeology Service and University of Bradford, Department of Archaeological Sciences.

Cornford, F.M.
1907 *Thucydides Mythistoricus.* Reprint, 1971, Philadelphia: University of Pennsylvania Press.

Costanzi Cobau, A.
1985 Excavated wallplasters: Conservation problems. In *Preventive measures during excavation and site protection,* 103–108. Rome: ICCROM.

Courty, A.M., P. Goldberg, and A. MacPhail, eds.
1990 *Soils and micromorphology in archaeology.* Cambridge: Cambridge University Press.

Cowgill, G.L.
1992 Toward a political history of Teotihuacan. In *Ideology and pre-Columbian civilization,* edited by A.A. Demarest and G.W. Conrad, 87–114. School of American Research Advanced Seminar Series. Santa Fe: School of American Research Press.

Croce, B.
1927 *Teoria e storia della storiografia,* 3d ed. Bari: Gius. Laterza & Figli.

Cronon, W.
1994 Inconsistent unity: The passion of Frank Lloyd Wright. In *Frank Lloyd Wright: Architect,* edited by T. Riley, 8–31. New York: Museum of Modern Art.

Daniel, G.
1963   *The idea of prehistory.* Cleveland: World Publishing Company.
1967   *The origins and growth of archaeology.* New York: Crowell.
Dar, S.
1982   *Settlement distribution in western Samaria in the days of the Second Temple, the Mishna, the Talmud and the Byzantine period* (in Hebrew). Tel Aviv: Society for the Protection of Nature.
1986   *Landscape and pattern: An archaeological survey of Samaria 800 BCE to 636 CE.* BAR International Series 308. Oxford: British Archaeological Reports.
Davies, A.M., and Y. Duhoux, eds.
1985   *Linear B: A 1984 survey.* Bibliothèque des Cahiers de L'Institut Linguistique de Louvain 26. Louvain-la-Neuve: Cabay.
Davis, H.
1998   Facing the crisis. Archaeology Online. Web site: *http://www.archaeology.org/online/features/loot/index.html.*
Davis, J.L., ed.
1998   *Sandy Pylos: An archaeological history from Nestor to Navarino.* Austin: University of Texas Press.
Davis, J.L., and J. Bennet
1999   Making Mycenaeans: Warfare, territorial expansion and representations of the other in the Pylian kingdom. In *Polemos*, vol. 1, edited by R. Laffineur, 105–120. Aegaeum 19. Liège and Austin: Histoire de l'art et archéologie de la Grèce antique, Université de Liège, and Program in Aegean Scripts and Prehistory, University of Texas at Austin.
Davis, J.L., and S.B. Sutton
1995   Response to A.J. Ammerman, "The dynamics of modern land use and the Acconia Survey." *Journal of Mediterranean Archaeology* 8:113–123.
Del Freo, M.
1996–97 Osservazioni su miceneo *ko-ma-we-te-ja*. Minos 31/32:145–158.
Demas, M.
1997   Summary of charters dealing with the archaeological heritage. In *The conservation of archaeological sites in the Mediterranean region*, edited by M. de la Torre, 151–153. Los Angeles: Getty Conservation Institute.
Demas, M., P-M. Lin, A. Agnew, and M. Taylor
1993   New materials for ancient worlds: The application of geosynthetics to the conservation of cultural sites. *Geosynthetics '93: Conference Proceedings*, 2:985–998. St. Paul: Industrial Fabrics Association International.

Demoule, J.-P., and C. Perlès
1993   The Greek Neolithic: A new review. *Journal of World Prehistory* 7:355–416.
Diaz-Andreu, M., and T. Champion, eds.
1996   *Nationalism and archaeology in Europe.* Boulder: Westview Press.
DiCenso, J.
1990   *Hermeneutics and the disclosure of truth: A study in the work of Heidegger, Gadamer, and Ricoeur.* Charlottesville: University Press of Virginia.
Dickinson, O.
1994   *The Aegean Bronze Age.* Cambridge: Cambridge University Press.
Dietz, S., L.L. Sebaï, and H. Ben Hassen, eds.
1995   *Africa Proconsularis: Regional studies in the Segermes Valley of northern Tunesia.* 2 vols. Aarhus: Aarhus University Press.
Dimacopoulou, A., and A. Lapourtas
1995   The legal protection of archaeological heritage in Greece in view of the European Union legislation: A review. *International Journal of Cultural Property* 2:311–323.
Dobres, M.-A., and J.E. Robb, eds.
2000   *Agency in archaeology.* New York: Routledge.
Douglas, M.
1970   *Natural symbols: Explorations in cosmology.* New York: Pantheon Books.
1982a   Introduction to group/grid analysis. In *Essays in the sociology of perception*, edited by M. Douglas, 1–18. London: Routledge and Kegan Paul.
1982b   Cultural bias. In *The active voice*, edited by M. Douglas, 183–254. London: Routledge and Kegan Paul.
Doukellis, P.N.
1988   Cadastres romains en Grèce: traces d'un réseau rural à Actia Nicopolis. *Dialogues d'histoire anciennes* 14:159–166.
Dousougli, A., and S. Morris
1994   Ancient towers on Leukas, Greece. In *Structures rurales et sociétés antiques*, edited by P.N. Doukellis and L.G. Mendoni, 215–225. Paris: Les Belles Lettres.
Dowdy, K., and M.R Taylor
1993   Investigations into the benefits of site reburial in the preservation of prehistoric plasters in archaeological ruins. *7th International Conference on the Study and Conservation of Earthen Architecture*, 480–487. Lisbon: DGEMN.
Dowley, T., ed.
1986   *Discovering the Bible.* Basingstoke: Marshall Pickering.

Drew, D.
  1999   *The lost chronicles of the Maya kings.* London: Weidenfeld and
              Nicolson.
Driessen, J.
  1990   *An early destruction in the Mycenean Palace at Knossos: A new
              interpretation of the excavation field-notes of the south-east area of the
              west wing.* Acta Archaeologica Lovanensia Monographiae 2.
              Louvain: Katholieke Universiteit Leuven.
  1997   Le palais de Cnossos au MR II-III: Combien de destructions? In
              La Crète mycénienne, edited by J. Driessen and A. Farnoux, 113–
              134. *Bulletin de correspondance héllenique,* Supplément 30. Paris:
              de Boccard Édition-Diffusion.
  1999   "The archaeology of a dream": The reconstruction of Minoan
              Palace architecture. *Journal of Mediterranean Archaeology* 12(1):
              121–127.
  2000   *The scribes of the room of the chariot tablets: Interdisciplinary
              approach to the study of a Linear B deposit.* Supplement to *Minos*
              16. Salamanca: Ediciones Universidad de Salamanca.
  2001   History and hierarchy: Preliminary observations on the settle-
              ment pattern in Minoan Crete. In *Urbanism in the Aegean Bronze
              Age,* edited by K. Branigan, 51–71. Sheffield Studies in Aegean
              Archaeology 4. Sheffield: Sheffield Academic Press.
Driessen, J., and C. MacDonald
  1997   *The troubled island. Minoan Crete before and after the Santorini erup-
              tion.* Aegaeum 17. Liège and Austin: Histoire de l'art et archéolo-
              gie de la Grèce antique, Université de Liège, and Program in
              Aegean Scripts and Prehistory, University of Texas at Austin.
Duhoux, Y.
  1976   *Aspects du vocabulaire économique mycénien (cadastre—artisanat—
              fiscalité).* Amsterdam: Adolf M. Hakkert.
  1988   Les contacts entre mycéniens et barbares d'après le vocabulaire
              du linéaire B. *Minos* 23:75–83.
  1994–95   Le mycénien connaissait-il la tmèse? *Minos* 29-30:177–186.
Dumézil, G.
  1958   *L'idéologie tripartie des Indo-Européens.* Collection Latomus 31.
              Brussels: Latomus.
Dunnell, R.C.
  1992   The notion site. In *Space, time, and archaeological landscapes,*
              edited by J. Rossignol and L.A. Wandsnider, 21–41. New York:
              Plenum Press.
Dunnell, R.C., and W.S. Dancey
  1983   The siteless survey: A regional scale data collection strategy.
              Advances in archaeological method and theory 6:267–287.

Dyson, S.L.
1998   *Ancient marbles to American shores: Classical archaeology in the United States.* Philadelphia: University of Pennsylvania Press.

Earle, T.
1997   *How chiefs come to power: The political economy in prehistory.* Stanford: Stanford University Press.

Ebert, J.I.
1988   Remote sensing in archaeological projection and prediction. In *Quantifying the present and predicting the past: Theory, method, and application of archaeological predictive modeling,* edited by W.J. Judge and L. Sebastian, 429–492. Washington, DC: U.S. Government Printing Office.

Economakis, R.
1994   *Acropolis restoration: The CCAM interventions.* London: Academy Editions.

Edmonds, M.
1999   *Ancestral geographies of the Neolithic: Landscapes, monuments and memory.* London: Routledge.

Edwards, I.E.S.
1949   *The pyramids of Egypt.* Harmondsworth, Middlesex: Penguin Books.

El-Baz, F.
1997   Space age archaeology. *Scientific American* 277(2):60–65.

Elia, R.J.
1993   U.S. cultural resource management and the ICAHM charter. In Special section: Managing the archaeological heritage, edited by H. Cleere. *Antiquity* 67(255):426–438.

Elon, A.
1971   *The Israelis, founders and sons.* New York: Holt, Rinehart and Winston.

Endere, M.L., and I. Podgorny
1997   Los gliptodontes son argentinos: La ley 9080 y la creación del patrimonio nacional. *Ciencia y Sociedad* 7(42):54–59.

Erickson, C.
2000   The Lake Titicaca Basin: A pre-Columbian built landscape. In *Imperfect balance: Landscape transformations in the Precolumbian Americas,* edited by D. Lentz, 311–356. New York: Columbia University Press.

Esin, U., and S. Harmankaya
1999   Asikli. In *Neolithic in Turkey,* edited by M. Özdogan and N. Basgelen, 115–132. Istanbul: Archeologie ver Sanat Yayinlari.

Evans, A.E.

1894　Primitive pictographs and a Prae-Phoenician script from Crete and the Peloponnese. *Journal of Hellenic Studies* 14:270–372.

1897　Further discoveries of Cretan and Aegean script, with Libyan and Proto-Egyptian comparisons. *Journal of Hellenic Studies* 17:327–395.

1900a　Knossos, I. The palace. *Annual of the British School at Athens* 6:3–70.

1900b　Writing in prehistoric Greece. *Proceedings of the British Association (Bradford)*, 897–899.

1900–01　The Palace of Minos: Provisional report of the excavations for the year 1901. *Annual of the British School at Athens* 7:1–120.

1901　Mycenaean tree and pillar cult and its Mediterranean relations. *Journal of Hellenic Studies* 21:99–204.

1901–02　The Palace of Minos: Provisional report of the excavations for the year 1902. *Annual of the British School at Athens* 8:1–124.

1902–03　The Palace of Minos: Provisional report of the excavations for the year 1903. *Annual of the British School at Athens* 9:1–153.

1904　The pictographic and linear scripts of Minoan Crete and their relations. *Proceedings of the British Academy* 1903–04:137–139.

1909　*Scripta Minoa I*. Oxford: Clarendon Press.

1921　*The palace of Minos at Knossos. Vol. 1: The Neolithic and Early and Middle Minoan Ages.* London: MacMillan.

1927　Work of reconstitution in the Palace of Knossos. *The Antiquaries Journal* 7:258–267.

1928　*The palace of Minos at Knossos. Vol. 2, Pt. 1: Fresh light on origins and external relations: The restoration in town and palace after seismic catastrophe towards close of M.M. III, and the beginnings of the new era. Pt. 2: Town-houses in Knossos of the new era and restored west palace section, with its state approach.* London: MacMillan.

1930　*The palace of Minos at Knossos. Vol. 3: The great transitional age in the northern and eastern sections of the palace: The most brilliant records of Minoan art and the evidences of an advanced religion.* London: MacMillan.

1935　*The palace of Minos at Knossos. Vol. 4, Pt. 1: Emergence of outer western enceinte, with new illustrations, artistic and religious, of the Middle Minoan phase: Chryselephantine 'Lady of Sports,' 'Snake Room' and full story of the cult: Late Minoan ceramic evolution and 'Palace Style.' Pt. 2: 'Camp-Stool' fresco—long-robed priests and beneficient genii; chryselephantine boy-god and ritual hair-offering; intaglio types, M.M. III–L.M. II; late hoards of sealings; deposits of inscribed tablets and the palace stores; Linear Script B and its mainland extension; closing palatial phase—'Room of the Throne' and final catastrophe. With epilogue on the discovery of 'Ring of Minos' and 'Temple Tomb.'* London: MacMillan.

1952   *Scripta Minoa II*, edited by J.L. Myres. Oxford: Clarendon Press.

Evans, J.

1943   *Time and chance: The story of Arthur Evans and his forebears.* London: Longman's Green.

Fagan, B.M.

1975   *The rape of the Nile: Tomb robbers, tourists, and archaeologists in Egypt.* New York: Scribner.

1988   Black day at Slack Farm. *Archaeology* 41(4):15–16, 73.

Fairbank, W.

1994   *Liang and Lin: Partners in exploring China's architectural past.* Philadelphia: University of Pennsylvania Press.

Falk, L., ed.

1991   *Historical archaeology in global perspective.* Washington, DC: Smithsonian Institution Press.

Falkenhausen, L. von

1986   Architecture. In *A consideration of the early Classic period in the Maya Lowlands*, edited by G.R. Willey and P. Mathews, 111–133. Publication no. 10. Albany: Institute for Mesoamerican Studies, State University of New York at Albany.

Farid, S.

2000   The Excavation process at Çatalhöyük. In *Towards reflexive method in archaeology: The example at Çatalhöyük by members of the Çatalhöyük teams*, edited by I. Hodder, 19–36. Cambridge: McDonald Institute for Archaeological Research and BIAA.

Farnoux, A.

1993   *Cnossos: l'archéologie d'un rêve.* Paris: Gallimard.

1996   *Knossos: Unearthing a legend.* London: Thames and Hudson.

Farrand, W.R.

2000   *Excavations of Franchthi Cave, Greece.* Fascicle 12: *Depositional history of Franchthi Cave. Stratigraphy, sedimentology, and chronology.* Bloomington and Indianapolis: Indiana University Press.

Fash, W.L., and R.J. Sharer

1991   Sociopolitical developments and methodological issues at Copán, Honduras: A conjunctive perspective. *Latin American Antiquity* 2:166–187.

Federspiel, B.

2001   The definition of the conservation profession and its field of operation: Issues in the 21st century. In *Past practice—Future prospects*, edited by A. Oddy and S. Smith, 75–79. British Museum Occasional Paper 145. London: British Museum.

Felstiner, J.
  1980   *Translating Neruda: The way to Machu Picchu.* Stanford: Stanford
            University Press.
Ferioli, P., E. Fiandra, and G.G. Fissore, eds.
  1996   *Administration in ancient societies.* Pubblicazioni del Centro Inter-
            nazionale di Ricerche Archeologiche Antropologiche e Storiche
            2. Turin: Scriptorium.
Ferioli, P., E. Fiandra, G.G. Fissore, and M. Frangipane, eds.
  1994   *Archives before writing.* Pubblicazioni del Centro Internazionale
            di Ricerche Archeologiche Antropologiche e Storiche 1. Turin:
            Scriptorium.
Ferguson, T.J.
  1996   Native Americans and the practice of archaeology. *Annual
            Review of Anthropology* 25:63–79.
Finkelstein, I.
  1988   *The archaeology of Israelite settlement.* Jerusalem: Keter.
Finkelstein, I., Z. Lederman, and S. Bunimovitz, eds.
  1997   *The highlands of many cultures.* Tel Aviv: Institute of Archaeology,
            Tel Aviv University.
Finlay, G.
  1869   *Paratereseis epi tes en Elvetiai kai Elladi proistorikes archaiologias
            (Observations on prehistoric archaeology in Switzerland and
            Greece)*(in Greek). Athens: Lakonia.
Fish, S.K., and S.A. Kowalewski
  1990   Introduction. In *The archaeology of regions,* edited by S. Fish and S.
            Kowalewski, 1–5. Washington, DC: Smithsonian Institution Press.
Flannery, K.V.
  1968   Archaeological systems theory and early Mesoamerica. In
            Anthropological archaeology in the Americas, 67–87. Washington,
            DC: Anthropological Society of Washington.
  1986   *Guilá Naquitz: Archaic foraging and early agriculture in Oaxaca,
            Mexico,* edited by K. V. Flannery. New York: Academic Press.
  1999   Process and agency in early state formation. *Cambridge Archaeo-
            logical Journal* 9:3–21.
Foley, R.
  1981   *Off-site archaeology and human adaptation in Eastern Africa.* BAR
            International Series 97. Oxford: British Archaeological Reports.
Forte, M., and A. Siliotti
  1997   *Virtual archaeology.* London: Thames and Hudson.
Fotiadis, M.
  1993   Regions of the imagination: Archaeologists, local people and the
            archaeological record in fieldwork, Greece. *Journal of European
            Archaeology* 1:151–170.

1995   Modernity and the past-still-present: Politics of time in the birth of regional archaeological projects in Greece. *American Journal of Archaeology* 99:59–78.

1997   Cultural identity and regional archaeological projects: Beyond ethical questions. *Archaeological Dialogues* 4:102–113.

Foucault, M.

1973   *The order of things: An archaeology of the human sciences.* New York: Vintage Books.

1977   *Discipline and punish: The birth of the prison,* translated by A. Sheridan. New York: Pantheon Books. Originally published as *Surveiller et punir: Naissance de la prison,* 1975. Paris: Gallimard.

Foundoukidis, E.

1940   Preface to *Manual on the technique of archaeological excavations.* Paris: International Institute of Intellectual Co-operation.

Foxhall, L.

1990   The dependant tenant: Land-leasing and labour in Italy and Greece. *Journal of Roman Studies* 80:97–114.

Francovich, R., and J. Buchanan

1995   Il progetto del parco archeominerario di Rocca di San Silvestro (Campiglia Marittima). In *I siti archeologici: Un problema di musealizzazione all'aperto,* edited by B. Amendolea, 176–195. Rome: Provincia di Roma/Gruppo Editoriale Internazionale.

Fresnais, J.

2001   *La protection du patrimoine en République populaire de Chine (1949–1999).* Ministère de l'Éducation nationale de la Recherche et de la Technologie, Comité des travaux historiques et scientifiques, Format 40. Paris: Éditions du C.T.H.S.

Fu Xinian

1998   *Jianzhushi lunwenji (Collected essays on the history of architecture).* Beijing: Wenwu chubanshe.

Fyfe, T.

1903   Painted plaster decoration at Knossos. *Journal of the Royal Institute of British Architects* 10:107–131.

1914   Some aspects of Greek architecture. *Journal of the Royal Institute of British Architects* 21:489–496.

1920   Greek studies. *Journal of the Royal Institute of British Architects* 27:107–131.

1926   The palace of Knossos: An example in conservation. *Journal of the Royal Institute of British Architects,* 26 June, 479–480.

1936   *Hellenistic architecture: An introductory study.* Cambridge: Cambridge University Press.

1942   *Architecture in Cambridge.* Cambridge: Cambridge University Press.

Gadamer, H.-G.

1975   *Truth and method.* New York: Seabury Press.

1981   *Reason in the age of science.* Cambridge, MA: MIT Press.

Gadon, E.

1989   *The once and future goddess.* San Francisco: Harper and Row.

Galaty, M.L., and W.A. Parkinson, eds.

1999   *Rethinking Mycenaean palaces: New interpretations of an old idea.* Los Angeles: The Cotsen Institute of Archaeology at UCLA.

Gallis, K.I.

1979   A short chronicle of Greek archaeological investigations in Thessaly from 1881 until the present day. In *La Thessalie: Actes de la table-ronde 21–24 Juillet 1975, Lyon,* edited by B. Helly, 1–30. Lyon: Maison de l'Orient.

1992   *Atlas proïstorikon oikismon tis anatolikis Thessalikis pediadas.* Larisa: Etaireia Istorikon Ereunon Thessalias.

Gamble, C.

1998   Paleolithic society and the release from proximity: A network approach to intimate relations. *World Archaeology* 29(3):426–449.

Gardiner, A.H.

1978   *Egypt of the pharaohs: An introduction.* Oxford: Oxford University Press.

Garnsey, P.

1979   Where did Italian peasants live? *Proceedings of the Cambridge Philological Society* 25:1–25.

Garrard, A., B. Byrd, B.P. Harvey, and F. Hivernel

1985   Prehistoric environment and settlement in the Azraq Basin: A report on the 1982 survey season. *Levant* 17:1–28.

Gaussen, J.

1980   *Le Paléolithique Supèrieur de Plein Air en Périgord.* Supplément 14, Gallia Préhistoire. Paris: Centre National de la Recherche Scientifique.

Gell, W.

1810   *The itinerary of Greece with a commentary on Pausanias and Strabo and an account of the monuments of antiquity at present existing in that country in the years 1801, 1802, 1805 and 1806.* London: T. Payne.

Georgiev, G.

1961   Kulturgruppen der Jungstein- und der Kupferzeit in der Ebene von Thrazien. In *L'Europe à la fin de l'age de pierre,* 45–100. Prague: Éditions de l'Académie tchécoslovaque des sciences.

Georgiev, G., N. Merpert, R. Katincharov, and D. Dimitrov

1979   *Ezero: Ranobronzovoto selishte.* Sofia: Arkheologicheski Institut BAN.

Gérard-Rousseau, M.
   1968   *Les mentions religieuses dans les tablettes mycéniennes.* Incunabula
            Graeca 29. Rome: Edizioni dell' Ateneo.
Geva, S.
   1992   Israeli biblical archaeology at its beginning (in Hebrew). *Zmanim*
            42:93–102.
Gibson, S.
   1995   Landscape archaeology and ancient agricultural field systems in
            Palestine. Ph.D. dissertation, University College, London.
Gill, M.A.V.
   1966   Seals and sealings: Some comments. The Knossos sealings with
            Linear B inscriptions. *Kadmos* 5:1–16.
Glassow, M.A.
   1990   Ethical issues brought about by the California Environmental
            Quality Act. In *Predicaments, pragmatics, and professionalism: Eth-
            ical conduct in archeology,* special publication number one, edited
            by J.N. Woodall, 37–47. Winston-Salem: Society of Professional
            Archeologists.
Glueck, N.
   1945   *The other side of the Jordan.* New Haven: Yale University Press.
   1959   *Rivers in the desert.* Philadelphia: Jewish Publication Society.
   1965   Further exploration in the Negev. *Bulletin of the American Schools
            of Oriental Research* 179:6-29.
Goring-Morris, A.N.
   1987   *At the edge: Terminal Pleistocene hunter-gatherers in the Negev and
            Sinai.* BAR International Series 361. Oxford: British Archaeo-
            logical Reports.
Grafton, A.
   1992   *New worlds, ancient texts: The power of tradition and the shock of
            discovery.* Harvard: Belknap Press.
Graham, J.W.
   1972   *The palaces of Crete.* Princeton: Princeton University Press.
Grant, C.
   1967   *Rock art of the American Indian.* New York: Thomas Crowell
            Company.
   1993   *The rock paintings of the Chumash: A study of a California Indian
            culture.* Berkeley: Santa Barbara Museum of Natural History.
            Originally printed in 1965, Berkeley: University of California
            Press.
Gray, D.H.F.
   1959   Linear B and archaeology. *Bulletin of the Institute of Classical Stud-
            ies* 6:47–57.

Greene, J.A.
1999   Preserving which past for whose future? The dilemma of cultural resource management in case studies from Tunisia, Cyprus and Jordan. *Conservation and management of archaeological sites* 3(1–2):43–60.

Gulizio, J., T.G. Palaima, and K. Pluta
2001   Religion in the room of the chariot tablets. In *Potnia*, edited by R. Hägg and R. Laffineur, 453–461. Aegaeum 22. Liège and Austin: Histoire de l'art et archéologie de la Grèce antique, Université de Liège, and Program in Aegean Scripts and Prehistory, University of Texas at Austin.

Hadjisavvas, S., and V. Karageorghis, eds.
2000   *The problem of unpublished excavations: Proceedings of a conference organized by the Department of Antiquities and the Anastasios G. Leventis Foundation. Nicosia, 25th–26th November, 1999.* Nicosia: Department of Antiquities and Anastasios G. Leventis Foundation.

Hägg, R.
1997a   Religious syncretism at Knossos? In *La Crète mycénienne*, edited by J. Driessen and A. Farnoux, 163–168. *Bulletin de correspondance hellénique*, Supplément 30. Paris: de Boccard Édition-Diffusion.

1997b   The function of the "Minoan Villa." *Proceedings of the Eighth International Symposium at the Swedish Institute at Athens, 6–8 June, 1992*, edited by R. Hägg.. Stockholm: Svenska Institutet i Athen.

Haiman, M.
1986   Archaeological survey of Israel map of Har Hamran — Southwest (198) 10–00. Jerusalem: Israel Department of Antiquities and Museums.

Hallager, E.
1996   *The Minoan roundel and other sealed documents in the neopalatial Linear A administration.* Aegaeum 14. Liège and Austin: Histoire de l'art et archéologie de la Grèce antique, Université de Liège, and Program in Aegean Scripts and Prehistory, University of Texas at Austin.

Halstead. P.
1992   The Mycenaean palatial economy: Making the most of the gaps in the evidence. *Proceedings of the Cambridge Philological Society* 38:57–86.

1994   The north-south divide: Regional paths to complexity in prehistoric Greece. In *Development and decline in the Mediterranean Bronze Age*, edited by C. Mathers and S. Stoddart, 195–219. Sheffield: J.R. Collis Publications.

1995 Late Bronze Age grain crops and Linear B ideograms *65, *120 and *121. *Annual of the British School at Athens* 90:229–234.

1999a Towards a model of Mycenaean palatial mobilization. In *Rethinking Mycanean palaces: New interpretations of an old idea*, edited by M.L. Galaty and W.A. Parkinson, 35–41. Los Angeles: The Cotsen Institute of Archaeology at UCLA.

1999b Surplus and share-croppers: The grain production strategies of Mycenaean palaces. In *Meletemata*, edited by P. Betancourt, V. Karageorghis, R. Laffineur, and W.-D. Niemeier, 319–326. Aegaeum 20. Liège and Austin: Histoire de l'art et archéologie de la Grèce antique, Université de Liège, and Program in Aegean Scripts and Prehistory, University of Texas at Austin..

1999c *Neolithic society in Greece*, edited by P. Halstead. Sheffield Studies in Aegean Archaeology 2. Sheffield: Sheffield Academic Press.

Hamilton, C.

2000 Faultlines: The construction of archaeological knowledge at Çatalhöyük. In *Towards reflexive method in archaeology: The example at Çatalhöyük by members of the Çatalhöyük teams*, edited by I. Hodder, 119–128. Cambridge: McDonald Institute of Archaeology and BIAA.

Hansen, J.M.

1991 *Excavations at Franchthi Cave, Greece*. Fascicle 7: *The palaeoethnobotany of Franchthi Cave*. Bloomington and Indianapolis: Indiana University Press.

Hassan, F.A.

1997 Beyond the surface: Comments on Hodder's "reflexive excavation methodology." *Antiquity* 71:1020–1025.

Hastings, C.M., and M.E. Moseley

1975 The adobes of Huaca del Sol and Huaca de la Luna. *American Antiquity* 40:196–203.

Hayes, P.

1995 The field survey: Its role and methodology. In *Ancient Akamas*. Vol. 1: *Settlement and environment*, edited by J. Fejfer, 171–186. Aarhus: Aarhus University Press.

Heidegger, M.

1971 *Poetry, language, thought*. Translated by A. Hofstadter. New York: Harper & Row.

Hellman, M.-C., P. Fraisse, and A. Jacques

1983 *Paris-Rome-Athènes. Le voyage en Grèce des architectes français aux XIXe et XXe siècles. Catalogue of the exhibition in Paris, Athens and Houston*. 2d ed. Paris: École nationale supérieure des Beaux-Arts.

Henry, D.
1995   Prehistoric cultural ecology and evolution: Insights from southern Jordan. New York: Plenum Press.
Herzfeld, M.
1987   Anthropology through the looking-glass: Critical ethnography in the margins of Europe. Cambridge: Cambridge University Press.
Herzog, Z.
1996   With time, we're getting worse. In Archaeology's publication problem, edited by H. Shanks, 87–110. Washington, DC: Biblical Archaeology Society.
Higgs, E.S.
1972   Papers in economic prehistory. Cambridge: Cambridge University.
Hiller S.
1980   The south propylaeum of the Palace of Knossos. Pepragmena tou Tetartou Diethnous Kretologikou Synedriou, Herakleion, 216–232.
1981   Mykenische Heiligtümer: Das Zeugnis der Linear B-Texte. In Sanctuaries and cults in the Aegean Bronze Age, edited by R. Hägg and N. Marinatos, 95–126. Acta Instituti Atheniensis regni Sueciae, series in 4°, 28. Stockholm: Paul Åströms Förlag.
Hiller, S., and O. Panagl
1976   Die frühgriechischen Texte aus mykenischer Zeit. Erträge der Forschung 49. Darmstadt: Wissenschaftliche Buchgesellschaft.
Hodder, I.
1985   Postprocessual archaeology. In Advances in archaeological method and theory, vol. 8, edited by M. Schiffer, 1–26. New York: Academic Press.
1986   Reading the past: Current approaches to interpretation in archaeology. Cambridge: Cambridge University Press.
1996   Çatalhöyük: 9000 year old housing and settlement in central Anatolia. In Housing and settlement in Anatolia: A historical perspective, edited by Y. Sey, 43–48. Habitat II, Istanbul: Türkiye Ekonomik ve Toplumsal Tarih Vakfi.
1997a   Always momentary, fluid and flexible: Towards a reflexive excavation methodology. Antiquity 71:691–700.
1997b   On the surface: Çatalhöyük 1993–95, edited by I. Hodder. Cambridge: British Institute of Archaeology at Ankara and McDonald Institute for Archaeological Research.
1999   The archaeological process. Oxford: Blackwell.
2000   Towards reflexive method in archaeology: The example at Çatalhöyük by members of the Çatalhöyük teams, edited by I. Hodder Cambridge: McDonald Institute for Archaeological Research and BIAA.

Hofstra, S.
  2000   Small things considered: The finds from LH IIIB Pylos in con-
          text. Ph.D. dissertation, University of Texas at Austin.
Holloway, M.
  1995   The preservation of the past. *Scientific American* 272(5):98–101.
Hood, R.
  1998   *Faces of archaeology in Greece: Caricatures by Piet de Jong.* Oxford:
          Leopard's Head Press.
Hood, S., and W. Taylor
  1981   *The Bronze Age palace at Knossos. Plans and sections.* Oxford: Brit-
          ish School at Athens.
Hope Simpson, R.
  1957   Identifying a Mycenaean state. *Annual of the British School at Ath-
          ens* 52:231–259.
  1966   The seven cities offered by Agamemnon to Achilles. *Annual of
          the British School at Athens* 61:113–131.
Hope Simpson, R., and O.T.P.K. Dickinson
  1979   *A Gazetteer of Aegean civilisation in the Bronze Age.* Vol. 1: *The
          mainland and islands.* Studies in Mediterranean Archaeology 52.
          Göteborg: Paul Åströms Förlag.
Hope Simpson, R., and J.F. Lazenby
  1970   *The Catalogue of Ships in Homer's* Iliad. Oxford: Oxford Univer-
          sity Press.
Horden, P., and N. Purcell
  2000   *The corrupting sea: A study of Mediterranean history.* Oxford:
          Blackwell.
Hurwit, J.M.
  1999   *The Athenian acropolis: History, mythology, and archaeology from
          the Neolithic era to the present.* Cambridge: Cambridge University
          Press.
Hyslop, J., Jr.
  1976   An archaeological investigation of the Lupaqa Kingdom and its
          origins. Ph.D. dissertation, Columbia University.
Inglis, F.
  2000   *The delicious history of the holiday.* London: Routledge.
Ingold, T.
  1995   Building, dwelling, living: How animals and people make them-
          selves at home in the world. In *Shifting contexts: Transformations
          in anthropological knowledge,* edited by M. Strathern, 57–80. Lon-
          don: Routledge.
International Museums Office
  1940   *Manual on the technique of archaeological excavations.* Paris: Inter-
          national Institute of Intellectual Co-operation.

Jacobsen, T.W., and W.R. Farrand
1987   *Excavations at Franchthi Cave, Greece.* Fascicle I: *Franchthi Cave and Paralia. Maps, plans, and sections.* Bloomington and Indianapolis: Indiana University Press.

Jameson, M.H., C.N. Runnels, and T. H. van Andel
1994   *A Greek countryside: The southern Argolid from prehistory to the present day.* Stanford: Stanford University Press.

Jansen, A.
1997   Bronze Age highways at Mycenae. *Echos du monde classique, Classical views,* n.s., 16:1–16.

Johnson, J., K. Osland, and J. Rudolph
1985   Archaeological site record for CA-SLO-79. Ms. on file at the Central Coast Information Center, Department of Anthropology, University of California, Santa Barbara.

Johnston, K.
2001   Broken fingers: Classic Maya scribe capture and polity consolidation. *Antiquity* 75:373–381.

Jokilehto, J.
1998   The context of the Venice Charter (1964). *Conservation and management of archaeological sites* 2(4):229–233.

1999   *A history of architectural conservation.* London: Butterworth-Heinemann, London.

Jones, C., and L. Satterthwaite
1982   *The monuments and inscriptions of Tikal.* Museum Monograph 44, Tikal Report 33A. Philadelphia: University of Pennsylvania Museum.

Kardulias, P.N.
1994   Archaeology in modern Greece: Bureaucracy, politics, and science. In *Beyond the site: Regional studies in the Aegean area,* edited by P.N. Kardulias, 373–387. Lanham: University Press of America.

Karetsou, A.
1997   To anaktoro meta ton Evans (The palace after Evans). *Kathemerini,* April 20:18–20.

Keller, D.R., and D.W. Rupp, eds.
1983   *Archaeological survey in the Mediterranean region.* BAR International Series 155. Oxford: British Archaeological Reports.

Killen, J.T.
1964   The wool industry of Crete in the late Bronze Age. *Annual of the British School at Athens* 59:1–15.

1985   The Linear B tablets and the Mycenaean economy. In *Linear B: A 1984 survey,* edited by A.M. Davies and Y. Duhoux, 241–305. Bibliothèque des Cahiers de L'Institut Linguistique de Louvain 26. Louvain-la-Neuve: Cabay.

1992   Observations on the Thebes sealings. In *Mykenaïka. Bulletin de correspondance hellénique*, Supplément 25, edited by J.-P. Olivier, 365–380. Paris: Diffusion de Boccard.

1994   Thebes sealings, Knossos tablets and Mycenaean state banquets. *Bulletin of the Institute of Classical Studies* 39:67–84.

1998   The Pylos Ta tablets revisited. *Bulletin de correspondance hellénique* 122:421–422

1999a   Mycenaean *o-pa*. In *Floreant studia mycenaea*, vol. 2, edited by S. Deger-Jalkotzy, S. Hiller, and O. Panagl, 325–341. Österreichische Akademie der Wissenschaften Philosophisch-Historische Klasse Denkschriften Band 274. Vienna: Verlag der Österreichischen Akademie der Wissenschaften.

1999b   Critique: A view from the tablets. In *Rethinking Mycenaean palaces: New interpretations of an old idea*, edited by M.L. Galaty and W.A. Parkinson, 87–90. Los Angeles: The Cotsen Institute of Archaeology at UCLA.

King, T.F.
1998   *Cultural resource laws and practice: An introductory guide*. Walnut Creek: AltaMira Press.

Klein, R.
2000   Archeology and the evolution of human behavior. *Evolutionary Anthropology* 9:17–36.

Klose, P.
1985   Das Grab des Königs Cuo von Zhongshan (gest. 308 v. Chr.). *Beiträge zur Allgemeinen und Vergleichenden Archäologie* 7:1–93.

Klynne, A.
1998   Reconstructions of Knossos: Artists' impressions, archaeological evidence and wishful thinking. *Journal of Mediterranean Archaeology* 11:206–229.

Knudson, R.
1989   North America's threatened heritage. *Archaeology* 42(1):71–73.

Kober, A.E.
1945   Evidence of inflection in the "chariot" tablets from Knossos. *American Journal of Archaeology* 49:143–151.

1946   Inflection in Linear Class B: I—Declension. *American Journal of Archaeology* 50:268–276.

1948   The Minoan scripts: Fact and theory. *American Journal of Archaeology* 52:82–103.

1949   "Total" in Minoan (Linear Class B). *Archiv Orientální* 17:386–398.

Koolhaas, R., and B. Mau
1995   *S, M, L, XL: Office for metropolitan architecture*. Rotterdam and New York: 010 Publishers and Monacelli.

Kourtessi-Philippakis, G.
1986   *Le Paléolithique de la Grèce continentale.* Paris: Sorbonne.
Krasniewicz, L.
1999   The Digital Imprint Project: Standards for digital publishing in
          archaeology. Web site: *http://www.anth.ucsb.edu/SAABulletin/*
          17.5/saa11.html.
Kristiansen, K.
1989   Perspectives on the archaeological heritage: History and future.
          In *Archaeological heritage management in the modern world,* edited
          by H. Cleere, 23–29. London: Unwin Hyman.
Kruft, H.-W.
1994   *A history of architectural theory from Vitruvius to the present.* Prince-
          ton: Princeton Architectural Press.
Landau, O.
1958   *Mykenisch-griechische Personennamen.* Studia Graeca et Latina
          Gothoburgensia 7. Göteborg: Akademische Abhandlung.
Laroche, D.
1996   Se anazitisi tis proklasikis archaiotitas (In search of pre-classical
          antiquity). Translated into Greek from French by K. Basba and
          A. Giakoumakatos. *Themata Chorou kai Technon* 27:194–199.
Larsen, M.T.
1996   *The conquest of Assyria: Excavations in an antique land, 1840–*
          1860. London and New York: Routledge.
Le Corbusier
1946   *Towards a new architecture.* Translated by F. Etchells. London:
          Architecture Press.
Ledderose, L.
2000   *Ten thousand things: Module and mass production in Chinese art.*
          The A.W. Mellon Lectures in the Fine Arts, 1998. Bollingen
          Series XXV:46. Princeton: Princeton University Press.
Lehner, M.
1997   *The complete pyramids.* New York: Thames and Hudson.
Lejeune, M.
1956   *Études mycéniennes. Actes du colloque international sur les textes*
          mycéniens (Gif-sur-Yvette, 3–7 avril 1956). Paris: Centre National
          de la Recherche Scientifique.
1972   *Phonétique historique du mycénien et du grec ancien.* Paris: Éditions
          Klincksieck.
Leveau, P.
1984   *Caesarea de Maurétanie: une ville romaine et ses campagnes.* Rome:
          École française de Rome.
Leveau, P., P. Sillières, and J.-P. Vallat
1993   *Campagnes de la Méditerranée romaine: Occident.* Paris: Hachette.

Levy, T.E.
1983 The emergence of specialized pastoralism in the southern Levant. *World Archaeology* 15:15–36.

Levy, T.E., ed.
1995 *The archaeology of society in the Holy Land.* London: Leicester University Press.

Liang Sicheng
1982–86 *Liang Sicheng wenji (Collected works of Liang Sicheng).* 4 vols. Beijing: Jianzhu gongcheng chubanshe.
1984a *A pictorial history of Chinese architecture,* edited by W. Fairbank. Cambridge, MA: MIT Press.
1984b *Yingzao fashi zhushi (A commented edition of the* Yingzao fashi), edited by Liang Sicheng. Taipei: Mingwen.

Lightfoot, K.
1995 Culture contact studies: Redefining the relationship between prehistoric and historical archaeology. *American Antiquity* 60: 199–217.

Lindgren, M.
1973 *The People of Pylos.* 2 vols. Boreas 3:1–2. Uppsala: Almqvist & Wiksell.

Llobera, M.
1996 Exploring the topography of mind: GIS, social space, and archaeology. *Antiquity* 70:612–622.

Lolos, Y.A.
1997 The Hadrianic aqueduct of Corinth (with an appendix of the Roman aqueducts in Greece). *Hesperia* 66:271–314.

Lorimer, H.L.
1950 *Homer and the monuments.* London: MacMillan.

Lubbock, J.
1865 *Pre-historic times, as illustrated by ancient remains, and the manners and customs of modern savages.* London: Frederic Norgate.

Luján, E.R.
1996–97 El léxico micénico de las telas. *Minos* 31/32:335–369.

Lyons, C.L., and J.K. Papadopoulos
2002 Archaeology and colonialism. In *The archaeology of colonialism,* edited by C.L. Lyons and J.K. Papadopoulos, 1–23. Los Angeles: The J. Paul Getty Trust.

Lyotard, J.-F.
1984 *The postmodern condition: A report of knowledge.* Minneapolis: University of Minnesota Press.

MacDonald, B.
1992 *The southern Ghors and northeast 'Araba archaeological survey.* Sheffield Archaeological Monographs 5. Sheffield: Department of Archaeology and Prehistory, University of Sheffield.

MacEnroe, J.
1995 Sir Arthur Evans and Edwardian Archaeology. *Classical Bulletin* 71:3–18.

MacGillivray, J.A.
2000 *Minotaur: Sir Arthur Evans and the archaeology of the Minoan myth.* London: Jonathan Cape.

MacNeish, R.S.
1981 Tehuacan's accomplishments. *Supplement to the Handbook of Middle American Indians* 1:31–47. Austin: University of Texas Press.
1992 *The origins of agriculture and settled life.* Norman: University of Oklahoma Press.

Marcus, J.
1976 The iconography of militarism at Monte Albán and neighboring sites in the Valley of Oaxaca. In *The origins of religious art and iconography in pre-Classic Mesoamerica*, edited by H.B. Nicholson, 123–139. Los Angeles: University of California, Los Angeles.
1980 Zapotec writing. *Scientific American* 242:50–64.
1983 Changing patterns of stone monuments after the fall of Monte Alban, A.D. 600–900. In *The Cloud People: Divergent evolution of the Zapotec and Mixtec civilizations*, edited by K.V. Flannery and J. Marcus, 191–197. New York: Academic Press.
1992 *Mesoamerican writing systems: Propaganda, myth and history in four ancient civilizations.* Princeton: Princeton University Press.
1995 Maya hieroglyphs: History or propaganda? In *Research frontiers in anthropology*, edited by C. Ember and M. Ember, 1–24. Englewood Cliffs: Prentice Hall.
1998 The peaks and valleys of ancient states: An extension of the dynamic model. In *Archaic states*, edited by G.M. Feinman and J. Marcus, 59–94. Sante Fe: SAR Press.

Marks, A.E., ed.
1976–83 *Prehistory and paleoenvironments in the Central Negev, Israel.* Vols. 1–3. Dallas: Southern Methodist University Press.

Martin, S., and N. Grube, eds.
2000 *Chronicle of the Maya kings and queens: Deciphering the dynasties of the ancient Maya.* London and New York: Thames & Hudson.

Mason, R., and E. Avrami
2002 Heritage values and challenges of conservation planning. In *Management planning for archaeological sites*, edited by G. Palumbo and J.M. Teutonico, 13–26. Los Angeles: Getty Conservation Institute.

Mathers, C., and S. Stoddart, eds.
1994 *Development and decline in the Mediterranean Bronze Age.* Sheffield Archaeological Monographs 8. Sheffield: J.R. Collis Publications.

Mattingly, D.

1996a   *Farming the desert: The UNESCO Libyan Valleys Archaeological Survey.* Vol 2: *Gazetteer and Pottery*, edited by D. Mattingly. Paris: UNESCO.

1996b   From one imperialism to another: Imperialism and the Mahgreb. In *Roman imperialism: Post-colonial perspectives*, edited by J. Webster and N. Cooper, 49–69. Leicester: School of Archaeological Studies, University of Leicester.

McDonald, W.A.

1942   Where did Nestor live? *American Journal of Archaeology* 46:538–545.

McDonald, W.A., and G.R. Rapp, Jr., eds.

1972   *The Minnesota Messenia expedition: Reconstructing a Bronze Age regional environment.* Minneapolis: University of Minnesota Press.

McDonald, W.A., and C.G. Thomas

1990   *Progress into the past. The rediscovery of Mycenaean civilization.* 2d ed. Bloomington and Indianapolis: Indiana University Press.

McEvoy, A.

1998   Market and ethics in U.S. property law. In *Who owns America: Social conflict over property rights*, edited by H.M. Jacobs, 94–113. Madison: University of Wisconsin Press.

McGuire, R.H.

1992   Archeology and the first Americans. *American Anthropologist* 94(4):816–836.

McGuire, R.H., and M. Schiffer

1983   A theory of architectural design. *Journal of Anthropological Archaeology* 2:277–303.

McInerney, J.

1999   *The folds of Parnassos: Land and ethnicity in ancient Phokis.* Austin: University of Texas Press.

McNeal, R.A.

1991   Archaeology and the destruction of the later Athenian Acropolis. *Antiquity* 65:49–63.

Mee, C.

1999   Regional survey projects and the prehistory of the Peloponnese. In *Le Peloponnèse: archéologie et histoire*, edited by J. Renard, 67–79. Rennes: Les Presses Universitaires.

Mee, C., and H. Forbes, eds.

1997   *A rough and rocky place: The landscape and settlement history of the Methana Peninsula, Greece.* Liverpool: Liverpool University Press.

Melena, J.L.
1983   Further thoughts on Mycenaean *o-pa*. In *Res Mycenaeae*, edited by A. Heubeck and G. Neumann, 258–286. Göttingen: Vandenhoeck and Ruprecht.

Melena, J.L., and T.G. Palaima
2001   100 years of Linear B from Knossos. *American Journal of Archaeology* 105:316–320.

Mellaart, J.
1967   *Çatal Hüyük: A Neolithic town in Anatolia*. London: Thames and Hudson.

Méndez, E.
1988   Tumba 5 de Huijazoo. *Arqueología* 2:7–16.

Meshel, Z., and I. Finkelstein, eds.
1980   *Sinai in antiquity* (in Hebrew). Tel Aviv: Hakibbutz Hameuhad.

Meskell, L., ed.
1998   *Archaeology under fire: Nationalism, politics and heritage in the eastern Mediterranean and Middle East*. London: Routledge.

Miller, A.G.
1995   *The painted tombs of Oaxaca, Mexico: Living with the dead*. Cambridge: Cambridge University Press.

Miller, N., J. Alchermes, and F.A. Cooper
1992   Macroregional survey of the Frankish Peloponnese. *American Journal of Archaeology* 96:366–367.

Minissi, F.
1978   *Conservazione dei beni storico artistici e ambientali*. Restauro e Musealizazzione. Rome: De Luca Editore.

Molina Montes, A.
1982   Archaeological buildings: Restoration or misrepresentation. In *Falsifications and misreconstructions of pre-Columbian art*, edited by E.H. Boone, 125–141. Washington, DC: Dumbarton Oaks.

Momigliano, N.
1999   *Duncan Mackenzie: A cautious canny highlander and the Palace of Minos at Knossos*. BICS Supplement 72. London: Institute of Classical Studies.

Moore, J.D.
1981   Chimú socio-economic organization: Preliminary data from Manchan, Casma Valley, Peru. *Ñawpa Pacha* 19:115–128.
1985   *Household economics and political integration: The lower class of the Chimú empire*. Ann Arbor: University Microfilms.
1989   Prehispanic beer in coastal Peru: Technology and social context of prehistoric production. *American Anthropologist* 91:682–695.

1992   Pattern and meaning in prehistoric Peruvian architecture: The architecture of social control in the Chimú state. *Latin American Antiquity* 3:95–113.

1995   The archaeology of dual organization in Andean South America: A theoretical review and case study. *Latin American Antiquity* 6(2):165–181

1996a   *Architecture and power in the ancient Andes: The archaeology of public buildings.* Cambridge: Cambridge University Press.

1996b   The archaeology of plazas and the proxemics of ritual: Three Andean traditions. *American Anthropologist* 98(4):789–802.

2002   Cultural landscapes and conceptions of social order in the north coast of Peru. Paper presented at the Society of American Archaeology 67th annual meeting, Denver, CO.

Moreland, J.
2001   *Archaeology and text.* London: Duckworth.

Morpurgo, A.
1963   *Mycenaeae graecitatis lexicon.* Incunabula Graeca 3. Rome: Edizioni dell' Ateneo.

Morris, I.
1987   *Burial and ancient society: The rise of the Greek city-state.* Cambridge: Cambridge University Press.

1994   Archaeologies of Greece. In *Classical Greece: Ancient histories and modern archaeologies*, edited by I. Morris, 8–47. Cambridge: Cambridge University Press.

2000   *Archaeology as cultural history: Words and things in Iron Age Greece.* Malden and Oxford: Blackwell.

Morris, S.
1989   A tale of two cities: The miniature frescoes from Thera and the origins of Greek poetry. *American Journal of Archaeology* 93:511–535.

1995   From modernism to manure: Perspectives on classical archaeology. *Antiquity* 69:182–185.

2001   The towers of ancient Leukas: Results of a topographic survey. *Hesperia* 70:285–347.

Muhly, J.
1992   The crisis years in the Mediterranean world: Transition or cultural disintegration? In *The crisis years: The 12th century* B.C.: *From beyond the Danube to the Tigris*, edited by W. Ward and M. Joukowsky, 2–10. Dubuque: Kendall and Hunt.

Müller, S.
1992   Delphes et sa région à l'époque mycénienne. *Bulletin de correspondance hellénique* 114(2):445–496.

Mulvany, M.
    2000   Unearthing public opinion: A poll shows Americans value archaeology. *American Archaeology* 4(3):9.

Myres, J.L.
    1941   Sir Arthur Evans. *Proceedings of the British Academy* 27:323–357.

Needham, J.
    1971   *Science and civilization in China.* Vol. 4, Pt. 3: *Civil Engineering and Nautics.* Cambridge: Cambridge University Press.

Nesbitt, K., ed.
    1996   *Theorizing a new agenda for architecture. An anthology of architectural theory 1965–1995.* Princeton: Princeton Architectural Press.

Nichols, D.L.
    1995   An overview of regional settlement pattern survey in Mesoamerica: 1960–1995. In *Arqueología Mesoamericana: Homenaje a William T. Sanders,* edited by A.G. Mastache, J.R. Parsons, R.S. Santley, and M.C. Serra Puche, 59–95. Mexico City: Instituto Nacional de Antropología e Historia, Mexico.

Nilsson, M.P.
    1932   *The Mycenaean origin of Greek mythology.* Berkeley: University of California Press.
    1941–50   *Geschichte der griechischen Religion.* Handbuch der Altertumswissenschaft 5(2). Munich: Beck.

Nohlen, K.
    1999   The partial re-erection of the Temple of Trajan at Pergamon in Turkey: A German Archaeological Institute project. *Conservation and management of archaeological sites* 3(1–2):91–102.

Nowicki, K.
    2000   *Defensible sites in Crete c. 1200–800 B.C.* Aegaeum 21. Liège: Université de Liège, Histoire de l'art et archéologie de la Grèce antique.

O'Brien, P.
    1989   Foucault's history of culture. In *The new cultural history,* edited by L. Hunt, 25–46. Berkeley: University of California Press.

O'Keefe, P.J., and L.V. Prott
    1984   *Law and the cultural heritage.* Vol. 1: *Discovery and excavation.* Abingdon: Professional Books.

Olivier, J.-P.
    1967   *Les Scribes de Cnossos.* Incunabula Graeca 17. Rome: Edizioni dell' Ateneo.
    1996   KN 115 et KH 115: Rectification. *Bulletin de correspondance hellénique* 120:823.

1996–97   El comercio micénico desde la documentación epigráfica. *Minos* 31/32:275–292.

1997   Die beschrifteten tonplomben (Klasse Wr). In *Die Tonplomben aus dem Nestorpalast von Pylos*, edited by I. Pini, 70–81. Mainz: Philipp von Zabern.

Oren, E.D.

1973   The overland route between Egypt and Canaan in the Early Bronze Age. *Israel Exploration Journal* 23:198–205.

Osborne, R.

1985   Buildings and residence on the land in Classical and Hellenistic Greece: The contribution of epigraphy. *Annual of the British School at Athens* 80:119–128.

Özdogan, M.

1983   Cultural heritage and dam projects in Turkey. An overview. Paper presented at the International Workshop on Cultural Heritage Management and Dams, University of Florida, February 14–16, 2000.

Page, D.

1959   *History and the Homeric Iliad*. Berkeley and Los Angeles: University of California Press.

Palaima, T.G.

1987   Mycenaean seals and sealings in their economic and administrative contexts. In *Tractata Mycenaea*, edited by P.H. Ilievski and L. Crepajac, 249–266. Skopje: Macedonian Academy of Sciences and Arts.

1988   *The scribes of Pylos*. Incunabula Graeca 87. Rome: Edizioni dell' Ateneo.

1990   *Aegean seals, sealings and administration*. Aegaeum 5. Liège: Histoire de l'art et archéologie de la Grèce antique, Université de Liège.

1991   Maritime matters in the Linear B texts. In *Thalassa. L'Égee préhistorique et la mer*, edited by R. Laffineur and L. Basch, 273–310. Aegaeum 7. Liège: Histoire de l'art et archéologie de la Grèce antique, Université de Liège.

1992–93   Ten reasons why KH 115 ≠ KN 115. *Minos* 27/28:261–281.

1993   Michael Ventris's blueprint. *Discovery, Research and Scholarship at The University of Texas at Austin* 13(2):20–26.

1995a   The nature of the Mycenaean *wanax*: Non-Indo-European origins and priestly functions. In *The role of the ruler in the prehistoric Aegean*, edited by P. Rehak, 119–139. Aegaeum 11. Liège and Austin: Histoire de l'art et archéologie de la Grèce antique, Université de Liège. and Program in Aegean Scripts and Prehistory, University of Texas at Austin.

1995b   The last days of the Pylos polity. In *Politeia: Society and state in the Aegean Bronze Age*, edited by R. Laffineur and W.-D. Niemeier, 623–633. Aegaeum 12. Liège and Austin: Histoire de l'art et archéologie de la Grèce antique, Université de Liège, and Program in Aegean Scripts and Prehistory, University of Texas at Austin.

1998   Linear B and the origins of Greek religion: '*di-wo-nu-so.*' In *The history of the Hellenic language and writing. From the second to the first millennium B.C.: Break or continuity?*, edited by N. Dimoudis and A. Kyriatsoulis, 205–222. Altenburg: DZA Verlag für Kultur und Wissenschaft GmBH.

1999   Kn02 - Tn 316. In *Floreant studia mycenaea*, vol. 2, edited by S. Deger-Jalkotzy, S. Hiller, and O. Panagl, 437–461. Österreichische Akademie der Wissenschaften Philosophisch-Historische Klasse Denkschriften Band 274. Vienna: Verlag der Österreichischen Akademie der Wissenschaften.

2000a   Themis in the Mycenaean lexicon and the etymology of the place-name *ti-mi-to a-ko*. *Faventia* 22:1:7–19.

2000b   Review of S. MacGillivray, "Minotaur: Sir Arthur Evans and the archaeology of the Minoan myth," *London Times Higher Education Supplement*, August 18:19.

2000c   The palaeography of Mycenaean inscribed sealings from Thebes and Pylos, their place within the Mycenaean administrative system and their links with the extra-palatial sphere. In *Minoisch-mykenische Glyptik: Stil, Ikonographie, Funktion*, edited by W. Mueller, 219–238. Corpus der minoischen und mykenischen Siegel, Beiheft 6. Mainz: Gebr. Mann Verlag.

2002   Special vs. normal Mycenaean: Hand 24 and writing in the service of the king? In *A-NA-QO-TA: Festschrift for J.T. Killen*, edited by J. Bennet and J. Driessen, 205-221. *Minos* 33/34. Salamanca: Ediciones Universidad de Salamanca.

N.D.a   Alice Elizabeth Kober. In *Women in archaeology*, edited by G. Cohen and M. Joukowsky. Forthcoming.

N.D.b   'Archives' and 'Scribes' and Information Hierarchy in Mycenaean Greek Linear B. In *Ancient archives and archival tradition: Concepts of record-keeping in the ancient world*, edited by M. Brosius. Oxford: Oxford University Press. Forthcoming.

N.D.c   Inside the mind of a Mycenaean "scribe": How Hand 2 wrote the Pylos Ta series. Paper presented at the conference Jornadas Micénicas held at the Universities of Alicante and Orihuela, Spain, February 17–19, 1999. Forthcoming.

N.D.d   Assessing the Linear B evidence for continuity from the Mycenaean period in the Boeotian cults of Poseidon (and Erinys) at

Onchestos (Telphousa–Haliartos). In *Boiotia Antiqua VII–VIII: Studies in Boiotian archaeology, history, and institutions (including papers presented at the IX International Conference on Boiotian Antiquities, Winnipeg, October 29–31, 1998)*, edited by J.M. Fossey and M.B. Cosmopoulos. Chicago: Ares Press. Forthcoming.

N.D.e   Fifty years ago in Mycenology: Reflections on our discipline. *Acts of the 11th International Mycenological Colloquium held in Austin, TX, May 7–13, 2000.* Forthcoming.

Palaima, T.G., E.I. Pope, and F. K. Reilly

2000   *Unlocking the secrets of ancient writing: The parallel lives of Michael Ventris and Linda Schele and the decipherment of Mycenaean and Mayan writing. Catalogue of an exhibition.* Austin: Program in Aegean Scripts and Prehistory, University of Texas at Austin.

Palaima, T., and J. Wright

1985   Ins and outs of the archive rooms at Pylos. *American Journal of Archaeology* 89:251–262.

Palmer, E.H.

1872   *The desert of the exodus.* New York: Harper and Brothers.

Palmer, L.R.

1960   Tomb or reception room? *Bulletin of the Institute of Classical Studies* 7:57–65.

1963   *The interpretation of Mycenaean Greek texts.* Oxford: Oxford University Press.

Palmer, L.R., and J. Boardman

1963   *On the Knossos tablets.* Oxford: Oxford University Press.

Palmer, R.

1989   Subsistence rations at Pylos and Knossos. *Minos* 24:89–124.

1992   Wheat and barley in Mycenaean society. In *Mykenaïka*, edited by J.-P. Olivier, 475–497. *Bulletin de correspondance hellénique*, Supplément 25. Paris: Diffusion de Boccard.

1994   *Wine in the Mycenaean palace economy.* Aegaeum 10. Liège and Austin: Histoire de l'art et archéologie de la Grèce antique, Université de Liège, and Program in Aegean Scripts and Prehistory, University of Texas at Austin.

1999   Perishable goods in Mycenaean texts. In *Floreant studia mycenaea*, vol. 2, edited by S. Deger-Jalkotzy, S. Hiller, and O. Panagl, 463–485. Österreichische Akademie der Wissenschaften Philosophisch-Historische Klasse Denkschriften Band 274. Vienna: Verlag der Österreichischen Akademie der Wissenschaften.

Palyvou, C.

1995a   Knossos, e poreia ton episkepton (Knossos, a visitor's route). *Kathemerini* April 20:23–25.

1995b   E poietike duname tou topiou. Morphologikes paratereseis pano sten Minoïke kai ten Pharaonike architektonike (The poetic power of the landscape: Morphological observations on Minoan and Pharaonic architecture). *Archaeologia* 55:33–44.

1999   *Akrotiri Theras: He oikodomike techne (Akrotiri Thera: The art of building)*. Athens: Athens Archaeological Society.

2000   Concepts of space in Aegean Bronze Age art and architecture. In *The wall paintings of Thera*, vol. 1, edited by S. Sherratt, 413–436. Athens: Thera Foundation.

Papadopoulos, J.K.

1993   To kill a cemetery: The Athenian Kerameikos and the Early Iron Age in the Aegean. *Journal of Mediterranean Archaeology* 6:175–206.

1994   Early Iron Age potters' marks in the Aegean. *Hesperia* 63:437–507.

1997   Knossos. In *The conservation of archaeological sites in the Mediterranean region*, edited by M. de la Torre, 93–125. Los Angeles: Getty Conservation Institute.

1999   Archaeology, myth-history and the tyranny of the text: Chalkidike, Torone and Thucydides. *Oxford Journal of Archaeology* 18:377–394.

Papageorgiou, L.

2000   "Unification of archaeological sites of Athens": The birth of an archaeological park? *Conservation and management of archaeological sites* 4(3):176–184.

Papathanassopoulos, G.A., ed.

1996   *Neolithic culture in Greece*. Athens: N.P. Goulandris Foundation.

Parsons, J.R.

1971   *Prehistoric settlement patterns of the Texcoco region, Mexico*. Memoirs 3. Ann Arbor: Museum of Anthropology, University of Michigan.

1972   Archaeological settlement patterns. *Annual Review of Anthropology* 1:127–150.

N.D.   Geological mapping with Rob Scholten in the Beaverhead Range, southwest Montana, and adjacent Idaho, summer 1960.

Parsons, J.R., E. Brumfiel, M. Parsons, and D. Wilson

1982   *Prehispanic settlement patterns in the southern Valley of Mexico: The Chalco-Xochimilco region*. Memoirs 14. Ann Arbor: Museum of Anthropology, University of Michigan.

Patterson, H., and M. Millett

1998   The Tiber Valley Project. *Papers of the British School at Rome* 66:1–20.

Patterson, H., F. di Gennaro, H. di Giuseppe, S. Fontana, V. Gaffney, A. Harrison, S.J. Keay, M. Millett, M. Rendeli, P. Roberts, S. Stoddart, and R. Witcher

2000   The Tiber Valley Project: The Tiber and Rome throughout two millennia. *Antiquity* 74:395–403.

Paynter, R.

1990   Afro-Americans in the Massachusetts historical landscape. In *The politics of the past*, edited by P. Gathercole and D. Lowenthal, 49–62. London: Unwin Hyman.

Peet, T.E.

1909   *The Stone and Bronze Ages in Italy and Sicily.* Oxford: Clarendon Press.

Pérez-Gómez, A.

1997   Modern architecture, abstraction and the poetic imagination. In *Cloud-Cuckoo-Land, an international journal of architectural criticism and theory.* Special Subjects Issue: Modernity of Architecture: A critical recognition, vol. 2, no. 1. Web site: *www.theo. tu-cottbus.de/wolke/eng/Subjects/subject971.html.*

Perlès, C.

1987   *Excavations at Franchthi Cave, Greece.* Fascicle 3: *Les industries lithiques taillées de Franchthi (Argolide, Grèce).* Tome 1: *Présentation générale et industries paléolithiques.* Bloomington and Indianapolis: Indiana University Press.

1990   *Excavations at Franchthi Cave, Greece.* Fascicle 5: *Les industries lithiques taillées de Franchthi (Argolide, Grèce).* Tome 2: *Les industries du mésolithique et du néolithique initial.* Bloomington and Indianapolis: Indiana University Press.

Perna, M., ed.

1998   *Administrative documents in the Aegean and their Near Eastern counterparts.* Pubblicazioni del Centro Internazionale di Ricerche Archeologiche, Antropologiche e Storiche 3. Turin: Scriptorium.

Philippides, D

1984   *Greek traditional architecture.* Vol. 3. Athens: Melissa.

Piggott, S.

1978   *Antiquity depicted: Aspects of archaeological illustration.* London and New York: Thames and Hudson.

Pini, I., ed.

1997   *Die Tonplomben aus dem Nestorpalast von Pylos.* Mainz: Philipp von Zabern.

Piteros, C., J.-P. Olivier, and J.L. Melena

1990   Les inscriptions en linéaire B des nodules de Thèbes (1982): La fouille, les documents, les possibilités d'interprétation. *Bulletin de correspondance hellénique* 104:103–184.

Platon, N.
1955   He archailogike kinesis en Krete (Archaeology in Crete). *Kretika Chronika* 9:554–555.
1956   He archailogike kinesis en Krete (Archaeology in Crete). *Kretika Chronika* 10:406–407.
1957   He archailogike kinesis en Krete (Archaeology in Crete). *Kretika Chronika* 11:328–329.
1958   He archailogike kinesis en Krete (Archaeology in Crete). *Kretika Chronika* 12:461–463
1959   He archailogike kinesis en Krete (Archaeology in Crete). *Kretika Chronika* 13:363–364
1960   He archailogike kinesis en Krete (Archaeology in Crete). *Kretika Chronika* 14:506.
1961   Problèmes de consolidation et de restauration des ruines Minoennes. In *Atti del Settimo Congresso Internazionale di Archeologia Classica*, 1:103–111. Rome: L'Erma di Bretschneider.

Plog, S., F. Plog, and W. Wait
1978   Decision making in modern surveys. *Advances in Archaeological Method and Theory* 1:384–421.

Pluta, K.
1996–97 A reconstruction of the Archives Complex at Pylos: Preliminary progress report. *Minos* 31/32:231–250.

Podany, J., N. Agnew, and M. Demas
1993   Preservation of excavated mosaics by reburial: Evaluation of some traditional and newly developed materials and techniques. In *Conservation, protection, presentation: Fifth Conference of the International Committee for the Conservation of Mosaics, Faro and Conimbriga, 4–8 October 1993*. Proceedings (Mosaics 6), 1–19. Lisbon: Instituto Portugues Museus.

Ponsich, M.
1974–79 *Implantation rurale antique sur le Bas-Guadalquivir*, 2 vols. Madrid: Laboratoire d'archéologie de la Casa de Vélasquez.

Pope, K.O., C.N. Runnels, and T.-L. Ku
1984   Dating Middle Palaeolithic red beds in southern Greece. *Nature* 312:264–266.

Popham, M.R.
1990   Reflections on "An Archaeology of Greece": Surveys and excavations. *Oxford Journal of Archaeology* 9(1):29–35.

Portugali, Y.
1982   A field methodology for regional archaeology (The Jezreel Valley Survey, 1981). *Tel Aviv* 9:170–188.

Potter, T.W.
1979   *The changing landscape of southern Etruria*. London: Paul Elek Limited.

Pred, A.
1984   Place as historically contingent process: Structuration and the time-geography of becoming places. *Annals of the Association of American Geographers* 74(2):279–297.

1990   *Making histories and constructing human geographies*. Boulder: Westview Press.

Preziosi, D.
1983   *Minoan architectural design: Formation and signification*. Berlin, New York, and Amsterdam: Mouton Publishers.

Preucel, R.
1995   The postprocessual condition. *Journal of Archaeological Research* 3(2):147–175.

Price, C.A.
1996   *Stone conservation: An overview of current research*. Los Angeles: Getty Conservation Institute.

Price, H.M., III
1991   *Disputing the dead: U.S. law on aboriginal remains and grave goods*. Columbia: University of Missouri Press.

Prip-Møller, J.
1937   *Chinese Buddhist monasteries: Their plan and its function as a setting for Buddhist monastic life*. Hong Kong: Hong Kong University Press. Reprint, 1982, Copenhagen and London: G.E.C. Gad and Oxford University Press.

Pritchett, W.K.
1965–91   *Studies in ancient Greek topography*, vols. 1–7. Berkeley: University of California Press.

Proskouriakoff, T.
1960   Historical implications of a pattern of dates at Piedras Negras, Guatemala. *American Antiquity* 25:454–475.

Ramos, M., and D. Duganne
2000   Exploring public perceptions and attitudes about archaeology. Harris Interactive and Society for American Archaeology Web site: *http://www.saa.org/Pubedu/nrptdraft4.pdf*.

Rapoport, A.
1969   *House form and culture*. Englewood Cliffs: Prentice-Hall.

1982   *Human aspects of urban form: Towards a man-environment approach to urban form and design*. Oxford: Pergamon Press.

Redfield, R.
1930   *Tepoztlan, a Mexican village: A study of folk life*. Chicago: University of Chicago Press.

Redman, C.L.

1973   Multistage fieldwork and analytical techniques. *American Antiquity* 38:61–79.

1978   *The rise of civilization: From early farmers to urban society in the ancient Near East.* San Francisco: W.H. Freeman.

1982   Archaeological survey and the study of Mesopotamian urban systems. *Journal of Field Archaeology* 9:375–382.

1986   *Qsar es-Seghir: An archaeological view of medieval life.* New York: Academic Press.

1993   *People of the Tonto Rim: Archaeological discovery in prehistoric Arizona.* Washington, DC: Smithsonian Institution Press.

1999   Human dimensions of ecosystem studies. *Ecosystems* 2:296–298.

Rees, G.

1999   *The remote sensing data book.* Cambridge: Cambridge University Press.

Rehak, P.

1995   *The role of the ruler in the prehistoric Aegean.* Aegaeum 11. Liège and Austin: Histoire de l'art et archéologie de la Grèce antique, Université de Liège, and Program in Aegean Scripts and Prehistory, University of Texas at Austin.

Reid, D.M.

2002   *Whose Pharaohs? Archaeology, museums, and Egyptian national identity from Napoleon to World War I.* Berkeley: University of California Press.

Renfrew, C.

1972   *The emergence of civilisation: The Cyclades and the Aegean in the third millennium B.C.* London: Methuen.

1980   The Great Tradition versus the Great Divide: Archaeology as anthropology? *American Journal of Archaeology* 84:287–298.

1987   *Archaeology and language: The puzzle of Indo-European origins.* London: Jonathan Cape.

1998   Word of Minos: The Minoan contribution to Mycenaean Greek and the linguistic geography of the Bronze Age Aegean. *Cambridge Archaeological Journal* 8(2):239–264.

2000   *Loot, legitimacy, and ownership: The ethical crisis in archaeology.* London: Duckworth.

Renfrew, C., and P. Bahn

2000   *Archaeology: Theories, methods and practice.* 3d ed. London: Thames and Hudson.

Renfrew, C., and K. Boyle, eds.

2000   *Archaeogenetics: DNA and the population prehistory of Europe.* Cambridge: McDonald Institute for Archaeological Research.

RIBA Journal
1945   Obituaries. *Journal of the Royal Institute of British Architects* 52:95.
Ricoeur, P.
1971   The model of the text: Meaningful action considered as text. *Social Research* 38:529–562.
Risch, E.
1966   Les differences dialectales dans le mycénien. In *Proceedings of the Cambridge colloquium on Mycenaean studies*, edited by L.R. Palmer and J. Chadwick, 150–157. Cambridge: Cambridge University Press.
1979   Die griechischen Dialekte in 2. vorchristlichen Jahrtausend. *Studi Micenei ed Egeo-Anatolici* 20:91–111.
Robinson, A.
1995   *The story of writing*. London: Thames and Hudson.
2002   *The man who deciphered Linear B*. London: Thames and Hudson.
Robinson, E., and E. Smith
1841   *Biblical researches in Palestine, Mount Sinai, and Arabia Petraea*. London: John Murray.
Role of the magazine, The
2000   *American Archaeology* 4(3):4.
Romano, D.G., and B.C. Schoenbrun
1993   A computerized architectural and topographical survey of ancient Corinth. *Journal of Field Archaeology* 20:177–190.
Rosen, A.M.
1986   *Cities of clay: The geoarchaeology of tells*. Chicago: University of Chicago Press.
Rosen, S.A.
1992   Nomads in archaeology: A response to Finkelstein and Perevoletsky. *Bulletin of the American Schools of Oriental Research* 287:75–85.
1994   Archaeological survey of Israel map of Makthesh Ramon (204). Jerusalem: Israel Antiquities Authority.
Roth, M.S., C.L. Lyons, and C. Merewether
1997   *Irresistible decay: Ruins reclaimed*. Los Angeles: Getty Research Institute.
Rothenberg, B.
1972   *Were these King Solomon's mines?* London: Stein and Day.
Rothenberg, B., and J. Glass
1992   The beginnings and development of early metallurgy and the settlement and chronology of the western Arabah from the Chalcolithic period to the Early Bronze IV. *Levant* 24:141–157.

Rotroff, S.
2001   Archaeologists on conservation: How codes of archaeological ethics and professional standards treat conservation. *Journal of the American Institute for Conservation* 40:137–146.

Ruijgh, C.J.
1967   *Études sur la grammaire et le vocabulaire du grec mycénien.* Amsterdam: A.M. Hakkert.
1985   Le mycénien et Homère. In *Linear B: A 1984 survey,* edited by A.M. Davies and Y. Duhoux, 143–190. Bibliothèque des Cahiers de L'Institut Linguistique de Louvain 26. Louvain-la-Neuve: Cabay.

Ruipérez, M.S., and J.L. Melena.
1990   *Los griegos micénicos.* Historia 16. Madrid: MELSA.
1996   *The Mycenaean Greeks,* translated by M. Panagiotidou. Athens: Institouto tou Bibliou, M. Kardamitsa.

Runnels, C.N.
1988   A prehistoric survey of Thessaly: New light on the Greek Middle Paleolithic. *Journal of Field Archaeology* 15:277–290.
1995   The Stone Age of Greece from the Palaeolithic to the advent of the Neolithic. *American Journal of Archaeology* 99:699–728.
2000   Anthropogenic soil erosion in prehistoric Greece: The contribution of regional surveys to the archaeology of environmental disruptions and human response. In *Environmental disaster and the archaeology of human response,* edited by G. Bawden and R.M. Ryecraft, 11–20. Albuquerque: University of New Mexico Press.

Runnels, C., and T. H. van Andel
1993   The Lower and Middle Paleolithic of Thessaly, Greece. *Journal of Field Archaeology* 20:299–317.

Runnels, C., T. H. van Andel, K. Zachos, and P. Paschos
1999   Human settlement and landscape in the Preveza region (Epirus) in the Pleistocene and early Holocene. In *The Palaeolithic archaeology of Greece and adjacent areas,* edited by G. Bailey, E. Adam, E. Panagopoulou, C. Perlès, and K. Zachos, 120–129. London: British School at Athens.

Ruz Lhuillier, A.
1973   *El Templo de las Inscripciones, Palenque.* Colección Científica, Arqueología 7. Mexico City: Instituto Nacional de Antropología e Historia.

Rykwert, J.
1972   *On Adam's house in paradise: The idea of the primitive hut in architectural history.* New York: Museum of Modern Art.

Sabloff, J.A., and J.S. Henderson, eds.
  1993   *Lowland Maya civilization in the eighth century A.D.* Washington,
          DC: Dumbarton Oaks Research Library and Collections.
Sacconi, A.
  1987   La tavoletta di Pilo Tn 316: Una registrazione di carratere eccezi-
          onale? In *Studies in Mycenaean and Classical Greek presented to
          John Chadwick*, edited by J.T. Killen, J.L. Melena, and J.-P. Oliv-
          ier, 551–556. *Minos* 20/22.
  1999   La tavoletta PY Ta 716 e le armi di rappresentanza nel mondo
          egeo. In *Epi ponton plazomenoi: Simposio italiano di Studi Egei dedi-
          cato a Luigi Bernabò Brea e Giovanni Pugliese Carratelli*, edited by
          V. La Rosa, D. Palermo, and L. Vagnetti, 285–289. Rome: Scuola
          Archeologica Italiana di Atene.
Sackett, J.
  1988   The Neuvic group: Upper Paleolithic open-air sites in the Peri-
          gord. In *Upper Pleistocene prehistory of western Eurasia*, edited by
          H. Dibble and A. Montet-White, 413–426. University Museum
          Monograph 54. Philadelphia: The University Museum, Univer-
          sity of Pennsylvania.
  1999   *The archaeology of Solvieux: An Upper Paleolithic open air site in
          France.* Monumenta Archaeologica 19. Institute of Archaeology,
          University of California, Los Angeles. Oxford: Oxbow Books.
  2000   Human antiquity and the old stone age: The nineteenth century
          background to paleoanthropology. *Evolutionary Anthropology*
          9:37–49.
Said, E.
  1978   *Orientalism.* New York: Pantheon Books.
  1983   *The world, the text, and the critic.* Cambridge, MA: Harvard Uni-
          versity Press.
Sanders, I.
  1982   *Roman Crete.* Warminster: Aris and Philips.
Sanders, W.T., J.R. Parsons, and R.S. Santley
  1979   *The Basin of Mexico.* New York: Academic Press.
Sandstrom, A.R.
  1991   *Corn is our blood: Culture and ethnic identity in a contemporary
          Aztec Indian village.* Norman: University of Oklahoma Press.
SARG
  1974   SARG: A co-operative approach towards understanding the
          locations of human settlement. *World Archaeology* 6:107–116.
Sarris, A., and R.E. Jones
  2000   Geophysical and related techniques applied to archaeological
          survey in the Mediterranean: A review. *Journal of Mediterranean
          Archaeology* 13:3–75.

Säve-Söderbergh, T.

1972 International salvage archaeology: Some organizational and technical aspects of the Nubian campaign. *Annales Academiae Regiae Scientarium Upsaliensis* 15/16:116–140.

Schachter, A.

1981 *Cults of Boiotia*. Vol. 1: *Acheloos to Hera*. Bulletin of the Institute of Classical Studies Supplement 38.1. London: Institute of Classical Studies.

1986 *Cults of Boiotia*. Vol. 2: *Herakles to Poseidon*. Bulletin of the Institute of Classical Studies Supplement 38.2. London: Institute of Classical Studies.

1994 *Cults of Boiotia*. Vol. 3: *Potnia to Zeus*. Bulletin of the Institute of Classical Studies Supplement 38.3. London: Institute of Classical Studies.

Schele, L.

1996 History, writing, and image in Maya art. *Art Bulletin* 78(3):412–416.

Schele, L., and P. Mathews

1998 *The code of kings*. New York: Simon and Schuster.

Schick, K.D., and N. Toth

1993 *Making silent stones speak*. New York: Simon and Schuster.

Schmid, M.

1998 Protective shelters at the archaeological sites of Mallia (Crete) and Kalavasos-Tenta (Cyprus). *Conservation and management of archaeological sites* 2(3):143–153.

Schnapp, A.

1993 *La conquête du passé: Aux origins de l'archéologie*. Paris: Editions Carré.

1996 *The discovery of the past*. London: British Museum.

Scot free!

1990 *Archaeology* 43(5):14–15.

Scully, V.

1991 *Architecture: The natural and the manmade*. New York: St. Martin's Press.

Seeden, H.

2000 Lebanon's archaeological heritage on trial in Beirut: What future for Beirut's past? In *Cultural resource management in contemporary society*, edited by F.P. McManamon and A. Hatton, 168–187. One World Archaeology 33. London: Routledge.

Shackleton, J.C.

1988 *Excavations at Franchthi Cave, Greece*. Fascicle 4: *Marine molluscan remains from Franchthi Cave*. Bloomington and Indianapolis: Indiana University Press.

Shane, O., and M. Küçük
1998   The world's first city. *Archaeology* 51:43–47.
2000   Presenting Çatalhöyük. In *Towards reflexive method in archaeology: The example at Çatalhöyük by members of the Çatalhöyük teams*, edited by I. Hodder, 218–228. Cambridge: McDonald Institute for Archaeological Research and BIAA.

Shankland, D.
2000   Villagers and the distant past: Three seasons' work at Küçükköy, Çatalhöyük. In *Towards reflexive method in archaeology: The example at Çatalhöyük*, edited by I. Hodder, 167–176. Cambridge: McDonald Institute for Archaeological Research and BIAA.

Sharypkin, S., K. Witczak, R. Sajkowski, and A. Korytko.
2000–01   *DO-SO-MO. Fascicula Mycenologica Polona.* Vols. 1–3. Olsztyn: Zaklad Poligrafii UWM w Olsztynie.

Shaw, J.
1973   *Minoan architecture: Materials and techniques.* Annuario della Scuola Archeologica di Atene e delle Missioni Italiane in Oriente, vol. 44. Rome: Scuola Archeologica di Atene.

Shelmerdine, C.W.
1973   The geography of the further province of Pylos. *American Journal of Archaeology* 77:276–278.
1981   Nichoria in context: A major town in the Pylos kingdom. *American Journal of Archaeology* 85:319–324.
1985   *The perfume industry of Mycenaean Pylos.* Göteborg: Paul Åströms Förlag.
1997   Review of Aegean prehistory VI: The palatial Bronze Age of the southern and central Greek mainland. *American Journal of Archaeology* 101:537–585.
1999   Administration in the Mycenaean palaces: Where's the chief? In *Rethinking Myceanaean palaces: New interpretations of an old idea*, edited by M.L. Galaty and W.A. Parkinson, 19–24. Los Angeles: The Cotsen Institute of Archaeology at UCLA.

Shelmerdine, C.W., and T.G. Palaima
1984a   *Pylos comes alive. Industry and administration in a Mycenaean palace.* New York: Archaeological Institute of America and Fordham University.
1984b   Mycenaean archaeology and the Pylos texts. *Archaeological Review from Cambridge* 3(2):76–89.

Shepheard, P.
1994   *What is architecture? An essay on landscapes, buildings and machines.* Cambridge, MA: MIT Press.

Sherratt, A.
1994   Core, periphery and margin: Perspectives on the Bronze Age. In *Development and decline in the Mediterranean Bronze Age*, edited by C. Mathers and S. Stoddart, 335–346. Sheffield Archaeological Monographs 8. Sheffield: J.R. Collis Publications.

Shi Zhangru
1954   Yin dai dishangjianzhu fuyuan zhi yili (First example of reconstruction of Late Shang period above-ground architecture). *Zhongyang Yanjiuyuan nianjian* 1:267–280.
1970   Yin dai dishangjianzhu fuyuan de di'erli (Second example of reconstruction of Late Shang period above-ground architecture). *Zhongyang Yanjiuyuan Minzuxue Yanjiusuo jikan* 29: 321–341.
1976   Yin dai dishangjianzhu fuyuan de disanli (Third example of reconstruction of Late Shang period above-ground architecture). *Guoli Taiwan Daxue Kaogu Renleixue jikan* 39/40:140–157.

Silberman, N.A.
1982   *Digging for god and country.* New York: Knopf.
1989   *Between past and present: Archaeology, ideology, and nationalism in the modern Middle East.* New York: H. Holt.
1990   The politics of the past: Archaeology and nationalism in the eastern Mediterranean. *Mediterranean Quarterly* 1:99–110.

Silberman, N.A., and D. Small, eds.
1997   *The archaeology of Israel: Constructing the past, interpreting the present.* Journal for the Study of the Old Testament, Supplement 237. Sheffield: Sheffield Academic Press.

Silva, A.C.
1999   *Salvamento arqueológico no Guadiana.* Memorias d'Odiana. Estudios Arqueológicos do Alqueva. Beja: EDIA.

Sirén, O.
1929   *A history of early Chinese art.* Vol. 4: *Architecture.* London: Benn.

Skeates, R.
2000   *Debating the archaeological heritage.* London: Duckworth.

Smart, B.
1986   The politics of truth and the problem of hegemony. In *Foucault: A critical reader*, edited by D.C. Hoy, 157–174. Oxford and New York: Blackwell.

Smith, J.T.
1997   *Roman villas: A study in social structure.* London and New York: Routledge.

Snodgrass, A.M.
1971   *The dark age of Greece: An archaeological survey of the eleventh to the eighth centuries* B.C. Edinburgh: Edinburgh University Press.

1985   The new archaeology and the classical archaeologist. *American Journal of Archaeology* 89:31–37.

1987   *An archaeology of Greece: The present state and future scope of a discipline.* Berkeley: University of California Press.

Snodgrass, A.M., and J.L. Bintliff

1988   Mediterranean survey and the city. *Antiquity* 62:57–71.

1991   Surveying ancient cities. *Scientific American* 264(3):88–93.

Speciale, M. S.

1999   La tavoletta PY Ta 716 e i sacrifici di animali. In *Epi ponton plazomenoi: Simposio italiano di Studi Egei dedicato a Luigi Bernabò Brea e Giovanni Pugliese Carratelli,* edited by V. La Rosa, D. Palermo, and L. Vagnetti, 291–297. Rome: Scuola Archeologica Italiana di Atene.

Spivey, N.

1994   Dung-heap trove. *Times Literary Supplement,* October 21:11.

Srejovic, D.

1988   The Neolithic of Serbia: A review of research. In *The Neolithic of Serbia: Archaeological research 1948–1988,* edited by D. Srejovic, 5–19. Belgrade: Center for Archaeological Research, University of Belgrade.

Staley, D.

1993   The antiquities market. *Journal of Field Archaeology* 20(3):347–355.

Stanish, C.

2001   The origins of the state in South America. *Annual Reviews in Anthropology* 30:41–64.

Stanley-Price, N.P.

1991   *Conservation of the Orpheus Mosaic at Paphos, Cyprus,* edited by N.P. Stanley-Price. Los Angeles: Getty Conservation Institute.

1995   *Conservation on archaeological excavations, with particular reference to the Mediterranean area,* edited by N.P. Stanley-Price. 2d. ed. Rome: ICCROM.

1997   The Roman villa at Piazza Armerina, Sicily. In *The conservation of archaeological sites in the Mediterranean region,* edited by M. de la Torre, 65–84. Los Angeles: The J. Paul Getty Trust.

Stark, B.L.

2000   Framing the Gulf Olmecs. In *Olmec art and archaeology in Mesoamerica,* edited by J.E. Clark and M.E. Pye, 31–53. Studies in the History of Art 58. Washington, DC: National Gallery of Art.

Starr, C.

1992   History and archaeology in the early first millennium B.C. In *Greece between east and west: 10th–8th centuries B.C.,* edited by

G. Kopcke and I. Tokumaru, 1–6. Mainz am Rhein: Verlag Philipp von Zabern.

Stein, C.A., and B.C. Cullen
1994 Satellite imagery and archaeology: A case-study from Nikopolis. *American Journal of Archaeology* 98:316.

Stevanovic, M.
2000 Visualizing and vocalizing the archaeological archival record: Narrative vs. image. In *Towards reflexive method in archaeology: The example at Çatalhöyük by members of the Çatalhöyük teams*, edited by I. Hodder, 235–238. Cambridge: McDonald Institute for Archaeological Research and BIAA.

Stevanovic, M., and R. Tringham
1998 The significance of Neolithic houses in the archaeological record of southeast Europe. In *Zbornik posvecen Dragoslavu Srejovicu*, edited by Z. Mikic, 193–208. Belgrade: Balkanoloski Institut.

Steward, J.H.
1955 *Theory of culture change*. Chicago: University of Illinois. Reprint, 1973, Bloomington: University of Indiana Press.

Stoddart, S., and C. Malone
2001 Editorial. *Antiquity* 75:234–236.

Stone, D.
1997 The development of an imperial territory: Romans, Africans and the transformation of the rural landscape of Tunisia. Ph.D. dissertation, University of Michigan.

Strassler, R.B., ed.
1996 *The landmark Thucydides. A comprehensive guide to the Peloponnesian War*. New York: Simon and Schuster.

Struever, S.
1968 Problems, methods, and organization: A disparity in the growth of archaeology. In *Anthropological archaeology in the Americas*, edited by B. Meggers, 131–151. Washington, DC: Anthropological Society of Washington.

Sued-Badillo, J.
1992 Facing up to Caribbean history. *American Antiquity* 57(4):599–607.

Sundwall, J.
1920 Zur Deutung kretischer Tontäfelchen. *Acta Academiae Aboensis Humaniora* 2:1–12.
1932a Zu dem minoischen Währungssystem. *Mélanges Gustave Glotz*, 2:827–829. Paris: Les Presses Universitaires de France.
1932b *Minoische Rechnungsurkunden*. Societas Scientiarum Fennica. Commentationes Humanarum Litterarum 4. Helsinki: Akademische Buchhandlung.

1936   Altkretische Urkundenstudien. *Acta Academiae Aboensis Humaniora* 10(2):1–45.

Sutton, S.B., ed.

2000   *Contingent countryside: Settlement, economy, and land use in the southern Argolid since 1700.* Palo Alto: Stanford University Press.

Szegedy-Maszak, A.

1987   True illusions: Early photographs of Athens. *The J. Paul Getty Museum Journal* 15:125–138.

Talalay, L.E.

1993   *Excavations at Franchthi Cave, Greece.* Fascicle 9: *Deities, dolls, and devices. Neolithic figurines from Franchthi Cave.* Bloomington and Indianapolis: Indiana University Press.

Tedlock, D.

1985   *Popol vuh: The definitive edition of the Mayan book of the dawn of life and the glories of gods and kings.* Translated by D. Tedlock. New York: Simon and Schuster.

Thomas, D.H.

1975   Nonsite sampling in archaeology: Up the creek without a site? In *Sampling in archaeology,* edited by J.W. Mueller, 61–81. Tucson: University of Arizona Press.

2000   *Skull wars: Kennewick Man, archaeology, and the battle for native American identity.* New York: Basic Books.

Thompson, R.J.E.

1996–97   Dialects in Mycenaean and Mycenaean among the dialects. *Minos* 31/32:313–333.

Tiano, P., C. Filareto, A. Granato, and F. Piacenti

1996   Methods and materials used for the conservation of monumental works in Italy. *Proceedings of the 9th International Congress on Deterioration of Stone, Berlin, Germany, 30.9–4.10 (1996),* 2: 885–893.

Tilley, C.

1994   *A phenomenology of landscape: Places, paths, and monuments.* Oxford: Berg.

1999   Landscapes and a sense of place. In *Metaphor and material culture,* edited by C. Tilley, 175–273. Oxford: Blackwell.

Todd, I.

1976   *Catal Hüyük in perspective.* Menlo Park: Cummings Publishing Company.

Todorova, H.

1978   *The Eneolithic period in Bulgaria in the fifth millenium B.C.* BAR International Series 49. Oxford: British Archaeological Reports.

Todorova, H., V. Vasiliev, I. Ianusevic, M. Koracheva, and P. Valev, eds.
1983   Ovcharovo. Sofia: Archaeological Institute of the Bulgarian Academy of Sciences.

Tokiwa Daijô and Sekino Tadashi
1926–29 Chûgoku bukkyô shiseki (Monuments of Chinese Buddhism). 5 vols. Tokyo.

Torrence, R.
1982   The obsidian quarries and their uses. In An island polity: The archaeology of exploitation in Melos, edited by C. Renfrew and J.M. Wagstaff, 193–221. Cambridge: Cambridge University Press.

Treuil, R., P. Darcque, J.-C. Poursat, and G. Touchais
1989   Les civilisations égéennes du Néolithique et de l'Âge du Bronze. Nouvelle Clio 1. Paris: Presses Universitaires de France.

Trigger, B.G.
1978   Time and traditions: Essays in archaeological interpretations. Edinburgh: Edinburgh University Press.
1980   Archaeology and the image of the American Indian. American Antiquity 45(4):662–676.
1989   A history of archaeological thought. Cambridge: Cambridge University Press.

Trik, A.S.
1963   The splendid tomb of Temple I at Tikal, Guatemala. Expedition 6(1):2–18.

Tringham, R.
1990   Introduction: The Selevac Archaeological Project. In Selevac: A Neolithic village in Yugoslavia, edited by R. Tringham and D. Krstic, 1–12. Monumenta Archaeologica No. 15. Los Angeles: Institute of Archaeology, University of California, Los Angeles.
1994   Engendered places in prehistory. Gender, place, and culture 1(2):169–203.
2000   The continuous house: A view from the deep past. In Beyond kinship: Social and material reproduction in house societies, edited by S. Gillespie and R. Joyce. Philadelphia: University of Pennsylvania Press.
N.D.   Expressing the feminist practice of archaeology through hypermedia opera. In Practising archaeology as a feminist, edited by M. Conkey and A. Wylie. Santa Fe: SAR Press. Forthcoming.

Tringham, R., B. Brukner, T. Kaiser, K. Borojevic, N. Russell, P. Steli, M. Stevanovic, and B. Voytek
1992   The Opovo Project: A study of socio-economic change in the Balkan Neolithic. 2nd preliminary report. Journal of Field Archaeology 19(3):351–386.

Tringham, R., and M. Conkey

1998   Rethinking figurines: A critical analysis of archaeology, feminism and popular culture. In *Ancient goddesses: The myths and the evidence*, edited by L. Goodison and C. Morris, 22–45. London: British Museum Press.

Tringham, R., and M. Stevanovic

2000   Different excavation styles create different windows into Çatalhöyük. In *Towards reflexive method in archaeology: The example at Çatalhöyük by members of the Çatalhöyük teams*, edited by I. Hodder, 111–118. Cambridge: McDonald Institute for Archaeological Research and BIAA.

Tsakanika, E.

N.D.   Earthquake resistant timber structures in prehistoric Greece, Ph.D. dissertation, National Technical University of Athens.

Uceda, S., and E. Mujica, eds.

1994   *Moche: propuestas y perspectivas. Actas del Primer Coloquio sobre la Cultura Moche, Trujillo, 12 al 16 de abril de 1993*. Travaux of the French Institute of Andean Studies, Tome 79. Trujillo: Universidad Nacional de la Libertad; Instituto Francés de Estudios Andinos; Asociación Peruana para el Fomento de las Ciencias Sociales.

Ucko, P.J., and R. Layton, eds.

1999   *The archaeology and anthropology of landscape*. London: Routledge.

UNESCO

1955   International principles governing archaeological excavations. Preliminary report. UNESCO/CUA/68. Paris: UNESCO

1974   Study of current policies concerning archaeological excavations: Suggestions for the housing of objects in the countries in which they were discovered. CC/MD/40. Paris: UNESCO.

1983   Conventions and recommendations of UNESCO concerning the protection of the cultural heritage. Paris: UNESCO.

Van Alfen, P.

1996–97   The LMIIIB inscribed stirrup jars as links in an administrative chain. *Minos* 31/32:251–274.

van Andel, T.H., and S.B. Sutton

1987   *Excavation at Franchthi Cave, Greece*. Fascicle 2: *Landscape and people of the Franchthi region*. Bloomington and Indianapolis: Indiana University Press.

van Dommelen, P.

1997   Colonial constructs: Colonialism and archaeology in the Mediterranean. *World Archaeology* 28(3):305–323.

van der Leeuw, S., and C.L. Redman
2002   Placing archaeology at the center of socio-natural sciences. *American Antiquity* 67:597–605.

Varias, C.
1993   Los documentos en lineal B de Micenas. Ensayo de interpretación global. Ph.D. dissertation, Universidad Autónoma de Barcelona.
1994–95   A tentative analysis of dialectal differences in the Linear B texts from Mycenae. *Minos* 29/30:135–157.

Ventris, M.G.F.
1940   Introducing the Minoan language. *American Journal of Archaeology* 44:494–520.
1952   Deciphering Europe's earliest scripts. *The Listener*, July 10:57–58
1955   Mycenaean furniture on the Pylos tablets. *Eranos* 53:3–4, 109–124.
1988   *Work notes on Minoan language research and other unedited papers*, edited by A. Sacconi. Incunabula Graeca 90. Rome: Edizioni dell' Ateneo.

Ventris, M.G.F., and J. Chadwick
1953   Evidence for Greek dialect in the Mycenaean archives. *Journal of Hellenic Studies* 73:84–103.
1956   *Documents in Mycenaean Greek*. Cambridge: Cambridge University Press.
1973   *Documents in Mycenaean Greek*. 2d ed. Cambridge: Cambridge University Press.

Vermeule, E.T.
1972   *Greece in the Bronze Age*. Chicago and London: University of Chicago Press.
1996   Archaeology and philology: The dirt and the word. *Transactions of the American Philological Association* 126:1–10.

Verona Charter (1997)
1999   On the use of ancient places of performance. *The Conservation and management of archaeological sites* 3(3):163–168.

Vilborg, E.
1960   *A tentative grammar of Mycenaean Greek*. Acta Universitatis Gothoburgensis 66. Göteborg: Almqvist & Wiksell.

Vitelli, K.D.
1993   *Excavations at Franchthi Cave, Greece*. Fascicle 8: *Franchthi Neolithic pottery*. Vol. 1: *Classification and ceramic phases 1 and 2*. Bloomington and Indianapolis: Indiana University Press.
1999   *Excavations at Franchthi Cave, Greece*. Fascicle 10: *Franchthi Neolithic pottery*. Vol. 2: *The later Neolithic ceramic phases 1 and 2*. Bloomington and Indianapolis: Indiana University Press.

Voorhies, B., and D. Kennett
1995   Buried sites on the Soconusco coastal plain, Chiapas, Mexico. *Journal of Field Archaeology* 22:65–79.

Wace, A.J.B., and F.H. Stubbings, eds.
1962   *A companion to Homer.* New York: MacMillan.

Wainwright, G.
2000   Time please. *Antiquity* 74:909–943.

Watson, A., and D. Keating
1999   Architecture and sound: An acoustic analysis of megalithic monuments in prehistoric Britain. *Antiquity* 73:326–335.

Watson, P. J., S. Leblanc, and C. Redman
1971   *Explanation in archaeology.* New York: Columbia University Press.

Webster, T.B.L.
1958   *From Mycenae to Homer.* Norwich: Jarrold and Sons Ltd.

Weinberg, S.
1970   The Stone Age in the Aegean. *Cambridge Ancient History* 1(1): 557–672.

Weingarten, J.
1986   The sealing structures of Minoan Crete: MM II Phaistos to the destruction of the Palace of Knossos. Pt. 1: The evidence until the LM I B destructions. *Oxford Journal of Archaeology* 5:279–296.
1988   The sealing structures of Minoan Crete: MM II Phaistos to the destruction of the Palace of Knossos. Pt. 2: The evidence from Knossos until the destruction of the Palace. *Oxford Journal of Archaeology* 7:1–25.

Whittle, A.
1996   *Europe in the Neolithic: The creation of new worlds.* Cambridge: Cambridge University Press.

Whitley, D.S.
1996   *A guide to rock art sites: Southern California and southern Nevada.* Missoula: Mountain Press Publishing Company.

Whitley, J.
1991   *Style and society in Dark Age Greece: The changing face of a pre-literate society 1100–700 B.C.* Cambridge: Cambridge University Press.

Whitley, J., M. Prent, and S. Thorne
1999   Praisos IV: A preliminary report on the 1993 and 1994 survey seasons. *Annual of the British School at Athens* 94:215–264.

Wiebe, K.D., A. Tegene, and B. Kuhn
1998   Land tenure, land policy, and the property rights debate. In *Who owns America: Social conflict over property rights,* edited by H.M. Jacobs, 79–93. Madison: University of Wisconsin Press.

Wiencke, M.H.
2000   Lerna IV: The architecture, pottery, and stratification of Lerna III. Princeton: American School of Classical Studies at Athens.

Wilkie, N.C.
1993   The Grevena Project. In Ancient Macedonia V: Papers read at the Fifth International Symposium held in Thessaloniki, October 10–15, 1989, 1747–1755. Hidryma Meleton Chersonesou tou Haimou, 240. Thessaloniki: Hidryma Meleton Chersonesou tou Haimou.

Wilkinson, T.J.
1982   The definition of ancient manured zones by means of extensive sherd-sampling techniques. Journal of Field Archaeology 9:323–333.

1989   Extensive sherd scatters and land use intensity: Some recent results. Journal of Field Archaeology 16:31–46.

2000   Regional approaches to Mesopotamian archaeology: The contribution of archaeological surveys. Journal of Archaeological Research 8:219–267.

Wilkinson, T.J., and S.T. Duhon
1990   Excavations at Franchthi Cave, Greece. Fascicle 6: Franchthi Paralia. The sediments, stratigraphy, and offshore investigations. Bloomington and Indianapolis: Indiana University Press.

Willey, G.R.
1953   Prehistoric settlement patterns in the Virú Valley, Peru. Bulletin 155. Washington, DC: Smithsonian Institution Bureau of American Ethnology.

1956   Introduction. In Prehistoric settlement patterns in the New World, edited by G. Willey, 1–2. Viking Fund Publications in Anthropology 23. New York: Wenner Gren.

1999   The Virú Valley project and settlement archaeology. Some reminiscences and contemporary comments. In Settlement pattern studies in the Americas. Fifty years since Virú, edited by B. Billman and G. Feinman, 9–11. Washington, DC: Smithsonian Institution Press.

Wiseman, J.R.
1978   The land of the ancient Corinthians. Studies in Mediterranean Archaeology 50. Göteborg: Paul Åströms Förlag.

1996   Space missions and ground truth: Satellite-age technologies yield a trove of new archaeological data. Archaeology 49(4):11–13.

Wolle, A., and R. Tringham
2000   Multiple Çatalhöyüks on the World Wide Web. In Towards reflexive method in archaeology: The example at Çatalhöyük by members of the Çatalhöyük teams, edited by I. Hodder, 207–218. Cambridge: McDonald Institute for Archaeological Research and BIAA.

Woolley, C.L., and T.E. Lawrence
1914   *The wilderness of Zin*. London: Palestine Exploration Fund.
Wright, F.L.
1945   *The living city*. New York: Horizon Press.
Wright, J.C.
1994   The spatial configuration of belief: The archaeology of Mycenaean religion. In *Placing the gods. Sanctuaries and sacred space in ancient Greece*, edited by S.E. Alcock and R. Osborne, 37–78. Oxford: Clarendon Press.

1995a   Empty cups and empty jugs: The social role of wine in Minoan and Mycenaean societies. In *The origins and ancient history of wine*, edited by P.E. McGovern, S.J. Fleming, and S.H. Katz, 287–309. Philadelphia: Gordon and Breach Publishers.

1995b   From chief to king in Mycenaean Greece. In *The role of the ruler in the prehistoric Aegean*, edited by P. Rehak, 63–80. Aegaeum 11. Liège: Université de Liège.
Wright, J.C., J.F. Cherry, J.L. Davis, E. Mantzourani, S.B. Sutton, and R.F. Sutton, Jr.
1990   The Nemea Valley Archaeological Project: A preliminary report. *Hesperia* 59:479–559.
Yang Hongxun
1987   *Jianzhu kaogu lunwenji* (Collected essays on architectural archaeology). Beijing: Wenwu chubanshe.
2001   *Gongdian kaogu tonglun* (General discussion of the archaeology of palace architecture). Zhongguo kaogu wenwu tonglun congshu. Beijing: Zijincheng chubanshe.
Zertal, A.
1988   The Israelite settlement in the hill-country of Manasseh (in Hebrew). Ph.D. dissertation, University of Haifa.
1992   *Seker Har Menasheh* (Manasseh hill-country survey). Tel Aviv: Misrad ha-bitahon.
Zerubavel, Y.
1995   *Recovered roots*. Chicago: University of Chicago Press.
Zevi, B.
1957   *Architecture as space: How to look at architecture*. Translated by M. Gendel. New York: Horizon Press.
1985   *Zhongguo gudai jianzhu jishushi* (History of ancient Chinese architecture). Beijing: Kexue chubanshe.
Zhongguo gudai jianzhu jishushi
1985   Beijing: Kexue chubanshe.

Zilhâo, J.

1998   The rock art of the Côa Valley, Portugal. Significance, conserva-
        tion and management. *Conservation and management of archaeo-
        logical sites* 2(4):193–206.

Zois, A.

1990   *I archaiologia stin Ellada.* Athens: Politipo.

1995   *Knossos: To ekstatiko orama* (Knossos: The ecstatic vision). Her-
        akleio: Panepistimiakes Ekdoseis Kritis.

Index